CROSSING PATHS

CROSSING *Paths*

• • • • • • • • • • • • • •

SCHUBERT, SCHUMANN, AND BRAHMS

John Daverio

OXFORD
UNIVERSITY PRESS
2002

OXFORD
UNIVERSITY PRESS

Oxford   New York

Auckland   Bangkok   Buenos Aires   Cape Town   Chennai
Dar es Salaam   Delhi   Hong Kong   Istanbul   Karachi   Kolkata
Kuala Lumpur   Madrid   Melbourne   Mexico City   Mumbai   Nairobi
São Paulo   Singapore   Taipei   Tokyo   Toronto

and an associated company in Berlin

Published by Oxford University Press, Inc.
198 Madison Avenue, New York, New York 10016

www.oup.com

Oxford is a registered trademark of Oxford University Press

Library of Congress Cataloging-in-Publication Data

Daverio, John.
Crossing paths: Schubert, Schumann, and Brahms / John Daverio.
p.   cm.
Includes bibliographical references (p.) and index.
ISBN 0-19-513296-3
1. Schubert, Franz, 1797–1828—Criticism and interpretation. 2. Schumann, Robert,
1810–1856—Criticism and interpretation. 3. Brahms, Johannes, 1833–1897—Criticism and
interpretation. 4. Music—Philosophy and aesthetics. I. Title.
ML390 .D335 2002
780'.92'243—dc21   2001038744

3   5   7   9   8   6   4   2

Printed in the United States of America
on acid-free paper

FOR EFFIE

Με την πάροδο του χρόνου, τα παλιά γίνονται καινούργια.
With the passage of time, old things become new.

—Nicostratus

ACKNOWLEDGMENTS

*E*VERY BOOK comes into being in a different way. This one grew in part from a number of lectures and less formal talks that I was asked to give between about 1996 and 1999. I would like to take this opportunity to thank those colleagues whose invitations to speak provided me with the opportunity to follow up on some of the aspects of nineteentʰ-century German music in general—and the music of Schubert, Schumann, and Brahms in particular—that I had been mulling over for some time. To this group belong Hennie Bordwin (indefatigable president of the American Schubert Institute), Marc Mandel (Boston Symphony Orchestra), Victor Rosenbaum (Longy School of Music), Annette Richards (Cornell University), Peter Smith (University of Notre Dame), and Neal Zaslaw (Cornell University).

Thanks are also due to Nancy Reich, "dean" of Clara Schumann scholars, for her immediate responses to my frequent queries on a wide range of Schumann-related issues; Styra Avins (Drew University), who made me aware of Brahms's special relationship to the cello; Antonius Bittmann (Rutgers University), who shared with me his work on the musical ciphers in Max Reger's Violin Sonata, Opus 72; and Stuart Feder, who called my attention to passages from Freud's *Interpretation of Dreams* that I would have otherwise overlooked. Several of my colleagues on the Board of Directors of the American Brahms Society—George Bozarth (University of Washington), David Brodbeck (University of Pittsburgh), Walter Frisch (Columbia University), Virginia Hancock (Reed College), Margit McCorkle, and the late David Epstein (Massachusetts Institute of Technology)—took the time to read and comment on drafts of individual chapters. I offer thanks to them, and to the reviewers of the complete draft, including Rufus Hallmark (Queens College), for their thoughtful suggestions.

I am also obliged to those among my musicological friends and colleagues— including Anna Maria Busse-Berger (University of California, Davis), Helen Greenwald (New England Conservatory), Lewis Lockwood (Harvard University), and Elizabeth Seitz (Boston University)—who cheerfully acted as sounding-boards for some of the ideas that went into this book.

As always, the staff at Boston University's Mugar Memorial Library—Holly Mockovak, Donald Denniston, and Olga Khurgin—responded promptly to my many, many requests.

Work on the final stages of this book coincided with my service as interim Director of the School of Music at Boston University, College of Fine Arts. I would like to express my gratitude to my extraordinary administrative assistant, Janice Filippi, who helped keep me sane.

I am doubly indebted to Maribeth Anderson Payne, former executive editor for music at Oxford University Press, first, for seeing this book through the earlier stages of the publication process; and second, for her long-standing support of my scholarly efforts. *Crossing Paths* would have been the third book I completed under Maribeth's editorial supervision. Without her guidance and encouragement, none of this work would have been brought to completion. Thanks are of course due to the entire editorial and production team at Oxford University Press, including Ellen Welch and Jessica Ryan, for all of their efforts on behalf of this book.

In conclusion I would like to offer special thanks to Eftychia Papanikolaou, my former advisee and now colleague and good friend, for her unwavering support of this and many of my other projects. Effie, this book is dedicated to you.

—J. D.
Boston, January 2002

CONTENTS

ABBREVIATIONS

AmZ	*Allgemeine musikalische Zeitung*
BBw	Johannes Brahms. *Briefwechsel*, 16 vols. Berlin: Deutsche Brahms Gesellschaft, 1907–22.
BBw 1 & 2	Johannes Brahms. *Briefwechsel. Johannes Brahms im Briefwechsel mit Heinrich und Elisabet von Herzogenberg*, 2 vols., ed. Max Kalbeck. Berlin: Deutsche Brahms Gesellschaft, 1907.
BBw 3	Johannes Brahms. *Briefwechsel. Johannes Brahms im Briefwechsel mit Karl Reinthaler, Max Bruch, et al.*, ed. Wilhelm Altmann. Berlin: Deutsche Brahms Gesellschaft, 1908.
BBw 5 & 6	Johannes Brahms. *Briefwechsel. Johannes Brahms im Briefwechsel mit Joseph Joachim*, ed. Andreas Moser. Berlin: Deutsche Brahms Gesellschaft, 1908 and 1912.
BBw 11	Johannes Brahms. *Briefwechsel. Johannes Brahms Briefe an Fritz Simrock*, ed. Max Kalbeck. Berlin: Deutsche Brahms Gesellschaft, 1919.
BLL	Johannes Brahms. *Life and Letters*, selected and annotated by Styra Avins, trans. Josef Eisinger and Styra Avins. Oxford: Oxford University Press, 1997.
BNF	F. Gustav Jansen, ed. *Robert Schumanns Briefe, Neue Folge*. Leipzig: Breitkopf und Härtel, 1904.
BrKG	Clara and Robert Schumann. *Briefwechsel: Kritische Gesamtausgabe*, 2 vols., ed. Eva Weissweiler. Frankfurt: Stroemfeld/Roter Stern, 1984.

CC   Clara and Robert Schumann. *The Complete Correspondence of Clara and Robert Schumann, Critical Edition*, 2 vols., ed. Eva Weissweiler, trans. Hildegard Fritsch and Ronald L. Crawford. New York: Peter Lang, 1994, 1996.

CS–JB   *Clara Schumann–Johannes Brahms: Briefe aus den Jahren 1853–1896*, ed. Berthold Litzmann, 2 vols. Hildesheim: Georg Olms; Wiesbaden: Breitkopf und Härtel, 1989. (Orig. publ. Leipzig, 1927.)

GS   Robert Schumann. *Gesammelte Schriften über Musik und Musiker*, 5th ed., 2 vols., ed. Martin Kreisig. Leipzig: Breitkopf und Härtel, 1914.

JAMS   *Journal of the American Musicological Society.*

JBr   Clara Schumann, ed. *Jugendbriefe von Robert Schumann*, 2d ed. Leipzig: Breitkopf und Härtel, 1886.

NA   Franz Schubert. *Neue Ausgabe sämtlicher Werke*, ed. International Schubert-Gesellschaft. Kassel: Bärenreiter, 1964 –.

NZfM   *Neue Zeitschrift für Musik*

SW 5   Johannes Brahms. *Sämtliche Werke*, vol. 5: *Konzerte für Streichinstrumente und Orchester*. Wiesbaden: Breitkopf und Härtel, 1926.

TB 1   Robert Schumann. *Tagebücher*, vol. 1: 1827–1838, ed. Georg Eismann. Leipzig: VEB Deutscher Verlag für Musik, 1971.

TB 2   Robert Schumann. *Tagebücher*, vol. 2: 1836–1854, ed. Gerd Nauhaus. Leipzig: VEB Deutscher Verlag für Musik, 1987.

TB 3   Robert Schumann. *Tagebücher*, vol. 3: *Haushaltbücher*, pts. I (1837–47) and 2 (1847–56), ed. Gerd Nauhaus. Leipzig: VEB Deutscher Verlag für Musik, 1982.

CROSSING PATHS

INTRODUCTION:

AT THE INTERSECTION

OF OLD AND NEW PATHS

*J*OHANNES BRAHMS was infamous for his rather sharp tongue. This trait, which seems to have intensified over the years, is much in evidence in the reminiscences of Richard Heuberger, a Viennese critic and composer who engaged Brahms in a series of discussions on musical matters between 1875 and 1897. Compared to Haydn, Brahms declared during a conversation in February 1896, the composers of the current generation were downright "miserable." Claiming that "everything today is in a state of ruin," Brahms went on to explain: "'Learning nothing' is to blame. . . . Neither Schumann, nor Wagner, nor I had a proper education. Talent, however, was decisive. Schumann went one way, Wagner another, and I a third. But none of us learned the right things. None of us passed through a proper school. —Indeed, we learned only *afterwards*. Well, it was a matter of diligence; more for one, less for the other."[1]

Quite apart from adding to the lore of Brahms the Curmudgeon, this passage introduces a metaphor that will play an important role in this book: the image of the "ways" or paths that nineteenth-century composers had to clear for themselves even if they were fortunate enough (as Schubert and Mendelssohn, for example, undoubtedly were) to have "passed through a proper school." The history of nineteenth-century music might well be construed as a dense network of such paths, together forming a congested map of which I will only be examining a limited part. And while Brahms was intent on pointing out, though without specifying, the divergent trajectories of three of the more significant paths in nineteenth-century music, I will focus on a trio of paths that converged often enough so that in retrospect we may recognize them as cutting a central artery in the musical landscape. The earliest of the paths I have in mind was charted by Schubert; Brahms identified the other two in conversation with Heuberger: Schumann's and his own.

Writing to his teacher Friedrich Wieck on 6 November 1829, less than a year after Schubert's death, Schumann referred to the recently deceased composer as his "one and only Schubert."[2] Nearly a quarter of a century later, Schumann would hail the young Brahms as the musical messiah who was destined to "give ideal expression to the times" in an essay titled, appropriately enough, "Neue Bahnen"—"New Paths."[3] Dispensing with the irony that he often used as a defense mechanism, Brahms wrote to an acquaintance in 1873 that "the memory of Schumann" was "sacred" to him, adding: "That noble, pure artist serves me constantly as a model." During the late 1880s, Brahms told his composition student Gustav Jenner that "there is no song by Schubert from which one cannot learn something."[4] These are only a few of the more prominent markers of a creative configuration that spanned much of the nineteenth century. It is the purpose of this book to explore some of the ways in which the strands in the configuration converged, intersected, ran parallel—and at times diverged as well.

The special affinities between and among Schubert, Schumann, and Brahms have hardly gone unremarked in the critical literature. Soon after their premieres in the 1840s, Schumann's symphonies in B♭ (Op. 38) and C (Op. 61) were viewed by some German music critics as successors to Schubert's "Great" C-major Symphony (D. 944), a work that Schumann himself was among the first to champion. Similarly, the 1868 premiere of Brahms's *Ein deutsches Requiem* at Bremen Cathedral prompted one writer to claim that in order "to estimate its worth, one must intimately understand the spirit of Schumann's compositions."[5] Especially within the last several decades or so, scholars have turned with increasing frequency to various pairings within our triumvirate of composers. With the publication of Marie Luise Maintz's excellent monograph on Schumann's reception of Schubert, students of the connections between these composers have at their disposal an indispensable point of reference for future work.[6] Elaborating on the trenchant criticism of Donald Francis Tovey, James Webster has demonstrated, in a now-classic two-part article, the extent to which Brahms's mature sonata forms were indebted to Schubertian models.[7] The ties between Schubert's colorful harmonic language and Brahms's—in particular as regards Neapolitan and other "flat-side" relationships—have been sensitively addressed by the theorists Christopher Wintle and Peter H. Smith.[8]

Sustained commentary on the links between Schumann and Brahms has been somewhat slower to materialize. Tovey, for one, pointedly excluded Schumann from the "main stream of musical history" on the grounds that the range of his musical thought was ill suited to the rhetorical demands of sonata form. In Tovey's opinion, Schumann lacked the "special powers" necessary to fashion coherent designs on the largest scale, so, "being a very clever man, [he] created for his larger works a kind of mosaic style, in which he imitates sonata forms only in so far as mosaics imitate pictures." Hence, while both Schubert and Brahms displayed a grasp of musical architecture that ensured their participation in the "main stream," Schumann the miniaturist created "a province for himself."[9] One of the principal scholars in recent times to argue that Schumann's "province" overlapped in fundamental ways with Brahms's is Constantin Floros, whose work on the piano music of both composers has uncovered points of contact in matters of aesthetic posture, poetic sensibility, and musical character.[10] While questioning the parallels that Floros draws between Schumann's alter egos, Florestan and Eusebius, on the one hand, and Brahms's identification with E. T. A. Hoffmann's mad Kapellmeister Johannes Kreisler, on the other, Siegfried Kross agrees that Schumann "pointed the way" to Brahms, especially in regard to the younger composer's study of Renaissance vocal polyphony and the instrumental works of Schubert.[11] In addition, the importance of Schumann's orchestral music for the development of Brahms's own symphonic thinking has been considered—albeit from rather different angles—in thought-provoking studies by Reinhold Brinkmann and David Brodbeck.[12] While hardly a comprehensive summary, this brief overview of the literature at least offers some sense for the range of critical discussion on the crossing paths of Schubert, Schumann, and Brahms.

Still, a fair amount remains to be done—and undone. Although writers including Walter Frisch and Harald Krebs have shown that Brahms's highly intricate approach to rhythmic and metric organization owes much to Schumann's experiments in this domain,[13] the relationship between the musical languages of the two composers has received less attention than it deserves. The same could be said for our understanding of Schumann's absorption of elements from Schubert's musical language as well.

While it is not my intent to provide an exhaustive survey of every intersection in the paths of Schubert, Schumann, and Brahms, I hope to shed light on some aspects of their interdependent musical languages that await more careful scrutiny and to revisit a few topics that are, in my opinion, worth a second look. One of these involves the command of extended temporal spans that, according to Tovey, was granted to Schubert and Brahms but denied to Schumann. In the pair of chapters that comprise part I of this book, I take a rather different stance, arguing instead that Schumann's methods of unfolding larger designs owe quite a bit to the inimitable blend of presence and pastness, immediacy and reminiscence, in the later instrumental works of his "one and only" Schubert. The three chapters of part II focus on an area where a small body of facts has generated an inordinately large body of fiction: the technique of musical encipherment that both Schumann and Brahms supposedly employed to translate their innermost feelings for Clara Wieck Schumann into tones. Issues of compositional strategy again constitute a central theme in the two chapters of part III, where in the course of sketching a genealogy for some of the characteristic features of Brahms's musical language I propose that the controversial music of Schumann's last years may have exercised a greater impact on Brahms than previously imagined.

Given that much of this study will be devoted to a consideration of the relationships between musical works, it might be appropriate at this point to reflect on some of the theoretical issues that such an intertextual approach raises. Ideally a means of mediating between the isolated artwork and the larger family to which it belongs, intertextual criticism is too often little more than a highfalutin expression for the license to ignore chronology and intent. E. M. Forster raised an additional red flag in a lively essay on the aims of art criticism. Invoking another loaded term, he noted wryly in a parenthetical aside that "criticism adores influences," the study of which may indeed be valuable, "but what meanwhile has become of Monteverdi's *Vespers,* or the Great Mosque at Dehli, or the *Frogs* of Aristophanes, or any other work which you happen to have in mind?" Forster's question is well worth pondering, not least because it reminds us that the danger inherent in the study of influences—the chief type of intertextual criticism—is its deflection of attention from the artwork at hand to other factors. "Straying this way into psychology and that way into history,"[14] the critic loses sight of what should, after all, be the centerpiece of the inquiry: the work of art itself.

Among the chief problems of one of the more estimable theories of influence, that of the literary critic Harold Bloom, is this tendency to stray, not so much into history as into psychology—and to remain there. According to Bloom, all great or "strong" poets establish their reputations by "misreading one another, so as to clear imaginative space for themselves." The relationship between poets and their predecessors engenders anxiety, "for what strong maker desires the realization that he has failed to create himself?"[15] Bloom's theory translates with remarkable ease into musical contexts, and indeed, it has provided several authors with a framework for dealing with topics that range from the late piano music of Brahms and the nineteenth-century symphony to the neoclassical turn in twentieth-century music.[16] At the same time, this trend has not met with unqualified approval. In his review of two Bloom-inspired studies, Richard Taruskin writes that Bloom's "agonistic theory" of poetic influence "is not a pretty thing. At its core is bleakness—a view of human nature founded on jealousy, territoriality, resentment, and of human relations founded on corrosive rivalry, contention, strife."[17] Moreover, to return to the sort of objection that Forster would have raised, the theory of influence as anxiety might be able to tell us something about the psychological state of the composer or poet, but it is often nearly impossible to detect signs of anxiety in the artwork under consideration. Brahms's supposed allusion to the "Ode to Joy" theme in the finale of his

First Symphony may well represent his anxiety of influence toward Beethoven, but listeners will be hard-pressed to detect even a trace of anxiety in Brahms's dignified, uplifting, and hymnlike tune. The anxiety, if there is any, must reside within Brahms's psyche.

Another branch of intertextual criticism is less concerned with influences per se than with allusions. Derived from the Latin *alludere,* meaning "to play with, jest, or refer to," an allusion, according to one standard dictionary definition, is "an implied indication or indirect reference . . . especially as utilized in literature."[18] Of course, there is nothing to prevent composers from employing comparable devices as well, and theorists of musical allusion have found an embarrassment of riches in the works of Brahms.[19] The practice of tracking down such references in his music, however, is not an activity that Brahms would have looked upon favorably. In a classic display of the curmudgeonly side of his personality, he wrote point-blank to the composer Otto Dessoff in the summer of 1878 that "one of the stupidest topics of stupid people is that of reminiscences,"[20] "reminiscences" (*Anklänge*) being the term that Brahms and his contemporaries generally used for what we would call allusions.[21] At the same time, Brahms freely admitted to incorporating allusive references into his works. In his most notorious confession to that effect, he quipped that "any jackass" could hear the resemblance between the main theme of the finale of his First Symphony (Op. 68) and the "Ode to Joy" theme of Beethoven's Ninth[22]; and commenting to Dessoff on the second theme of the first movement of his Second Symphony (Op. 73), he wrote: "You know that I too have stolen on this occasion."[23] The question is whether Brahms made use of allusions with the frequency that some writers maintain and, if so, what criteria should we invoke to determine the deeper meanings of this practice?

One thing is certain: the identification of musical allusions is by and large a subjective endeavor. Unless the composer is obliging enough to supply the source of the allusion—as Brahms was in indicating that the opening bars of his song "Unüberwindlich" (Op. 72, no. 5) were adapted from the theme of Domenico Scarlatti's Sonata in D major (K. 223)[24]—critics are left to exercise their own judgment in deciding whether or not an allusion has actually been made. Given the subjective nature of the process, I would like to relate a personal experience that will help to clarify the stance on musical allusions taken in this book. I first heard Schumann's Third Symphony (Op. 97), the "Rhenish," in the early 1970s, from my seat in the violin section of the Berkshire Music Center Orchestra at Tanglewood. About two-thirds of the way through the first movement, when we had reached a spot where the violin parts thin out enough to allow the players to attend to events in other precincts of the orchestra (m. 449), I was struck by the fact that the lower winds and strings proceeded with a melodic idea that seemed to be directly imported from one of the Brahms symphonies (the Third, Op. 90, as it turned out). While not having a very precise sense for the chronology of nineteenth-century music, I was nonetheless aware that Brahms's symphony had to have been composed some years after Schumann's. Still, I distinctly remember thinking: *Schumann just stole a tune from Brahms*—a thought that evaporated as soon as the violin part demanded my full attention about a dozen bars later. Writing thirty years after this little incident took place, I realize that it has something to offer on the nature of musical allusions, at least as I understand them. The point is that given the parenthetical character of the passage from the "Rhenish," it sounds *as if Schumann were* alluding to a musical idea drawn from a source outside of the work, whatever the source may have been. (If a specific source is needed, the most likely candidate would be a transitional passage from the slow movement of Schumann's own Symphony No. 1.) In short, it seems to me that in order for something to qualify as an allusion it must embody this quality of "calling by name"—a quality often lacking in many of the passages that have been adduced as allusions in Brahms's output.

As I see it, the problem with an overly zealous pursuit of allusive references in the music of Brahms (or of any other composer for that matter) is twofold. First, it tends to produce an atomistic view of the musical text; and second, it too often confuses allusion with a more generalized stylistic resonance. Once the search for allusions has begun, it is a potentially endless process, which threatens to reduce the text to a string of particles patched together from other sources. Likewise, in failing to distinguish between the phenomenology of the allusion—the calling of a (possibly unspecified) source by name— and the numerous stylistic affinities with other musical works that every composition displays, we run the risk of conflating two quite distinct properties.[25] For these reasons, the approach to the topic of musical allusions in the body of this study can best be described as a cautious one.

I have reserved for last a few words on the most decorous variety of intertextual criticism—actually, another theory of poetic influence. Proceeding from the premise that the genuinely original aspects of the creative artist's work are those in which "the dead poets . . . assert their immortality most vigorously," T. S. Eliot argued in his 1919 essay "Tradition and the Individual Talent" that the poet is engaged in "a continual surrender of himself as he is at the moment to something which is more valuable"—and the "something" he meant was tradition.[26] At first blush, this would appear to represent the diametric opposite of the Bloomian position. Whereas Bloom's aspiring poet wages a fierce oedipal struggle with imperious predecessors, Eliot's displays an attitude of homage and reverence to respected ancestors. While the poet, according to Bloom's model, attempts to overcome the past, the poet in Eliot's scheme embraces it. Instead of the repression of domineering forces, we have benign submission to a superior authority. Or do we? Perhaps the poet, for Eliot, is not such a passive receptacle, for as he also maintained, tradition "cannot be inherited, and if you want it you must obtain it by great labour."[27] In other words, Eliot's poet does not surrender to tradition; he (or she) earns it.

Their differences aside, all three models of intertextual criticism that I have described address the relationship between the individual and the collective, the will to originality and the force of tradition, the demands of the present and the urgings of the past. What distinguishes them is a matter of emphasis. Sooner or later, critics who subscribe to Bloom's theory will argue for the artist's repression of the past.[28] Implicit in the search for allusive sources is the belief that every apparently original utterance in a new text has its basis in an older one. Finally, from Eliot's point of view, the truly distinctive poetic voices are the ones that manage to re-create the past. Of the three models, it seems to me that Eliot's best addresses an inescapable fact, namely, that every individual creation is necessarily of smaller dimensions than the totality of past creations that had an impact on its making.

At the same time, the approach employed in this study is not exactly congruent with Eliot's. Informed by the nineteenth-century critic Friedrich Schlegel's admonition that "it is equally fatal for the mind to have a system or to have none,"[29] my method is admittedly an eclectic one. Although I have been rather critical of Bloom's theory, I will from time to time (and perhaps unwittingly) invoke some of its premises. Like Bloom, I, too, will stray into psychology—especially in considering aspects of homage in the creativity of Schumann and Brahms—but I will also make every effort to return to the artwork itself. Likewise, the musical works considered in the following pages will often be viewed as force fields of tensions among the past, the present, and the future, an idea that has obvious parallels in the writings of Bloom and Eliot. My take on this issue, however, owes less to Bloom's theory of the anxiety of influence or to Eliot's thoughts on tradition and individuality than to the cultural criticism of Walter Benjamin. His 1936 essay "The Storyteller," for instance, helped to sharpen my view on the interweaving of memory, tradition, and experience implicit in the subtle variety of musical storytelling practiced by Schubert, Schumann, and Brahms.[30] In a broader sense, my thinking on the historical character of art has been shaped by Benjamin's conviction that the literary artwork is a "microcosm," or more precisely a "microeon," which contains within itself traces of both its prehistory (the processes that brought it into being) and its afterlife (the factors that sustain its impact on future creators).[31] This insight can, I think, be put to good use in a musical context. Hence the metaphor of "crossing paths," as employed here, is intended not to suggest the accidental convergence of disparate lines but the charged intersection of pre- and posthistory.

This book is organized as a series of meeting points between at least two such paths. In part I (chapters 1 and 2), I will try to show that Schumann's conception of the larger musical forms was predicated upon his sensitivity to the complementary modes of temporal unfolding in Schubert's late instrumental music: what he called heavenly length, on the one hand, and musing on the past, on the other. Both part II (chapters 3–5) and part III (chapters 6 and 7) focus on various intersections between the paths of Schumann and Brahms, though here I will also take into account the paths of some other members of their extended family as well, namely, Clara Wieck Schumann and Joseph Joachim.

Chapters 3 and 4, which are devoted to a reexamination of Schumann and Brahms's practice of encoding extramusical references in their works, should be read as a unit. The general thrust of the argument is that neither composer was particularly interested in music's cryptographic potential and that the cultural points of reference for their so-called musical ciphers lie in other domains: in the world of Biedermeier parlor games and children's books and in the rich store of proverbs and maxims that formed a vital part of both composers' heritage. Having ruled out the techniques of cryptography as the agency for Schumann's and Brahms's projection of lived experience in tone, I turn in chapter 5 to a more likely metaphor for this process: the tendency of those who are in love to perceive images of the beloved object in every space, no matter how tiny. This tendency, I propose, finds a musical analogue in Schumann's (and, to an extent, Brahms's) fondness for making interpolations into, or digressions from, the principal musical narrative, a quality that lends the music an imagistic, pictographic character and that can in turn be traced to the strategies of temporal unfolding that Schumann learned from Schubert.

Although Schumann is often portrayed as a quintessentially Romantic dreamer, I suggest in chapter 6 that Brahms must have viewed him as a shrewd tactician as well. Finally, chapter 7 offers a kind of musical genealogy for a single work, Brahms's "Double" Concerto for Violin, Cello, and Orchestra (Op. 102), in an attempt to sort out the dense network of paths in a composition that testifies to a career-long preoccupation with the ethos of the Schumann circle.

As I have noted earlier, the yield of this exercise in intertextuality makes no claims to completeness. If, however, it succeeds in deepening our understanding of the interdependence between self-discovery and creative engagement with the past, the exercise will not have been in vain.

Part I.

SCHUMANN'S ONE AND

ONLY SCHUBERT

CHAPTER I.

SCHUMANN AND SCHUBERT'S

"IMMORTAL" PIANO TRIO

IN E FLAT, D. 929

*I*F IMPACT ON LATER GENERATIONS were in itself a measure of a composer's stature, then Schubert's significance for the history of music would be assured on this point alone. Johannes Brahms was only one of many composers who could justifiably claim that his love for Schubert was "a serious one, precisely because it is not a passing fancy." Commenting on Schubert's symphonies, which Brahms had edited for the Breitkopf und Härtel collected edition, Dvořák noted in a similar vein: "The more I study them, the more I marvel."[1] An abiding source of inspiration for nineteenth-century composers from Mendelssohn to Bruckner, Schubert's music continued to cast its spell well into the twentieth century. While Schubertian echoes have long been acknowledged in the works of Mahler, Schoenberg, and Berg, they can also be detected in compositions nearer to our own day such as Luciano Berio's *Rendering*, based on Schubert's sketches for a Symphony in D (D. 936a), Edison Denisov's *Lazarus*, and John Harbison's *November 19, 1828*, a piano quartet named after the date of Schubert's death. As Alex Ross reports in a recent *New Yorker* article, György Ligeti recognized Schubert's late String Quartet in G (D. 887) as "a crucial influence on [his] current style."[2]

I

Though impossible to prove with absolute certainty, it could be argued that Schubert made a more immediate, long-lasting, and profound effect on one composer more than any other: Robert Schumann. The documentary evidence leaves little doubt that although the two obviously never met, Schumann harbored feelings for the older composer the likes of which we usually reserve for our most intimate friends. According to the testimony of Emil Flechsig (Schumann's roommate during his days as a law student in Leipzig), the news of Schubert's death in November 1828 threw Schumann into such a state of agitation that he "sobbed the whole night long."[3] Schumann himself described his year of legal studies in Leipzig (from May 1828 to May 1829) as a time of "revelling in Jean Paul and Schubert."[4] Jean Paul, of course, was the pen name of Johann Paul Friedrich Richter, author of a long series of idiosyncratic (and for many modern readers impenetrable) novels that counted among Schumann's favorite specimens of imaginative prose. In a number of his diary entries from the late 1820s, Schumann went so far as to equate his experiences as a reader with his response to his newly found musical idol: "Schubert," he wrote in August 1828, "expresses Jean Paul, Novalis, and E. T. A. Hoffmann in tones."[5] Similarly, Schumann informed his piano teacher Friedrich Wieck in a letter of 6 November 1829 that "when I play Schubert, it's as if I were reading a novel composed by Jean Paul."[6] Another remark from the same letter is even more suggestive: "Apart from Schubert's music, none exists that is so psychologically unusual in the course and connection of its ideas . . . While others used a diary to set down their momentary feelings, Schubert used a piece of manuscript paper."[7]

In order to form a clear picture of Schubert's meaning for Schumann, we will first need to consider which of Schubert's works he knew and when he came in contact with them. Needless to say, Schumann did not have ready access to the totality of Schubert's output, and indeed, by our standards, his knowledge of it was spotty. (The "Unfinished" Symphony, D. 759, which did not see the light of day until 1865, is only one of the mainstays of the Schubert canon that Schumann would not have known.) Yet considering that during the 1820s and 1830s Schubert's music was little circulated outside of Vienna, it is all the more remarkable that Schumann learned as much of it as he did.

The musical affinity between the two composers was already acknowledged during Schumann's lifetime. In an 1846 review of his Piano Quartet in E flat (Op. 47), for instance, the critic August Kahlert stated unequivocally: "In my opinion, Schumann is most closely related to Schubert."[8] Only recently, however, has a systematic study of Schumann's outlook on Schubert and his music appeared: Marie Luise Maintz's *Franz Schubert in der Rezeption Robert Schumanns.*[9] Rather than recapitulate at length the material presented in this excellent book, I will offer only a brief survey of the high points in Schumann's engagement with Schubert's output. This, in turn, will serve as the background for an examination of Schumann's multifaceted response to Schubert's Piano Trio in E flat, D. 929, a work whose significance for the younger composer warrants closer attention.

II

Schumann's love affair with the music of Schubert began soon after he matriculated at the University of Leipzig in the spring of 1828. Among the first of Schubert's pieces to attract his attention was the celebrated ballad "Erlkönig," which, according to Flechsig, he played from start to finish time and again.[10] At about this time, Schumann also developed a passion for Schubert's variations and polonaises for piano, four hands. In July 1828, he dubbed the Variations on a Theme from Hérold's Marie (D. 908) a "perfect novel in tones" ["ein vollkomner Tonroman"], noting further a month later that the work was "too sublime and otherworldly for the man of today."[11] Between August 1828 and January of the following year, Schubert's Polonaises (D. 824 and 599)—"thunderstorms with romantic rainbows spreading over the solemnly slumbering world"—figured prominently in Schumann's convivial music making with his friends and his sister-in-law Therese.[12] These sessions must have fueled Schumann's creative impulses, for in the late summer of 1828 we find him working on his own set of polonaises for piano, four hands (VIII Polonaises, WoO 20). Although the collection was never published, Schumann salvaged some material from the fourth and seventh polonaises in Nos. 11 and 5, respectively, of his Papillons, Op. 2. Furthermore, the VIII Polonaises clearly attest to Schumann's early attempts to emulate Schubert's style. The easygoing, unbuttoned character of Schumann's writing for piano, the emphasis on the Neapolitan and other flat-side harmonies, the frequent modulations by third—all of these features recall comparable traits in Schubert's music.

During the same period, Schumann also became acquainted with some of Schubert's more ambitious compositions. In a diary entry of 13 August 1828, he wrote that in the "Wanderer" Fantasy (D. 760) Schubert "tried to summon up an entire orchestra with only two hands; the inspired opening is a seraphic hymn of praise to the godhead."[13] Reflecting further on the same piece, Schumann penned an "Evening Fantasy in X Major" in which he described the "free fantasy" as the medium for the most elevated musical thoughts, for it combines "the strict law of the measure with alternately lyrical and free metric groupings."[14] Between late November 1828 and March 1829, Schubert's Piano Trio in E flat became an intense object of study, and, as we shall see, it elicited a more far-reaching creative reaction from Schumann than any of Schubert's other works up to that point. Another of Schubert's major chamber works occupied Schumann later in 1829, the C-major String Quintet (D. 956), which he asked Wieck to send him in November of that year.[15]

Schubert's so-called Sehnsuchtswalzer, or "Yearning Waltz" (which is actually comprised of two pieces, the Waltz in A flat, D. 365, and the Deutscher, D. 972), provided the theme for a set of variations composed by Schumann in 1833. (As early as 4 March 1829, he contemplated writing a Fantasie on the Sehnsuchtswalzer.)[16] Like the VIII Polonaises, the variations remained unpublished, and here, too, Schumann drew on some of the music in a later compositional effort: the lengthy introductory section of the variation set became the *Préambule* to *Carnaval*, Op. 9, completed early in 1835.

Schumann's designation of the year 1834 as the most important of his life[17] was motivated in part by his founding—along with Wieck, Ludwig Schunke, and Julius Knorr—of the *Neue Leipziger Zeitschrift für Musik* (soon renamed the *Neue Zeitschrift für Musik*), the critical mouthpiece for an all-out crusade against philistinism in the contemporary musical scene. Schubert's music, a prime representative of the poetic spirit advocated by Schumann and his half-imaginary cohorts, the *Davidsbündler*, was a favored object of critical attention, particularly between 1835 and 1840. During those years, Schumann published substantial critiques of a number of Schubert's later compositions, focusing on keyboard works such as the Impromptus (D. 935) and *16 Deutsche und 2 Ecossaisen* (D. 783); the Sonatas in A minor (D. 845), D (D. 850), G (D. 894), C minor (D. 958), A (D. 959), and B flat (D. 960); and the Sonata in C ("Grand Duo") for Piano, Four Hands (D. 812). Among Schubert's chamber works, Schumann bestowed special praise—in either brief reviews or passing references—on the String Quartet in D minor (*Der Tod und das Mädchen*, D. 810), the Piano Trio in B flat (D. 898), and, most especially, the Piano Trio in E flat. In a concise but laudatory account of a series of works for choral forces and piano (*Gebet*, D. 815; *Nachthelle*, D. 892; *Ständchen*, D. 920; *Mirjams Siegesgesang*, D. 942), Schumann expressed his fervent hopes for the rapid appearance of Schubert's masses and operas in print, adding that "Vienna possesses no greater musical treasures than these."[18] Finally, Schubert's "Great" C-major Symphony (D. 944) was the subject of one of Schumann's most significant essays.

Conspicuously absent from this list are Schubert's lieder, a portion of his output toward which Schumann harbored an attitude that most contemporary observers will find rather odd. Having at first reacted positively to his earliest steady exposure to this repertory (at musical soirées held at the home of Dr. Ernst August Carus and his wife, Agnes, in the winter of 1828 in Leipzig),[19] Schumann subsequently adopted a cooler stance toward Schubert's songs. In sketching the history of the German lied in an 1843 review of songs by Robert Franz and others, he downplayed Schubert's role in the development of the genre, tracing its recent flowering to three other sources: Bach, Beethoven (whose influence, according to Schumann, can be felt in Schubert's songs), and the new school of lyric poetry exemplified by writers such as Rückert, Eichendorff, Uhland, and Heine.[20] Furthermore, Schumann was rather critical of two aspects of Schubert's approach to song composition: his supposed lack of discrimination in the choice of poetry ("Telemann, who demanded that a respectable composer should be able to set a billboard to music, would have found his man in Schubert"), a factor that, in Schumann's opinion, could take its toll on the musical setting; and Schubert's fondness for persistent accompanimental figures, which, as Schumann wrote, "threatened the delicate life of the poem."[21]

Schumann's outlook was considerably more prescient when it came to Schubert's instrumental music. While attempting to gain a foothold in Vienna late in 1838 and early in 1839, Schumann paid several visits to Ferdinand Schubert, who introduced him to much of his brother Franz's unpublished music, including operas, four Masses, and four or five symphonies.[22] Of all these pieces, the one that impressed Schumann most was the C-major Symphony. Almost surely composed in 1825, though subjected to revision over the course of the next year or two,[23] the symphony had not yet been performed when Schumann came upon it. He quickly rectified this situation, arranging for a public premiere with the Leipzig Gewandhaus orchestra under Mendelssohn's direction on 21 March 1839, and also for publication of the score by the venerable firm of Breitkopf und Härtel. While the Gewandhaus orchestra was preparing for another rendition of the work later in 1839, Schumann wrote breathlessly to his colleague Ernst Becker: "At today's rehearsal I heard part of Schubert's [C-major] Symphony—all the ideals of my life unfolded in this piece, which is the greatest achievement in instrumental music after Beethoven, not even Spohr and Mendelssohn excepted. . . . It has stimulated me to take up symphonic composition soon again, and when I am peacefully united with Clara, I think that something will come of my plan."[24] On the same day he sent an equally enthusiastic report to Clara herself, extolling the symphony's ingenious instrumentation and—to quote one of his more celebrated epithets—its "heavenly length."[25]

Schumann reiterated both of these points in his most extended pronouncement on Schubert's symphony, an essay published in the 10 March 1840 issue of the *Neue Zeitschrift*. (In a highly symbolic gesture, he drafted the essay with a pen he had found on Beethoven's grave during his stay in Vienna.) Here it might be instructive to restore Schumann's famous sound bite on the symphony's sprawling dimensions to its context: "Consider also the heavenly length of the symphony, like a thick novel in four volumes by Jean Paul, who was also incapable of coming to an end, and to be sure for the best of reasons: to allow the reader, at a later point, to re-create it for himself."[26] Much as in his diary entries of the late 1820s, Schumann thus drew a parallel between the narrative strategies of a favored author and a revered composer. In addressing Schubert's deft handling of his orchestral forces, Schumann marveled at his ability to make it seem as though the instruments "converse like human voices and chorus."[27] Yet for Schumann the chief token of the work's enduring value lay elsewhere—in "its relationship of complete independence from Beethoven's symphonies."[28]

On the last point, Schumann no doubt overstated his case. As several writers have observed, Schubert's C-major Symphony proceeds along a path already cleared in Beethoven's Seventh Symphony, particularly as regards the shape and pacing of its first and second movements.[29] Yet almost immediately after asserting the absolute distinction between Schubert's and Beethoven's symphonic styles, Schumann qualified his stance: "Conscious of his more modest powers, Schubert refrains from imitating the grotesque forms and audacious relationships that we encounter in Beethoven's later works."[30] Given the context (a discussion of the early nineteenth-century symphony) Schumann must have been thinking of one of Beethoven's "later works" more than any other: the Ninth Symphony. In other words, he was most deeply impressed by Schubert's creation of a monumental idiom that derived its sustenance from sources quite different from those that animated the last of Beethoven's symphonic works. Or, to put it in more general terms, Schubert had demonstrated to Schumann that it was still possible to make an original contribution to a genre whose potential had been seemingly exhausted by Beethoven. While Schubert's treatment of the orchestra may have been comparable in some ways to Beethoven's, the instrumental colors of the C-major Symphony (Schumann spoke of its "brilliance and novelty") bore Schubert's distinctive imprint. Also like Beethoven, Schubert stretched the temporal scale of the symphonic form to its outer limits—extending it both in "length and breadth"—but his means toward that end were quite different from Beethoven's. Imbued with "heavenly length," Schubert's symphonic forms opened a window onto infinity.

Not surprisingly then, Schumann's own tendencies as a symphonist reveal a deep debt to Schubert's example. Echoes of Schubert's C-major Symphony are perhaps most clearly audible in Schumann's Symphony No. 1 in B flat, Op. 38—the first product of his so-called symphonic year, 1841—and Symphony No. 2 in C, Op. 61, both of which are dominated by brass mottos whose lineage can be traced to the opening horn melody of Schubert's symphony.[31] The kinship between Schubert's C-major Symphony and Schumann's symphony in the same key is especially pronounced, and understandably so: Schumann set to work on his symphony just days after attending a December 1845 peformance of Schubert's symphony in Dresden.[32] Surely the martial, triplet-driven fanfares of Schubert's first movement were ringing in his ears when he conceived the buoyant reprise of his own C-major Symphony's opening movement.

At the same time, Schumann's symphonies in B♭ and C are not his only works in the larger forms that demonstrate a deep awareness of Schubert's alternative to Beethovenian paradigms, nor was Schubert's C-major Symphony the only source for Schumann's understanding of that alternative. Over a decade before his rediscovery of Schubert's symphony, Schumann became intensely attached to a composition in which the Schubertian world of fresh instrumental colors and heavenly lengths would have been fully revealed to him—which brings us to the Piano Trio in E flat.

III

Given Schumann's fondness for Schubert's dances, it is easy to see why he was so profoundly affected by the Piano Trio in E flat. Its technical and musical challenges notwithstanding, the trio is thoroughly informed by the spirit of the dance, from the infectious rhythms of the triple-time first movement to the lilting $\frac{6}{8}$ tunes of the finale. Only the slow movement, whose attraction for Schumann lay in a wholly other domain, offers momentary contrast to the often-boisterous strains of the other movements. In a word, Schumann discovered in Schubert's trio an idealized embodiment of the dance, a musical type to which he responded with visceral immediacy throughout his creative life.

Schumann expressed his high regard for Schubert's trio in no uncertain terms in a June 1838 review of the late piano sonatas in C minor, A, and B♭; as fine as these compositions were, Schumann was unable to put them in the same class as the trio, which he "always considered . . . to be Schubert's last as well as his most independent and individual work."[33] Similarly, while commenting on Mendelssohn's Piano Trio in D minor, Op. 49, in a review of December 1840, Schumann dubbed his friend's work "the master trio of the present, just as Beethoven's trios in B flat [Op. 97] and D [Op. 70, no. 1] and Franz Schubert's in E flat were the master trios of theirs."[34] Schumann's most revealing remarks on Schubert's trio can be found in a brief review published in a December 1836 issue of the *Neue Zeitschrift*. "About a decade ago," he wrote, "Schubert's Piano Trio in E flat swept through the musical world like an angry portent from the skies." Conjecturing that the Piano Trio in B flat was written a short time before its companion piece,[35] he argued further that the two works bore little resemblance to each other:

> Inwardly they differ in essential ways. The first movement of the E-flat work is a product of deep anger and boundless longing, while that of the B-flat trio is graceful, intimate, and virginal. The slow movement, which in the former is a sigh intensified to the point of an anguished cry of the heart, appears in the latter as a blissful dream, an ebbing and flowing of beautiful human feeling. The Scherzos are similar, though I prefer the one in the second trio [in E b]. As for the finales, I cannot decide. In a word, the second trio is more active, masculine, and dramatic, while in contrast, the other one is passive, feminine, and lyrical.[36]

As in his review of the C-major Symphony, Schumann seems to have been indulging in a bit of wishful thinking. For some critics, the similarities between the trios (especially evident in a number of melodic figures shared by their opening movements)[37] are just as compelling as their differences. Moreover, the binary oppositions through which Schumann defined the essential character of the two works—active/passive, masculine/feminine, dramatic/

lyrical—are at once overly schematic and, in several crucial instances, down-right contrary to aural experience. The exuberant principal theme of the B♭ Trio's first movement is just as "active" (or "masculine") as its counterpart in the Trio in E flat; conversely, the latter is just as rich in lyrical effusions as its supposedly "passive" (or "feminine") cousin. Yet despite Schumann's exaggeration of the affective disparities between the trios—to say nothing of the purple prose and gendered rhetoric—his remarks are highly significant: first, because they offer a clue to his idiosyncratic understanding of the piece; and second, because that understanding would resonate with his own compositional efforts. In order to measure the trio's effect on Schumann's creativity, we will have to return to his initial encounter with the work.

Schumann first heard Schubert's Piano Trio in E flat on 30 November 1828 at a musical soirée at Wieck's home, where it was rendered by Adolph Wendler, an attorney and amateur pianist; Christian Müller, a violinist; and Johann Grabau, a cellist in the Gewandhaus orchestra. Schumann was also present when the trio was performed by the same players at a similar gathering held four days later. In typical fashion, he entrusted his reactions to his diary, writing on 30 November: "enraptured by [Schubert's] trio"; and on 4 December: "home at 3am—excited night with Schubert's immortal trio ringing in my ears—frightful dreams."³⁸ One of the guests at both events was Heinrich Probst, whose publishing firm had issued the trio a little over a month before. Also present was Gottfried Wilhelm Fink, editor of the *Allgemeine musikalische Zeitung* and at the time one of the principal music critics in the German-speaking world. Reading Fink's review of the trio—one of a handful of serious accounts of Schubert's instrumental pieces to appear in print in the late 1820s—is tantamount to eavesdropping on the discussions prompted by the readings of the work for the inner circle of Leipzig's musical elite. What impressed Fink most was the trio's affective ambivalence, its ineffable blend of good humor and melancholy. Consider his remarks on the recurrence of the main theme of the slow movement in the finale: "In a wondrously moving way, the plaintive *Romanze* of the second movement often enters into the impetuous play of pain and joy [in the fourth movement]. From time to time we perceive voices of recollection, although these reminiscences are drowned out by the turbulence of the present moment which, veiled in mist, spreads over the otherwise amiable morning of the future."³⁹ In a word, he viewed the trio as a masterpiece of psychological portraiture, an interpretation with which Schumann—given his sensitivity to the psychologically unusual relationships in Schubert's music—would have wholeheartedly concurred. And chances are, Schumann was also taken by the relationship between the trio's slow movement and finale, in ways that will soon become apparent.

In the weeks and months after these initial encounters, references to Schubert's trio appear frequently in Schumann's diaries. Moreover, the period encompassed by these references—late November 1828 through mid-March 1829—coincides almost exactly with Schumann's participation in a group he had organized for the express purpose of studying the literature for piano trio and piano quartet. Comprised of three amateur string players (Johann Friedrich Täglichsbeck, violin; Christoph Soergel, viola; Christian Glock, cello), with Schumann himself at the keyboard, the ensemble focused on the chamber music for piano and strings of Mozart, Beethoven, Ferdinand Ries, J. L. Dussek, Prince Louis Ferdinand, and Georges Onslow. But the mainstay of the group's repertory was Schubert's Piano Trio in E flat, which figured in its sessions of 7 December 1828 and 19 January, 31 January, and 13 March 1829.[40] Schumann's diary entry for 13 March provides a wonderful sense of the flavor of these gatherings: "Evening: 14th quartet session. [We played] Beethoven's "Archduke" Trio [Op. 97] ([a] bizarre [piece]), Dussek's Quartet in E flat (Op. 57), Quartet Op. V (went well), [drank] much Bavarian beer— longwinded conversation about the students' and peasants' associations— good cheer—late in the evening, the first movement of Schubert's Piano Trio [in E flat]—very noble music—gallopade—beautiful sleep."[41]

The "Quartet Op. V" to which Schumann referred was a compositional project of his own: a piano quartet in C minor that occupied him during the four-month life span of his chamber group. Having begun sketching it in late November 1828, Schumann completed a draft of the composition on the morning of 21 March 1829, and that evening the entire four-movement piece (Allegro molto affettuoso, Minuetto. Presto, Andante, and Allegro giusto. Presto) garnered praise from his colleagues.[42] On 25 March he checked through the score "note for note . . . behind closed doors," no doubt in preparation for another run-through at the final meeting of his group on 28 March 1829. Schumann's diary conveys no further reports on the piece until 7 January 1830, when we read: "The quartet will be cobbled into a symphony."[43]

Although this plan was never realized, and while Schumann opted not to see the quartet version through to publication, he nonetheless retained fond memories of his youthful effort. In a diary entry written sometime between 1846 and 1850, he accorded it a special place in his compositional development: "I remember very well a passage in one of my pieces ([composed in] 1828), about which I said to myself: this is *Romantic;* a spirit different from that of my earlier music came into view and a new poetic life revealed itself for the first time (the passage in question was the Trio of a Scherzo [*sic*] from a Piano Quartet [in C minor])."[44] A wistful E-minor dance tune notable for its lilting dactylic rhythms, the theme of the Trio is presented first by the violin, while the quietly pulsing chords in the piano part produce delicious *appoggiature* between D♯ and E in the third and seventh bars. (See Ex. 1-1a.) The second half of the Trio opens with a variant of the tune in the cello, evocatively accompanied by pizzicati in the violin and viola and appoggiatura-laden harmonies in the piano. (See Ex. 1-1b.) Although there are unmistakable melodic

Example 1-1a: Schumann, Piano Quartet in C minor, second movement, Minuetto.
Presto, Trio section, mm. 1–8

similarities between the Trio theme and the opening gesture of Beethoven's
Piano Trio in C minor (Op. 1, no. 3),[45] it is tempting to speculate that the
"new poetic life" to which Schumann alluded in his diary came to him principally by way of Schubert. As we will soon observe, this hypothesis is supported by (among other factors) the fate of the Trio theme in the finale of
Schumann's quartet.

An impressive achievement for someone with essentially no formal training in composition, Schumann's C-minor Piano Quartet is particularly significant for our purposes as a document of the aspiring artist's reception of
Schubert. Schumann's very first reference to the quartet, in a diary entry of 31
November 1828, makes an implicit connection between the work's genesis

Example 1-1b: Schumann, Piano Quartet in C minor, second movement, Trio, mm. 17–24

and Schubert's death: "My quartet—Schubert is dead—dismay."[46] As indicated in entries of 31 January and 13 March 1829, Schumann and his friends often rehearsed portions of his quartet and Schubert's E flat–Major Piano Trio on the same evening.[47] Furthermore, the musical parallels between the works are too striking, and too numerous, to be purely coincidental. To cite an obvious instance: the glittering passagework for piano in the first movement and finale of Schubert's trio is echoed at many points in the corresponding movements of Schumann's quartet. Likewise, the "listener-friendly" canon[48] that frames Schubert's Scherzo may have inspired the playful imitative textures of Schumann's Minuetto. For the most part, Schumann's forays into canonic writing are limited to brief passages that involve the rapid-fire exchange of scalar fragments, but in one case the interplay develops into a bona fide canon of nearly a dozen bars between violin and piano, the other instruments engaging in free imitation.

Two other aspects of Schubert's musical language—both of them much in evidence in the Piano Trio in E flat—seem to have made a particularly strong impression on Schumann at this point in his compositional career: its inimitable harmonic colors and its rhythmic verve. Elaborating on a metaphor first suggested by Tovey, Richard Cohn has recently shown that Schubert's tonal world can be compared to a "star cluster" or constellation, a "decentered network" whose sense derives less from the relationship of triadic harmonies to a governing tonic than from the voice-leading relationships among the harmonies themselves.[49] As a prime example of Schubert's "cyclic" approach to tonality, Cohn cites the coda of the first movement of the Piano Trio in E flat (see Ex. 1-2 for the opening phase of this section), a passage that features modal mixture (E♭ major versus E♭ minor in mm. 585–88), augmented-sixth chords used as passing sonorities (m. 590), enharmonic reinterpretation (C♭/B in mm. 605–6), and modulation by third (E♭–C♭/B–G–E♭).[50]

All of these manifestations of Schubert's decentered tonal universe—and several others besides—surface with great regularity in Schumann's C-minor Piano Quartet. The closing paragraph of the finale's exposition, for instance, offers a veritable lexicon of Schubertian tonal practices. Within the space of ten bars, Schumann moves through a colorful series of diminished-seventh, Neapolitan, and augmented-sixth sonorities, effecting the transitions between them, much like Schubert, through both semitonal voice leading and enharmonic sleight of hand. While the tonal pillars of the coda are comprised of harmonies with roots a minor third apart (A minor / C minor), this pairing of third-related keys is in turn embedded in a larger progression characterized by modal mixture: C major (from the midpoint of the second group) versus C minor (the tonal goal of the exposition). Thus, on both the local and global levels, Schumann evokes the tonal properties associated with the "star clusters" of his model, though without lapsing into merely slavish imitation. Indeed, it could be argued that the overall tonal physiognomy of Schumann's quartet represents a mirror image of its counterpart in Schumann's trio. Whereas Schubert's is an E♭-major work in which C minor plays an important role (as the key of the slow movement and of the second main thematic idea from the finale), Schumann's quartet reverses the relative weight of these keys, offering C minor as tonic and E♭ as subsidiary tonality (in the exposition of the first movement and the recapitulation of the finale).

The quality of harmonic flux in Schumann's finale is heightened by the quick tempo (*Allegro giusto. Presto*) and even more by the almost obsessive repetition of a single rhythmic cell: ♩.♪♩. Here, too, Schumann took his cue from Schubert. The Piano Trio in E flat, like many of Schubert's later sonata-style works, makes extensive use of a kind of "isorhythmic" variation tech-

Example 1-2: Schubert, Piano Trio in E flat (D. 929), Allegro, mm. 585–605

(continued)

nique whereby a compact rhythmic cell is combined with an ever-changing array of melodic shapes over the course of a protracted temporal span. The second main thematic idea of the opening movement, for instance, is pervaded by melodically varied repetitions of a simple rhythmic pattern: a quarter note followed by four eighths. Likewise, the marchlike accompaniment to the slow movement's main theme (♩ ♩ ♩ ♩♪) gradually assumes the character of a per-

Example 1-2. *continued*

sistent ostinato. In the Trio of the Scherzo, Schubert uses the quarter-plus-eighths pattern from the first movement as a foil to a suave melody in the cello. Finally, each of the last movement's principal thematic groups is linked with a discrete rhythmic gesture: three upbeat eighths plus a quarter for the first group, steadily repeated eighths for the second (where Schumann evokes the *cimbalon* of the gypsy band), and metrically displaced duple groupings (♩♪♪ ♪♪♩♪♪♩♪) during the course of the closing section. While this procedure obviously owes something to Beethoven, Schubert made it his own through the sheer obstinacy of his rhythmic repetitions and his frequent coupling of the latter with kaleidoscopic shifts in harmonic color.

If anything, Schumann was even more persistent than Schubert in his employment of the "isorhythmic" strategy in the finale of his C-minor Piano Quartet. The propulsive dactylic rhythm cited earlier runs through a high percentage of the movement's 582 bars, energizing the accompaniment and, in some cases, informing the thematic substance as well. The most striking realization of the latter possibility comes at the climax of the movement, where the wistful E-minor theme from the Trio of the Minuetto serves as the point of departure for the jubilant Più presto that brings the work to a close in C major. (See Ex. 1-3.)

This gesture of transformed recall also resonates with Schubert's Piano Trio in E flat. As we have seen, in his review of the trio G. W. Fink called special attention to the intrusion of the slow movement's main theme into the boisterous world of the finale. Like a voice from afar, it recurs at two points in the last movement, first in the development section and next in the coda,

Example 1-3: Schumann, Piano Quartet in C minor, Allegro giusto. Presto, mm. 546–53

thereby imparting a distinctly epic quality to the work as a whole.[51] In a sense, an epic or, more specifically, balladic quality is built into the theme itself (see Ex. 1-4), a derivative of the Swedish folk song "Se solen sjunker" ("The sun has set") in an arrangement by the Swedish tenor Isaak Albert Berg. As we now know, Schubert almost surely heard the song in late November 1827 at the home of his friends the Fröhlichs, who hosted a gathering at which Berg was also a guest.[52] In addition to the "walking" eighth-note accompaniment of the original song, Schubert appropriated a number of melodic elements from his source, reordering them to suit his own ends. As they appear in Schubert's version of the tune, these elements include: the ornamental slide into the second bar, the leap down a fifth near the beginning of the third phrase, the falling octaves between the third and fourth phrases, and the expressive contour of the final phrase.[53] Tinged with a faintly modal character that wavers between C-Aeolian and G-Dorian, this nostalgic tune strikes us as a musical emblem for distance in time—and hence a perfect vehicle for recall.[54] In crafting the two extended passages where this material returns in the final movement, Schubert deftly integrated the folk tune with its new context, assimilating it gracefully to the prevalent $\frac{6}{8}$ meter and surrounding it with the paired eighths that had already served as an accompanimental pattern earlier in the movement.

In Fink's description, these "voices of recollection" are "drowned out by the turbulence of the present moment."[55] Yet one might just as easily argue that the voices are transformed into an *utterance of* the turbulent present. When the melody from the slow movement recurs in the finale's development section, it appears in B minor, thus retaining its nostalgic character despite the transposition down a half step from its original pitch level. This scenario is drastically altered in the coda. Schubert begins by moving directly from the first phrase of the tune to the third, both of which are presented in a languid, E♭-minor context. Having dispensed with the parenthetical octave leaps that follow in the initial version, he then takes the melody in an unsuspected direction, shifting from minor to major for the tune's fourth and final phrase and reinforcing the gesture of triumph by means of dynamics (*forte* and *fortissimo*) and instrumental color (violin and cello in octaves). The coda's overall affective progress from melancholy reflection to unbridled joy may well have had programmatic implications for Schubert. The text of the original folk song circles around the quintessentially Romantic themes of loss (of both time and hope) and separation (from a distant beloved):

See the sun is going down behind the peak of the high mountain,
Before night's shadows you flee, O beautiful hope.
Farewell, farewell, ah, the friend forgot about
His true dear bride.
La, la, la, la.[56]

Example 1-4: Piano Trio in E flat, Andante con moto, mm. 1–21

(continued)

Example 1-4. *continued*

Schubert's jubilant coda rescues the dejected speaker from his temporal and emotional dilemma. In the final stages of the Piano Trio in E flat, lost time and hope are recaptured as the distant beloved becomes a vivid presence.

Although there is little chance that Schumann would have been aware of the specific poetic background for Schubert's trio, he clearly grasped its affective meaning through the rhetorical power of the music alone. This is evident in part from his description of the slow movement, in his 1836 review of both piano trios, as "a sigh intensified to the point of an anguished cry of the heart."[57] The "sigh" is no doubt a metaphor for the plangent main theme itself, which Schubert intensifies into an "anguished cry of the heart" in a series of passionate developments based on motivic elements from the theme itself, especially in the latter half of the movement. In these passages, he unleashes the latent heroic power of the folk-derived tune, though as Schumann must have realized, Schubert's efforts to dispel the anguish embodied in the developmental interludes collapse into resignation and defeat: the slow movement ends with eerie, disembodied allusions to its opening melody. At this point the narrative is thus left in a state of suspended animation, its definitive move toward triumph withheld until the concluding paragraphs of the finale. When Schumann described the essential character of the trio as "active" and "masculine," it was in all likelihood this fundamental plotline that he had in mind.

Viewed against this background, the C-minor Piano Quartet represents an early attempt on Schumann's part to replicate a narrative pattern that had been deeply impressed upon him by his experience of Schubert's Piano Trio in E flat. To be sure, the motion from despair to struggle to ultimate triumph is an affective paradigm that we tend to associate first and foremost with the middle-period works of Beethoven, and justifiably so. What is most striking about Schumann's approach, then, is that he chose to realize this paradigm in ways that are clearly redolent of Schubert, through the transformation of a melancholy conceit—the wistful Trio theme of his youthful piano quartet—

into an emblem of joyous reconciliation—the jubilant variant of the theme in the coda of the quartet's finale.

Schumann paved the way for the decisive gesture of triumph in his Piano Quartet both overtly and covertly. Already in the third movement, Andante, we hear an evocative allusion to the Trio theme just before the recapitulation; fluctuating between G minor and G major, this passage was intended for horn in the projected symphonic version—a highly appropriate choice, for the tone of that instrument, more than any other, offered the Romantic imagination a potent symbol of distances near and far. The finale in turn brings fleeting references to ideas from each of the preceding movements—a fragment from the first movement's second theme, an allusion to the opening idea of the Andante, and, in the retransition to the reprise, a hint of the Trio theme itself—all of them swept up in the ostinato rhythm that propels the music inexorably forward. At the same time, Schumann prepares for the climactic restatement of the Trio theme in more subtle ways as well. As can be easily seen by comparing Examples 1-1a and 1-3, the rhythmic pattern of the original version of the theme is subjected to an exact diminution (by two-thirds) at the high point of the finale. The diminuted pattern, in turn, has already been the topic of considerable discussion in the finale's development section. Divorced from its initial melodic content, it is filled with ever-new shapes, thus providing a subliminal preview of the main attraction: the C-major transfiguration of the theme that signals the denouement of the musical narrative. Schumann's covert strategy for motivating the final gesture of the quartet speaks eloquently to his creative engagement with his model. While obviously dependent on Schubert's "isorhythmic" technique, so far as I know, Schumann's use of the procedure in this case is without a specific precedent in the older composer's works.

IV

If Schumann ultimately decided not to put the finishing touches on his C-minor Piano Quartet and send it off for publication, it is not difficult to understand why. Despite many impressive passages, it is a deeply flawed work, requiring not just minor adjustments but also major surgery to make it fit for public consumption. Only in the second movement, Minuetto, does Schumann seem to have convincingly channeled the flow of his musical ideas. In contrast, the Andante suffers from the overly zealous repetition of often-uninspired figuration, while the development sections of both the opening movement and finale strike this listener as rather diffuse, rambling on without a clear sense of direction. At least in the outer movements, the problem lies mainly with the young composer's idiosyncratic approach to tonal planning. As if in intentional defiance of the traditional modus operandi, Schumann continually circles back to the tonic in both developments, thereby under-cutting the articulative force of the definitive return to tonic harmony at the point of recapitulation. In short, he appears to have been striving for heavenly length (even if he hadn't yet formulated this expression) without quite know-ing how to achieve it. This might be an appropriate place, then, to consider how Schubert did. The Piano Trio in E flat—a primer of techniques intended to generate heavenly length—will serve as our primary point of reference.

On the whole, Schubert broadened the temporal frame of his musical ar-guments in two ways: through expansion from within and through incre-mental addition.[58] Of course, the two processes are closely related: sequence, a favored means of prolonging the motion from one point to another and thus of amplifying the music's dimensions from within, is obviously an addi-tive device as well. In the Piano Trio in E flat, as in any number of Schubert's mature works, sequence is frequently coupled with excursions into flat-side tonal regions to produce what Tovey called purple patches. One such mo-ment occurs during the first group of the opening movement, where Schu-bert lingers on the flat mediant (G♭) while en route to a half-cadence on the dominant. When this strategy is projected over even larger temporal spans, the result is often one of Schubert's so-called three-key expositions. (The label is hardly accurate, but for better or worse, it seems to have stuck.) In the ex-position of the trio's first movement, for instance, Schubert enriches the long-range motion from tonic to dominant with a series of sequentially elaborated phrases whose harmonic starting point is the flat-submediant minor (enhar-monically respelled as B minor). Outright digressions constitute another vari-ety of expansion from within. Wedged between the reprise of the main and subsidiary ideas in the slow movement is an extended developmental inter-lude (mm. 103–27) that one might conceivably excise without many listeners being the wiser. To do so, however, would be ill advised, for it is precisely here that Schubert realizes the explosive potential of his main theme. In ret-rospect, the digression turns out to be the affective center of the movement.

The foundation for Schubert's techniques of incremental addition is the variation principle. Bound by no fixed law of continuation, a chain of varia-tions is capable of infinite expansion and thus a favored agency of heavenly length. While the theme-and-variations form is common enough in the slow movements of multimovement cycles, Schubert often transferred this ap-proach to sites within the cyclic structure where we would least expect it, namely, to the main sections of the sonata-allegro design. Traditionally con-ceived as a medium for dynamic, goal-directed arguments, the sonata form in Schubert's hands becomes a vehicle for leisurely unfolding.[59] Perhaps the most striking instance of this practice (or the most "notorious," depending on one's point of view) comes in the development of the trio's opening movement,[60] which Schubert casts as a series of three nearly analogous para-graphs, the second and third presenting the music of the first transposed and rescored.[61] Given the essentially lyrical, ruminative quality of the thematic material (a lovingly spun-out derivative of one of the closing ideas from the exposition), these paragraphs might well be construed as the successive strophes of a song without words. At times Schubert uses this sort of melodic parallelism to give shape to a movement as a whole. The massive 748-measure finale of the trio exhibits this tendency on the largest scale, the movement's recapitulation and coda running largely parallel with its exposition and development, respectively.[62] With both procedures—the strophic variations of the first movement's development section and the "parallel" form of the finale—Schubert demonstrated how the stock-in-trade of the born song composer could be transformed into guarantors of heavenly length in the instrumental genres.

Schumann's understanding of these strategies deepened considerably as he acquired a broader knowledge of Schubert's output during the course of the 1830s. Imitation gave way to emulation as Schumann discovered increasingly sophisticated means of bending Schubertian techniques to his own expressive purposes. Not surprisingly, Schumann's piano works of this period reflect a close study of Schubert's mature contributions to the various genres of keyboard music. (In the following chapter, we will see how one of Schubert's later works in particular—the first of the four Impromptus, D. 935—resonated with Schumann's own interest in music's capacity to evoke different temporal states.) Similarly, Schumann's achievements as a symphonist are unthinkable without the revelation that accompanied his rediscovery of Schubert's C-major Symphony. Of course, two of the features Schumann so admired in that work—its boundless rhythmic energy and its luxuriant expansiveness—would have been familiar to him from his earlier encounter with the Piano Trio in E flat. From this perspective, Schubert's symphony was not quite so revelatory as Schumann claimed, its specific contribution to his creative development consisting in a heightened awareness of how the motivators of heavenly length might function in a symphonic context.[63]

The Piano Trio in E flat continued to serve Schumann as a touchstone of creativity well after he had attained full artistic maturity. Indeed, the love affair that began in November 1828 during an evening of convivial music making culminated with the drafting of the Piano Quintet in E flat (Op. 44) and its slightly later counterpart, the Piano Quartet in E flat (Op. 47), between September and November of 1842, at the height of a year devoted principally to the composition of chamber music. Although it would be naive to suggest that Schubert's trio was the only model for these works—or even that Schumann required a specific model at this stage of his career—the Schubertian echoes in Schumann's Piano Quintet and Piano Quartet are too numerous to be ascribed to mere coincidence. Apart from obvious similarities in key (E♭) and medium (strings and piano), these products of Schumann's chamber music year also share a number of topical and textural features with Schu-

bert's trio. Take, for example, the main theme of the C-minor slow movement, In Modo d'una Marcia, of Schumann's Piano Quintet. Directed to play
molto p ma marcato, the violin presents a somber tune that evokes the opening
idea of Schubert's slow movement—a plangent cello solo accompanied by
the marchlike tread of the piano—in both key and character. Likewise, the
canonic textures that figure prominently in the Scherzo movements of Schumann's Piano Quintet (Trio I) and Piano Quartet (reprise of the Scherzo's
opening section, and Trio I) may call to mind the "listener-friendly" canon of
the Scherzo from Schubert's trio.[64] Finally, Schumann's quintet and quartet
embrace the entire spectrum of techniques that Schubert regularly employed
to produce the heavenly length of his largest designs. The greater part of the
development section from the first movement of Schumann's Piano Quintet,
for instance, is occupied by a pair of ruminative strophic variations, the second a step lower than the first. A Schubertian three-key exposition provides
the tonal framework for the finale of Schumann's Piano Quartet. Moreover,
the finales of the quintet and quartet are cast in "parallel" forms (with ample
codas) that culminate in the climactic return of an important idea from an
earlier stage in the four-movement cycle. In light of these points of contact,
we can only conclude that August Kahlert—whose review of the Piano Quartet was quoted earlier in this chapter—was absolutely justified in identifying
Schubert as Schumann's closest musical relative.[65]

At the same time, there is not a single passage from either the Piano Quintet or Piano Quartet that could be mistaken for Schubert. The often dense,
almost orchestrally conceived textures of Schumann's quintet stand in marked
contrast to the generally more transparent sound world of Schubert's chamber music for piano and strings. Equally remote from Schubert is the rather
abstracted, neoclassical pose that Schumann adopted with some regularity in
his Piano Quartet (especially in the opening movement). Likewise, the climactic recall of the opening music at the conclusion of Schumann's Piano
Quintet (see Ex. 1-5) is only obliquely related to Schubert's method of bringing down the curtain on his Piano Trio in E flat. The steady buildup of tension toward dominant harmony, the dramatic pause on the dominant itself,
the ensuing double fugato on the principal ideas of the first movement *and*
finale, the exhilarating drive to the final cadence—none of this bears direct
comparison with the closing pages of Schubert's trio. The rhetorical force of
Schumann's coda suggests Beethoven, but even here the fit is not quite right.
Beethoven's final movements often drive toward a moment of apotheosis,
and, with increasing frequency in the later works, his finales may also include
reminiscences of music from earlier movements; but rarely, if at all, does
Beethoven bring these two strategies together.[66] In other words, the coda of
Schumann's quintet finale at once represents a synthesis of Schubertian and
Beethovenian strategies and an individualized solution to the problem of
crafting an effective denouement for a multimovement composition.

Example 1-5: Schumann, Piano Quintet (Op. 44), Allegro ma non troppo, mm. 316–30

(continued)

Example 1-5. *continued*

Schumann's tendency to synthesize apparently incompatible models and to imbue the result with a quirkiness all his own is even more strongly pronounced in the less well known Piano Quartet in E flat. For this reason, it will be instructive to examine this work more closely. Our focus will be Schumann's means of ensuring closure on the large scale, a process already set in motion in the coda of the third movement. The final fourteen measures of this Andante cantabile surely count among the most evocative passages in all of Schumann's chamber music. (See Ex. 1-6.) Devoid of any ostensible connection with the sentimental lyricism of the movement's principal themes, the coda conjures up a psychological state in which time and space seem to have been abrogated. The quality of temporal suspension emanates from the combined effects of several features, which include the hushed, *pianissimo* dynamic level, the tied notes in the upper strings, and the cello's tonic pedal on B♭ (Schumann underscores the latter by asking the cellist to tune the C string down a step). Hovering over the pedal is a mysteriously ascending line spun out of sequential elaborations of a three-note cell. Comprised of a falling fifth and a rising sixth, the cell is caught up in a process whereby ascent and descent are confounded at an even higher level: while the melodic path of the sequences leads steadily upward through transpositions at the interval of a fourth, the harmonic trajectory moves in the opposite direction, downward by fifth. This process of spatial disorientation continues in the ensuing bars, where the upper strings and piano proceed in contrary motion with a series of delicately articulated scalar fragments that eventually dissolve into a mur-

mur. The result is an extraordinary musical evocation of weightlessness and timelessness, of sublime removal into a realm where the laws of gravity and temporal succession no longer hold sway. Appropriately enough, the coda ends with a pair of tentative echoes of the three-note cell, its intervallic content altered to embrace a falling fifth and a rising octave.

I have devoted considerable space to describing this remarkable passage because, as we will soon observe, it undergoes an equally remarkable series of transformations in the course of the finale. Indeed, as if to awaken his listeners from a pleasant daydream in the rudest manner possible, Schumann launches into the last movement of the quartet with a forceful call-to-arms whose shape is clearly that of the tiny cell from the slow movement's coda.[67] (See Ex. 1-7.) The call-to-arms gives way to a flurry of sequentially descending sixteenths in the upper strings and piano that in turn becomes the point of departure for a bustling fugato initiated by the viola. Drawing on a strategy he would have encountered while assiduously studying the string quartets of Haydn and Mozart in March 1842, Schumann casts his first group as a fugal exposition, replete with four subject–answer entries and a countersubject that moves in contrary motion with the fugato theme.[68] But if the design of the movement's opening theme group speaks to Schumann's engagement with the tradition of the fugal finale in the classical string quartet, the exposition as a whole is patterned after one of Schubert's "three-key" plans. Schumann articulates each phase of the design with utter clarity, beginning with the fugato theme in the tonic, E♭, proceeding with a pair of transitional phrases initiated by a passionate C-minor melody in the cello, and closing with a series of phrases in the dominant. The entire process, however, takes

Example 1-6: Schumann, Piano Quartet (Op. 47), Andante cantabile, mm. 117–30

(continued)

Example 1-6. *continued*

up only 62 bars: hardly a display of heavenly length. On the contrary, the exposition of Schumann's finale is just as compact as its 186-bar counterpart in the first movement of Schubert's Piano Trio in E flat is discursive. In fact, Schumann's rapid progress through the various phases of his exposition—coupled with several abrupt shifts in character—creates a kind of nervous momentum that contrasts sharply with the leisurely pace of Schubert's larger forms. Moreover, Schumann increases the sense of urgency by means of a tightly wrought web of thematic relationships: the closing group in the dominant draws on an episodic idea from the slow movement and also makes a parting reference to the passionate cello tune from the transition.

Another Schubertian paradigm, the strophic variation form, appears in an equally unusual light in the development section of the finale. The subject of Schumann's variations is far removed from the sumptuously lyrical music we encounter at the comparable juncture in the first movement of Schubert's trio. Less a theme than a constellation of motivic fragments, it is comprised of five segments: (1) an introductory unit that recalls the music of sublime removal from the preceding slow movement; (2) a stretto on the opening motto theme ("call-to-arms" plus descending sixteenths), which, as we have seen, derives from the coda of the previous movement; (3) another stretto, this one centered on the emphatic initial gesture of the motto, which figures here in a less than cordial dialogue between strings and piano; (4) a brief reference to the episodic theme from the slow movement (already a topic of discussion in the exposition); and (5) a playful series of imitative sequences on another melodic gesture from the slow-movement episode. This rather complex affair is abbreviated considerably in the two variations that follow: moving from G♭ major to the dominant of B♭, the first offers only segments b (the motto) and e; the second also opens with segment b, but like the "theme," it then proceeds with segment c. Since the latter is based on the opening "call-to-arms" and since the harmonic trajectory of the second variation replicates that of its predecessor at the lower fifth (C♭ to V/E♭), Schumann is able to lead smoothly and logically into the recapitulation of the opening motto in the tonic.

Much as in the exposition, the development of Schumann's finale thus invokes the structure, though not the character, of a Schubertian model. Unlike the development sections of most of Schubert's later sonata-form movements, Schumann's development is notable for its contrapuntal density, its closely argued motivic relationships, its concision, its nervous energy, and its drive toward the reprise. On the one hand, several of these qualities point to Beethoven rather than Schubert; on the other, the overall framework in which Schumann presents his ideas is quite unlike anything in Beethoven and departs in significant ways from Schubert as well. In short, the development enacts a synthesis of disparate tendencies, and the result is noticeably greater than the sum of the influences that went into its making.

Similar claims could be made for the recapitulation. Immediately after the whole ensemble proclaims the initial motto theme in the tonic, the music embarks on an unusual path. Instead of proceeding with the fugato, as expected, Schumann introduces a self-contained binary unit in A♭ that at first appears to bear no clear relationship to what precedes or follows it. (See Ex. 1-8.) Of course, for Schumann, such moments are really not so unusual at all; comparable digressions from the main thrust of the musical argument are standard fare in his keyboard music of the previous decade. Lyrical in tone, the episode from the piano-quartet finale also assumes the character of an exercise in double counterpoint, its two chief melodic strands consisting of a descending chromatic line in the viola part and a winding, sequential idea in the

Example 1-7: Schumann, Piano Quartet, finale: vivace, mm. 1–12

(continued)

piano. In attending more closely to the second strand, we begin to under-stand the method in Schumann's madness: the sinuous figure in the piano is a derivative of the countersubject in the fugato that opens the movement, precisely the music that is withheld at this stage of the reprise. (Cf. Ex. 1-8 and Ex. 1-7, mm. 3–11, viola; mm. 12–15, piano; mm. 17–19, violin and piano.) A distant relative of the sudden detours in Schubert's larger forms (recall, for instance, the digression that occurs at the corresponding spot in the slow movement of the Piano Trio in E flat), Schumann's episodic aside is far more radical than its possible models, in terms of both the absolute contrast be-

tween the episode and its surroundings and the quirky logic that justifies this interruption in the normal flow of events.

While the remainder of the recapitulation unfolds with nearly textbook regularity, things take another odd turn with the onset of the coda. Opening with a restatement at the lower fifth of the entire constellation of motives that served as the "theme" of the development's strophic variations, Schumann seems to invoke the sort of parallel form by means of which Schubert imparted structural clarity to the mammoth finale of his Piano Trio in E flat. In Schumann's finale, however, the exact parallelism breaks down rather sooner than in Schubert's, extending only through the initial segment of the first variation. Again, the musical path veers in an unexpected direction (cutting immediately to the last segment of the second variation), and again, there is an underlying logic to Schumann's strategy. The goal toward which he aspires is a grand restatement of the opening motto, imitatively fanned out by the whole ensemble in a three-voice stretto. With this gesture of apotheosis, Schumann in effect tacks yet another coda onto the coda already in progress, a move that some listeners may well find excessive. Yet here, too, the procedure is not without justification, for Schumann is intent on discovering a satisfactory resolution not only for the finale but also for the four-movement cycle as a whole.

Example 1-8: Schumann, Piano Quartet, finale, mm. 147–64

(continued)

The reprise of the motto works itself up to a fermata on the dominant, and then, in one last display of contrapuntal ingenuity, Schumann devotes the next thirty bars or so to a new fugato on the motto theme that rivals the opening paragraph of the movement in rhythmic drive and transformational power. All of these gestures—the triumphant return, the surge toward dominant harmony, the release of tension with yet another contrapuntal transformation of the motto—lend a dimension to the proceedings that is "epic" in the fullest sense of the term: Schumann not only calls up the past; more to the point, he makes the past vividly present. With the terminal coda of the finale we thus reach the last stage of a process that began with the moments of sublime removal at the end of the slow movement. In tracing a great affective arc from dreamy reflection to decisive action, Schumann invokes the path he had taken many years before in his Piano Quartet in C minor, a path already traversed in Schubert's Piano Trio in E flat. Of course, as a mature artist Schumann was able to realize his aims in ways that were clearly beyond him a decade before: what in 1828 was only the promise of future successes had evolved by 1842 into mastery of the whole range of contrapuntal and motivic techniques. Moreover, it was precisely in his handling of these techniques that the mature Schumann set himself apart from the model of his youth.

In closing, then, a few words about the terminal fugato of Schumann's Piano Quartet in E flat—a passage where he allowed free reign to his skills in counterpoint and motivic development. (See Ex. 1-9.) The fugato is based on a contrapuntal combination of the two elements that had been presented successively in the initial motto theme: the "call-to-arms," extended from three to thirteen pitches to form an angular, rhetorically charged subject (given first to the viola); and the sequentially descending sixteenth-note pattern, also amplified in its new context to provide a rhythmically driving countersubject (initially in the piano). Stated fourteen times in whole or in part (at various pitch levels, in closely overlapping entries, and with the relative position of subject and countersubject sometimes inverted), this contrapuntal unit also embodies a rather extraordinary motivic property. Indeed, it allows us to view its melodic sources—the motto theme, the finale's opening fugato, the three-note cell from the coda of the slow movement—in a new light. Combining features from all of its previous incarnations, the closing fugato reveals the latent connections among them.

As shown in Example 1-10, the subject is grounded in a chain of descending thirds that can be parsed into two complete cycles, each spanning a double octave from B♭ to B♭. (By inverting three of the thirds into sixths, Schumann is able to keep what would otherwise have occupied a full four octaves within a comfortable range.) Similarly, the countersubject outlines a complementary (if not quite so extravagant) pattern of descent in thirds. (See Ex. 1-11.) Hence Schumann practically forces us to realize, if we haven't already, that the motto theme itself elaborates a single cycle of the same downward spiral.

Example 1-9: Schumann, Piano Quartet, finale, mm. 277–84

Example 1-10: Schumann, Piano Quartet, finale, closing fugato subject

Example 1-11: Schumann, Piano Quartet, finale, closing fugato countersubject

Example 1-12: Schumann, Piano Quartet, finale, motto theme

(See Ex. 1-12.) In returning to the subject of the closing fugato, we observe that its descending thirds might also be grouped into cycles of descending fifths, an interpretation suggested by the gap between B♭ and E♭ at the beginning of the subject and between C and F near the end. (See Ex. 1-10.) This alternate intervallic cycle in turn resonates with Schumann's treatment of the three-note cell in the coda of the slow movement; as observed earlier, the otherworldly quality of this passage derives in part from a series of transpositions down by fifth. The decidedly earthbound close of the finale evokes the tonal trajectory of the slow movement's coda in another way as well: Schumann initially answers the fugato subject at the lower fifth, A♭. (See Ex. 1-9, mm. 281–84.)

Schumann's Piano Quartet in E flat is thus situated at a crossroads. On the one hand, it offers the listener a compelling—and strikingly original—synthesis of earlier models and practices. While its structural underpinnings hearken to Schubert, its intense motivicism and rhythmic urgency suggest a Beethovenian source. The contrapuntal tour de force of its closing pages points back even further still, to the fugues of J. S. Bach. On the other hand, the work looks well into the future: the chains of cascading thirds that run through its final paragraphs would become a staple of Brahms's musical vocabulary. Schumann's quartet takes us on an incredible journey, a journey initiated by his experience of Schubert's "immortal" Piano Trio in E flat.

CHAPTER 2.

THE GESTUS OF REMEMBERING:

SCHUMANN'S CRITIQUE OF

SCHUBERT'S IMPROMPTUS, D. 935

HE PUBLICATION OF SEVERAL large-scale instrumental works by Franz Schubert in the late 1820s and 1830s elicited little reaction from contemporary critics. G. W. Fink's thoughtful—and poetic—review of the Piano Trio in E flat, from which I have already quoted in the previous chapter, was one of only a few exceptions that prove the rule.[1] Yet the critical voice that broke the near silence with the greatest regularity belonged to Robert Schumann. Between 1834 (when he and a small group of like-minded thinkers founded the *Neue Zeitschrift für Musik*) and 1840, Schumann turned repeatedly to Schubert's instrumental music, illuminating the special magic of pieces that ranged in weight from the comparatively slight *16 Deutsche und 2 Ecossaisen* (D. 783) to the colossal Symphony in C major (D. 944).[2]

I

What was it that drew Schumann so ineluctably to Schubert's music? As we have seen, Schumann accorded much significance to what he perceived to be Schubert's departure from Beethovenian formal models, his demonstration that Beethoven's path was not the only path to grandeur and sublimity in the larger instrumental genres. And of course, Schumann located the principal tenet of this declaration of independence from Beethoven in the "heavenly length" of Schubert's broadest designs. By the same token, heavenly length was not the only quality that distinguished Schubert's approach; equally deci-

47

sive, in Schumann's opinion, was the unique constellation of features that lent to Schubert's music its inimitable melancholy and wistfulness. Writing to Friedrich Wieck in 1829, Schumann also marveled at the "psychologically unusual . . . course and connection of [Schubert's] musical ideas."[3] In alluding to the specifically psychological dimension of Schubert's musical language, Schumann calls our attention to the older composer's ability to represent or evoke a whole panoply of mental states, attitudes, and processes in tone.

According to the philosopher Martin Heidegger, the totality of these mental postures can be subsumed under three fundamental modes of consciousness or "ways of being in the world," each of which he further linked with a distinct temporal orientation. In the first mode, the individual is totally absorbed in contemplation and hence removed from the present into the past; the second mode constitutes a "moment of vision," the point at which the individual becomes acutely aware of the existence in the present of an object or action; finally, the third mode is characterized by resoluteness or purpose, thus necessitating a frame of mind directed at the future. The possibilities of this scheme for art criticism were recognized by the aesthetician Emil Staiger, who found in each of Heidegger's temporal modes the essence of the three canonical genres of poetry: the lyric, the epos, and the drama. In Staiger's view, the essential character of lyric poetry lay not only in its disclosure of a mood but also in its tendency to represent a mental state that favored contemplation of and, ultimately, complete immersion in the past. "In the flow of the lyric," he wrote, "we hear the stream of transience."[4] The epic poet also dips liberally into the well of the past, but rather than losing himself in the process, he summons what is far away into the here-and-now, allowing it to stand before our eyes as a vivid presence and thereby lending permanence to the transitory.[5] In contrast, the dramatist neither meditates nor objectifies; the most volatile of the artistic types, he "throws himself . . . toward a presupposed future."[6] Staiger sums up his entire theory in three succinct phrases: "lyric existence remembers, epic existence presents, dramatic existence projects."[7]

Having made this detour into psychology, philosophy, and aesthetics, we are better poised, I think, to understand the nature of Schumann's intense attraction to Schubert. Briefly stated, Schumann heard in Schubert's music a unique and alluring exploration of the relationship between affective character and temporal unfolding. In chapter 1, we considered Schumann's reactions, as listener and composer, to Schubert's "epic" shaping of time in his Piano Trio in E flat, a work that closes with a triumphant gesture of thematic recall and thus gives primacy of place to the temporality of presence in the musical experience.[8] Here I would like to suggest that Schumann, as a critic, was equally sensitive to the temporality of pastness in Schubert's instrumental music and to its bearing on the emotional character of large-scale musical designs. Indeed, this was another area where Schubert, at least in Schumann's view, asserted his independence from Beethovenian paradigms: whereas Beethoven, especially in the symphonic works of his "heroic" phase, tended to drive headlong from the present into the future, in emulation of the teleological thrust of drama, Schubert often treated the present as a mere pretext for summoning up and then immersing himself in the past.[9]

Schumann voiced his thoughts on the unique temporal quality of Schubert's music as early as August 1828, in a diary entry where he described the Adagio of the "Wanderer" Fantasy (D. 760) as "a gentle reflection on lived experience."[10] Writing five years later in the metaphoric vein that had become the hallmark of his prose style, he equated the *Sehnsuchtswalzer* with "memories of lost youth and a thousand loves."[11] Yet one area of Schubert's output more than any other seems to have impressed Schumann for its embodiment of the temporality of pastness: the set of four Impromptus, D. 935. Published posthumously in 1839 by the Viennese firm of Diabelli as Op. 142, the Impromptus were greeted by the virtual silence that typically attended the appearance in print of Schubert's more extended works. Ignored by the venerable *Allgemeine musikalische Zeitung*, the Impromptus did, however, inspire a suggestive response from Schumann, whose review of the collection was published in the 14 December 1838 issue of the *Neue Zeitschrift*. Although I will be quoting from Schumann's review in the course of the subsequent discussion, it may be useful to reproduce it in full at this point.[12] For ease of reference, the sentences have been numbered from 1 through 14:

[1] Would that he had lived to see how people now revere him; this would have inspired him to the highest degree. [2] Now that he has long rested in peace, we should carefully collect and chronicle what he has left behind; nothing survives that does not give witness to his spirit; in only a very few works [of other composers] is the seal of their creator so clearly imprinted. [3] Hence every page of the first two Impromptus seems to whisper "Franz Schubert"; we discover him anew as we recognize him in his inexhaustible moods, and as he charms, deceives, and then grips us. [4] Yet I can hardly believe that Schubert really called these movements "Impromptus"; the first is so obviously the first movement of a sonata, so perfectly executed and self-contained [*so vollkommen ausgeführt und abgeschlossen*] that there can be no doubt. [5] I consider the second Impromptu to be the second movement of the same sonata; in key and character it is closely related to the first. [6] As far as the closing movements are concerned, Schubert's friends must know whether or not he completed the sonata; one might perhaps regard the fourth Impromptu as the finale, but while the key confirms this supposition, the rather casual design speaks against it. [7] Of course, these are suppositions that only an examination of the original manuscript would clarify. [8] But I do not consider them of little consequence; to be sure, titles and superscriptions matter little; on the other hand, a sonata is such a fine ornament in the wreath of a composer's

works that I would gladly add another one to Schubert's many, indeed twenty. [9] So far as the third Impromptu is concerned, I would have hardly taken it to be one of Schubert's efforts, except, perhaps, a youthful one; it is a set of by-and-large undistinguished variations on an equally undistinguished theme. [10] The variations are totally lacking in invention and fantasy, qualities that Schubert has displayed so creatively in other works of this genre. [11] If one plays the first two Impromptus in succession and joins them to the fourth one, in order to make a lively close, the result may not be a complete sonata, but at least we will have one more beautiful memory [Erinnerung] of Schubert. [12] If one is already familiar with his style, only a single play-through will be necessary to grasp the work perfectly. [13] In the first movement, the delicate, fantastic embroidery between the quiet melodic passages might well lull us to sleep; the whole movement was conceived in an hour of suffering, as if musing on the past [wie im Nachdenken an Vergangenes]. [14] The second movement has the more meditative [beschaulichen] character we often find in Schubert's works; in contrast, the third movement (fourth Impromptu) seems to pout, though quietly and kindly: one can hardly miss the point; in many places it reminded me of Beethoven's "Rage over a Lost Penny," a very comical but little-known piece.

One phrase in particular from this critique merits closer attention: in line 11 Schumann writes that the first, second, and fourth Impromptus constitute "one more beautiful memory [Erinnerung] of Schubert." Taken at face value, this remark simply implies that the Impromptus (or, to be precise, the three that Schumann judged worthy of the mature Schubert) represented a welcome addition to the growing body of Schubert's published instrumental music. But interpreted as a figurative expression and viewed in the context of Schumann's comments on the individual Impromptus, the phrase invites us to examine more closely the musical representation of memory in these pieces.[13]

II

After completing the Impromptus (D. 935) in late December 1827, Schubert had little success in placing them with a publisher. Tobias Haslinger, who had recently issued two other Impromptus by Schubert (D. 899, nos. 1 and 2), showed little interest in the new set. Similarly Schott, the Mainz firm to which Schubert sent the pieces in April 1828, responded in October with a withering reply; apparently the publisher's Parisian contacts found them to be "too difficult for little pieces [Kleinigkeiten] and therefore unmarketable in France."[14] Since Schubert had designated the pieces as "Impromptus," Schott probably expected something along the lines of the fashionable salon pieces for piano produced in sizable quantities during the initial decades of the nineteenth century by the Czech composer Václav Jan Tomášek and his pupil Jan Václav Voříšek. Named after poetic genres such as the eclogue (an idyllic soliloquy or dialogue), rhapsody (verses of an emotional or ecstatic character), and dithyramb (the ancient choric hymn dedicated to Dionysus), Tomášek's piano pieces tended to be modest in scope and were especially notable for their elegant melodies, rippling accompaniments, and pastoral tone.[15] Voříšek followed suit with his six Impromptus, Op. 7 (issued by the Viennese publisher Mechetti in 1822), adding to the stylistic palette of his teacher's works a propensity for chromatic part writing redolent in some ways of Schubert.[16] Like the eclogue, rhapsody, and dithyramb, this genre also had a poetic source: during the course of the eighteenth century, the term "impromptu" was used to designate the brief, epigrammatic verses improvised between the acts of plays. But most important of all from the perspective of the musical marketplace in the early nineteenth century, the miniatures of Tomášek and Voříšek were tailor-made for amateur pianists who could manage a certain amount of flashy but not very difficult passagework. Schubert's Impromptus were of an entirely different order; cast for the most part in rather large forms, they posed far greater challenges to players and listeners than the charming character pieces of Tomášek and Voříšek. To borrow a phrase from current theorists of musical reception: these Czech composers set the terms of the "generic contract" that Schubert either ignored or abrogated in his Impromptus, D. 935.[17]

Schumann was also struck by the discrepancy between the title "Impromptus" and the actual substance of Schubert's pieces, a discrepancy he found to be especially pronounced in the F-minor work that opens the set. To quote line 4 of his review: "Yet I can hardly believe that Schubert really called these movements 'Impromptus'; the first is so obviously the first movement of a sonata, so perfectly executed and self-contained [so vollkommen ausgeführt und abgeschlossen] that there can be no doubt."[18] As shown in Table 2-1, the Impromptu is comprised of two roughly corresponding parts plus a brief epilogue based on the initial music. Both parts in turn fall into five sections (labeled A–E in Table 2-1), each of which projects a distinct character. The F-minor section A, with its eloquent dotted rhythms, pregnant pauses, and abrupt dynamic shifts, displays a markedly rhetorical profile; in contrast, the murmuring figuration of section B projects an air of pathos. The move toward Ab having been effected during the last phrases of section B, section C presents a series of bravura cadential flourishes in that key, which holds throughout the idyllic theme and two variations of section D. Part I closes with section E, a full-fledged binary form conceived as a wistful exchange between treble and bass. After this ruminative dialogue without words, a brief retransition leads to part II, where Schubert restates all the attendant sections of part I, now anchored in F minor-major. The Impromptu concludes with an abbreviated return to section A in the tonic, F minor.

Table 2-1: Overview of Schubert, Impromptdu in F minor, D. 935, no. 1 (Op. posth. 142, no. 1)

Part I				
A	B	C	D	E
Rhetorical	Pathetic	Bravura	Idylic Variation	Dialogue w.o. Words
(1st group)	(trans.)	(trans.)	(2nd group)	(closing)
f	f to V/A^b	A^b to V/A^b	A^b	a^b to C^b; C^b/a^b to A^b
1–13	13–30	30–44	45–66	182–224
Part II				
A	B	C	D	E
Rhetorical	Pathetic	Bravura	Idylic Variation	Dialogue w.o. Words
f	f to V/F	F to V/F	F	f to A^b; A^b/f to F
115–27	127–44	144–58	159–80	182–224
Epilogue				
A				
Rhetorical				
f				
226–34				

The overall structure of the F-minor Impromptu thus exhibits the sort of parallelism with which Schubert had framed the sonata-form argument of the finale of his Piano Trio in E flat,[19] though here we are obviously not dealing with a typical example of sonata-allegro form. First, there is nothing that remotely resembles a development section. In addition, the lengthy, episodic section E is difficult to square with the conventional paradigm. At the same time, the Impromptu is hardly devoid of features generally encountered in sonata-form movements. In terms of function, section A approximates a first group, sections B and C a transition, section D a second group, and section E a closing group. Furthermore, since part I moves from minor tonic (f) to relative major (A♭), whereas part II remains within the orbit of the minor and major tonic, the two larger divisions of the movement relate much like exposition and recapitulation. Thus, while the Impromptu cannot be said to be "in" sonata form, it certainly draws on the rhetorical markers of that design.[20] Moreover, it displays the "symmetry of construction" that Schumann associated with sonata form elsewhere in his writings and that he invoked in the "parallel" designs of many of his own sonata-form movements, including the original finale of the G-minor Piano Sonata (Presto passionato), the finale of the *Concert sans orchestre* (Op. 14), the opening and closing movements of the Fantasie (Op. 17), and the finales of the A-major String Quartet (Op. 41, no. 3), the Piano Quintet (Op. 44), and the Piano Quartet (Op. 47).[21]

The next stage of Schumann's argument brings us nearer to our central theme: the quality of pastness that imparts to the Impromptus their special temporal character. In Schumann's opinion, the first, second, and possibly fourth Impromptus were movements of a sonata that Schubert may or may not have finished. (Schumann wrote off the third Impromptu in B♭ rather harshly, in line 9, as "a set of by-and-large undistinguished variations on an equally undistinguished theme."[22]) To quote lines 5 and 6 of his review: "I consider the second Impromptu to be the second movement of the same sonata; in key [A♭] and character it is closely related to the first. As far as the closing movements are concerned, Schubert's friends must know whether or not he completed the sonata; one might perhaps regard the fourth Impromptu as the finale, but while the key [F minor] confirms this supposition, the rather casual design speaks against it." The humorous quality of the fourth Impromptu (which, as Schumann observes in line 14, "seems to pout") is also in keeping with the affective character traditionally expected of a final movement in an early nineteenth-century sonata cycle. In this case, the comic effect is largely a result of Schubert's playful handling of rhythm and meter: the combination of triple groupings in the right hand with duple groupings in the left; the alternation of the notated $\frac{3}{8}$ meter with an implied $\frac{3}{4}$ and unexpected stresses on the second and third beats of the measure. But whereas the finales of multimovement works are often cast in "casual" designs such as the rondo, the form of Schubert's concluding Impromptu—A B A′ plus coda—is more readily linked with the character piece than with the final movement of a sonata.

In short, Schumann was suggesting that Schubert may have embedded the remnants of a sonata in what appeared, on first hearing, to be a collection of character pieces—an observation that in turn led him to describe Impromptus 1, 2, and 4 as "one more beautiful memory of Schubert." Consider the phrase in the context of line 11 from his review: "If one plays the first two Impromptus in succession and joins them to the fourth one, in order to make a lively close, the result may not be a complete sonata, but at least we will have one more beautiful memory [Erinnerung] of Schubert." Had Schumann examined the autograph of D. 935, he would have been disappointed, for the evidence it provides on the unity of the set is ambiguous.[23] Schumann's musicological skills, however, are of less interest for our purposes than the implicit parallels he draws between incompletion and memory on the one hand and fragmentation and pastness on the other.

Since every product of memory possesses a fragmentary quality, the fragment can be readily construed as a metaphor for memory. This is not to say, however, that all fragments are emblems of past experience. Only the fragment that points to an absent whole that necessarily precedes it in time, thus revealing itself as a torso or ruin, can be viewed as a figurative expression of pastness. Schumann made this point epigrammatically in a fanciful dialogue published in 1836: "A monument is a ruin facing forward (just as a ruin is a monument facing backward.)"[24] Since, for Schumann, all but the third of the D. 935 Impromptus were fragments or ruins of a sonata, they were at the same time "monuments facing backward" and thus looked toward the past.

Keeping this in mind, we might interpret Schumann's hypothesis that concerns the fragmentary sonata embedded in the D. 935 set as a metaphoric statement of the temporality of pastness in the Impromptus.

Schumann spells this out in his comments on the first two Impromptus (lines 13 and 14), the movements about whose status as fragments of a sonata he had no doubt: "In the first movement, the delicate, fantastic embroidery between the quiet melodic passages might well lull us to sleep; the whole movement was conceived in an hour of suffering, as if musing on the past [*wie im Nachdenken an Vergangenes*]. The second movement has the more meditative [*beschaulichen*] character we often find in Schubert's works." Thus in Schumann's reading, both Impromptus bore the unmistakable imprint of pastness. The second, cast in ABA form, alternates between what he once called the visionary keys of A♭ and D♭.[25] Meditative or contemplative in character, the movement reflects chiefly on itself. (See Exs. 2-1a and 2-1b.) The central Trio in D♭ (section B) can be heard as a meditation on the music of section A; while its quietly pulsing inner-voice pedal on A♭ recalls the E♭-pedal of the opening material, the accentuation of the pedal in the Trio subtly echoes the sarabande rhythm with which the movement begins.[26] In describing the first Impromptu as a rumination on the past, Schumann hit upon one of the most characteristic—and uncanny— aspects of Schubert's music: its richness in musical ideas that, already on their first appearance, are imbued with the quality of a reminiscence. Consider the opening of section B (see Ex. 2-2.). There is something tentative, disembodied about this music: we hear an idea attempting to take shape—a series of repeated notes embellished by lower and upper neighbors—though it is veiled by the broken texture of the pattern in the right hand. (If, as Henri Bergson claimed, memory arises at "the intersection of mind and matter," then section B of the Impromptu surely counts as a striking representation of memory in tones.[27]) Later, in section D, the veiled idea from section B assumes a more tangible shape (see Ex. 2-3), but while the pitch level of the idea is the same in both passages, the brooding F minor of section B is replaced by a mellow and stable A♭ major in section D.[28] In other words, section D seems to embody the presence lacking in section B, while conversely, section B might be interpreted on first hearing as an only partially successful attempt to call up an idea in memory.[29]

Schubert's predilection for suffusing the present with an aura of pastness is even more evident in the passage described by Schumann as consisting of "delicate, fantastic embroidery" that "might well lull us to sleep." Here he was surely alluding to the wordless dialogue of section E. Most probably Schumann was captivated by the sublime inwardness of this passage, by its projection of a sense of removal from the temporal presence of the earlier music into a realm summoned up from the recesses of memory. Texture, rhythm, and harmony contribute equally to this effect (see Ex. 2-4). The accompanimental arpeggios (or, in Schumann's words, "the delicate, fantastic

Example 2-1a: Schubert, Impromptu in A flat, D. 935, no. 2, mm. 1–8

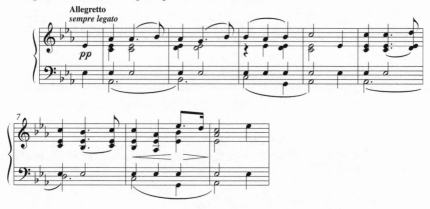

Example 2-1b: Schubert, Impromptu in A flat, D. 935, no. 2, opening of Trio

embroidery") displace the downbeat by an eighth note, thus creating a mild but perceptible metric dissonance that envelops the wordless duet in a haze—the haze through which half-forgotten events and images are brought to consciousness. The shift from A♭ major to A♭ minor during the brief transition into section E further intensifies the impression of motion from one temporal plane to another.

The effect of this transitional passage can be compared to a process enacted repeatedly in an artwork that is thoroughly suffused with the aura of pastness: Proust's *A la recherche du temps perdu.* In the first and most celebrated of the novel's *moments bienheureux* (fortuitous moments) the taste of a madeleine dipped in lime-blossom tea is the catalyst for the narrator's detailed and nuanced recollection of myriad scenes from his youth. Products of the *mémoire involuntaire,* such fortuitous moments occur when something ex-

Example 2-2: Schubert, Impromptu in F minor, D. 935, no. 1, section B, opening

Example 2-3: Schubert, Impromptu in F minor, D. 935, no. 1, section D, opening

perienced in the present triggers the memory of something experienced in the past by means of what Proust calls the miracle of analogy. Each phase of this process can be mapped onto a corresponding phase in Schubert's F-minor Impromptu: the cascading A♭-major arpeggios that link sections D and E articulate a moment in the present, the evocative dialogue without words unfolds as a memory of things past, and the emergence of the delicate, accompanimental embroidery of the wordless dialogue from the preceding arpeggios owes its existence to the "miracle of analogy." According to Proust, the "present scene" is always victorious over the "distant scene"—as it surely is in Schubert's Impromptu when the dialogue without words gives way to a reprise of the rather austere music of section A—but in spite of this, the "vanquished" scene, the one that emanates from the past, is still "the more beautiful of the two."[30] And indeed, the interior journeys traced by the dialogues without words in both parts of the F-minor Impromptu surely represent the most strikingly beautiful moments in the piece.[31] The closing passages of Schubert's Impromptu thus embody a very different temporal character from that of the corresponding moments in the finale of his Piano Trio in

Example 2-4: Schubert, Impromptu in F minor, D. 935, no. 1, mm. 66–71

E flat. Whereas in the latter a memory of things past (the melancholy principal theme of the slow movement) is fully absorbed into the present moment (the triumphant coda of the finale), the evocative vision of past experience in the Impromptu vanishes, like a mirage, without a trace. If the close of the Piano Trio stages a celebration of presence, the final bars of the Impromptu, in contrast, leave us yearning for an irretrievable moment in the past.

Even the generic character of the F-minor Impromptu aspires to a condition of pastness. Rather than conforming to a single generic code, the piece draws on a wide array of genres: the opening movement of a sonata, the virtuoso variations on well-known opera tunes that some composers of the early nineteenth century subsumed under the title "Impromptu,"[32] and the poetic miniature for piano of the type cultivated by Tomášek and Vořišek. Schubert not only invokes the markers of all these genres in the F-minor Impromptu; he also reflects upon them as if from afar. As we have observed, the piece recalls the sonata form in scope, substance, and design, or, as Schumann put it, the F-minor Impromptu is as "perfectly executed and self-contained" as the first movement of a sonata, though it was hardly made to order from a prefabricated mold. In addition, echoes of the virtuoso impromptu can be heard in the improvisatory flourishes of section A, the outbursts of bravura in section C, and the patterned figures of the variations that comprise section D. Finally, in the ruminative section E we hear memories of a lyric keyboard piece that itself recalls a lied or dialogue. A self-contained miniature nestled in a much larger design, Section E quite literally reflects upon the surrounding music, not through motivic recollection but rather by mirroring the tonal trajectory of the entire Impromptu (minor tonic to relative major in the first half, minor tonic to major tonic in the second).

Is it too much to suggest, therefore, that the F-minor Impromptu not only enacts a musical representation of *memory* but also actually embodies *memories* of the various musical genres? And is this not simply another way of defining Schubert's role in the profound transformation undergone by the notion of genre itself in the early nineteenth century? For an early German Romantic critic such as Friedrich Schlegel, "one might just as well claim that there are *infinitely many* poetic genres, or that there is only *one* progressive genre."[33] By this he meant that the tendency in modern literature was toward a metagenre ("*one* progressive genre") in which the poet attempted to synthesize the discrete poetic types of earlier periods. As a result of this process, the individual genres were transformed into an array of fluid qualities: the lyric poem became a lyrical tone, the drama a dramatic manner, the idyll an idyllic aura, the romance a romantic flavor, and so forth for all of the "infinitely many" genres.[34]

Schumann the critic was deeply cognizant of the musical analogues of this shift. In his view, genres that included the sonata and variation had outrun their life course, but as he noted in 1839, "This is entirely in keeping with the order of things; for rather than repeat ourselves for centuries, we should seek out new possibilities."[35] Of all the composers of the preceding generation, it was Schubert who, in Schumann's opinion, offered the clearest premonition of what these new possibilities might entail. In keeping with the Romantic outlook on freedom as both a right and a calling, Schumann once praised Schubert for his "disregard for strict, mathematical forms."[36] On one hand, Schubert asserted his freedom from the strict forms by exploring the outer reaches of infinity, hence the heavenly length that characterizes not only the C-major Symphony but also the G-major String Quartet (D. 887), the C-major String Quintet (D. 956), and, of course, the Piano Trio in E flat, Schumann's favorite among Schubert's late chamber works. On the other hand, Schubert's disregard for tried-and-true paradigms just as often pointed in the opposite direction, that is, toward an excavation of the past. In other words, heavenly length and the temporality of pastness prove to be flip sides of the same coin. While the former was an agency of Schubert's epic breadth, the latter went hand in hand with his tendency toward lyric inwardness. In both cases, the product was that "psychologically unusual course and connection of musical ideas" that attracted Schumann to Schubert's music in the first place.

III

Schumann's critical writings and his music stand in a reciprocal relationship. While many of his compositions represent an attempt to realize in tone the ideals he crusaded for in the pages of the *Neue Zeitschrift für Musik,* his comments on the works of other composers often open a window onto his own creativity. This is surely the case for much of what he had to say about Schubert. Hence Schumann's observations on the recollective quality of Schubert's F-minor Impromptu serve to heighten our awareness of the remarkable affinities between both composers' musical representations of temporal character. And although Schumann's music tends toward heavenly length less often than Schubert's, it is every bit as rich in evocations of the past.

In some instances, the temporality of pastness in Schumann's works emerges in moments of self-reflection, as when, at the conclusions of *Dichterliebe* and *Frauenliebe und Leben,* the piano meditates quietly on music heard earlier in the song cycles. Alternatively, Schumann often concentrates his sites of pastness in the self-absorbed digressions of which he, like Schubert, was so fond. The "Im Legendenton" section from the first movement of the C-major Fantasie (Op. 17) serves as a classic example. (See Ex. 2-5.) Embedded within a varied reprise of the movement's opening theme group, this dreamy aside—and a gargantuan one at that, occupying nearly a hundred bars—transports us into a realm far removed from that of the surrounding music. The passage calls up an image of a pianist improvising at the keyboard (Schumann himself no doubt) who loses his previous train of thought, perhaps intentionally, and indulges in a strange but wondrous reverie. That this new improvisation is oriented toward the past is clear enough from the indication in the score: "Im Legendenton," that is, "in the tone of a legend," a tale from days long gone by.[37] But even the listener who does not have access to the score (and since we are witnessing an improvisation, a score is obviously not involved) will have little difficulty in determining the temporal orientation of the music. The plangent, folklike quality of the main theme, the austere harmonies, the tonal shift in the "plagal" direction as we proceed from the first phrase (G minor) to the second (C minor), the subsequent allusions to melodic strands from earlier in the movement: all of this draws us ever more deeply into the past.[38]

For Schumann, the contrast between temporal modes becomes just as effective a means of shaping a musical argument as the more traditional contrasts between keys or themes. Composed in 1849, the *Concertstück,* or *Introduction und Allegro appassionato* for piano and orchestra (Op. 92) plays on the opposition of two sound worlds, one a signifier for distance in time, the other firmly rooted in the present. The former realm dominates the G-major introduction, which opens with a four-bar lyrical fragment in the clarinet answered

Example 2-5: Schumann, Fantasie (Op. 17), first movement, mm. 129–43

by an evocative horn call; delicate arpeggios in the piano echo the melodic contour of both ideas. By way of contrast, the Allegro jolts us into another temporal plane with an abrupt shift into E minor and a full orchestral presentation of a martial figure punctuated by triplet fanfares. Reminiscences of the horn call from the introduction insinuate themselves into the musical flow at several points in the ensuing exposition—during the transition to the second group, as a foil to the lyrical second theme, and immediately before the piano's subsequent outburst of virtuoso display—but Schumann reserves the principal conflict between sound worlds for the development. Twice during that section the clarinet melody from the introduction intrudes on the proceedings, and in both instances the sense of removal into a distant realm is enhanced by means of instrumental color: in place of the original clarinet line, we hear the entire wind band, accompanied first by pizzicato triplets in the violas and then by rolling figuration in the piano solo. The same voices from afar make a final appearance in the coda, and here the quality of temporal displacement is even more clearly underscored than in the development, hinging not only on instrumental sonority (upper wind tone, continuous piano arpeggios, string pizzicati) but on tonal juxta-position as well (B♭ major in a G-major context). The tension between these emblems of pastness and the presence embodied in the music that surrounds them is finally resolved when the solo piano integrates both the horn call and the dreamy clarinet melody into the brilliant passagework that brings the *Concertstück* to a close.[39]

Just as in Schubert's music, the images of pastness in Schumann's fre-quently appear to arise from the workings of the *mémoire involuntaire*. In a sensitive and eloquently argued study, Berthold Hoeckner has described the musical representation of this recollective faculty in the *Davidsbündlertänze* (Op. 6). Schumann invokes the *mémoire involuntaire* in the penultimate piece of the eighteen-movement cycle ("Wie aus der Ferne"), where he summons up the melancholy but tender music of the second piece ("Innig"). To quote Hoeckner: "As a distant memory flashing back closely, [this] is the most mag-ical moment of the cycle: not a 'mask,' as Schumann said, but a 'face.'"[40] And the "face," Hoeckner further observes, belongs to Clara Wieck, whose *Valses romantiques* provided Schumann with the musical figure—a series of re-peated F♯s—that unleashed the floodgates of memory in the closing phases of the *Davidsbündlertänze*.[41]

Indeed, Schumann's most compelling representations of the *mémoire invol-untaire* are perhaps those in which the origin of the reminiscence lies outside the piece in which it occurs, for here the arc that connects present and past spans the greatest distances. Such *moments bienheureux* occur with some fre-quency in Schumann's keyboard music of the 1830s (the fleeting reminiscence of the first waltz of *Papillons* in "Florestan" from *Carnaval* offers a case in point), and they appear in the later chamber music as well. Two examples in particular invite comparison with Schubert's practice. The *moment bienheu-reux* in the eighth and last of the *Novelletten* (Op. 21)—designated a "Stimme aus der Ferne," or "voice from the distance"—emerges from the jaunty music of the movement's second Trio section, transforming presence into pastness through "the miracle of analogy." An allusion to the elegant and supple melody of the "Notturno" from Clara Wieck's *Soirées musicales* (Op. 6), this reminiscence of things past floats in atop the accompanimental figuration previously coupled with the Trio's marchlike opening idea.[42] Clara is also bound up with the *moments bienheureux* in the first movement of the F-major Piano Trio (Op. 80), which evoke one of her favorites among Schumann's lieder: "Dein Bildniss wunderselig" from the Eichendorff *Liederkreis* (Op. 39). And perhaps it is not a coincidence that these lyrical excursions are intro-duced in much the same way as the dialogues without words in Schubert's F-minor Impromptu, over rippling arpeggios carried over from the immedi-ately preceding music, and that they surface in spots roughly analogous to

those in which the wordless dialogues appear in Schubert's piece: just after
the exposition and again during the coda. It was surely passages of this sort
that Theodor Adorno had in mind when he attributed to Schumann the discovery of "the musical gestus of remembering, [of] looking and listening
back."[43] There is good reason to believe that Schumann's principal mentor in
this rarefied art was Franz Schubert.

Part II.

UTTERING "CLARA" IN TONES

CHAPTER 3.

SCHUMANN: CRYPTOGRAPHER

OR PICTOGRAPHER?

*T*HEY EXCHANGED their first kiss in November 1835, on the steps outside her father's house. He was twenty-five; she was only sixteen. When her father learned of their bond, he flew into a rage, forbidding them to have even the slightest contact. Secretly engaged in August 1837, they were not married until 12 September 1840, battle-scarred victors in a legal struggle that had dragged on for over a year. Their love for each other was unconditional, boundless, so that even if they didn't live happily ever after, they lived together happily for over a decade. Lest there be any doubt, the main characters in this story are Robert and Clara Schumann, one of the most remarkable artist couples in the history of Western music. Not surprisingly, their emotional lives affected their artistry. This process was especially decisive for Robert Schumann, whose letters eloquently confirm his desire to inscribe his beloved into the very fabric of his music. "There is only one thought," he wrote to her on 9 October 1837, "that I would like to portray [*hinmahlen*] in large letters and chords: *Clara*."[1]

Only one other figure harbored comparably intense feelings for Clara. A gifted young pianist and composer from Hamburg named Johannes Brahms, he came knocking at the door of the Schumanns' town house in Düsseldorf on 30 September 1853. Although his love for Clara was of a different order from Schumann's, it had no less profound an effect on his creativity. Echoing Schumann, Brahms likened this effect to portraiture. While working on the Adagio of his D-minor Piano Concerto (Op. 15) in December 1856, he wrote to Clara: "I'm painting a gentle portrait of you [*auch male ich an einem sanften Porträt von dir*]".[2]

That Clara served as a muse to both her husband and Brahms is beyond question. That both men sought to portray her in their music is equally certain. But how did they do it? How did Schumann and Brahms utter "Clara" in tones? This chapter and the next consider one of the most frequently offered responses: the hypothesis that several of Schumann's and Brahms's works contain cryptic references to Clara's name, musical ciphers for "Clara" that act as sonorous emblems for a beloved image. This is precisely the sort of approach that underlies Schumann's *Carnaval*. Here the letters in the name Asch, the hometown of his erstwhile sweetheart, Ernestine von Fricken, are translated into musical pitches—more or less in the manner of the old *soggetto cavato* technique—the result being a series of motivic cells, or Sphinxes, as Schumann calls them. (In German, "As" is the word for A♭, while the word for the letter "S", "Es," also designates the pitch E♭; the letter "H" is used to indicate the pitch B, whereas the letter "B" stands for B♭. Thus "Asch" can be enciphered musically as either A♭–C–B or A–E♭–C–B.) Brahms also made use of ciphers. A musical equivalent for the first name of one of his amours, Agathe von Siebold, found its way into the first movement of his G-major String Sextet (Op. 36). Given these examples, it is tempting to think that of all women, Clara must certainly have been the subject of a similar procedure in the music of Schumann and Brahms.

This hypothesis has by no means been universally accepted. Many Schumann specialists simply ignore it. Although other writers have voiced their skepticism,[3] even some of the skeptics are willing to concede that it describes *the kind of thing that Schumann might have done.* Interestingly enough, the theory is invoked most often by writers on Brahms, many of whom assume that Schumann must have passed on his musical code name for Clara, and the system that generated it, to his young protégé.[4] Having been absorbed into the popular wisdom on Schumann and Brahms since it was first proposed in the 1960s, the hypothesis warrants careful scrutiny. As we shall see, it does not stand up well.

Why, then, is the inquiry even worth pursuing? Why should it matter to us that Schumann and Brahms either did or did not translate the name Clara into tones? These questions not only situate us at the intersection of several crossing paths (Schumann's, Brahms's, Clara Schumann's); they also compel us to reflect on the relationship between lived experience and artistic creativity, the twin coordinates whose settings must be closely regulated if we want to produce meaningful statements about the nature of figures like the Schumanns and Brahms. If the setting is askew, then biography degenerates into myth, as it usually does when the point of departure is one of life's intangibles—such as a beloved image whose essence is only dimly captured in a name—from which we hope to gain insights into the meaning of artworks. If, however, we ground our observations in artistic practice, an activity far more conducive than life to precise description, we stand a better chance of learning something about the inner lives of our creative subjects.

So, while my argument will deal initially with negatives (with what Schumann and Brahms probably did *not* do), its ultimate aim is to offer positive responses to issues that remain unresolved: Given our knowledge of Schumann's actual practice of musical encipherment, how can we best interpret it? Was he a practitioner of cryptography, or is there another context for his compositional procedures? Similar questions will be posed on Brahms in chapter 4. Then we will be in a position to understand how both composers might have uttered "Clara" in tones, the subject of chapter 5. For now, we had better begin at the beginning, with the hypothesis that Schumann was a musical cryptographer and that a favorite among his encrypted messages was "Clara."

I

First some definitions. *Cryptology,* or the science of codes, is comprised of two branches: *cryptography,* the art of making codes, and *cryptanalysis,* the art of breaking them. "Cryptograph," a closely related term, first appears in Edgar Allan Poe's short story "The Gold-Bug," where it refers to a text in which something has been encoded. Every cryptographer, or maker of codes, will begin with a *plaintext,* the text marked for transformation into a code or cipher. Many of these terms have Greek roots. "Cryptograph," for instance, derives from the verbs "kryvo" (aorist form: "ékrypsa"), which means "hide," and "gráfo," which means "write." Hence a cryptograph is a piece of hidden or secret writing, while a cryptographer is a crafter of such texts.

Strictly speaking, "codes" and "ciphers" are not quite synonymous, even though the terms are often used interchangeably. In a code the words or phrases of the plaintext are replaced by an alternate set of syllables, letters, words, or phrases, while in a cipher each letter of the plaintext is replaced by another character or group of characters. Of the many types of cipher, the most common by far is the substitution cipher, where every letter in the plaintext is replaced by an individual letter, numeral, or other character in accordance with a predetermined system or pattern. This system is called a key and will in turn be employed by the cryptanalyst (who either knows it outright or discovers it through a process of logical inference) to uncover the text embedded in a cryptograph.[5]

In a series of articles and book chapters published in the late 1960s and early 1970s, the British critic Eric Sams argued that Robert Schumann was a musical cryptographer, a practitioner of the art of secret writing in tones.[6] In two articles published in 1971, he made the same case for Johannes Brahms.[7] Since, in Sams's view, Brahms "learned his musical letters" from his mentor,[8] it will be important for us to review the argument for Schumann's engagement with musical cryptography.

The title of Sams's first article on this topic, published in 1965, asks: "Did Schumann Use Ciphers?" Well, yes, of course he did. In addition to his encipherment of **Asch** (henceforth, plaintexts will appear in boldface type) in *Carnaval,* there are several other instances of this practice in his works, beginning in 1830 with his Op. 1, the *Theme sur le nom Abegg varié pour le pianoforte* (the plaintext, **Abegg,** may refer to a young woman from Mannheim by the name of Pauline Comtesse d'Abegg),[9] and ending in 1853 with his contributions to the "F.A.E." Sonata for Violin and Piano. Dedicated to the violinist Joseph Joachim, the sonata was composed jointly by Schumann (second and fourth movements), Albert Dietrich (first movement), and Brahms (Scherzo), all of whose contributions drew either directly or indirectly on the plaintext **FAE,** the first letters of the words comprising Joachim's personal motto, "frei aber einsam" ("free but lonely").

Sams's rhetorical question was prompted by what he took to be an anomaly, namely, that none of these well-known cases involved **Clara,** "the name that meant more to [Schumann] than any other in the world."[10] Indeed, his entire argument would proceed as a chain of deductions from the premise that Schumann must have had a Clara cipher: "Of course, [Schumann] could have transcribed Clara's name in music, and if he could have done [so] then it was a good working hypothesis that he did."[11] Whereas other writers, including Robert Haven Schauffler and Roger Fiske, had already suggested that Schumann's music incorporated themes or motives associated with Clara[12]— the most often cited of which is comprised of a stepwise descent through the interval of a fifth, as in the opening melody of the Fantasie for Piano (Op. 17)—Sams proposed something quite different. He maintained that in addition to the simple system of substitution cipher in pieces like the "Abegg" Variations and *Carnaval,* where each letter in the plaintext is replaced by its precise pitch equivalent, Schumann invented another, considerably more complex system in the mid-1830s specifically for **Clara.**

Beginning with the obvious, Sams substitutes pitches for the "musical" first, third, and fifth letters of Clara's name and fills in the blank second and fourth spaces to produce the stepwise pattern C–B($\flat$)–A–G($\sharp$)–A, noting that one of its forms (C–B$\flat$–A–G$\sharp$–A) initiates the opening vocal melody of "Die Lotosblume," the seventh song of *Myrthen.*[13] Yet Sams rejects this pattern as the basic form of the Clara cipher,[14] and for reasons that are not difficult to surmise. First, in the one documented instance where Schumann shows us how he would have enciphered a name that contained "nonmusical" letters— his own—he did not substitute pitches for the letters without pitch equivalents. The instance in question is the tenth piece of *Carnaval*—**A.S.C.H_S.C.H.A.** *(Lettres Dansantes)*—where the musical cells suggested by the title are comparable to the *soggetti cavati,* or subjects "carved" out of the letters of a name,

Figure 3-1: Sams's key to Schuman's putative cipher system, from "Did Schuman Use Ciphers?" *Musical Times* 106 (1965), p. 586

much beloved of Renaissance composers such as Josquin des Pres.[15] Second, and more important for Sams's line of reasoning, there is no apparent justification for substituting the l in Clara's name with B($\flat$) and the r with G($\sharp$). Thus the basic form of the Clara cipher must be sought elsewhere, just as the key to its construction must be of a different order from that which generated the Abegg and *Carnaval* ciphers.

Figure 3-1 presents the putative key to Schumann's alternate cipher system, as given in Sam's 1965 article. As we can see, Sams's cipher table consists of a scale that embraces the pitches from g′ to g″, each of which is aligned with several plaintext letters. These in turn appear in three vertical rows or lines to produce what Sams calls a three-line alphabetical arrangement. Hence pitch classes A through F can be used to encipher three plaintext letters, while for pitch class G there are as many as six possibilities.

How does Sams arrive at this seemingly odd construction, where, for instance, the pitch E substitutes for its letter equivalent (E), but B substitutes for A? Again, the argument unfolds deductively from a premise: the assumption that Schumann sought a musical means of uniting Clara's name with his own or, more precisely, with the names of his respectively introverted and extroverted alter egos, Eusebius and Florestan. In his 1967 article "Why Florestan and Eusebius?" Sams goes even further, arguing that Schumann's selection of these names for his conflicted inner selves was actually motivated by his desire for a symbolic union with Clara: "Schumann would have begun by asking what names, beginning with E and F, could be directly related to himself, to each other, and to Clara."[16] The special relationship Sams is looking for arises not only from the proximity of the initials "C" (for "Clara"), "E" (for "Eusebius"), and "F" (for "Florestan") but also from the proximity of Clara's and Eusebius's name days—12 and 14 August, respectively—a fact first noted by Schumann in 1835.[17] After asking us to imagine a cipher table that consists of two elements—a scale from g′ to g″ and under it a "top line" of plaintext comprised of a blank space and the letters from A to G—Sams continues as follows: "Once admit the idea that nothing can be allowed to come between E for Eusebius and C for Clara, and it follows that the letter D must be displaced from its position on the top line of the cipher table and put elsewhere."[18]

Pitches:	g′	a′	b′	c″	d″	e″	f″	g″
Plaintext:	?	?	**A**	**B**	**C**	**E**	**F**	**G**

Figure 3-2: The basis for Sams's key

The result of this operation is given as Figure 3-2. With most of the top line in place, Sams is now poised to deduce the remainder of the cipher table. After filling in the second line by working backward and forward from the letter **L**, he proceeds directly from the **P** at the end of this line to **Q** at the beginning of the third, from which point he simply moves in strict alphabetical sequence through **X**. All that remains is to find spots for the unused letters **D**, **H**, **Y**, and **Z**. Since **Z**, in German, sounds as **TS**, it is, in Sam's view, dispensable. **D** and **H** are arbitrarily placed under the pitches G and A, while **Y** is simply omitted without comment. With these adjustments, Sams's table as given in Figure 3-1 is now complete.

Why, one might ask, does the second line of plaintext letters begin with **I** and not **H**, a logical choice given the terminal **G** of the first line? Although Sams does not offer a rationale, his decision is easily accounted for. As it stands, the table will produce the following encipherment of Clara's name: D–C(♯)–B–A(♯)–B. If **H** had fallen into place as expected, as the first letter in the second line, then all the remaining letters would obviously shift one slot to the right, yielding D–D–B–B–B for **Clara,** not a very compelling result. Furthermore, and quite conveniently, the pitch configuration D–C(♯)–B–A(♯)–B corresponds exactly to a pattern that Roger Fiske identified, in his 1964 article "A Schumann Mystery," as an important musical motive in Schumann's *Davidsbündlertänze* (Op. 6).[19]

Armed with the cryptographic tools offered by the cipher table, Sams can now maintain with confidence that the pitch cell D–C(♯)–B–A(♯)–B not only stands for Clara but actually utters her name in tones. And given his keen eye for appearances of the putative cipher in its many guises—transposed, embedded within larger patterns, or altered in any number of other ways—Sams is able to locate it in a wide sampling of Schumann's music. Extending his net well beyond the *Davidsbündlertänze*, Sams finds derivatives of the Clara cipher in *Myrthen* (no. 18: "Wenn durch die Piazzetta"), the Heine *Liederkreis*, Op. 24 (no. 2: "Es treibt mich hin"), and *Dichterliebe*, Op. 48 (no. 2: "Aus meinen Thränen spriessen").[20] In his second major article on the topic, "The Schumann Ciphers" (1966), Sams points to additional examples in the Heine *Liederkreis* and *Dichterliebe* and also uncovers references in the Eichendorff *Liederkreis* (Op. 39), the Fantasie (Op. 17), and the Fourth Symphony in D minor (Op. 120).[21] The search for musical cryptographs yields especially rich results in the latter work, dubbed by Sams "the symphony that was to be called Clara" after an entry Schumann made in his diary before drafting the original

Example 3-1: Schumann, Symphony in D minor, Lebhaft, m. 1

version of the D-minor Symphony in 1841.[22] Example 3-1 presents but one of
the eleven appearances of the Clara cipher cited by Sams in his discussion of
the work. Here we may observe how the putative cipher, transposed up a
minor third, insinuates itself into a significant thematic element, in this case
the main idea of the *Lebhaft* near the beginning of the symphony.

Of course, the cipher table is capable of rendering musical equivalents of
far more than just **Clara.** Indeed, Sams demonstrates its potential for generating a whole range of hidden messages in Schumann's music. Already in "Did
Schumann Use Ciphers?" we discover that "Und wüssten's die Blumen" from
Dichterliebe transmits the words "Noch ruf' ich mei[ne] Clara" ("I still cry out
for my Clara"); the seventeenth piece from *Carnaval* speaks its title, **Paganini;**
the Overture to *Julius Cäsar* (Op. 128) does much the same (albeit with a
spelling that departs slightly from that in the published title, i.e., **Caesar** as
opposed to **Cäsar**); and the first of the *Nachtstücke* (Op. 23) yields the name of
Schumann's brother **Eduard,** whose death in early April 1839 may have influenced the genesis of the cycle.[23] Further discoveries emerge in a brief article
published in 1966, "The Schumann Ciphers—a Coda," where Sams reads "Ich
liebe dich" ("I love you") out of a melody appended to a letter from Schumann
to Clara, and in an essay on the Overture to *Hermann and Dorothea* (Op. 136),
where Sams argues for the encipherment of **Hermann, Dorothea,** and **Clara**
in one of the less well known of Schumann's orchestral works.[24]

Sensitive to the fact that many readers might remain unconvinced by the
remarkable chain of inferences he draws from two basic premises, Sams does
offer an interesting piece of empirical evidence to support his hypothesis. In
fact, it is presented as the trump card of the argument. Near the conclusion
of "Did Schumann Use Ciphers?" we learn that the "likely source" for Schumann's putative system was a manual of cryptography by Johann Ludwig
Klüber (1762–1837), a diplomat and specialist in states' rights who held profes-
sorial appointments in Erlangen and Heidelberg between 1786 and 1817, subsequently entered the Prussian civil service, and retired in 1824 to devote himself
to writing about constitutional law. The volume that concerns us, *Kryptographik: Lehrbuch der Geheimschreibekunst,* appeared in 1809, and according to Sams,
"there are indications that [Schumann] used it all through his creative life."[25]
Sams elaborates on this suggestive remark in "The Schumann Ciphers," conjecturing that Klüber's book found its way into August Schumann's book
dealership in Zwickau and from there into the hands of his son Robert,
"whose interest in cryptography was to be immense and enduring."[26]

To support his claims for Schumann's dependence on and fascination with Klüber's manual, Sams points out correspondences of two types: those between Schumann's putative system and the musical cipher described by Klüber and those between passages in the composer's writings and parallel excerpts from the *Kryptographik*. The principal correspondences of the first type, as given by Sams in "The Schumann Ciphers," may be summarized as follows: the use of musical pitches as substitutes for plaintext letters (twenty-four in all), flats and sharps (the latter have a "special meaning" for Klüber), a three-line alphabetical arrangement of plaintext letters, a fully constructed key or cipher system (presented by Klüber in the shape of a circle or wheel), and allowances for "frequent changes of cipher setting" (i.e., transposition).[27] As for what Sams calls non-cipher correspondences—which he addresses in a later article titled "A Schumann Primer?" (1970) by aligning various selections from Klüber's book and Schumann's letters, diaries, and critical writings— these touch on a variety of topics, which include hieroglyphics, numerical permutations, a "musical language of flowers" or *Blumensprache,* a method for composing letters in code, sign language, and "sympathetic" or invisible ink.[28] To those readers with lingering doubts, Sams poses two questions: How could Klüber's book "be found to have unique and detailed correspondences with Schumann's letters, diaries and critical writings—unless he had read it? And how could that same manual be found to have unique and detailed correspondences with a cipher system inferred from his music—unless he had used it?"[29] This, in its basic outlines, is the case for the Clara cipher and the system used to create it.

Sam's first article on the topic, "Did Schumann Use Ciphers?," sparked off a lively series of responses in the October 1965 issue of the *Musical Times.* In the first, Nicholas Temperley observed that the putative cipher system "works" because its extreme flexibility allows one "to extract words from any musical material." Sams, he maintained, was "very far . . . from having given his cipher any real test," the first requirement of which would involve "laying down all the rules of his code." In Temperley's view, such a test is especially needed since in every case but one—the decipherment of the name **Caesar** from Schumann's Overture, Op. 128—Sams must allow for some kind of "breach" (e.g., arbitrary selection or rejection of pitches) "before the notes can be made to yield the desired significant words."[30] In contrast to Temperley, Malcolm Boyd found the argument for a Clara cipher "entirely convincing" and further suggested that Sams's findings might well shed light on the music of Brahms, "who must have chanced upon the cipher while Robert was out of the room . . . [and] hastily made a copy of it."[31] (Sams would pursue this line of inquiry in his 1971 article "Brahms and His Clara Themes," which details the role of the Clara cipher in Brahms's Piano Trio, Op. 8, his C-minor Piano Quartet, Op. 60, and a number of solo and ensemble lieder.)

In some ways, these two opposing reactions prefigure the subsequent reception of Sams's theory. As a rule, writers on Schumann can hardly be said
to have embraced it. Some, as noted earlier, make no mention of it at all,
while others refer to it only in passing.[32] A few find it plausible that Schumann had a musical cipher for **Clara** but otherwise feel that Sams went too
far.[33] For reasons that are difficult to explain, Sams's work has been accepted
much more readily in the Brahms literature. Many recent Brahmsians take
Schumann's encipherment of Clara's name as a near certainty,[34] though with
a slight twist. Almost without exception, writers on Brahms cite the pitch
configuration C–B($\flat$)–A–G($\sharp$)–A (as opposed to D–C($\sharp$)–B–A($\sharp$)–B) as the
basic form of the Clara cipher. Yet as we have seen in our review of Sams's argument, Sams himself rejected the pattern that began on C as the cipher's
basic form, probably because it contradicts Schumann's documented practice
and also because of the lack of justification for the choice of B($\flat$) and G($\sharp$). To
complicate matters even further, Sams implies in some of his writings that
C–B($\flat$)–A–G($\sharp$)–A may indeed have been the basic form of the cipher.[35]
These discrepancies bode ill for the validity of the theory as a whole. And to
be sure, a close examination of Sams's work reveals it to be riddled with logical inconsistencies and otherwise characterized by wild surmise, a troubling
disregard for and misinterpretation of the documentary evidence, and an
inattention to the evidence provided by the music itself. What's more, the
trump card in the argument, Klüber's *Kryptographik,* turns out to be a joker.

Let us reconsider the links in the chain of deductions that comprise Sams's
argument. To repeat, Sams proceeds from the assumption that Schumann
must have enciphered Clara's name in tones. Why should we accept this
premise? If we knew for certain that Schumann regularly fashioned musical
ciphers for the names of those who were closest to him—relatives such as his
brother Eduard or his sister Emilie, close friends such as Ludwig Schunke,
Felix Mendelssohn, or Ferdinand Hiller—then we might be justified in sus-
pecting that he made one for Clara, too. As it stands, we have firm evidence
that Schumann bestowed a musical cipher on only one member of his circle:
the Danish composer Niels Gade, whose last name generates the melodic
material of the diminutive "Nordisches Lied," the forty-first piece in the *Album
für die Jugend* (Op. 68). Obviously, **Gade** lends itself beautifully to musical
treatment because each of its constituent letters has a precise pitch equivalent.[36] Likewise, all of the absolutely certain examples of musical encipherment from Schumann's output involve plaintexts that are conducive to the
simple substitution of pitches for the corresponding letters. These observations seem to suggest that Schumann was drawn to a plaintext primarily by
its musical potential and not by its personal meaning for him.

Thus, while it is certainly *possible* that Schumann constructed a musical cipher out of **Clara,** there is little justification for assuming that he *probably* did

so. Allow me to suggest a more likely scenario. If Schumann wanted to create a Clara cipher, chances are he would have treated her name just as he did his own in *Carnaval;* that is, he would have enciphered only the musical letters as pitches.[37] Clearly the musical yield of the procedure is slight: the *soggetto cavato* C–A–A. In fact, it is even slighter than this, for in the summer of 1838 Schumann began to spell Clara's name with a "K" instead of a "C," leaving only one musical letter. In a letter of 31 August 1838 he addresses her as "Clärchen oder Klärchen," chides himself for not being able to decide on a spelling, but concludes that "Klärchen" is the "kindlier" form—perhaps because it also happened to be the name of the heroine in Goethe's *Egmont,* one of Schumann's favorite plays.[38] In any event, from that point forward Schumann generally rendered his beloved's name as "K.," "Kl.," "Klara," or "Klärchen" in his correspondence, diaries, and household account books (Clara, however, continued to spell her name with a "C"). Might he have felt that although his beloved Klara was extraordinarily musical, her name simply was not?

Moving on to the second premise of Sams's argument, the notion that Schumann's putative cipher system arose from his desire for a symbolic union with Clara, we soon discover that it is as implausible as the first. Recall that, according to Sams, Schumann christened his alter egos "Eusebius" and "Florestan" precisely in order to facilitate the desired union, which takes place symbolically and literally when the plaintext letters **C, E,** and **F** meet on the top line of letters in the key to Schumann's putative cipher system. Also, keep in mind that Sams dates the system to 1835 or so, the period when Schumann's love for Clara came into full bloom. Yet we know from Schumann's diaries that Eusebius and Florestan entered his imaginative universe in 1831: "Florestan the Improviser" appears first, in an entry of 15 June, as one of the characters in a projected novel titled *Die Wunderkinder,* while Eusebius turns up soon thereafter, on 1 July.[39] Thus, if we accept Sams's assumption that the invention of Eusebius and Florestan was motivated by Schumann's longing for a symbolic bond with Clara, then we must date his longing—together with its counterpart, the supposed cipher system—to the year 1831. Neither the assumption nor its corollary accords well with the facts. In the first place, there is no evidence for Clara's having in any way influenced the creation of Eusebius and Florestan. (True, Schumann found a place for Clara in *Die Wunderkinder,* under the name Cilia or Zilia, but his plot sketches for the novel put her in closer touch with the famed violin virtuoso Paganini than with Florestan.[40]) Second, it is difficult to believe that Schumann was seriously contemplating any kind of union with Clara in the summer of 1831, more than four years before they exchanged their first kiss and at a time when his future bride was not yet twelve years old.

While neither of Sams's premises holds up well, what are we to make of the musical evidence he offers? Of the instances of the supposed Clara cipher (and its derivatives) he identifies in the *Davidsbündlertänze* and other works associated in one way or another with Clara? Before considering these examples of what Schumann might have done, it may be useful to have a clear understanding of what he actually did on other occasions. And if the gap between Schumann's actual practice and his supposed practice should prove to be too wide, then surely the validity of the latter will be open to question.

So far as I can determine, there are nine instances in which Schumann's use of musical ciphers is beyond dispute. These are listed in Table 3-1. On the basis of a comment in a letter from Schumann to Clara of April 1838, where he observes that "Ehe," the German word for "marriage," is a "musical word" and even writes out its pitch equivalent (E–B–E), we might also want to add "Mondnacht," the fifth song from the Eichendorff *Liederkreis* (Op. 39), to the list. Composed in May 1840, when marriage was very much on Schumann's mind, this song makes prominent use of the pitch cell E–B–E.[41]

The items in Table 3-1 are more or less evenly spread over the twenty-three-year period from 1830 to 1853, that is, over nearly the whole of Schumann's creative life. (If Schumann did construct an alternate system to encipher **Clara,** it must have coexisted with the one employed here.) Note that the favored medium for these cases—which range in length from a two-measure fragment to a twenty-one-piece cycle—is the solo keyboard, generally the piano, the instrument of choice in the bourgeois salon. The salon, in turn, was equally receptive to combinations that involved the piano and a melody instrument (such as Schumann's two movements for the "F.A.E." Sonata) or piano and voice. In other words, all of our indisputable cipher pieces (and "Mondnacht" as well) were conceived against the backdrop of an interior space where artist members of the bourgeois class would gather after dinner to make or listen to music (see items 1, 2, 4, 6, and 9), to give piano lessons, sometimes to their own children (items 7 and 8), to read letters (item 5), or to peruse the latest issue of a music journal (item 3). We can readily understand why Clara was reluctant to perform all but a small sampling of her husband's piano music in public: like the cipher pieces on our list, this repertory was less suited to the concert hall than to the intimate setting provided by the bourgeois drawing room.

Turning to Schumann's treatment of musical ciphers in the cases where their presence is certain, we can easily detect a number of patterns that governed their use. These can be presented as a series of guidelines for the construction and elaboration of musical ciphers, as "rules" of a "game" that involved letters and pitches. The game strikes me as a particularly apt metaphor for Schumann's approach, for it concords nicely with what he and his contemporaries tended to think of compositions based on ciphers. Writing to Ignaz Moscheles on 23 August 1837 about *Carnaval,* Schumann predicted that "deciphering my musical masked ball will be a real game for you."[42] In an 1840 review of Liszt's performances in Dresden and Leipzig, he lumped his *Carnaval* together with other musical "Spielereien" (i.e., amusements, frivo-

Table 3-1: Schumann's cipher pieces and fragments: The indisputable cases

1. *Theme sur le nom Abegg varié pour le pianoforte,* Op. 1
   Date of composition: 1830
   Plaintext: **Abegg**

2. *Carnaval, Scenes mignonnes . . . sur quatre notes,* Op. 9
   Date of composition: 1834–35
   Plaintext: **Asch**

3. 2-bar cadential figure in Schumann's fanciful review: "Bericht an Jeanquirit in Augsburg über den letzten kunsthistorischen Ball beim Redacteur"
   Date: 1837
   Plaintext: **Beda**
   Comments: review published in *Neue Zeitschrift für Musik* 6 (1837), pp. 159–161

4. "Rätsel," no. 16 from *Myrthen,* Op. 25
   Date of composition: 1840
   Plaintext: **H**
   Comments: In German, the letter "H" is called "Ha"

5. 4-bar fragment, setting of "Auf Wiedersehn"
   Date: 5 January 1844 (letter to Johann Verhulst)
   Plaintext: **Gade ade!**

6. *Sechs Fugen über den Namen BACH für Orgel oder Pianoforte mit Pedal,* Op. 60
   Date of composition: 1845
   Plaintext: **Bach**

7. "Rebus," originally intended for *Album für die Jugend,* Op. 68
   Date of composition: 1848
   Plaintext: **Lass das Fade, fass das Ächte**
   Comments: also in *Album für Constanze Jacobi* (1849)

8. "Nordisches Lied" [no. 41], from *Album für die Jugend,* Op. 68
   Date of composition: 1848
   Plaintext: **Gade**

9. "F.A.E." Sonata for Violin and Piano, Intermezzo (movement 2), and finale (movement 4):
   Date of composition: 1853
   Plaintext: **FAE** (= initials of Joachim's motto, "frei aber einsam")
   Comment: The title page of the manuscript of the sonata is in Schumann's hand and reads: *F.A.E. / In Erwartung der Ankunft des / verehrten und geliebten Freundes / Joseph Joachim / schrieben diese Sonate / Robert Schumann, Albert Dietrich / und Joh. Brahms.* (F.A.E. / In anticipation of the arrival of their / honored and beloved friend / Joseph Joachim / this sonata was written / by Robert Schumann, Albert Dietrich / and Joh. Brahms.) Note that **F.A.E.** is embedded, in retrograde, in the words: "Erwartung . . . Ankunft . . . Freundes."

lous games).[43] And when, in another letter to Moscheles, Schumann appeared to write off what has since proven to be one of his best-loved works, claiming that *Carnaval* was "devoid of artistic worth,"[44] he was in effect saying: "My *Carnaval* is not really a serious work of art: it's only a game." Though tinged with sarcasm, Ludwig Rellstab's 1832 review of Schumann's *Abegg* Variations makes a similar point: "I would like to set the talented composer even more complicated tasks to perform . . . And once he got the hang of it, I would give him still other themes, apart from the well-known **Bach** and **Fasch**, such as **Eis** [= ice cream *and* E♯] (even though the theme would consist of only one note), **Caffé** [coffee] . . . **Fisch** [fish], **Hase** [rabbit], and **Schaaf** [sheep], so that a whole luncheon would ensue."[45] For both composer and critic, the musical cipher piece is a harmless diversion that one had best not take too seriously, and Rellstab's suggested plaintexts, fanciful though they may be in their invocations of the dinner table, remind us that such games found a natural place in the bourgeois interior.

Now in order to play the game, a composer must obviously begin by constructing a musical cipher. The rules employed by Schumann toward this end can be stated as follows:

1. You may encipher a proper name, either real (e.g., **Gade**) or fictional (**Beda**), a place name (**Asch**), a single letter (**H**), a brief expression or maxim (**Lass das Fade . . .**), or an acronym (**F.A.E.**).

2. Every letter, or sometimes pair of letters, must have a precise musical equivalent. We have already encountered some special cases conditioned by the nature of the German language: **B** = B♭, **H** = B, **As** = A♭, **Es** or **S** = E♭. Here are a few more that turn up in "Rebus": **ß** = E♭, **Ä** = A-E, **T** = D (obviously because it sounds like **D**).

As for the manner in which Schumann presents, manipulates, and otherwise develops his musical ciphers over the course of a composition:

3. A piece (or fragment) should begin immediately with the basic form of the enciphered word or phrase. There are only a very few exceptions to this rule (e.g., "Pierrot" and "Paganini" from *Carnaval*).

4. The basic form may be associated with any rhythm, articulation, or dynamic, but note repetitions are rare unless the plaintext itself includes a repeated letter (e.g., **Abegg**). Arbitrary note repetitions should not occur during the first presentation of the basic form.

5. Generally, the basic form should appear first in the melody, though an initial placement in the bass is a possibility. The basic form and its derivatives may migrate from melody to bass or vice versa.

6. The basic form should dominate in a piece (or fragment).

7. When the basic form or its derivatives appear within the body of a piece, they should be placed at phrase beginnings.

8. The pitch material of the basic form may be elaborated or developed in any number of ways: It may appear transposed, in sequence (exact or free), in inversion, in retrograde; it may initiate longer melodic ideas; or individual pitches from the basic form may be chromatically altered or displaced by alternate pitches to generate new thematic ideas. There are some further possibilities, although they are to be employed sparingly: the basic form may be embedded in a longer phrase, its pitches may be permuted, or different forms of the basic cell may be contrapuntally combined. *But please remember:* the basic form must be presented first; all subsequent forms issue from it.

With these rules in hand, we are now ready to evaluate those cases in which Schumann supposedly used the Clara cipher. Since we should not rule out the possibility that an alternate system was devised for the encipherment of **Clara** or any other plaintext, Schumann cannot be held to rules 1 and 2, both of which concern the construction of a particular kind of musical cipher. What will, however, command our attention are the rules that concern the cipher's presentation and elaboration (nos. 3–8). For if there are too many discrepancies between Schumann's documented practice and the treatment of the supposed cipher, then we will have to accept what seems to me an unlikely conclusion, namely, that Schumann not only invented an alternate system for the generation of musical ciphers, but that he also fabricated a new set of rules for their treatment.

As a test case, let us consider the *Davidsbündlertänze,* a composition in which the pitch configuration D–C(♯)–B–A(♯)–B is said to play an important role. As Sams points out, this cycle of character pieces was intimately linked with Clara.[46] Schumann himself, in a letter of 5 January 1838, confided to her that the work was "teeming with wedding thoughts."[47] Even more tantalizing is a comment from the letter that accompanied the deluxe edition of the published score he sent to Clara about a month later: "My Clara will find out what's in the *Tänze,* which are dedicated to her more than anything else of mine."[48] Drafted in a state of exultation in August and September 1837, just after Clara and Schumann were secretly engaged, the cycle bears the opus number "6," the same number as Clara's own *Soirées musicales,* the collection of piano pieces from which Schumann quotes at the very beginning of the *Davidsbündlertänze.*[49] Thus, in terms of both musical and documentary evidence, this cycle would seem to be a prime candidate for the Clara cipher.

Building on the observations of Roger Fiske, Sams locates the putative cipher in five of the cycle's sixteen pieces: no. 4, "Ungeduldig"; no. 5, "Einfach"; no. 11, "Einfach"; no. 13, "Wild und lustig"; and no. 16, "Mit gutem Humor."[50] Unfortunately, an examination of the cipher's treatment in light of the rules outlined earlier does not yield encouraging results. (See Exs. 3-2a–c.) In no. 4, the cipher appears at the very beginning (and also at the return of the open-

Example 3-2a: *Davidsbündlertänze*, no. 4, mm. 1–5

Example 3-2b: *Davidsbündlertänze*, no. 5, mm. 1–2

Example 3-2c: *Davidsbündlertänze*, no. 11, mm. 1–2

Example 3-2d: *Davidsbündlertänze*, no. 13, mm. 1–4

Example 3-2e: *Davidsbündlertänze,* no. 16, mm. 33–41

ing music in mm. 25ff.), but in retrograde, and on successive downbeats of the bass part, thus violating rules 3, 5, 6, and 8. Both phrases of the opening melody of no. 5 begin with an incomplete form of the cipher in retrograde, contrary to rules 3, 6, and 8 (the same material also rounds off the piece). Rules 3, 6, and 8 are also broken in no. 11 (both phrases of its main melody open with the retrograde form of the cipher) and no. 13, where the cipher first appears in retrograde, embedded in the opening idea. In no. 16, the basic form of the cipher is withheld until the last seven measures of the piece and is embedded in a larger melodic pattern, thus violating rules 3 and 8. Note that the basic form of the supposed cipher hardly figures at all in any of these movements, a strange thing indeed for the work that, according to Sams, most clearly utters **Clara** in tones. No doubt the pitch configuration B–A(♯)–B–C(♯)–D (the retrograde of the cipher) contributes something to the motivic unity of the *Davidsbündlertänze,* but it hardly pervades the cycle from beginning to end in the way that, let's say, the Sphinxes do in *Carnaval.* Nor is its treatment comparable to that of the Sphinxes or any other of Schumann's documented musical ciphers.

It would be tedious to repeat this exercise for the other compositions in which Sams claimed to have discovered Clara ciphers. Let me say only that even the examples drawn from the Fantasie (Op. 17), the Eichendorff *Liederkreis,* and the Fourth Symphony[51]—pieces for which there is some documentary evidence that establishes a close connection with Clara (and thus a possible rationale for the hunt for ciphers)—manage to violate at least one of Schumann's rules 3–8 and generally break two or three at the same time. In fact, I can find only one case where the behavior of the putative cipher is more or less in line with the composer's documented practice: "Die Lotosblume" from *Myrthen*. Yet even this case is problematic, first because we cannot be certain that C–Bb–A–G#–A, the configuration with which the first and third vocal phrases begin, represents the basic form of the cipher; and second because, in contrast to his usual procedure, Schumann starts straightaway by repeating the first, second, and fifth pitches in the configuration, thus stuttering (rather than merely uttering) Clara's name in tones: **C–C–L–LARA–A.**

We are left with two alternatives: either we conclude that D–C(#)–B–A(#)–B and its derivatives were not genuine musical ciphers for Schumann because they break too many of the rules that he is otherwise known to have followed; or, as suggested earlier, we assume he had alternatives to rules 3–8 for pieces based on the **Clara** cipher system. I think we can safely dismiss the second alternative, for the new rules would boil down to a single statement that runs something like this: One may present the musical cipher in any one of its possible forms—basic, transposed, inverted, in retrograde; either complete or fragmentary; either as a distinct motivic idea or as an element embedded in a larger idea—at any point in a phrase or an entire composition. Clearly, this is hardly a rule, and without rules, we have no game.

Finally, we cannot ignore Sams's claim that Schumann made use of Klüber's *Kryptographik* as an aid in the construction of an alternate cipher system. It should be kept in mind, however, that the evidence for this hypothesis is entirely circumstantial, as nowhere in the surviving documents (letters, diaries, household account books, various and sundry notebooks, reading lists) does Schumann refer to the volume—an odd circumstance if, as Sams maintains, he "had a copy by him all his life."[52] The strength of the claim thus rests on what Sams calls unique and detailed correspondences between Schumann's putative system and Klüber's musical cipher and between various passages in Schumann's writings and parallel spots in Klüber's manual.[53] Sams's presentation of this material is troubling in a number of respects. First, he never provides a clear description of Klüber's method for the construction of musical ciphers. In fact, in all of his articles and book chapters Sams quotes only one short sentence from the section of Klüber's book that deals with the topic: "Draw lines for music notes round in a circle."[54] Furthermore, most of the passages cited from the *Kryptographik* for comparison with Schumann's writings are fragments that, torn from their original context, mean little in themselves. Finally, Sams does not provide page-number citations for any of the material he either quotes or paraphrases from Klüber's book, so that someone who wishes to verify Sams's exposition is faced with a wearisome and time-consuming task. None of this inspires confidence in his findings.

Klüber's manual, the full title of which is *Kryptographik: Lehrbuch der Geheimschreibekunst (Chiffrir- und Dechiffrirkunst) in Staats- und Privatgeschäften* (Tübingen: Cotta, 1809), is a comprehensive and carefully researched study of the field of cryptology as it was understood in the early nineteenth century. As Klüber says on the opening page of the book, he undertook his study because "the art of secret writing is so frequently used in both governmental and private affairs . . . that it seemed worth the effort to make a coherent whole out of all that had been discovered and practiced for centuries" (p. i). The *Kryptographik* falls into two parts. The first and by far longer part, titled "Chiffrirkunst," deals with cryptography per se, that is, with the various techniques for devising ciphers and codes (pp. 1–418); here Klüber gives especially thorough coverage to letter-substitution ciphers, or *Buchstabenschrift* (pp. 82–229), though he treats a wide variety of other types of secret writing as well, including numerical ciphers, figural and "color" ciphers, abbreviated script, astronomical and mnemonic ciphers, and "invisible" script. The second part of the book, devoted to *Dechiffrirkunst*, addresses the practice of cryptanalysis and consists mainly of an account of the orthographic properties of German, French, English, Italian, Spanish, Dutch, and Latin—information of particular importance for the would-be decipherer of an encrypted message who does not possess a key (pp. 421–72).

Klüber discusses the cryptographic potential of musical symbols in the section of the manual's first part devoted to *Zeichenschrift* (symbolic or "sign" script), under which rubric he also considers sign language, a Morse code–like system (*Punctirchiffre*), and ciphers comprised of lines (pp. 230–75). His discussion of a musical cipher technique (*Musikchiffre* or, as he also calls it, *Musique parlante*) addresses three principal topics: the construction of a musical cipher wheel according to the principles of "circular writing" (*Cirkularschreibenschrift*), the employment of the wheel to encipher plaintexts, and the decipherment of messages transmitted in this way (pp. 264–75).

Klüber's cipher wheel, reproduced here as Figure 3-3, is made up of two superimposed disks (*Scheiben*): a fixed outer disk and a movable inner one (marked off by the heavy line just above the pitches). The outer disk is further comprised of two rings, while the inner disk contains only one. All three rings are in turn divided into twenty-six equal segments, which are filled in as follows as we move inward from the outermost ring of the wheel:

a. Outer disk, outer ring: 12 time signatures, 14 empty spaces
b. Outer disk, inner ring: letters of the alphabet in their usual order, ampersand
c. Inner disk, single ring: 11 individual pitches, 15 pairs of pitches (all chosen at random)
d. Inner disk, central portion: C, G (treble), and F (bass) clefs

Now we are ready to encipher a message. Let's take as our plaintext the phrase: **Clara, ich liebe dich** (Clara, I love you). We begin by turning the inner disk to any of its twenty-six possible locations (I will leave it as it ap-

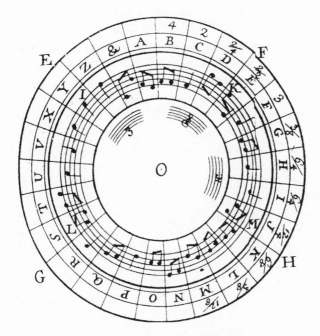

Figure 3-3: Klüber's musical cipher wheel

pears in Fig. 3-4). Since clef and time signature are mutually dependent, we have the following choices, given the present position of the two disks: our musical cipher may be notated either in treble clef + 2/4, or bass clef + 6/4 (I have chosen the former). Now we simply replace each of the letters in the plaintext with the pitch or pitches directly beneath them in the inner disk of the wheel. Klüber also suggests that we use flats or sharps to mark off the beginnings of words in the plaintext. The result of our little exercise in cryptography is given as Example 3-3. No doubt the wide leaps and augmented intervals lend the melody a Webernian quality that is quite foreign to Schumann's style; nonetheless, the message will get across, provided—as Klüber stresses (p. 267)—the recipient has a copy of the cipher wheel.

Now even the reader who cannot translate the German text of the *Kryptographik* can easily tell, simply by examining the cipher wheel, that there are significant discrepancies between Klüber's *Musikchiffre* and the system that Sams ascribes to Schumann. While the plaintext letters of the latter begin with the unusual sequence **D–H–A–B–C–E–F–G** (see Fig. 3-1), the letters in Klüber's cipher wheel are presented in the normal alphabetical order. Whereas Schumann's putative system features a "three-line arrangement" of plaintext letters, Klüber arranges his plaintext letters in a single line, bent into the shape of a circle (Sams's assertions to the contrary, I have been unable to find a single example of a "three-line arrangement" anywhere in the *Kryptographik;*

Example 3-3: **Clara, ich liebe dich,** enciphered according to Klüber's method

C l   a   r   a,   i   c   h   l   i   e   b   e   d   i   c   h

the "one-line arrangement" seems to be the norm in Klüber's many charts and diagrams). Moreover, while three plaintext letters in the putative system generally share one symbol (i.e., musical pitch), *each* plaintext letter in Klüber's cipher wheel is linked with its own symbol or symbols. In addition, whereas each of the letters in the putative system is associated with a single pitch, Klüber links fifteen of his plaintext letters with a pair of pitches. Actually, in practicing *musique parlante* one might want to substitute three, four, five, or more pitches for some or all plaintext letters, since Klüber's only requirement is that each letter should be linked with a *different* musical symbol or set of symbols. This brings us to another telling difference between the two systems: The pitches in Klüber's cipher wheel were assigned in a purely arbitrary manner; the pitches in Schumann's putative system were not. Indeed, the latter system is predicated on the emphatically nonarbirtary relationships among Clara, Eusebius and Florestan, the initials "C," "E," and "F," and the pitches D, E, and F. Finally, two features of Klüber's system play no part whatsoever in the method ascribed to Schumann: the interdependence of time signature and clef and the use of accidentals to indicate the beginnings of words. If there are "unique and detailed correspondences" between the two cipher systems, this observer has failed to locate them. In fact, apart from the principle of substitution (a common feature of many ciphers), the systems share no features at all.

The supposed parallels between Schumann and Klüber that Sams calls "non-cipher correspondences" are equally unconvincing. Some are purely fanciful, including the connection Sams draws between Beda, a character modeled to an extent on Clara from one of Schumann's most imaginative pieces of poetic criticism,[55] and the Venerable Bede, whose eighth-century treatise on the expressive and rhetorical use of manual gestures is cited by Klüber in his discussion of sign language.[56] Several correspondences involve what would have been common knowledge for a person with Schumann's background. His mere mention of "hieroglyphs" in a letter of July 1827 to his school chum Emil Flechsig and allusion to "sympathetic" (i.e., invisible) ink in a February 1854 letter to Joachim hardly count as evidence that he had read Klüber's account of these topics.[57] Had Schumann written as well about the decipherment of hieroglyphic writing or about the various chemical solutions used to produce different types of invisible ink, both of which topics are considered at some length in the *Kryptographik,* then we might have cause to speculate on his familiarity with Klüber's manual.[58] As it is, Schumann did no such thing.

In still other cases, the noncipher correspondences concern material that Schumann most probably encountered in sources other than Klüber's *Kryptographik*. True, he tells us, in a diary entry of 27 May 1832, that a "musical language of flowers" ("musikalische Blumensprache") was one of his "earliest ideas"[59] and Klüber details the allegorical meanings of about sixty flowers under the section heading "Blumenchiffre der Morgenländer" ("Flowercipher[s] of the Occident," pp. 281–84). But Klüber and Schumann were by no means the only figures from the first half of the nineteenth century who expressed interest in the signifying potential of flowers. In one of the explanatory essays appended to the *Westöstlicher Divan*, Goethe devotes considerable space to "der sogenannte Blumensprache" ("the so-called language of the flowers"), which he defines as the practice of "imparting a meaning to individual flowers in order to transmit that meaning as secret writing [*Geheimschrift*] in a bouquet."[60] Although Goethe's herbarium is not quite as large as Klüber's, he, too, lists a number of flowers, each of which is linked with a brief phrase that at once rhymes with the name of the flower and conveys an additional meaning (e.g., "Myrten—will dich bewirten" / "The myrtle [the traditional wedding blossom]—wants to offer you its hospitality").[61] In the immediately following essay, called "Chiffer" (Cipher or Code), Goethe includes a poem conceived in imitation of the lyrics exchanged by young lovers who looked to the fourteenth-century poet Hafiz as a kindred spirit.[62] Interestingly enough, Schumann made a musical setting of this very poem and published it (under the title "Liebeslied") in 1850 as the fifth piece of his *Lieder und Gesänge*, Op. 51. Since Schumann cherished Goethe's works from his teenage years until the end of his creative life, wouldn't it be sensible to infer that Schumann's interest in *Blumensprache*—which found consummate expression in the twenty-six songs of *Myrthen*, presented as a wedding gift to Clara—owed more to Goethe than to Klüber?

The only one of Sams's noncipher correspondences that carries the least bit of weight is the one between what Klüber calls network- or lattice-cipher ("Netz-oder Gitterchiffre," pp. 183–225)—in which successive integers in a simple numerical sequence are made to generate entirely new sequences[63]— and a series of similar calculations that Schumann entered into his diary in March 1830.[64] But even here, he may have been merely indulging in a mathematical exercise picked up during his early student days at the Zwickau Lyceum (1820–28). And of course, even if Schumann did construct a "lattice" of numbers on Klüber's model, our principal point stands: there is not an iota of evidence that Schumann used the *Kryptographik* to construct a specifically *musical* cipher system.

Both in his account of the supposed correspondences between Schumann's and Klüber's writings and his interpretation of other documents that appear to speak to the composer's receptivity to cryptography Sams makes a simple error: he mistakes poetry for prose. By taking this most poetically minded of composers at his word, Sams reads literally what was often meant to be understood figuratively. I will cite just one example of his misreading, which, incidentally, has managed to slip into the Brahms literature as well: the notion that Schumann's D-minor Symphony was conceived as a "Clara symphony."[65] This claim is based on a diary entry made by Schumann in March 1841, soon after he drafted the First Symphony in B flat (Op. 38): "Really, my next symphony will be called 'Klara,' and in it I shall portray her with flutes, oboes, and harps. Now what does my little Klara [*Klärchen*] think of that?"[66] The problem is this: while the entry dates from 14–21 March, Schumann did not begin sketching the supposed Clara symphony in D minor until over two months later, in late May; in the interim, between 12 April and 8 May, he drafted the orchestral work that would be published in 1846 as *Ouverture, Scherzo und Finale* (Op. 52).[67] It took Schumann some time to settle on a title for the new composition. Initially he referred to it as a "Suite," but in late April or eary May Clara reported: "We still don't know what to call it."[68] By mid-May it had been dubbed a Symphonette, and in a letter of 5 November 1842 to the publisher Friedrich Hofmeister, Schumann called it his "Second Symphony (Overture, Scherzo and Finale for orchestra)."[69] Thus isn't the E-major *Ouverture, Scherzo und Finale* just as likely (or even more likely) to have been the "Clara symphony" as the later Symphony in D minor? Indeed, this possibility is supported by a diary entry made in mid-April 1841 and thus falling within the period when Schumann was in the thick of composing the E-major work: "Klara's heart is always clear [*klar*] and bright and lovely . . . all this is contained in my music."[70] Should we not conclude, therefore, that the *Ouverture, Scherzo und Finale,* and not the D-minor Symphony, was the "Clara symphony"? Probably not. In fact, it would be equally misguided to identify either work as *the* Clara symphony. Both of them are Clara symphonies, just as nearly everything Schumann composed between about 1835 and 1843 is a Clara something-or-other. That is, when Schumann promised in March 1841 to call his next symphony Klara, he was writing poetry, not prose (his allusion to "harps" is the tip-off: he never used them in his purely orchestral works). The diary entry should be read as a figurative expression of Schumann's conviction that every note he wrote in some way embodied Clara, and in 1841 most of those notes happened to be written for orchestra.

To find traces of Schumann's embodiment of Clara in four- and five-note cells that supposedly utter "Clara" is a naive, musically unconvincing, and ultimately pointless enterprise: naive because the images of a loved one cannot be translated directly into pitches, unconvincing because as often as not the pitch cells do not coincide with musically significant ideas, and pointless because the argument for Schumann's invention of a cipher to encipher **Clara** is absolutely without foundation. Hasn't the time come, then, to cast this theory aside? And having recognized Schumann's Clara cipher as a fiction, shouldn't we do the same with Brahms's, for how could Brahms have learned something from his mentor that never existed in the first place?

II

Biography is necessarily grounded in simple statements of fact ("she was born in . . . ," "they lived for ten years in . . . ," "he died in . . . "). But as soon as biographers begin to interpret the raw data of their subjects' lives, as indeed they must, biography runs the risk of lapsing into mythology. On that account, I have dealt at length with the hypothesis that concerns the Clara cipher, for it seems to me that it feeds directly into a quasi-fictional or mythic image of Schumann—and also of Brahms, insofar as he is supposed to have adopted his mentor's techniques of encipherment.

Consider the character portrait of Schumann that emerges from Sams's work: it is made up in equal parts of withdrawal and reclusiveness ("of all composers [Schumann was] at once the most wayward and the most inward"),[71] waning inventive powers ("When the music stopped pouring out it could be ciphered out"),[72] and, finally, madness (the *lettres dansantes* in *Carnaval* might easily be construed as a counterpart of the alphabetical lists of towns and rivers that Schumann compiled from an atlas during his final months in the asylum at Endenich).[73] This portrait of Schumann corresponds rather closely to the image of the cryptographer in world literature. The main character of Edgar Allan Poe's "The Gold-Bug," William Legrand, is a misanthropic recluse, "subject to perverse moods of alternate enthusiasm and melancholy,"[74] whose decipherment of an encrypted message on a tattered parchment leads him to buried treasure. Adrian Leverkühn, the syphilitic composer-protagonist of Thomas Mann's *Doktor Faustus*, fashions a "note-cipher" out of the musical letters in *hetæra esmerelda*, a species of butterfly (B, E, A, E, E♭), and, as Mann says: "Leverkühn was not the first composer, nor will he be the last, who loved to put mysteries, magic formulas, and charms into his work. The fact displays the inborn tendency of music to superstitious rites and observances, the symbolism of numbers and letters."[75] Thus in describing Schumann as a cryptographer we are hardly making a neutral biographical observation. On the contrary, we may be contributing to the formation of a mythic image by placing the composer in the company of shady figures who traffic in "mysteries," "magic formulas," and "superstitious rites."[76]

In what sense, however, is this a mythic image? For aren't there at least nine cases where Schumann undoubtedly *did* make use of musical ciphers? And on the strength of these cases alone, aren't we justified in calling Schumann a cryptographer and identifying at least some of his works as musical cryptographs? Actually, the justification proves to be slight on both counts.

Recall, first, the etymology of the terms that contain the stem "crypto-," which means "hide." A cryptographer is someone who hides messages by translating them into a kind of secret text, a cryptograph. As Klüber puts it, "The art of secret writing, also known as cryptography or stenography, shows us how to inscribe thoughts in such a way that what has been written, or its actual contents, will remain a secret" (p. 3).

By this standard, Schumann was a rather inept cryptographer. The gesture in his musical cipher pieces is almost invariably one of revelation, not concealment. Take the "Abegg" Variations. The plaintext is there for all to see, boldly announced in the title: *Theme sur le nom Abegg varié pour le pianoforte.* The same holds true for the "B-A-C-H" Fugues and the "F.A.E." Sonata. Likewise, the full title of *Carnaval* tells us that the cycle is based "on four notes," while the plaintext(s) associated with them can be inferred easily from the three Sphinxes that appear between the eighth and ninth pieces, "Replique" and "Papillons." In some instances, Schumann provides an explanatory remark that all but reveals the encrypted text (e.g., the comment that accompanies the final **Ha** of the song "Räthsel," discussed later (pp. 97–98). In "Nordisches Lied (Gruss an G.)," the title clearly points us in the direction of the plaintext: the name of a "Nordic" (i.e., Scandinavian) composer that begins with the letter **G.** Who, other than Niels **Gade,** could it be? Thus Schumann's cipher pieces are hardly the "musical cabala" that they have sometimes been made out to be.[77] In general, Schumann behaves less like a cabalist or cryptographer than like an excited child who, during a game of hide-and-seek, gives himself away by giggling from behind the sofa or under the table.[78]

Likewise, the nature of the signs in Schumann's cipher pieces is cryptographic in only a very rudimentary sense. The signs in a genuine cryptograph are arbitrary as opposed to natural; that is, the cryptographic signifier possesses no inherent property that motivates it to function as it does. When Klüber assigns pitches to the letters in the outer disk of his cipher wheel, he does so in a purely random manner, prescribing only that every letter should be linked with a different musical sign. In only one case do plaintext and cipher text correspond (**E/E**; see Fig. 3-3). From a cryptographer's perspective, this makes eminently good sense, for the point of the whole operation is to create a cipher text that can only be understood by those for whom the message is intended. Now the signs in Schumann's cipher pieces are not quite "natural," but neither are they totally arbitrary. For nearly a millennium, musical pitches have been designated by letters of the alphabet, at least in the West, thus establishing in the minds of musicians a rather close relationship between the pitch that now sounds at 440 vibrations per second and the letter "A." This is the relationship that Schumann exploits in his cipher pieces, a relationship with only limited cryptographic potential. A bona fide cryptographer would never encipher his friend Gade's name with the pitches G, A, D,

53‡‡†305)) 6*;4826)4‡.)4‡) ;806*;48†8¶60))85;1‡(;:‡*8†83
(88) 5*†;46(;88*96*?;8)*‡(;485) ;5*†2:*‡(;4956*2 (5*—4)
8¶8* ;40692 85);) 6†8) 4‡‡;1 (‡9;48081 ;8:8‡1 ;48†85;4) 485†
528806*81 (‡9;48;(88;4(‡?34;48)4‡;161 ;:188;‡?;

Figure 3-4: The cryptograph from Poe's "The Gold-Bug"

and E, since the resultant musical cipher, instead of concealing the plaintext,
essentially blurts it out.

The same point can be made by comparing the appearance of a genuine
piece of secret writing—the text that ultimately leads Legrand to the treasure of Captain Kidd in Poe's "Gold-Bug"—with that of one of Schumann's
cipher pieces, "Arlequin" from *Carnaval*. (Cf. Fig. 3.4 and Ex. 3.4.) The cryptograph from Poe's story strikes the viewer as a meaningless hodgepodge of
punctuation marks, numerals, and other symbols, while Schumann's score
will appear perfectly coherent to anyone who reads music. Of course, not
every cryptograph resembles Poe's chaotic jumble of signs; a skillful cryptographer might just as well encipher a message into a text that possesses a coherent meaning of its own. The point is simply this: cryptographic method
lends itself to the creation of texts with no inherent meaning of their own,
texts whose meaning will remain obscure so long as the receiver is ignorant
of the key. Schumann's method never results in texts of this kind.

Hence we may either pronounce Schumann a failed cryptographer and
call the argument to a halt or—to opt for what I think is a more sensible al-

Example 3-4: Schumann, "Arlequin," mm. 1–8 (from *Carnaval*)

ternative—conclude that his musical cipher pieces are poorly described by the term "cryptograph." Perhaps if viewed in light of another, more appropriate category, their essential qualities might emerge more clearly. That category, I would like to suggest, is the pictograph, a representational object with markedly different cultural connotations from the cryptograph. While the latter belongs to the imaginative world of the suspense tale, a world characterized by skulduggery and stealth, the pictograph inhabits a realm of children's books, parlor games, and other bourgeois pastimes prevalent during the period between 1815 and the revolutions of 1848–49 known as the Biedermeier era. Whereas cryptographs are emblems of mystery and secrecy, the pictographs of the Biedermeier period were agencies of humor and playfulness, of education and moral uplift.

Of all of Schumann's cipher pieces, there is one in which the pictographic character and the cultural motifs associated with it are especially pronounced: an eight-bar piece for piano called "Rebus," which, after it was composed in the autumn of 1848, remained unpublished during Schumann's lifetime. (See Ex. 3-5.) Despite its brevity and its location on the periphery of the composer's creative output, it contains the key to a number of more extended and apparently more central compositions.

A rebus is a representation of a name, word, or phrase in which some or all of the verbal units—or any number of their syllables—are rendered as pictorial images. In short, a rebus is a kind of picture puzzle. In Schumann's piano piece, the pictures are musical pitches that, taken together, yield a melody harmonized by Schumann in block-chordal, chorale style. Indeed the title, "Rebus," directs us to interpret the symbols on the page as *images to be named*. Schumann provides the letter L—for which, of course, there is no direct musical equivalent—but from that point on, he leaves us on our own. In naming the pitches in the melody, we arrive at a sequence of letters (A, S, and so forth) that in turn form words: **Lass das Fade, fass das Ächte** [= **Echte**], roughly translatable as: "Don't concern yourself with trifles, seize only what's genuine." In short, the plaintext emerges less through a process of decipherment than through the mere act of *calling symbols by their names*.

In the Biedermeier era, rebuses tended to appear in one context more than any other: the children's books of all types—primers, alphabet books, catechisms, storybooks—that were produced in increasing numbers during precisely these years. According to Walter Benjamin, an astute and sensitive critic of this fascinating byway of early nineteenth-century culture, the most striking aspect of these publications was the craftsmanship that went into the production of their colorful illustrations. In Benjamin's view, colors immerse "the child's imagination in a dream state," thereby inducing a mood in which the child is receptive to learning, for "nowhere is sensuous, nostalgia-free contemplation as much at home as in color."[79] The rebus offered a marvelous opportunity for the creation of what Benjamin called a "resplendent, self-sufficient

Example 3-5: Schumann, "Rebus"

world" of illustrations,[80] witness one of the most popular children's books of the period, the *Sittensprüche des Buchs Jesus Sirach für Kinder und junge Leute aus allen Ständen mit Bildern welche die vornehmsten Wörter ausdrücken* (Moral sayings from the Book of Jesus Sirach [Ecclesiastes, one of the fifteen books of the biblical Apocrypha] for children and young people of all classes with pictures that express the most distinguished words). In this volume, first published at the end of the eighteenth century, the maxims of the second-century Jewish pedagogue Jesus ben Sira are transmitted as rebuses. (See Fig. 3-5.)

The world of children's books intersected with Schumann's world on a number of points. Several of his closest associates were among the most skilled illustrators of these volumes, among them Johann Peter Lyser—a member of the circle whose discussions led to the founding of the *Neue Zeitschrift für Musik* in 1834—and Ludwig Richter, with whom Schumann was on close terms during his Dresden days in the late 1840s.[81] In planning for the publication of his *Album für die Jugend,* Schumann hoped that its forty-three pieces would be coupled with forty-three illustrations, by Richter and several other Dresden artists. Here Schumann may have taken as his model an illustrated alphabet book on which several of his Dresden associates had recently collaborated: *ABC-Buch für kleine und große Kinder, gezeichnet von Dresdener Künstlern, mit Erzählungen und Liedern von R. Reinick und Singweisen von Ferdinand Hiller* [1845] (ABC book for small and large children, illustrated by Dresden artists, with tales and lyric poems by R. Reinick and melodies by Ferdinand Hiller). Unfortunately, it was impossible to carry out this plan in time for the Christmas 1848 publication deadline of the *Album für die Jugend;* in the end, Richter illustrated only the title page of the volume, a lithograph comprised of ten vignettes, each of which is associated with one of the pieces in the collection.[82]

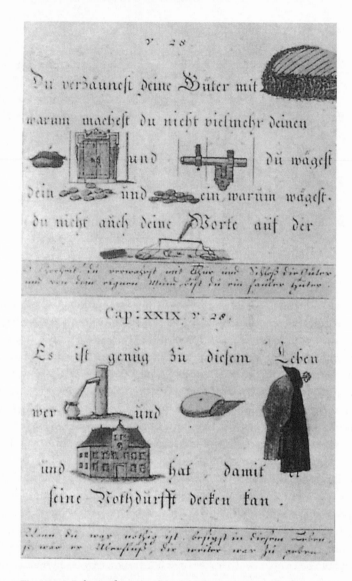

Figure 3-5: Rebuses from *Sittensprüche des Buchs Jesus Sirach* . . .
(publ. Nuremberg, late eighteenth century). Reprinted by permission, Suhrkamp Verlag, Frankfurt am Main.

As it turns out, Schumann's "Rebus" was also closely bound up with the
prehistory of the *Album für die Jugend,* a specifically *musical* book for children
that became a best-selling item soon after its publication in December 1848.
Several months before, Schumann had presented his oldest daughter, Marie,
with a manuscript volume titled *Stückchen für's Clavier / Zu Marie'chens 7tem
Geburtstag / den 1sten September 1848 / gemacht vom Papa* (Small pieces for
piano / written on the occasion of dear little Marie's seventh birthday /

1 September 1848 by Papa). Comprised of eight diminutive compositions, most of which eventually found their way into the *Album für die Jugend,* the birthday album soon became the nucleus of a larger project: thirty-four training pieces for piano interspersed with nineteen aphorisms intended for the edification of the fledgling musician. The collection was also supposed to include a brief "course in music history" or "music history in examples," which consisted of arrangements by Schumann of famous works or melodies by ten other composers, who ranged from Bach and Handel to Schubert and Mendelssohn.[83] (One of these arrangements had already appeared as the fifth item in the *Stückchen* for Marie: a transcription for piano of the main tune of Zerlina's aria "Vedrai, carino" from Mozart's *Don Giovanni.*) Although Schumann, with Clara's help, made fair copies of about a half-dozen of these arrangements, intending to send them along to the engraver who was preparing the *Album für die Jugend,* he ultimately decided, for reasons that are not entirely clear, to omit them from the published collection. The same fate befell a number of the freely composed pieces for the *Album,* among them the eight-bar "Rebus," which, according to an early listing of the volume's contents, was to appear as its fifteenth piece.[84] Nonetheless, Schumann managed to put some of these rejected items to good use, appending them to the original eight pieces in Marie's birthday album to form a little booklet, or *Klavierbüchlein,* that could be called into service in her piano lessons.[85] Six items were recycled in this way: five of the transcriptions from the "course in music history" (pieces by Bach, Handel, Mozart, Beethoven, and Schubert) and "Rebus" as well.[86] Interestingly enough, the latter is also transmitted on the single manuscript page (*Albumblatt*), dated 8 January 1849, that the composer contributed to the musical commonplace book of his friend Constanze Jacobi (*Album für Constanze Jacobi*).[87] Thus the little piece made its way into a volume that functioned in the adult world much like an illustrated book did in the world of the child.

Although any sort of verbal material might appear as a rebus, one type in particular was most often presented in picture-puzzle form: maxims and proverbs. What better way to imprint a sense for ethical codes of behavior on the mind of the developing child than through the medium of pictorial representation? Chances are a child would be little impressed by a verbal admonition like the following, from Ecclesiastes 28:24–25: "Just as you enclose your garden with a thorn hedge, and lock up your silver and gold, so weigh your words and measure them, and make a door and a bolt for your mouth." If, however, the imagery of this prescription was made to take on a sensuous life of its own—as it is in the illustrated *Sittensprüche des Buchs Jesus Sirach . . .* (see Fig. 3-5 for the presentation of this passage as a rebus)—the same child would probably respond much more immediately to the content of the text. What's more, he or she might never forget the text. Benjamin took this observation a step further by linking it to the Platonic doctrine of *anamnesis*—

of calling to memory things that were known all along: "by remembering, [children] learn."[88] Recollection brings suppressed knowledge to the surface of consciousness, and insofar as images set this process in motion, the rebuses in publications such as the *Sittensprüche des Buchs Jesus Sirach* . . . served as powerful agencies in the moral education of the young.

Whether Schumann possessed this volume I cannot say (though as a child he almost certainly had books like it).[89] At the same time, the importance of maxims and proverbs for Schumann the man and the musician is beyond question. Just as he probably first learned them during his childhood, so as an adult he passed them on to his own children. At the end of the *Erinnerungsbüchelchen für unsere Kinder* (Little book of memories for our children)—a notebook Schumann maintained between 1846 and 1852 for the express purpose of recording landmark events in the young lives of his children Marie, Elise, Julie, Emil, Ludwig, and Ferdinand—we find four proverbs, one from Ecclesiastes ("Riches and strength lift up the heart, but the fear of the Lord is above them both") and three from a collection by E. M. Arndt.[90]

During the same period, Schumann also created analogues for this body of folk wisdom that would speak directly to young musicians, either verbally or in tones. Consider the *Musikalische Haus- und Lebensregeln* (Musical rules to use at home and to live by), first published as a supplement to the 3 May 1850 issue of the *Neue Zeitschrift für Musik,* though they were originally meant for inclusion in the *Album für die Jugend.*[91] Schumann clearly modeled the didactic aphorisms of this collection on the maxims and proverbs known to him through both biblical and popular sources—not, of course, as regards content but rather in terms of rhetoric, syntax, and tone. Compare, for instance, the injunction from Ecclesiastes copied into the *Erinnerungsbüchelchen*— "Riches and strength lift up the heart, but the fear of the Lord is above them both"—with the following excerpt from the musical *Lebensregeln:* "Flashy passagework changes with the times; technical accomplishment is of value only when it serves a higher purpose."[92]

As for Schumann's transmission of the wit and wisdom of proverbs through the medium of music, the earlier stages in the genesis of the *Album für die Jugend* provide us with two striking examples. The first is a twelve-bar canon (not included in the printed collection) titled after the old German saying: "Aus ist der Schmaus" ("The party's over").[93] With the second example, we return to Schumann's "Rebus," the plaintext of which enjoins the young musician not to waste his or her time with "trifles" but rather to "seize only what's genuine." (Wordplay is a typical feature of maxims and proverbs in all languages, and unfortunately, the interaction of alliteration, assonance, and rhyme that characterizes "Lass das Fade, fass das Ächte" is all but lost in translation.) While this tiny composition has all the pithiness of the saying that generated its melody, Schumann's evocation of the Lutheran chorale is entirely in line with the moralizing tone of the enciphered message. What we have then is a musical analogue for the biblical proverbs represented in volumes such as the illustrated *Sittensprüche*.

This brings us to two other cultural motifs associated with the Biedermeier picture puzzle: tradition and craft. Proverbs and maxims, the favored objects of representation in children's books of the period, are handed down from older to younger generations, often through the medium of oral transmission. Intended to overcome the contingencies of time and place by ensuring continuity between one generation and the next, this process creates the links in the chain that we call tradition. And it is to tradition, albeit a specifically musical one, that the plaintext of Schumann's "Rebus" refers. It tells the young musician to ignore the merely fashionable or trifling musical products of the day (**das Fade**) and to embrace what is of genuine or lasting value (**das Ächte**), that is, the achievements of the composers who together comprise the Austro-German tradition that extends from Bach to Mendelssohn—and presumably to Schumann himself. This message is made crystal clear in the amplified birthday album for Marie, where Schumann's "Rebus" appears together with selections from his "music history in examples." The plaintext of his musical picture puzzle directs the child—Schumann's own daughter—to cherish the music-historical tradition embodied in those examples.[94]

If proverbs and maxims are conduits for the transmission of wisdom through the ages, then the focal point of the tradition to which Schumann's "Rebus" alludes is the notion of musical craft. For Schumann, as for many of his predecessors and successors, compositional craft was nearly synonymous with mastery of the entire spectrum of contrapuntal techniques, from simple, "species" writing to double counterpoint, canon, and fugue.[95] But before tackling this rarefied art, the beginning composer must acquire a firm command of a more fundamental practice: harmonization in the strict, four-part style. An idiom that found its classic expression in the chorales of Bach, it constitutes the bedrock of the young composer's craft. Thus Schumann's "Rebus," conceived as a little exercise in the art of chorale-style harmonization, is an emblem of that craft.

In all likelihood, however, the novice would not be given a melody such as that of Schumann's "Rebus" for his or her first assignment in chorale-style writing. Featuring no fewer than four ungainly leaps of a tritone (between A and E♭ and D and A♭) and lacking a clear tonal center, the pitch sequence is hardly conducive to realization in the four-part style. Whether or not Schumann was responsible for the plaintext that generated this wayward melodic pattern is beside the point; one way or the other, he was faced with a difficult task. As a first step toward rationalizing this seemingly random array of pitches, he imposed rhythmic order both at the local level (through repetition of the anapestic pattern short–short–long) and on the larger scale (by articulating the whole into two balanced phrases of four bars each). The only key capable of grounding the peculiar melody in a tonal center is the one that

Schumann chose: D minor. While he treated the final pitch (E) as the fifth of a dominant harmony, he underscored the tonic at the midpoint of the piece by holding the F at the end of the first phrase for a full five beats (longer than any other pitch) and harmonizing it with a D-minor chord. Hence owing to the nature of the preestablished series of pitches, the customary relationship between antecedent and consequent is turned on its head, the second phrase offering a rejoinder or "question" to the "answer" of the first. In his approach to the melody's irksome E♭s and A♭, Schumann also made a virtue out of necessity, invoking in both phrases the harmonic pun on the chord B♭–D–F–A♭, which at first suggests the dominant of E♭ but resolves as the German augmented-sixth chord of D minor (mm. 2–3, 6). Finally, the contingency of the melodic pattern is balanced by the directional force of the bass line: an embellished descent through the tetrachord D–C–B♭–A, which circles back to the tonic pitch (D) at the end of the first phrase but remains poised on the dominant (A) at the conclusion of the second. Underlying every aspect of Schumann's musical realization of the plaintext is a desire to make rational what initially appears to be irrational, and this, in the final analysis, is the aim of craftsmanship in all fields.

With the notion of craft, we have not yet exhausted the cultural motifs embedded in Schumann's little piano piece. As noted previously, in and of themselves the words of a proverb may have little effect on a child. But how amused a young pianist will be upon discovering how those words emanate from the pitches of the melodic line in Schumann's "Rebus," for he or she is at once engaged in a game. Illustrated books such as the *Sittensprüche* proved to be so popular for the very same reason: the amusement derived from identifying the images in a rebus and from observing how a coherent thought can emerge from a fanciful combination of letters, words, and images makes the child receptive to the sometimes-bitter medicine served up in a maxim or proverb.[96] Here I part company with Benjamin, who believed that the illustrations in Biedermeier children's books "[were] not there to be enjoyed" but rather "to be used like cooking recipes."[97] On the contrary, the enjoyment that children experience while participating in a game with images and words allows the process of learning to take its course without their even being conscious of it. Learning to play the piano (or any other instrument) also requires the child to swallow some bitter medicine. But Schumann, like all good pedagogues, knew how to temper bitterness with playfulness. Absorbed by a game whose rules hinge on the relationship between pitches and letters, the young interpreter of Schumann's "Rebus" at the same time learns the rudiments of musical craft.

Despite the seriousness of its enciphered message, the little piece also has a humorous dimension. After all, humor arises from our sudden realization of the unusual consequences that can be drawn from the chance similarities between apparently different things, in this case musical pitches and letters of the alphabet. This, at least, was how humor was understood by Schumann's favorite author, Jean Paul.[98] In a memorable scene from his *Flegeljahre*—of all his novels, the one that Schumann treasured most—Jean Paul underscored the essentially humorous quality of musical substitution ciphers. While Walt Harnisch, one of the novel's twin-brother protagonists, is tuning a ramshackle piano in the home of a bookbinder named Paßvogel, three of its A, C, and B strings snap simultaneously. The startled onlookers cry out, "Ach!" in unison, but Paßvogel, having observed that the mishap occurred while Walt was tuning one of the B♭ strings, realizes that the pitches B♭, A, C, and B yield not only the musical letters in **Harnisch** but also the name **Bach.** The bookbinder announces the second discovery with a witticism, which, given its terseness and rhyming cadence, has all the rhetorical force of a proverb: "Aus dem Ach wird ja ein Bach" ("Indeed, 'Bach' comes out of 'Ach' ").[99] Just as Paßvogel's little pun ("Bach" is the German word for "brook") dissolves the momentary tension inadvertently created by Walt's attempt to tune the piano, so it also exposes the practice of musical encipherment as a game, an innocent diversion, and an agency of humor.[100] In this way, the musical cipher takes its place next to the colored illustrations and rebuses of Biedermeier children's books, a body of literature over which Jean Paul has been said to preside like a "patron saint."[101]

To summarize, the rebus, a kind of pictograph frequently encountered in illustrated books of the Biedermeier era, opens many windows onto early nineteenth-century German culture. It touches on three other cultural objects—the children's book, the maxim or proverb, and the parlor game—as well as on the varied array of qualities, visual, craftsmanly, educational, ethical, and humorous, bound up with those objects. Taken together, these objects and qualities form a constellation of motifs that provide us with a context for understanding key aspects of the Biedermeier world. The entire constellation can in turn be read out of one of Schumann's most unassuming works, a tiny piano piece originally intended for the *Album für die Jugend* in which the letters of the alphabet are enciphered as musical pitches.

Wouldn't it be sensible to assume, therefore, that the same constellation of cultural motifs informs Schumann's other cipher pieces and fragments as well? Since they require us to interpret musical pitches as images-to-be-named, they *all* partake of the fundamental property of the rebus. In some cases, the imagistic character of Schumann's musical ciphers emerges from the actual physical layout of a score. The Sphinxes in *Carnaval*, for instance, are meant to be seen but not played (rather like the children of earlier times were supposed to be seen but not heard). Arranged horizontally as three sets of breves, they gape wide-eyed at the reader of the score.[102] The "riddle" posed in the humorous song of the same name ("Räthsel," from *Myrthen*) asks us to determine the element shared by "Himmel" (heaven), "Hölle" (hell), and a long list of other words, which ends with "Hauch" (breath). The

Example 3-6: Schumann, 4-measure fragment on **Gade ade!**

answer, the letter **H,** appears as the final B in the voice and piano parts. But according to Schumann's explanatory note, the singer should not sing this pitch, though he or she will presumably breathe it out (in German, the letter **H** and the pitch B are both called **Ha**). Hence the last image in the voice part, the pitch B, is in effect a rebus, a visual signifier for "breath" or "breathing." The four-measure fragment on **Gade ade!** (see Ex. 3-6) has much the same look on the page as the "Rebus" for piano, though here the plaintext is enciphered in the bass instead of the melodic line. Note in addition that this diminutive setting of the words "Auf Wiedersehn, auf Wiedersehn!" is a cadence, and a final one at that, as indicated by the double bar. As Schumann related in the letter of January 1844 that transmits the fragment, he also copied it into the album of his young colleague and friend Niels Gade, who had taken up residence in Leipzig in October 1843 and was about to embark on a brief journey. Since Gade's stay in Leipzig was about to come to an end, at least for the time being, the four-bar fragment can be interpreted as a musical pictograph for "parting" or "departure." The pictorial quality of the two-measure fragment on **Beda** is just as pronounced. This, too, is a cadence (replete with fermatas and double bar), and appropriately enough, Schumann placed it at the end of his "Bericht an Jeanquirit," a review, disguised as a short story, of several sets of dances for piano (see Fig. 3-6). Schumann appended a verbal postscript (*Nachschrift*) immediately below the **Beda** fragment). Both its terminal placement and its cadential character suggest that the fragment is intended as an imagistic rendering, a rebus, of the "Finis" that is often printed at the conclusion of stories and plays.

Another of Schumann's cipher pieces, the "Nordisches Lied," relates directly to two of the cultural objects associated with the rebus: the children's book and the maxim. Indeed, it appears as the antepenultimate item in Schumann's musical book of instructional pieces for children, the *Album für die Jugend*. Moreover, its terse structure (twenty bars, grouped in an 8 + 12 pattern) and its evocation of the four-part chorale style recall Schumann's approach to

zieht und erzählt: »an feinem Korb wäre ich Schuld;
der Vater Redacteur hätte Beda'n ausdrücklich verbo=
ten, mit mir (Florestan) zu tanzen, da ich ein Erz=
romantifer, ein drei Viertel Faust sei, vor dem sich zu
hüten, wie vor einer Lißt'schen Composition, — Beda uns
aber wahrscheinlich unsrer großen Aehnlichkeit wegen ver=
wechselt und ihm den Korb gegeben, der eigentlich mir
bestimmt, — daher das plötzliche Abtreten Beda's, die
von de Knapp nach dem Willen des Vaters vom wah=
ren Bestand der Sache unterrichtet worden 2c.« Und
diefer Redacteur, diefer phantasielose Zopf, deffen friti=
sches Stimmgabelverfahren ich der Welt noch einmal
aufdecken will, macht mir auf der Treppe noch den An=
trag, daß ich ihm etwas für seine »Neuste« über die
eben gehörten Tanzmusifen liefern möchte, versichert mir,
daß er mich an sein Haus (an Ambrosia, der ein
Mann fehlt, natürlich, da sie schon einer ist) zu ketten
wünsche u. dgl. Jeanquirit, daß ich ihm etwas Dumpfes
antwortete, wäre zu erwarten gewesen; daß ich aber Be=
da's wegen wie ein Lamm vor ihm stand und nichts
sagte, beim Himmel, verzeihe ich mir nie. Und doch hat
an Allem nur Chopin die Schuld.   FF.

Nachschrift. Wie ich's vorausgesehen! — Nr. 37.
der Neusten enthält eine Recension unsers Carnavals:
»das wären einmal wieder Zwiebelmonstra, bei denen
man vor lauter Mitleid nicht zum Weinen kommen könne:
— Componisten sollten ihre Werfe doch erst die Linie pas=
siren lassen, ehe sie entstöpselten, — sollten nicht denken,
daß wenn. sie ihren Nullen von Gedanken Schwänzchen
anhingen, gleich Neunen daraus würden 2c.« —

    NB. De Knapp hat sich in voriger Nacht aus dem
Staube gemacht. —   ____ ____

Figure 3-6: Schuman, 2-measure fragment on **Beda**

the maxim **Lass das Fade . . .** in "Rebus." Both the children's book and the
maxim provide the context for several other pieces as well. The motley
troupe of *commedia dell'arte* characters after which a number of the pieces in
Carnaval are named (Pierrot, Arlequin, Pantalon, Colombine) have momentarily relinquished their places in an illustrated book for children in order to
put in cameo appearances in Schumann's cycle.[103] Schumann's contributions

to the "F.A.E." Sonata are in turn based on the maxim or motto that Joachim adopted to reflect his personal situation in the mid-1850s: **Frei aber einsam** (his engagement to Gisela von Arnim having been broken off in 1853, Joachim was "free but lonely").

Moreover, all of Schumann's cipher pieces can be viewed as a variety of Biedermeier parlor game: diversions for the player who, seated at the piano in a bourgeois drawing room, attempts to guess their meaning (an easy but amusing task) and for the composer who constructed them in the first place. Like all games, compositional and otherwise, this one has rules: the eight principles outlined earlier in this chapter (see pp. 77–78). Here we need only observe that Schumann plays the game with varying degrees of subtlety and sophistication. Not surprisingly, the fragments and shorter pieces tend to be the simplest, while in the more substantial compositions—the "Abegg" Variations, *Carnaval,* the "B-A-C-H" Fugues, and the pair of movements from the "F.A.E." Sonata—he often treats his musical ciphers as a mere springboard for elaborations and developments of the most far-reaching kind. Several of the larger pieces (the "B-A-C-H" Fugues and the second movement, Intermezzo, of the "F.A.E." Sonata) and one of the smaller ones as well ("Nordisches Lied") afford Schumann the opportunity to display his formidable contrapuntal skills. But even in those pieces where the composer's craft is most apparent, as regards either the linear development of motives or their integration into a contrapuntal fabric, good humor still prevails. And it is probably not by chance that the humorous element is most evident in the compositions that draw on the imaginative world of Jean Paul: the *Abegg* Variations and *Carnaval,* both of which evoke the kind of madcap masked ball that serves as the climax of *Flegeljahre.*[104]

To say that Schumann was not primarily a cryptographer but rather a pictographer is to say not very much at all. But at the same time, the wide array of motifs bound up with the rebus, one of the Biedermeier era's favored types of pictograph, allows us to understand the extent to which a slice of Schumann's output—his compositions based on musical ciphers—was bound up with the culture in which he lived and worked. In addition, the cultural motifs embedded in Schumann's cipher pieces also have something to tell us about Schumann the man. They lend further support to what we can also infer about his personality from letters, diaries, household account books, and other documents, namely, that he was a keen observer of the world of the child, a solicitous father, a committed and imaginative pedagogue, a bourgeois whose ethical sensibility was nurtured by a rich store of proverbs and folk wisdom, a conservator of artistic traditions, and an individual whose quirky sense of humor came straight out of the world of Jean Paul. To be sure, Schumann was much else besides: a poet, a dreamer, and, periodically, a depressive; but an image of the composer that fails to give due weight to the other character types I have enumerated will soon degenerate into a mythic image.

Two qualifications are in order. First, the cultural motifs associated with the Biedermeier picture puzzle resonate well beyond Schumann's cipher pieces and the immediate context in which they first appeared. His engagement with the world of the child and of children's books, for example, did not begin and end with the *Album für die Jugend*. The same motif informs the *Kinderscenen* (Op. 15)[105] as well as the entire series of pedagogical collections that followed on the heels of the *Album für die Jugend*: the *Lieder-Album für die Jugend* (Op. 79), *Ball-Scenen* for piano, four hands (Op. 109), *Drei Clavier-Sonaten für die Jugend* (Op. 118), and *Kinderball* for piano, four hands (Op. 130). Second, the cultural motifs related to the pictograph are not the only motifs embedded in Schumann's cipher pieces. One key motif that I have not considered thus far derives from the specifically musical culture that Schumann at once inherited and helped to shape: the notion of homage.

For Schumann and the composers of succeeding generations, the cipher piece often served as a means of paying tribute to another creative figure. J. S. Bach, who had himself woven the **Bach** cipher into the unfinished Contrapunctus 14 of his *Die Kunst der Fuge,* was a favored recipient of this kind of attention. Apart from Schumann, many other composers—including Liszt, Reger, Busoni, d'Indy, Schoenberg, and Webern—wrote pieces based either in whole or in part on the same musical cipher. And Bach was not the only artist singled out in this way. Responding to a call for scores from the *Revue musicale,* Debussy, Ravel, Dukas, and several other French composers wrote piano pieces on the name **Haydn** to commemorate the one hundredth anniversary of the composer's death (1809/1909).[106] Similarly, in the *Kammerkonzert* for violin, piano, and thirteen wind instruments, conceived in 1925 as a fiftieth birthday gift for his mentor Arnold Schoenberg, Berg applied the technique of the *soggetto cavato* to Schoenberg's name, Webern's, and his own.

A number of Schumann's cipher pieces likewise served as what the French would call *hommages* to respected colleagues. His contributions to the "F.A.E." Sonata for Joachim not only grew out of the musical cipher for the young violinist-composer's personal motto; they also formed part of a work whose performing medium (violin and piano) was obviously tailored to fit the dedicatee. In the "Nordisches Lied (Gruss an G.)," Schumann "greets" his Danish contemporary in two ways: first, by transforming his name into the musical motive that pervades the texture of the piece; and second, by consciously imitating the "Nordic" national style that Schumann himself and other German critics had attributed to Gade, a style characterized by folklike melodies, modally inflected harmonies, and a generally melancholy tone.[107]

It is certainly no accident that Schumann's *hommages* make striking use of contrapuntal artifice—witness the treatment of musical ciphers as migrating *cantus firmi* in the "Nordisches Lied" and the Intermezzo of the "F.A.E." Sonata or the subjection of the **Bach** motive to inversion, retrograde, and augmentation in the Op. 60 fugues—for in these pieces one craftsman speaks directly to another. Furthermore, in addressing his colleagues in a language imbued with counterpoint, Schumann brought himself and his addressees within the orbit of the same venerable tradition. As we shall see in the next chapter, the family of motifs clustered around the *hommage*—stylistic imitation, commemorative spirit, contrapuntal artifice, veneration for tradition—also assumes a central role in the cipher pieces of the artist whom Schumann hailed as a musical messiah in October 1853: Johannes Brahms.

CHAPTER 4.

BRAHMS'S MUSICAL CIPHERS:

ACTS OF HOMAGE AND GESTURES

OF EFFACEMENT

*D*ISCUSSIONS OF MUSICAL CIPHERS tend to include a fair amount of speculation, much of it groundless. It is for this reason that, in considering the broader meaning of Schumann's practice of musical encipherment, I have proceeded from the "rules" that can be inferred from his works indisputably based on musical ciphers. To put it another way: before speculating on what Schumann might have done, we need to have a clear idea of what he is known to have done. The same formula holds true for Brahms. Admittedly, the younger composer seems to have gone out of his way to obstruct an inquiry of this sort. Unlike Schumann, he never announced a plaintext in the title of a composition, nor did he provide many overt clues as to the identity of his plaintexts. Moreover, there are very few cases from his output where we can be certain that musical ciphers are even involved, and several of these amount only to brief works or sections from movements of larger works. Thus it will not be easy to arrive at definite conclusions regarding the nature of his cipher technique. But despite the challenge of reconstructing the rules of the game in which Brahms engaged, the evidence we do have at our disposal will allow for more than just tentative observations.

I

Table 4-1 presents the handful of cases for which Brahms's employment of ciphers is more or less assured. These in turn fall into three categories, which

Table 4-1: Brahms's ciphers

---

1. *Des jungen Kreislers Schatzkästlein,* nos. 225, 226, 228, 320
   Date: (? late 1840s–1854)
   Plaintext: **f.a.e.**

2. "F.A.E." Sonata for Violin and Piano, Scherzo (movement 3), WoO2
   Date: late October 1853
   Plaintext: **f.a.e.**
   Comments: oblique relationship to plaintext

3. Piano Sonata No. 3 in F minor, Finale, *Allegro moderato ma rubato* (movement 5)
   Date: complete draft by late October/early November 1853
   Plaintext: **f.a.e.**
   Comments: musical cipher used for episode that begins in m. 39

4. Fugue in A-flat minor for Organ, WoO8
   Date: April to early June 1856
   Plaintext: **Brahms** (probably)

5. "Und gehst du über den Kirchhof," no. 10 of *Zwölf Lieder und Romanzen für Frauenchor a capella* (and piano ad libitum), Op. 44
   Date: probably between summer 1859 and early 1860
   Plaintext: **Agathe**

6. String Sextet in G, Op. 36
   Date: September 1864
   Plaintext: **Agathe**
   Comments: musical cipher used in first movement, second group, closing theme (mm. 162ff. and mm. 496ff.)

---

depend on the strength of the evidence: certain or nearly certain (items 1, 3, 5, and 6); probable (item 4); and one case where a composition stands in an indirect relation to a musical cipher (item 2). The first entry on the list refers to the "signed" excerpts from *Des jungen Kreislers Schatzkästlein,* a group of four notebooks comprised largely of excerpts (over 600 of them) from the works of Brahms's favorite authors, including Jean Paul, Goethe, and Novalis. Compiled for the most part between about 1850 and 1854 and named after the young Brahms's alter ego, E. T. A. Hoffmann's fictional Kappellmeister Johannes Kreisler, the *Schatzkästlein* includes seventeen quotations ascribed to Joseph Joachim, most of which are identified by the initials "f.a.e." or their pitch equivalents.[1] This configuration of pitches assumes a thematically significant role in one nearly certain case, the finale of the Third Piano Sonata (Op. 5). The two other items in this category both employ the musical subject that Brahms carved out of the first name of Agathe von Siebold, Brahms's inamorata, the daughter of a Göttingen professor, in the summer of 1858 (a painful break came in January 1859). Quick-witted, attractive, and blessed with a lovely soprano voice, Agathe was introduced to Brahms through Julius Otto Grimm, a close friend of the composer and Agathe's music teacher (at the time, Grimm was engaged to her good friend "Pine" Ritmüller). Comprised of the pitches A, G, A, B, and E, the Agathe cipher (or, more precisely, *soggetto cavato*) is treated as an ostinato in Brahms's choral partsong "Und gehst du über den Kirchhof" and assumes an almost identical motivic guise at the climax of the second group in the opening movement of the G-major String Sextet, Op. 36. (See Exs. 4-1a–b.) Documentary evidence for the link between Agathe and the musical cipher, however, comes three decades after the fact, in a letter of 27 September 1894 from Joachim, who had recently visited Brahms's old flame while on holiday in Göttingen. Immediately after mentioning her name in the letter to Brahms, Joachim adds its musical equivalent, and in almost precisely the form it takes in the G-major Sextet (see Ex. 4-1c).[2]

Example 4-1a: Brahms, "Und gehst du über den Kirchhof" (Op. 44, no. 10), mm. 1–6

Example 4-1b: Brahms, String Sextet in G major (Op. 36), first movement, mm. 163–68 (violin 1 & viola 1)

Example 4-1c: The Agathe cipher, as given in Joachim's letter to Brahms of 27 September 1894

This leaves us with two somewhat unusual cases: the Scherzo of the "F.A.E." Sonata and the A flat–minor Fugue for Organ (WoO8). Brahms's Scherzo does not draw directly on the basic form of the musical cipher that figures so prominently in the other movements of the sonata. Instead, the second halves of the Scherzo's A section and central Trio contain an arching melodic line, distinguished by an upward leap of an octave, that recalls the violin's initial gesture in Albert Dietrich's contribution to the sonata, the opening Allegro. (Cf. Exs. 4-2a–c.) In mm. 19–21 of the Allegro, Dietrich combines a straightforward melodic version of the F–A–E cell with the upwardly striving figure (marked **x** in Exs. 4-2a–c).[3] Since Brahms's Scherzo employs an idea associated at an earlier point in the sonata with the basic form of the musical cipher, it stands in an oblique relationship to the F–A–E cell itself.

Finally, although the A flat–minor Fugue almost surely belongs on our list, we cannot be absolutely certain about the identity of its plaintext. In July 1856, Brahms wrote to the music critic Adolf Schubring: "The [enclosed] music is at once a reply [to an earlier letter from Schubring] and my signature, because I'm really not inclined to inscribe the latter at the bottom of the page. You will certainly be able to perceive the name [in the music] and proceed accordingly with your response, namely, return [the music] to me with thorough critiques, and please, do so as quickly as possible, for I do not have copies of the fugues and must practice them."[4] The fugues to which Brahms alluded were most probably the pair he had been working on during the spring of 1856, both for organ: the Fugue in A-flat minor, WoO8 (completed between April and early June, when he sent a copy to Joachim and Clara), and the Fugue, with Prelude, in A minor, WoO9 (which Clara and Joachim received in May and June, respectively). Since in his letter to Schubring Brahms equates the "music" (*Noten*, literally, the "notes") with his "signature" (*Namenunterschrift*) and expresses his confidence in Schubring's ability to "perceive the name" (*sehen . . . den Namen heraus*) embedded in the notes, it is safe to assume that we are dealing with a musical cipher piece or pieces based on the letters in Brahms's name.[5] Yet the plaintext might have taken any one of the following forms, all of which appear in the composer's correspondence and manuscripts of the mid-1850s: **Brahms, Johannes Brahms, Johannes, J. B., J. Brahms,** or **Johs. Brahms.**[6] Of these, the most likely candidate is the first, **Brahms** (**Johannes** adds only one new musical letter, **E,** which does not appear in the subject of either fugue), and of the two organ works, the one whose primary melodic material bears the closest relationship with the likely plaintext is the Fugue in A-flat minor. As shown in Example 4.3a, its subject yields four of the musical letters in the composer's last name ($C^\flat/B = $ **H,** $B^\flat = $ **B,** $E^\flat = $ **S,** $B^{\flat\flat}/A = $ **A**), while the A-minor fugue subject (Ex. 4-3b) yields only two (**B** and **A**).[7]

In viewing the entries in Table 4-1 as a group, note that they span a limited period, the decade from the early 1850s to the early 1860s, and that several

Example 4-2a: Brahms, "F.A.E." Sonata, Scherzo, mm. 31–33

Example 4-2b: Dietrich, "F.A.E." Sonata, first movement, mm. 1–4

Example 4-2c: Dietrich, "F.A.E." Sonata, first movement, mm. 19–21

items cluster around the years 1853–56, the period when Brahms's involve-
ment with the Schumann circle was most intense. The significance of this experience for the young Brahms can hardly be overestimated, for of all the
composers of the Austro-German line whom he so deeply revered, only one
was a living presence, the figure he sometimes addressed, with a mixture of
adulation and affection, as "Mynheer Domine": Robert Schumann.[8] Brahms's

Example 4-3a: Brahms, Fugue in A-flat minor (WoO8), subject

Example 4-3b: Brahms, Fugue in A minor (WoO9), subject

cipher pieces represent only one manifestation of the rarefied atmosphere in which the young composer lived and worked while he was most directly under Schumann's sway.

Just as Schumann's pieces based on musical ciphers were cast for media associated with the bourgeois drawing room, so, too, were the majority of Brahms's. The single exception, the partsong "Und gehst du über den Kirchhof," was conceived for an institution that was just as deeply implicated in bourgeois musical life as the private salon: the amateur choral society for women (*Frauenchor*), an offshoot of the mixed choruses (*Chorvereine*) and men's choruses (*Männerchöre*) that served as powerful outlets for both cultural enrichment and conviviality during the Biedermeier era and beyond. In other words, both Schumann's and Brahms's musical cipher pieces drew on a network of genres—keyboard music, instrumental chamber music, lied, choral partsong—that was a perfect conduit for two of the chief markers of bourgeois culture: intimacy and high-minded diversion.

Not surprisingly, the rules of Brahms's game with musical ciphers—in the certain and nearly certain cases from Table 4-1—correspond almost exactly to Schumann's:

1. One may encipher a proper name or the acronym for a brief expression.
2. Replace every musical letter in the plaintext with its precise pitch equivalent.
3. The enciphered plaintext, in its basic form, should occur at the beginning of the piece or should articulate an important sectional division.

4. The basic form may be associated with any rhythm, articulation, or dynamic, but repetitions of individual pitches or groups of pitches are to be avoided.
5. Generally, the basic form should appear first in an upper part, less often in the bass.
6. Generally, the basic form should dominate in the piece or section.
7. The basic form should be treated as a self-sufficient musical motive.
8. The basic form can be developed in various ways: it may be transposed, treated in sequence, or melodically altered or transformed; it may initiate longer melodic ideas; it may be contrapuntally combined with other melodic ideas; individual pitches from the cell may be chromatically altered or displaced by alternate pitches to generate new thematic ideas, *but the basic form of the cell should be presented first.* It generates all subsequent forms.

In light of the near agreement between these rules and Schumann's, it is fair to assume that Brahms's approach was conditioned to a large degree by the musical cipher pieces of his mentor. Of Brahms's familiarity with Schumann's contributions to the "F.A.E." Sonata there can be no doubt. Moreover, among Brahms's favorites from Schumann's works was the one that illustrates the older composer's techniques of musical encipherment most fully: *Carnaval.* In a letter to Clara of 15 December 1854, Brahms reported on his performance of the work at a private soirée, and writing to her on 25 November 1855 he expressed his desire to present it in public at some point in the future.[9] From his correspondence we know that Brahms began to study Schumann's music in earnest no later than the summer of 1854, and most probably his studies—often undertaken in the library of the Schumanns' town house in Düsseldorf—would have led him to the cipher piece on Gade's name from the *Album für die Jugend,* one of the most widely known of Schumann's keyboard collections, and to the Fugues on "B-A-C-H" (Op. 60) as well.[10]

Brahms was also intimately aware of the musical cipher techniques practiced by another disciple of Schumann: Joseph Joachim, Brahms's fast friend since the two met in 1853 and the figure who was responsible for Brahms's admission to the Schumann circle. A fascinating project in which they both engaged a few years thereafter is especially relevant to our discussion. At Brahms's urging, the two friends began to trade off contrapuntal assignments of their own making during the spring of 1856, and they continued to do so at various points up through October 1861, although the exchange was carried on most assiduously between April and July 1856. As described in David Brodbeck's thorough account, this dialogue in tones produced some quite remarkable results.[11] Among the products of Brahms's side of the exchange were a number of substantial compositions, including the Fugue in A-flat minor and the Prelude and Fugue in A minor, several canonic settings of the Mass Ordinary (*Missa canonica,* WoO 18), the "Geistliches Lied" for chorus and organ, and earlier versions of two of the three *Geistliche Chöre* (Op. 37). While Joachim's contributions to the exchange were less ambitious, being comprised mainly of brief exercises and fragments, many of them make striking use of musical ciphers. In addition to the tried-and-true "B-A-C-H" motive, which appears in a series of fugal subjects and answers, Joachim wove his personal cipher, F-A-E, into a number of contrapuntal fragments, several of which also contain encipherments of the name **Gisela** (**Gis** = G♯; **E** = E; **la** = the solfége syllable for A).[12] The latter two ciphers are closely related, both in terms of their musical content (G♯–A–E inverts the intervallic pattern of F–A–E) and their personal connotation for Joachim. Indeed, it was owing to his broken engagement with Gisela von Arnim, daughter of the poetess Bettina von Arnim née Brentano, that he was "frei aber einsam."[13] Already in 1853, just after the breakup with Gisela, Joachim had explored the musical relationships between the two ciphers in his *Drei Stücke* for violin and piano, Op. 5. This composition and the exercises motivated by the contrapuntal exchange with Brahms constitute a repertory from which we can glean the rules that Joachim followed in his own game with musical ciphers.

Again, the results are not surprising: Joachim's rules are nearly identical to Schumann's and Brahms's, a further sign that we are dealing with a mutually shared practice grounded in the techniques that Schumann had evolved in the 1830s. Of the three composers, however, Joachim was by far the most liberal in his approach. Two of his rules depart in small but significant ways from Schumann's:

1. Two musical ciphers may be combined to form a continuous melodic entity (e.g., in the two-voice canon on the bass line F–A–E–G♯–E–A [June 1856]; see also 2b).
2. A piece or fragment should generally begin with the basic form of the cipher but may also open with:
   a. its retrograde (fugue subject and answer on E–A–F [April 1856]),
   b. a reordered presentation of the pitches in the basic form ("Schulfuchserei" [Pedantry], comic seven-voice double canon on the bass G♯–E–A–F–E; plaintext = **Gisela** + **F.A.E.** [April 1856]), or
   c. a melodically embellished variant (fugue subject and answer on E–A–F [April 1856]).

Joachim's rules 2b and 2c, both of which are exemplified by items from the contrapuntal exchange, may have influenced Brahms's handling of musical ciphers, for together they account for his unusual encipherment of the probable plaintext (**Brahms**) in the A flat–minor Fugue. (See Ex. 4-3a.) The rearrangement of the musical letters in the plaintext (C♭/B = **H**, B♭ = **B**, E♭ = **S**, B♭♭/A = **A**, . . . E♭ = **S**; instead of B♭ = **B** , A = **A**, B = **H**, E♭ = **S**) is in line with Joachim's rule 2b, while the embellishment of the cipher with six noncipher pitches (the fifth through tenth notes of the fugue subject) falls under rule 2c. The fugue's date of composition lends weight to this conjecture: Brahms drafted the work between April and early June 1856, just after Joachim began to modify the rules of the musical cipher game in his side of the contrapuntal exchange with his friend.

Leaving conjecture aside and returning to the principles of musical encipherment that Brahms unquestionably followed, we might now put them to use much as we did Schumann's rules, that is, as a means of assessing Brahms's supposed practice.[14] The results of this exercise are just as telling as those we reached in examining Schumann's putative methods. Let us begin with the plaintext **F.A.F.,** the initials of the expression "frei aber froh" ("free but happy"), which, according to Max Kalbeck, served as the Brahmsian counterpart to Joachim's "frei aber einsam."[15] For Kalbeck, musical equivalents of this motto play a leading role in the Third Symphony (Op. 90) and also appear with some regularity in the A-minor String Quartet (Op. 51, no. 2), the *Balladen* for piano (Op. 10), the First Piano Concerto (Op. 15), the First Symphony (Op. 68), and the "Tragic" Overture (Op. 81). Since Michael Musgrave has already mounted a strong case against the authenticity of this motto on both documentary and musical grounds,[16] I will limit myself to a summary of the chief points in his argument. In terms of the documentary evidence, all we have to rely on is Kalbeck's (not always reliable) word. So far as the musical evidence is concerned, if Brahms did construct a musical cipher on **F.A.F.,** then he broke his own rules every time he worked it into one of his compositions. Nowhere in the examples mentioned earlier does Brahms feature the putative cipher in its basic form (F–A–F). Rather, it appears in a number of "derived" versions that involve chromatic alteration (F–A♭–F in the Third Symphony; F♯–A–F♯ in the *Balladen* and the First Piano Concerto), transposition and inversion (First Symphony), or wholesale reformulation (A–F–A in the A-minor String Quartet). Not even Joachim's departures from the fundamental rules of the game will account for these supposed derivatives of the F–A–F cell.

Equally problematic is Brahms's purported use of Joachim's motto, the pitch cell F–A–E, in the opening movement of the A-minor String Quartet and in the "Double" Concerto for Violin, Cello, and Orchestra (Op. 102).[17] Here, too, he seems to have ignored (or fundamentally altered) his own principles of musical encipherment with surprising frequency. In violation of the rules that address the primacy of the basic form of a musical cipher (nos. 3, 6, and 8), Brahms relies almost totally on a variety of apparently derived forms in both works. At the very beginning of the string quartet, for instance, the first violin states a configuration in which the basic form is arbitrarily prefaced by the pitch A, which yields A–F–A–E. In the outer movements of the "Double" Concerto, we encounter variants that involve the rearrangement and/or repetition of elements of the basic form, often coupled with transposition (e.g., C–B–E and F–E–A in the first movement and A–E–E–F–E–E in the main theme of the finale), whereas the basic form itself is conspicuously absent. The fact that these configurations are often nestled in the middle of longer phrases, where they may or may not function as self-sufficient motivic units, increases the suspicion that we are not in fact dealing with bona fide musical ciphers.[18]

Finally, we should consider Brahms's employment of the putative musical cipher(s) for **Clara**. First, it should be emphasized that the documentary evidence for Brahms's encipherment of **Clara** is nil. If any such material exists to support the claim, it is surely among the best kept of musicological secrets. This fact, however, has not deterred writers from pinpointing various forms of the supposed Clara cipher (C–B–A–G♯–A or D–C♯–B–A♯–B)[19] in a number of Brahms's works, including: the Scherzo of the Piano Trio in B (Op. 8), the Variations for Piano (Op. 9), the finale of the First Piano Concerto, the third movement of the Second Serenade for Orchestra (Op. 16), the Intermezzo of the G-minor Piano Quartet (Op. 25), the first movement of the C-minor Piano Quartet (Op. 60), the first movement of the First Symphony, the Prelude and Fugue in A minor for Organ, and the Chorale Prelude and Fugue on "O Traurigkeit, o Herzeleid" (WoO 7), also for organ.

Let us turn to the works from this group most frequently associated with the putative Clara cipher: the Piano Trio in B and the C-minor Piano Quartet.[20] Both works were drafted in earlier and later versions, and in both cases the earlier form discloses special biographical links with Clara. The first version of the Trio, completed in January 1854, was privately dedicated to her,[21] while the no longer extant C♯-minor version of the C-minor Piano Quartet occupied Brahms during precisely the period when he was struggling to come to terms with his amorous feelings for Clara, the years 1855–56.[22] The biographical overtones of the C-minor Piano Quartet have often been cited in the Brahms literature. When the composer showed his friend Hermann Dieters the first movement of the work—in what form it is impossible to say—in the summer of 1868, he asked him to "imagine a man who is about to shoot himself, and for whom there is no other way out."[23] And when, in the mid-1870s, Brahms sent copies of the final version of the Piano Quartet to his friend Theodor Billroth and the publisher Fritz Simrock, he made even more explicit comparisons between the feelings embodied in the work and those of Goethe's fictional Werther, whose love for an older (and unattainable) woman precipitates his suicide.[24] Thus both the B-major Piano Trio and the C-minor Quartet would appear to be ideal candidates for musical cells that utter **Clara** in tones. Unfortunately, the music itself tells us otherwise.

While the pitch configuration D–C♯–B–A♯–B appears in the opening theme of the Scherzo of the Piano Trio (see Ex. 4-4; the theme is the same in

Example 4-4: Brahms, Piano Trio in B (Op. 8), Scherzo, mm. 1–4

both versions of the work), contrary to Brahms's usual practice, it occupies the middle and ending, as opposed to the opening, of the phrase (cf. Brahms's rule 3); furthermore, it is not, in and of itself, musically significant, beginning as it does midway through a musical idea in progress (cf. Brahms's rule 7). The derivative of the supposed cipher that heads off the plaintive main theme of the first movement of the C-minor Piano Quartet (Ex. 4-5) is certainly of musical significance, but again, it contradicts Brahms's documented method: first, because it involves an initial presentation of the cell in transposed form (cf. rules 3 and 8), and second, because it contains a threefold repetition of a group of pitches from the cell, the sighing figure E♭–D (cf. rule 4).

Similarly, all of the remaining cases put forward as examples of the Clara cipher break one or more of Brahms's rules 3–8. While the pattern can be inferred from all of these examples, it often occurs in the "wrong" portion of the phrase (First Piano Concerto, finale, mm. 2–4; First Symphony, first movement, mm. 44–45; Prelude and Fugue in A minor, m. 19; Chorale Prelude and Fugue, "O Traurigkeit," mm. 16–17), or appears initially in a derived form, either in retrograde or transposed (First Piano Concerto, finale; Second Serenade for Orchestra, third movement; G-minor Piano Quartet, Intermezzo), or is first stated in a chromatically altered form (Second Serenade, third movement), or fails to present all of the requisite pitches (Prelude and Fugue in A minor).[25] Only one case, the eleventh of the Variations (Op. 9), approximates Brahms's customary practice, but even here there is a problem: the first pitch, C, is repeated three times (cf. Brahms's rule 4), so that the music, much as in Schumann's "Die Lotosblume," stammers out **C-C-C-Clara.** (See Ex. 4-6.) Thus even on the almost non-existent chance that Brahms thought of the pitch cell C–B–A–G♯–A as a Clara cipher, it has little or nothing of importance to tell us about the music.

Example 4-5: Brahms, Piano Quartet in C minor (Op. 60), first movement, mm. 1–10

Example 4-6: Brahms, Variations for Piano (Op. 9), variation 11, mm. 1–3

II

Ciphers, whether real or imagined, can create a false sense of satisfaction in the critic, for they imply that the meaning of a text is coextensive with the meaning of its enciphered plaintext. Ciphers thus relieve the critic of a burden: that of probing beneath the surface of a text for meaning. Thus we might ask, apart from the obvious meanings conveyed by the plaintexts **F.A.E.** and **Agathe,** what significance did the practice of musical encipherment have for Brahms? Up to a point, it meant much the same to him as it did to Schumann. Many of the cultural motifs embedded in Schumann's cipher pieces resonate with Brahms's as well. Like Schumann's, all of Brahms's compositions based on ciphers are pictographs or rebuses in the sense that an image comprised of musical symbols stands for a word or group of words. The essence of the rebus is best conveyed, however, in the tiniest of his forays into musical encipherment: the F.A.E. ciphers affixed to excerpts 225, 226, 228, and 230 from the *Schatzkästlein.* (See Ex. 4-7.) Much as in Schumann's **Beda** fragment, these ciphers on F.A.E. serve as visual representations of a printed or written inscription, in this case a signature appended to a quotation: "—Joseph Joachim." Likewise, all of Brahms's cipher pieces are "games" insofar as they adhere to a set of prescribed rules. And while the products of Brahms's game with musical ciphers can hardly be described as humorous—the A flat–minor Fugue, to take the most obvious example, is deadly serious from start to finish—humor is not entirely lacking (in, for example, the buoyant music that Brahms spins out of the Agathe motive in the G-major Sextet).

For Brahms, the most important of the motifs we previously located in Schumann's cipher pieces is undoubtedly the *hommage* to a revered predecessor or contemporary. The Scherzo of the "F.A.E." Sonata is at once a show of repect for Joachim, whose artistry inspired the project in the first place, and for another of Schumann's disciples, the young composer Albert Dietrich. Invoking the latter, Brahms alludes directly to Dietrich's first-movement theme in the main section of his Scherzo and treats it imitatively in the central Trio. Likewise, Brahms pays homage to a pair of artists in the finale of his Third Piano Sonata, completed on the heels of the "F.A.E." Sonata in late October and early November 1853. As George Bozarth has noted, the first episode (mm. 39–70) in this rather freely structured movement is based on the F–A–E cell,[26] thus establishing an unmistakable connection with Joachim. At the

Example 4-7: Brahms, *Schatzkästlein des jungen Kreislers,* excerpt 226

Es gibt einen Grad der Technik, der zu Geist,
weil zur Vollkommenheit wird.

same time, the episode points just as clearly to Schumann, more specifically, to his Intermezzo for the "F.A.E." Sonata, which almost surely served as the model for the presentation and elaboration of the F–A–E cell in Brahms's sonata movement. (See Exs. 4-8a–b.) On its initial appearance in the finale of Brahms's sonata, the cell occurs at the very same pitch level at which the violin first states it in Schumann's movement. In both cases, the cell is linked with similar rhythmic values, dynamics (*piano*), and articulations (*legato*), and in both cases it is coupled with comparable accompanimental patterns (cf. Brahms's murmuring sixteenths and Schumann's rolling triplets). Melodic sequence, whether exact (Brahms) or free (Schumann), offers the primary means of elaboration in both movements. Moreover, the opening harmonies of Brahms's episode—F, A minor, and D minor—neatly encapsulate the poignant interplay of third-related tonalities (F major versus A minor and D minor) in Schumann's Intermezzo. Taken together, these factors account for Brahms's beautiful re-creation of the dreamy mood that pervades his model— but there is more. In light of the grounding of both the evocation (Brahms's episode) and its model (Schumann's Intermezzo) in a common idea (Joachim's motto), what we have is a realization in tone of one of Joachim's quotations from the *Schatzkästlein*: "The disciples assembled around a master, who together with their master form a school, are like the Milky Way in the firmament of art history; alone they would attract little notice, but together they emit a bright, cheerful luster."[27]

The most impressive of Brahms's musical *hommages* of the mid-1850s, however, is the A flat–minor Fugue for organ. Most probably based on a musical

Example 4-8a: Brahms, Third Piano Sonata (Op. 5), finale, mm. 39–42

Example 4-8b: Schumann, "F.A.E." Sonata, Intermezzo, mm. 1–6

cipher derived from the composer's own name, this work, like the Scherzo of the "F.A.E." Sonata and the finale of the Third Piano Sonata, is deeply bound up with the Schumann circle. A product of the contrapuntal exchange with Joachim, it was presented to Clara Schumann in early June 1856 on the occasion of her husband's forty-sixth (and, as it would turn out, his last) birthday. And although the manuscript bore the warm dedication "Ganz eigentlich für meine Clara" ("Totally and truly for my Clara"), at a deeper level, the work was dedicated to Schumann.[28]

In the A flat–minor Fugue, as in the Scherzo of the "F.A.E." Sonata and the Third Piano Sonata, gestures of homage are conveyed through a network of thematic reminiscences. David Brodbeck has drawn convincing links between the chromatically charged subject of the fugue and the second principal theme from Schumann's Overture to his "dramatic poem" (*dramatisches Gedicht*), *Manfred,* one of the young Brahms's favorite works.[29] (See Ex. 4-9.) Yet *Manfred* is only one of the several works of his mentor to which Brahms alluded. The shape of Brahms's subject also recalls that of the subject of Schumann's Fugue no. 4 on "B-A-C-H." (See Ex. 4-10.) Nor does the resemblance between the two fugues end here. Both are tours de force of contrapuntal technique, rich in affective countermelodies and notable for their employment of many other tricks of the contrapuntist's trade: melodic inversion (and retrograde, in Schumann's fugue), rhythmic augmentation and diminution (in Brahms's fugue), motivic combinations of every kind, pedal points, and stretto. One of Brahms's countermelodies, a sequentially rising pattern coupled only three measures into the piece with an inverted form of the subject (which also serves as fugal answer), evokes the solemn theme, first presented by trombone choir, of the fourth movement of the "Rhenish" Symphony, another of Schumann's celebrated contrapuntal essays. (See Exs. 4-11a–b.)

What is most striking here is the fact that in each case Brahms alludes to works in which Schumann demonstrates his absolute command of the art of counterpoint, viewed for centuries by German composers as the sine qua non of musical craft. (Contrapuntal craftsmanship is no less in evidence in the *Manfred* Overture than it is in the "B-A-C-H" Fugues and the fourth movement of the "Rhenish" Symphony.[30]) It practically goes without saying that the notion of craft was a crucial element in Brahms's ethic of musical com-

Example 4-9: Schumann, Overture to *Manfred,* mm. 52–57

Example 4-10: Schumann, Fugue no. 4 on "B-A-C-H," subject

Example 4-11a: Brahms, Fugue in A-flat minor, mm. 1–4

Example 4-11b: Schumann, "Rhenish" Symphony, fourth movement, trombone chorale, mm. 1–3

position. Many of the excerpts in the *Schatzkästlein* touch on this topic, among them the following passage ascribed to Joachim: "**Craftsmen and Artists.** Those of you who take up random, everyday things and render them as useful but merely fashionable objects, beware: the next generation will hurl your work into the past only to exchange it for the newest, most fashionable bit of finery, but those of you who have a sense for what endures eternally, you master builders who create a temple of the arts with age-old stones, your work will be esteemed and valued by people of all lands for years to come, even if it only survives as a ruin."[31] The same conceit takes an almost metaphysical turn in another aphorism attributed to Joachim, who obviously valued craftsmanship just as highly as his friend Brahms: "There is a level of technique that attains to spirit [*Geist*] because it achieves perfection."[32] Both of these excerpts in turn resonate with the thought conveyed by Schumann, in much simpler language, through the plaintext of his little "Rebus" for piano: "Don't concern yourself with trifles; seize only what's genuine."

With his A flat–minor Fugue, Brahms thus asserted his worthiness of admission into the guild of German craftsmen-composers that counted among its most distinguished members such figures as J. S. Bach, Beethoven—and Schumann. The significance of the fugue for Brahms's place within this venerable tradition was not lost on either Joachim or Clara Schumann.[33] On 20 June 1856, two weeks after receiving a copy of the work, Joachim wrote to

Gisela von Arnim that it "combine[d] depth and tenderness of feeling with a wealth of musical art so nobly that even Bach and Beethoven have scarcely surpassed it."[34] The following day, Clara shared with Joachim the deep impression that Brahms's fugue had made on her, musing, "Isn't it as though a holy appearance hovers over the whole thing?"[35] The identity of the "holy appearance" is not difficult to guess. In a diary entry made just after Brahms presented her with the work, she referred to it as a "wunderbar schöne, innige Fuge" ("wondrously beautiful, intimate fugue"),[36] a description that includes one of Schumann's favored expressive designations: "innig." Is it too much to suggest, therefore, that in Brahms's A flat–minor Fugue Clara sensed the presence of her husband's spirit, hovering over the work like a "holy appearance"?

Of course, by late June 1856 Schumann was in no state to express an opinion on the matter even if one been sought. When, in April, Brahms visited Schumann at the asylum in Endenich where the composer had been remanded after attempting suicide in February 1854, he was genuinely alarmed by the apparent turn for the worse in the older man's condition. Highly excitable, babbling incoherently, and unable to comprehend fully what was said to him, Schumann passed his time by making alphabetical lists of names picked out of an atlas. What's more, his doctor, Franz Richarz, had all but given up hope of Schumann's recovery.[37] Brahms must have realized that the end was near, as indeed it was: Schumann died on 29 July 1856. Furthermore, Brahms's realization would have come during precisely the period when he was engaged in the composition of the A flat–minor Fugue.

Given these factors, it would seem plausible that Brahms's fugue was not only an *hommage* to Schumann but also a lament, a *deploration* before the fact, on the imminent death of his mentor. Another evocation of Schumann's creative output lends weight to this supposition. The A flat–minor Fugue vividly calls up the sound world of the final scene of *Manfred*, a melodrama in which deeply affective music for chorus and orchestra provides the backdrop for the spoken dialogue between the dying title character and an abbot. Both compositions are characterized by a pervasive melancholy tone, an aura of solemn religiosity enhanced by the organ (which accompanies the chorus in Schumann's scene), an austere contrapuntal style (double fugato in the scene from *Manfred*), and flat keys (A♭ minor for Brahms, E♭ minor for Schumann). What is implicit in Brahms's fugue is made explicit by the words intoned by the chorus in Schumann's *Manfred:* "Requiem in aeternam dona eis . . . "

In sum, Brahms's A flat–minor Fugue embodies the whole constellation of motifs associated with the *hommage:* evocations of a revered predecessor's work, craft, veneration for tradition, and commemorative spirit. These elements, more than the probable plaintext enciphered in the fugue, disclose its meaning. In this, as in their points of contact with the rebus and the parlor game, Brahms's cipher pieces are absolutely in line with Schumann's. But what of the other cultural motifs linked with Schumann's practice of musical encipherment: the children's book and the world of the child, the maxim and its pedagogical intent? Do they, too, impinge on Brahms's cipher technique?

All of these motifs do indeed have a place in Brahms's world—though not primarily in his compositions based on ciphers. His arrangements of fourteen *Volks-Kinderlieder* for voice and piano, completed in 1858 and dedicated to the Schumann children, clearly speak to an interest in the world of the child.[38] Interestingly enough, the best represented of the authors quoted in the *Schatzkästlein*, with no fewer than 124 excerpts, is Jean Paul, the "patron saint" of children's books.[39] Brahms's sense for the folk wisdom transmitted in maxims is demonstrated by a little commonplace book that dates from 1855 into which he copied 135 German proverbs (*Deutsche Sprichworte*), either for his own pleasure or for the edification of Schumann's children. Headed by the epigraph "Good maxims, wise lessons one must practice, not just hear," this collection is the ethical pendant to the poetic and aesthetic excerpts in the *Schatzkästlein*.[40] Finally, Brahms's pedagogical inclinations found an outlet in his five *Studien* for piano, composed between 1852 and 1859 and based on pieces by Chopin, Weber, and Bach (an analogue of the "little course in music history" originally intended for inclusion in Schumann's *Album für die Jugend*) and his 51 *Übungen* for piano, completed by 1893. Thus while Brahms's world clearly intersected with Schumann's, the two worlds did not coincide on every point, even during the period when Brahms's contact with the Schumann circle was closest. In the long run, this was all to the good, for as Joachim put it in one of his aphorisms from the *Schatzkästlein*: "We must take care that the spirit of the genius we admire most does not become a flame in which we will perish like helplessly twittering butterflies."[41]

The wisest disciples, in other words, are those who maintain a certain distance between themselves and their masters. Brahms's cipher pieces offer a small but telling example of this stance. Several of them introduce a motif that runs directly counter to Schumann's practice, which goes hand in hand with a process of effacement. In both the Scherzo of the "F.A.E." Sonata and the Fugue in A-flat minor, the plaintexts (or probable plaintext, in the case of the fugue) exist at two levels of remove from the musical surface. As we have seen, the Scherzo relates only indirectly to the F–A–E cell, drawing primarily on an idea associated with the cell at an earlier stage of the sonata. Likewise, the plaintext of the fugue appears to have been deliberately obscured by a series of precompositional operations (omission of "nonmusical" letters, reordering of plaintext letters) so that we cannot be absolutely sure of its identity. Here Brahms acts less like a cryptographer than a chemist, transforming a verbal subject so thoroughly into a musical one that no trace of the original plaintext remains. In these works, the plaintext thus functions as a mere *pretext* that ultimately has no bearing on the aesthetic significance of the finished product.

While the effacement of plaintexts is a matter of precompositional planning in the Scherzo and the A flat–minor Fugue, the same process is actually written into the musical texts of the pair of compositions that employ the Agathe cipher: the partsong "Und gehst du über den Kirchhof" and the G-major String Sextet. The overriding trajectory in both is from a clear statement of the musical motive based on the plaintext to its transformation and, finally, its withdrawal. The basic form of the Agathe cipher runs throughout the first and third strophes of the partsong like a doleful ostinato; sounding five times in all, it is shared by the two lower vocal lines (Altos I and II) and the ad libitum piano part. But when the tonality shifts from E minor to E major for the alternating second and fourth strophes, the Agathe motive undergoes a decisive shift in character and quality. Rhythmically altered, and shorn of its last pitch (E), it is subsumed into—and obliterated by—the final cadential gesture.

The process of effacement is effected more subtly in the first movement of the G-major Sextet. Here the Agathe cipher provides the motivic material for the closing paragraphs of the movement's exposition and recapitulation (mm. 162–213 and 496–547, respectively). These passages are shaped in two broad arches or waves, the first initiated by a climactic tutti, the second by a quieter and more lyrical closing theme. Each wave begins with presentations of the basic form of the Agathe motive that soon give way to phrases in which the motive is gradually dismantled through procedures that include detachment of the motive's central three pitches (a stepwise ascent that spans a third, G–A–B), sequential elaboration and inversion (of the three-note cell), transposition, free reshaping, and relegation of the motive and its derivatives to the inner voices of the texture. In the final bars of the movement, the motive is utterly dissolved, its central three-note cell swallowed up in the concluding cadence.

Thus Brahms's Agathe pieces interweave aesthetic and biographical factors. One of our chief sources of information regarding the latter is an autobiographical sketch drafted late in life by Agathe herself and titled *Allerlei aus meinem Leben / Für meine Kinder aufgeschrieben* (Autobiographical miscellany / written for my children).[42] In the portion of the sketch headed "In memoriam J. B.," Agathe recounts the circumstances that led up to her break with Brahms in the form of a folktale whose main characters are "a lively and hot-blooded young maiden" and "the youth" with whom she fell in love, but whose feelings were "not as strong and deep as hers." Indeed, he refused to formalize their bond on the flimsy grounds that he could not "wear fetters." Compelled by "duty and honor" to break with the young man, the maiden "wept and wept for years over the death of her happiness." And even though she eventually found fulfillment in her marriage to another, "the memory [*Andenken*] of her immense love for the youth . . . was never, never extinguished."[43]

While Brahms certainly never read this tale, many of its motifs resonate with his Agathe pieces. "Und gehst du über den Kirchhof," for instance, is a bittersweet lament in folk-song style, the text of which tells of a young lover, now dead and buried, who like Agathe "loved too ardently" ("hatte zu heiß geliebt"). The G-major Sextet, the work in which Brahms is said to have claimed that he "freed" himself from his "last great love,"[44] is more reflective of the "youth's" attitude than the "maiden's." Whereas she preserved the memory of their love to the end of her days, he effaced it through his treatment of the musical motive generated from her name.[45] The precedent for Brahms's approach lies ready to hand in Joachim's cipher pieces. Just as Joachim neutralized the pain of his failed love affair with Gisela von Arnim by taking her name as the point of departure for a game with musical ciphers, so Brahms wrote **Agathe** into his music as a means of writing Agathe von Siebold out of his life.

The effacement of a love gone wrong: with this motif we circle back to Clara Schumann. Brahms's correspondence during the roughly two-year period between the early summer of 1854 and the summer of 1856 leaves little room for doubt that his initial feelings of admiration and respect for Schumann's wife soon blossomed into full-scale passion. Consider the following passage from a letter to Joachim of 19 June 1854: "I believe I admire and honor [Frau Schumann] no more highly than I love and am in love with her. I often have to restrain myself forcibly just from quietly embracing her and even—: I don't know, it seems to me so natural, as though she could not take it at all amiss. I think I can't love a young girl any more, at least I have entirely forgotten them; after all, they merely promise the Heaven which Clara shows us unlocked."[46] Many of Brahms's letters from this period to Clara herself contain thinly veiled declarations of love. In one of the most fanciful of these, he speaks through the Brahmin Prince Kamarez-zemán, a character from the tales in the *1001 Nights:* " 'Would to God it were permitted me today, instead of sending this letter, to repeat to thee in person that I am dying of love for thee.'"[47] Although it is highly improbable that Brahms ever entered into a sexual relationship with Clara,[48] it is nonetheless clear that as a young man of twenty-one or twenty-two he was deeply in love with her. Then, at some point after Schumann's death in July 1856, something went awry. We note a change in Brahms's correspondence with Clara during the autumn of that year: the tone becomes somewhat cooler, more detached, noticeably less impassioned.[49] Brahms and Clara remained remarkably close until the end of their lives, managing repeatedly to patch over the disagreements and misunderstandings that are apt to beset any relationship that extends over a forty-year period—but as best we can tell from the surviving evidence, the passion that he felt for her in the mid-1850s would never flare up again.

Wouldn't Clara, therefore, have been a likely candidate for the kind of procedures that helped Brahms to efface his love for Agathe? In other words,

despite the absence of hard evidence, isn't it still possible that musical encipherments of **Clara** are embedded in some of Brahms's compositions of the
1850s and 1860s and in the later works whose origins can be traced back to
that period? I think not. In the first place, there is little reason to suppose that
Brahms would have responded musically to Clara in the same way he did to
Agathe. His warm feelings for Agathe in the summer of 1858 were probably
genuine and perhaps even reached a certain level of intensity, but ultimately,
they were quite ordinary. In contrast, his feelings for Clara, especially during
the critical years 1854–56, represented a rather *extra*ordinary mixture of love,
awe, and veneration.[50]

Like Schumann before him, Brahms almost surely attempted to embody
Clara in tones. But, as I will argue in chapter 5, both composers must have
done so in extraordinary ways, as would only befit a figure who played such
an extraordinary role in their lives. Schumann concluded his review of
Clara's Opus 6, a set of piano pieces titled *Soirées musicales,* by observing that
"some things just can't be expressed through the letters of the alphabet."[51]
Schumann and Brahms would have agreed that one of those "things" was
Clara Wieck Schumann.

CHAPTER 5.

THE FOLDED FAN

How helpful of Proust to remark
that "one cannot read a novel without
ascribing to the heroine the traits
of the one we love"
—Alain de Botton,
How Proust Can Change Your Life, *1997*

ECONSTRUCTING THE CONSCIOUSNESS of a subject who is not present to speak on his or her own behalf can be a risky business. Yet so far as Robert Schumann is concerned, one thing is certain: for the last two decades of his life, his perception of the world around him was permeated with visions of Clara. Writing to her in February 1836, soon after the death of his mother, he confided that her "bright image shines through the darkness," thus allowing him to bear his burden more easily.[1] Several years later, when Schumann was struggling to gain a foothold as a critic and composer in Vienna, Clara's image was every bit as much a consoling presence. "Often I'd like to run away," he wrote to her on 11 November 1838, "but then I see you before me, your eyes full of love and faithfulness, and you say 'Just be patient'—then I'm so happy again, for you are my bride lying in my arms."[2] Even his responses to musical compositions were colored by imaginary representations of Clara. "I recognized you so completely in it," he reported on receiving a copy of her A flat–major Romance in May 1839, "my girl of old with the dreamy look."[3] Fifteen years later, Brahms would react similarly while immersing himself in his mentor's music in the Schumanns' Düsseldorf flat: "I too gaze ever more deeply into a pair of wondrously beautiful eyes, which gaze at me now from out of the *Davidsbündlertänze* and the *Kreisleriana*."[4] No doubt those eyes belonged to Clara, to whom he wrote on 8 December 1854: "I do see you often, as good as in person; for instance, at the trill in the final passages of the Andante of the C-major Symphony [third movement of Schumann's Symphony No. 2, Op. 61], and at the pedal points of great fugues, when you suddenly appear to me as St. Cecaelia!"[5] That Schumann and the young Brahms experienced reality in this way is only to be expected—after all, they were both very much in love.

I

While it is common enough for lovers to apprehend traces of their beloved in the sights and sounds of the surrounding world, this phenomenon first became a popular theme in art when it was appropriated by the Romantics and their immediate predecessors. Wandering through a garden in springtime, the lovesick speaker in Friedrich von Matthison's *Adelaide*—a poem set by Beethoven in the mid-1790s and published as his Opus 46—sees the image of his beloved wherever his glance happens to settle, whether it be on a flowing stream, the Alpine snow, or "the golden clouds of fading day." Similarly, the enamored girl of Adalbert von Chamisso's *Frauenliebe und Leben*—poems that would provide the textual basis for one of Schumann's most famous song cycles—is blind to everything *except* the image of her beloved: "Wherever I look," she muses at the beginning of the cycle, "I see only him." In contrast to Chamisso's protagonist, the lyrical subject of Eichendorff's "Dein Bildniss wunderselig" (set by Schumann as the second song of his *Liederkreis,* Op. 39) internalizes his perceptions, retaining deep within the recesses of his heart a "wondrous image" of his inamorata that "gazes back" at him "brightly and merrily."

With increasing frequency, Romantic artists imbued this universal experience with particularity as they attempted to replicate it in the products of their creativity. Arguably the most sensual of the arts, music proved to be a fertile medium for endeavors of this kind. Consider, for instance, Berlioz's *Symphonie fantastique.* According to the initial program, published with the first edition of the full score in 1845, the symphony's central character is a "young musician" who "sees for the first time a woman embodying all the charms of the ideal being he has dreamt about, and with whom he falls desperately in love." Furthermore, whether "in the midst of *the tumult of a party*" or "in the peaceful contemplation of the beauties of nature," he cannot escape from the "beloved image," which both "hovers before him and disturbs his peace of mind."[6] Intent upon simulating the artist's obsessive preoccupation with his beloved, Berlioz had the perfect means at his disposal in the form of the melodic *idée fixe* that winds its ways through each of the symphony's five movements. The desire to create aural embodiments of a beloved image persisted in the works of the more Romantically inclined composers of the twentieth century as well. One such figure was Edward Elgar, who prefaced his Violin Concerto of 1910 with the inscription "AQUI esta ENCERRADA el ALMA de . . ." ("HERE is ENSHRINED the SOUL of . . ."). While the identity of the "enshrined" being is cloaked in mystery, the composer's aim—the embodiment of a cherished being in tone—could not be clearer. In a similar vein, Alban Berg's Violin Concerto of 1935—a work that surely represents one of the last gasps of Romanticism—is dedicated "Dem Andenken eines Engels" ("To the memory of an angel"). Granted, Berg was not in love with Manon Gropius, the "angel" of his inscription, who died tragically at the age of nineteen from infantile paralysis. Still, we now know that in addition to the "official," Manon-related program of the concerto, there was at least one other, "secret" program as well, built around the musical images of Berg's amours: Hanna Fuchs-Robettin and a Carinthian peasant girl by whom he may have fathered a child.[7]

Yet of all the composers who strove to inscribe the object of their passion into the fabric of their works, none did so as purposefully—or as frequently—as Robert Schumann. His correspondence with Clara during the period of their enforced separation leaves no doubt as to his intentions. On 3 August 1838 he exhorted her to play his *Kreisleriana:* "There's a wild love in a few movements—and your life and mine, and many of your looks." Writing to his "dear bride" on 30 June 1839, he declared: "In the *Novelletten,* you appear in every imaginable situation and disposition, and these pieces also contain other irresistible things about you. . . . I maintain that only someone who is familiar with eyes like yours and who has touched lips like yours could write *Novelletten.*"[8] These passages represent only a small sampling from a body of quotations large enough to fill an album of considerable dimensions. And although the comparable passages from Brahms's surviving correspondence are fewer, they are just as telling. As he informed Clara on 30 December 1856, while drafting the slow movement of his Piano Concerto in D minor: "I'm painting a gentle portrait of you, which will then become an Adagio."[9] The conclusion is obvious: like Schumann before him, Brahms strove just as assiduously to capture the image of Clara in tone.

But to reiterate a question posed earlier, in chapter 3, how, exactly, did Schumann and Brahms realize their aim? Having ruled out the practice of cryptography as a viable medium for their aural embodiments of Clara, we must look elsewhere. A more appropriate metaphor—"appropriate" in the sense that it resonates with both lived experience and artistic practice—can, I think, be found in Walter Benjamin's *One-Way Street,* a collection of miniessays written between 1923 and 1926 and published in 1928. The entry titled "FAN" deserves to be quoted in full:

> Most people probably will have had the following experience: if you are in love, or even just intensely preoccupied with someone else, then you will find the other person's portrait in nearly every book. Indeed, the beloved will appear as both protagonist and antagonist. In tales, novels and novellas you will encounter [the beloved] in ever new metamorphoses. Thus it follows from this that the faculty of imagination is the gift of making inter-

polations into infinitely small spaces, of conceiving every intensity as an extensiveness, thereby discovering in it a newly compressed fullness—in short, of receiving every image as if it were that of a folded fan that only in unfolding draws breath and presents, by way of its new expanse, the features of the beloved object within.[10]

Alternately folding and unfolding, concealing and revealing, compressing and expanding, the fan is a potent symbol for the dialectics—and the actual physical tokens—of sensual love. Indeed, it is hardly a coincidence that the fans that became so popular among the upper strata of Western European society in the seventeenth and eighteenth centuries were often decorated with frankly erotic drawings, executed in minute detail by skilled artisans in imitation of Oriental models. An emblem of Eros, the fan as described by Benjamin is also an emblem for the quintessentially Romantic artwork, an entity caught up in a perpetual dialectic of enfoldment and unfurling, disclosure and revelation, intensification and expansion.

The folded and unfolding fan is the central term in a constellation of motifs that, taken together, will help us to bridge the gap between a beloved image and the inscription of that image in a work of art. As Benjamin pointed out in another context, the fan is not only a signifier for the erotic experience but also a metaphor for the process of remembrance. Commenting in *A Berlin Chronicle* on the "form" assumed by that process in the works of Proust, he noted that whoever "has once begun to open the fan of memory never comes to the end of its segments. No image satisfies him, for he has seen that it can be unfolded, and only in its folds does the truth reside—that image, that taste, that touch for whose sake all this has been unfurled and dissected; and now remembrance progresses from small to smallest details, from the smallest to the infinitesimal, while that which it encounters in these microcosms grows ever mightier."[11] Defined a few pages later as "the capacity for [making] endless interpolations into what has been," the "mysterious work of remembrance" therefore corresponds to the faculty of imagination as described in the miniessay on the fan.[12]

Products of the twin faculties of memory and imagination, the interpolations that reside in the folds of the fan possess the clarity and vividness of an image—and not just of any image. Insofar as they disclose to the perceptive beholder the tiniest details, these interpolations bear comparison with specifically *photographic* imagery, the final term in our constellation of fan-related motifs. Characterized soon after its invention in the 1830s as a "mirror that remembers,"[13] photography does considerably more than produce mere copies of what appears before the camera's lens: it has the uncanny power to disclose those aspects of physical reality that are inaccessible to the naked eye. Or as Benjamin put it in his "Little History of Photography":

It is through photography that we first discover the existence of [the] optical unconscious, just as we discover the instinctual unconscious through psychoanalysis. Details of structure, cellular tissue, [things] with which technology and medicine are normally concerned—all this is, in its origins, more native to the camera than the atmospheric landscape or the soulful portrait. Yet, at the same time, photography reveals in [these] material physiognomic aspects, image worlds, which dwell in the smallest things—meaningful yet covert enough to find a hiding place in waking dreams."[14]

Hence just as the fan is a symbol of the bittersweet mixture of imagination and remembrance implicit in the erotic experience, so can the photograph, a gateway to the "optical unconscious," be identified as a symbol of revelation. And since the photograph and the fan alike are receptacles for deeply buried memories, it is clear that this family of motifs embraces the totality of relations between the lover and the object of his or her affections.

The structural property shared by all of our principal motifs—the fan, the faculty of memory, and the photographic image—is what Benjamin calls the gift or capacity of making endless interpolations, and it is this property, in turn, that enabled musical alchemists like Schumann and Brahms to transmute their lived experiences into works of art. Both were masters of the technique of interpolation, and it is probably not by chance that they practiced it best in precisely those works inspired by Clara's muse. (Conversely, imagistic renderings of Schumann and Brahms insinuated themselves into Clara's own compositions.) What we hear in the opening movement of Schumann's Fantasie (Op. 17) and the Adagio of Brahms's D-minor Piano Concerto—to name only two of the better-known "Clara" pieces—is an attempt to imbue the musical surface with the quality of a consciousness gripped by a deep preoccupation with a beloved object, an endeavor that lends to so many of the works of Schumann and Brahms the texture of a folded and unfolding fan. In the pages that follow, we will further explore the significance of this metaphor and its attendant motifs for an understanding of Schumann's and Brahms's embodiment of Clara in tone.

II

In writing about music, it is fairly common to draw comparisons between aural and visual modes of perception. Schumann himself did so on a number of occasions; in a letter of 9 June 1839, for instance, he encouraged Clara to share her thoughts on the first movement of his Fantasie (Op. 17), asking: "Doesn't it bring many images [Bilder] to your mind?"[15] Yet in what sense is the analogy between musical and visual perceptions justified?

According to Roland Barthes, Schumann's music is notable above all for its imagistic quality, a feature he locates in the interruptions that constantly ruffle the musical surface and that are, in the critic's words, "consubstantial with the entire Schumannian oeuvre." For Barthes, the "sequence of intermezzi" that he equates with Schumann's output does not serve primarily "to make contrasts speak but rather to fulfill a radiant writing, which is then recognizable much closer to painted space than to the spoken chain. Music, in short, at this level, is an image, not a language."[16] The homology that Barthes proposes between Schumann's music, on the one hand, and visible images, on the other, acquires greater force if we assume that the imagery he has in mind is chiefly photographic, as opposed to painterly, in nature. After all, both music and photography operate under the sign of ephemerality, even though that property manifests itself differently in each medium: while music is a figure for transience itself, photography represents an attempt to capture the transient moment, to freeze it for eternity. Hence, it follows that music will assume a photographic quality when its discursive course is suspended, diverted from its expected path for the purpose of seizing upon a single moment in the temporal continuum.

Schumann's music abounds in discontinuous effects of just this kind (indeed, for Barthes, it consists of *nothing but* temporal discontinuities), and it is here, in the interstices between what would normally be successive moments in the steady flow of time, that Schumann is most apt to situate the interpolations that imbue his music with the texture of an unfolding fan. The opening movement of the Piano Sonata in F-sharp minor (Op. 11), "dedicated" to Clara by "Florestan and Eusebius," offers an excellent case in point. Originally conceived in 1832 as an independent composition titled *Fandango*, it underwent some rather extraordinary changes before assuming its final form in 1835. (A triple-time dance of Castilian-Andalusian origin, the fandango was originally associated with courtship ceremonies, making it an appropriate model for Florestan and Eusebius's offering to Clara; although Schumann's *Fandango* is cast in duple time, it projects the rhythmic verve and emulates the clicking castanets of the actual dance.) In addition to prefacing the movement with a slow introduction, Schumann amplified the body of the *Fandango* in ways that are of particular significance for the metaphor we are developing. Instead of beginning straightaway with the repetitive anapestic rhythm of the fandango theme, the main Allegro section of the sonata movement opens with a drummed motive that outlines a perfect fifth, and the same motive, rendered *forte* in octaves, puts in an appearance after each of the following two statements of the complete fandango theme. (Schumann also combines bits of the motive with portions of the theme itself.) The drummed motive was almost surely derived from the opening bars of Clara's "Scène fantastique: Le Ballets des Revenants," a short piano piece composed in 1833 and published in 1836 as the fourth item in her *Quatre pièces caractéris-*

tiques (Op. 5). Although Clara initially drums out a tritone, the gestural similarities between her motive (which eventually does span a perfect fifth) and Schumann's are unmistakable. (Cf. Exs. 5-1 and 5-2.) Premonitions and after-echoes of the motive figure prominently in the first and second movements of Schumann's sonata, witness the quietly descending fifth at the conclusion of the first movement's slow introduction and the muted asides, which feature the same intervallic gesture, in the slow movement, an "Aria" based on one of Schumann's early songs.[17] In all of these instances we observe Schumann in the process of making interpolations into the folds of preexistent musical textures—and what emerges from the folds are humorous evocations of Clara. Both parties, moreover, seem to have indulged in the same game: while Schumann's sonata playfully alludes to Clara's "Scène fantastique," the rhythmic profile of the second half of Clara's piece is suspiciously close to that of Schumann's *Fandango*.

Not all of Schumann's interpolations impinge upon the temporal flow as do those in the F sharp–minor Sonata. At times they unfold as discrete lines in a multilayered texture, highlighting the spatial character of the music by mediating between surface and foundation, height and depth. Schumann offers a graphic representation of this interplay of textural layers in the *Humoreske* (Op. 20). The fourth section of this affectively mutable piece, marked *Hastig* ("hasty"), features a wistful upper line, gracefully embellished in the right hand and supported by a melodic bass line and offbeat chords in the left. Embedded between these textural strands is yet another part which Schu-

Example 5-1: Schumann, Piano Sonata No. 1 in F-sharp minor, Op. 11, first movement, mm. 53–56

Example 5-2: Clara Schumann, "Scene fantastique," Op. 5, no. 4, mm. 1–4

mann notates in small notes on a third staff and designates as an *Innere Stimme*. (See Ex. 5-3.) Replicating the melodic contour of the right-hand line at the lower octave, the "inner voice" provides a shadowy simulacrum of that line, a kind of musical X ray intended only for the eyes of the player. Whether or not the *Innere Stimme* was meant as a specific invocation of Clara is difficult to say. A possible clue as to its meaning, however, may be found in a letter Schumann wrote to her on 3 November 1837, about sixteen months before the *Humoreske* was completed. Noting his inability to find the words that could adequately convey his love for her, he went on to say: "My feelings are so strong, but I can express so little. —An inner voice must tell you—"[18] Viewed against the backdrop of these remarks, the *Innere Stimme* of the *Humoreske*—inaudible but (just barely) visible—points vividly to the experience of a lover who perceives the image of his beloved wherever he looks.

And just as the motivic asides in Schumann's F sharp–minor Sonata are implicated in an exchange of creative ideas between musical lovers, so, too, are the layered interpolations in the *Humoreske,* albeit unconsciously. Commenting on Clara's recently drafted Romance in G minor (Op. 11 no. 2) in a letter of 10 July 1839, Schumann reaffirmed his conviction "that we have to be

Example 5-3: Schumann, *Humoreske,* mm. 251–58

man and wife. You complement me as a composer just as I do you. Each of your ideas comes from my soul, just as I owe all of my music to you." Two days later, he provided a concrete example of this phenomenon. After observing that an "extremely intimate yet passionate" passage from the middle section (Allegro appassionato) of Clara's Romance reminded him of Beethoven, he added: "In March, I had a very similar thought; you will find it in the *Humoreske*. Our sympathies are just too remarkable."[19] Although the two works were conceived independently—the *Humoreske* in March of 1839 and the Romance in June of the same year—in Schumann's opinion, they seemed to flow from one and the same spiritual source. According to Janina Klassen, the spot from the *Humoreske* that Schumann was probably thinking of occurs just past the midpoint of the piece during a section marked *Innig* (mm. 672ff.). Klassen is almost surely right; Schumann's music, at this juncture of the *Humoreske,* resonates with Clara's in terms of melodic shape, rhythmic profile, and even tonal orientation (an excursion to G♭ in a B♭-major context).[20] At the same time, there is another and even more telling affinity between the pieces. As Klassen also observes, Clara's Romance is characterized by a deft interlacing of registral strands, especially in the framing Andante sections of the work, where a flowing line appears by turns at every level of the texture, almost in the manner of a migrating cantus firmus.[21] In other words, it is possible that Schumann perceived an image of himself not only in the isolated melodic details of the Romance but also in its richly interwoven textural layers—audible counterparts of the inaudible *Innere Stimme* of his *Humoreske.*

For the sake of clarity, I have described each of Schumann's principal types of interpolation—the episodic, or temporally disruptive, and the layered—as if they were separate strategies. In practice, however, both methods of making insertions were interdependent, often working together to enhance the fanlike quality of a piece or movement. For instance, one of the more significant ideas in the opening movement of the Fantasie (Op. 17) first arises from an inner layer of the texture during the course of the transition between the first and second thematic groups in the exposition (mm. 33–41). Initiated by an emphatic ascent through scale steps 5, 3, and 1 of the minor triad, this idea later recurs, in a somewhat altered rhythmic guise, as the chief conceit of the "Im Legendenton" section that begins at m. 129 and extends all the way to m. 224. Having already identified this mammoth digression as a site of pastness and thus a counterpart of the moments of suspended time in Schubert's late instrumental music,[22] we are now in a position to observe how Schumann directed this Schubert-inspired technique toward his own expressive ends: the musical embodiment of erotic yearning. In the opening movement of the Fantasie, Schumann presents the fan of Eros both in its folded state and also as it would be perceived by one who is deeply in love, that is, in the process of unfolding. The gestures on either side of the "Im Legendenton" (mm. 127–28 and m. 225, respectively) correspond to a pair of adjacent measures in the exposition (mm. 28–29) that bridge the gap between the close of one phrase and the beginning of the next. In other words, Schumann has quite literally interpolated a nearly 100-bar aside into an "infinitely small space" (to quote Benjamin's miniessay on the fan): the caesura between successive phrases. What we first apprehended as just another fold in the musical texture subsequently unfolds, in the "Im Legendenton" section, and in doing so "draws breath and presents, by way of its new expanse, the features of the beloved object within." While the earlier, layered interpolation afforded a glimpse of those features, it is only with the unfolding of the "Im Legendenton" that Schumann allows us to behold them in vivid detail.

From what we know of the genesis of the first movement of the Fantasie, it is obvious that Clara was the "beloved object" who inspired its creation. As a result of Nicholas Marston's masterful sleuthing, we can be all but certain that this movement was conceived as an independent fantasy, titled *Ruines*, in June 1836, hence during a period when Schumann's personal life itself was in ruins; in fact, it was at just this time that Clara, acting under her father's orders, insisted that Schumann return her love letters.[23] Almost two years later, in a letter of 18 March 1838, he would describe the opening movement of what had since grown into a three-movement work as a "deep lament" for Clara,[24] invoking a phrase that leads us back to the music of "Im Legendenton." Initially exuding an atmosphere of wistful resignation and eventually building toward a climax of intense pathos, this passage constitutes the melancholy center of Schumann's "deep lament."[25]

Here the playful sharing of ideas that characterized the creative interchange between Schumann's Sonata in F-sharp minor and Clara's "Scène fantastique" takes a doleful turn. As Berthold Hoeckner has suggested, the principal melodic idea of Schumann's "Im Legendenton" was fashioned as a minor-mode variant of the theme of Clara's *Romance variée* (Op. 3), a supposition strengthened by the fact that the "Im Legendenton" originally bore the designation "Romanza" in Schumann's autograph.[26] If this designation aims to capture the underlying amorous character of the passage, its subsequent titles—"Legende," "Erzählend im Legendenton" (Narrated in the manner of a legend), and finally "Im Legenden Ton"—speak to the temporality of pastness inherent in those moments where Schumann, intent on converting the fleeting moment into an infinity, lingers dreamily on melodic threads introduced earlier in the movement.[27] Both of these qualities—eroticism and reminiscence—are closely related, for as Stephen Downes observes in a sensitively argued essay on Schumann's Fantasie, Erato, the muse of love poetry, was also the daughter of Mnemosyne, or Memory.[28] In short, the opening movement of the Fantasie in general, and the "Im Legendenton" in particular, would seem to encapsulate the entire panoply of moods associated with the erotic experience: bittersweet melancholy, dreamy reflection, and wistful reminiscence. Hence what emanates from the folds of the fan in Schumann's fantasy movement is not only an image of Clara, the beloved object who occasioned its composition, but a musical rendering of a universal condition.

While the episodic interpolation takes precedence over its layered counterpart in projecting the message of the first movement of the Fantasie, the reverse holds true in the *Davidsbündlertänze* (Op. 6). Named after the Davidsbund, Schumann's half-imaginary band of crusaders against philistinism in music, and completed in rough draft by September 1837—soon after Clara agreed to Schumann's proposal that they enter into a "second alliance"[29]— this cycle of eighteen dances clearly reflects his elation over the prospect that the long-awaited union with his beloved was finally at hand. (As things turned out, it would not take place until nearly three years later.) The *Davidsbündlertänze*, Schumann wrote to Clara in January 1838, are "full of wedding thoughts," noting further in a letter of 6 February 1838 that they were "dedicated" to her "more than anything else" he had written up to that point.[30] Schumann returned to the nuptial theme in the second of these letters, claiming that the "story" of the cycle was a "Polterabend" (the traditional bachelor's party before a wedding) and leaving it to Clara to "imagine the beginning and the end."[31] Although this implies that the "beginning" and "end" of the skeletal program lie somewhere outside the bounds of the music itself, they, too, can be integrated within the overall scheme of the cycle.

In my reading, the bachelor's party does not actually get under way until the third movement (Etwas hahnbüchen), the first in a series of generally exuberant dances—which included waltzes, polkas, and a tarantella—that extends up through no. 16 ("Mit gutem Humor"). The remaining pairs of dances serve as a frame, thus yielding the following design:

"Beginning"	"Polterabend"	"End"
Nos. 1–2	Nos. 3–16	Nos. 17–18

This reading is supported by the affective, gestural, and tonal properties of the widely spaced dances that together delineate the inner frame: no. 2, a heartfelt waltz in B minor signed "E." for "Eusebius" and further designated *Innig* ("intimate"); and no. 17, a joint creation of "F. u. E." (Florestan and Eusebius), which calls up, "as if from the distance" (*wie aus der Ferne*), first a sensuous waltz in B major and then a reprise of the music of No. 2.[32] Both movements are expressions of longing for a distant beloved whose identity Schumann reveals through a pair of strategically placed interpolations.

As paradoxical as it may sound, the cycle opens with an interpolation: a tiny insertion that prefaces the true beginning of the first dance at m. 6 and that takes the form of a quotation of the first two bars of Clara's Mazurka in G major, the fifth piece of *her* Op. 6, *Soirées musicales*. Specifically designated as a "Motto von C[lara] W[ieck]," this phrase gives rise to a complementary unit from which Schumann extracts a single, long-held pitch: b'.[33] (Cf. Exs. 5-4 and 5-5.) A complementary interpolation in no. 16 in turn heralds the

Example 5-4: Clara Schumann, Mazurka (*Soirées musicales,* Op. 6, no. 5) mm. 1–2

Example 5-5: Schumann, *Davidsbündlertänze* (Op. 6), first movement, mm. 1–8

"end" of the cycle. While it begins with humorously cross-accented rhythms that cannot be definitively ascribed to any of the standard dance types, the main part of the movement reveals itself to be a mazurka through the characteristic rhythmic pattern that punctuates its main cadences (♩♪ | ♩ ♩). In evoking the mazurka, Schumann thus paves the way for the reemergence of a musical image of Clara in the movement's Trio section, where small clusters of emphatically repeated pitches fill in the interstices between ethereal phrases in the piano's upper register. An allusion to Clara's *Valses romantiques* of 1835, the repeated-note motive proceeds from F♯ and ultimately settles on the same pitch with a pedal that at once echoes the sustained B at the beginning of the cycle and provides an imperceptible transition into its closing phase.[34] In terms of Schumann's program for the cycle as a whole then, the "beginning" is dominated by an image of the beloved object that recedes in the ensuing "bachelor's party" and only rises to the surface toward the "end." And while Schumann's employment of episodic references to Clara's own works contributes to this impression, his subtle play with layered interpolations provides an even more crucial means of ensuring the same effect.

In his review of the *Soirées musicales,* Schumann drew attention to Clara's ability "to entangle and unravel the more secretive, deeply spun threads of harmony." Mesmerized by the "strangely intertwined arabesques" in Clara's pieces, he also compared them to "pearls" that only rarely floated "on the surface," remaining for the most part buried "in the depths."[35] In his *Davids-bündlertänze,* Schumann not only borrowed a memorable thematic idea from Clara's collection—the two-bar opening gesture of her Mazurka in G—but also attempted to simulate the interplay of surface and depth to which he alluded in his review of her Op. 6. This interplay is evident in a melodic thread that straddles the cycle's beginning and end, linking one to the other by way of a stepwise descent from B, the pitch that Schumann extracted from his extension of Clara's motto, to C, the tonal and melodic goal of the final dance (no. 18).

The initial segment of the thread, B–A–G, occupies the surface of the first dance, articulating the descent from the third to the first scale degree in a G-major context. With the second dance, Eusebius's languorous waltz in B minor, the thread begins its motion toward the "depths" as the segment G–F♯ retreats into an inner layer of the texture. After a long interruption—the central bachelor's party—Schumann picks up the thread in no. 16, embedding the G–F♯ cell in an inner voice of the mazurka cadences that prefigure the end of the cycle. Momentarily rising to the surface with the repeated F♯s derived from Clara's *Valses romantiques,* the melodic thread once again dips toward the interior in the "distant music" of no. 17 ("Wie aus der Ferne"), first in the form of a gently pulsating inner-voice pedal on F♯ and then as a sighing accompaniment (G–F♯) to the reprise of Eusebius's B-minor waltz. The uppermost pitch in the final B-minor triad of no. 17, F♯, then gives way to F in the dissonant haze out of which the concluding movement emerges. According to Schumann's inscription in the first edition of the *Davidsbündlertänze,* Eusebius "added" this delicate waltz "needlessly" ("Zum Überfluss"), while at the same time "his eyes told of much bliss" ("sprach aber viel Seligkeit aus seinen Augen"). His eyes also betray a mildly ironic intent, for the last movement is hardly a needless afterthought. On the contrary, it is precisely here that the melodic thread once more reclaims the musical surface, proceeding through E and D to C (scale steps 3–2–1 of the C-major tonic) and thus completing the descent initiated at the beginning of the cycle.[36] In short, the last dance of the cycle represents a moment of revelation, and Schumann underscores its revelatory character by coupling the reemergence of the guiding motivic thread from an interior layer with a turn to a crystalline texture that seems to resound from an otherworldly music box. A programmatically oriented listener might well imagine that at this point only two figures—Eusebius and Clara—remain on the dance floor. But even without prior knowledge of the cycle's implication in the details of the composer's personal life, the listener who is attuned to Schumann's subtle play with depth and surface (or concealment and disclosure) will perceive in the concluding waltz of the *Davidsbündlertänze* a dream image of union with a distant beloved.

As we have seen, the interpolations in Schumann's earlier keyboard music, whether episodic or layered, often allude unmistakably to Clara's own compositions. One of the most striking of these allusions occurs in the last of Schumann's *Novelletten* (Op. 21, no. 8) when a *Stimme aus der Ferne* (voice from the distance) soars in with an extended reference to the main melody of the "Notturno" from Clara's *Soirées musicales* (Op. 6, no. 2).[37] In chapter 2 we observed how this gesture, as the product of an involuntary musical memory, creates an effect not unlike that of a Proustian *moment bienheureux*.[38] Here it will be instructive to consider that observation in the light of Schumann's placement of the allusions to Clara's theme within the design of the eighth *Novellette* as a whole. The movement is a sprawling affair, its unusually large dimensions, as Berthold Hoeckner has pointed out, a consequence of its growth out of a pair of *Novelletten*, in D and B♭, to which Schumann added an opening section in F♯ minor. The resultant design is comparable to that of the sets of wooden dolls that one is apt to find in a Russian toy store, for as Hoeckner puts it, Schumann generates "a series of interlocking *Novelletten* within a *Novellette*, setting up the 'Voice from afar' in different tonal and expressive contexts."[39] Indeed, the first reference to Clara's "Notturno" functions as an episode within the marchlike "Trio II" in D major that an unsuspecting listener would probably identify as the C section of a rondo pattern: A–B–A–C, and so forth. In other words, the *Stimme aus der Ferne* is not just an interpolation but an interpolation *within* an interpolation and thus a musical analogue of the unfolding "fan of memory," which, to repeat Benjamin's description, "progresses from small to smallest details, from the smallest to the infinitesimal, while that which it encounters in these microcosms grows ever mightier."[40] Schumann's *Novellette* offers more than an intimation of this endless process, for its Trio II is not followed by a reprise of the opening F♯-minor A section but instead gives way to a lengthy *Fortsetzung und Schluss* (continuation and conclusion)—for all intents and purposes a mammoth interpolation tacked onto the immediately preceding music. Like the initial phases of the *Novellette*, the *Fortsetzung und Schluss* displays an episodic, rondolike structure—aba cdxdc a—and at the midpoint of its central episode, the spot I have designated with the letter "x," comes none other than an apotheotic statement of the "Notturno" melody, and at the tonal level in which Clara originally conceived it, F major.

An interpolation-within-an-interpolation-within-an-interpolation, this pivotal statement recalls a phenomenon that Schuman related to Clara in a letter written while he was working on the *Novelletten* early in 1838: "Sometimes it feels as if a great many alleys were running pell-mell through my heart and as if my thoughts and feelings were bustling about in there . . . just as people do, and they were asking one another, 'Where does this one lead?'—to Clara— 'and this one?'—to Clara—everything leads to you."[41] For Schumann, Clara occupied the "enigmatic center" of a labyrinth that, as Benjamin observed, arises from the attempt to recall a past life in memory; as the fan of memory unfolds, it greets us with "passageways that always, in the most diverse periods of life, guide us to the friend, the betrayer, [and] the beloved."[42] In the interlocking interpolations of the eighth *Novellette*, no less than in the episodic and layered interpolations of the Fantasie and the *Davidsbündlertänze*, Schumann gave musical shape to a universal experience.

III

It should now be clear that the imagistic quality of Schumann's music goes hand in hand with its implication in an exchange of creative ideas with Clara. After the couple were finally wed in September 1840, this exchange underwent a noticeable shift. Previously centered on the various types of Romantic keyboard music—the fantasy, sonata, and character piece—it subsequently manifested itself in the genres of song and chamber music. And whereas before their marriage it was generally Schumann who alluded to Clara's music, Clara made increasing reference to the works of her husband in the period after their wedding. One of her compositions more than any other offers an especially good example of the new terms under which the exchange evolved. A setting of Heinrich Heine's poem "Ihr Bildnis" for voice and piano, it marks a crucial point in an ongoing process of creative give-and-take that would culminate in one of Schumann's most evocative renderings of a beloved image in tone, the opening movement of his Piano Trio in F (Op. 80).

Presented to Schumann in December 1840 along with two other songs as a gift for the first Christmas the couple celebrated as man and wife, Clara's setting of *Ihr Bildnis* was not published until 1843, when it appeared in a somewhat revised form as the first song of her *Sechs Lieder* (Op. 13).[43] The model for Clara's song was one of the most resplendent lyrical gems of Schumann's "year of song": the second item, "Intermezzo," of his Eichendorff *Liederkreis* (Op. 39), a song whose opening words—"Dein Bildniss wunderselig" ("Your wondrous image")—clearly resonate with the title of Clara's Heine setting.[44] The key image in both texts is itself an image. In Heine's poem, it figures as the portrait of a distant beloved who seems to come to life, her eyes sparkling and her lips curling into a smile. (Clara, in her 1840 setting of the text, underlined the bitter irony in the lover's ultimate realization that his beloved is irrevocably lost by harmonizing the cadential tonic pitch of the last vocal phrase with a pungent diminished-seventh chord.) Similarly, the "wondrous image" in Eichendorff's poem is a portrait of the beloved that resides in the depths of the lover's heart and that joyfully gazes back at him (or her).

Clara affirms the relationship with Schumann's song at the very outset of hers with a melodic turn on scale steps 4, 6, and 5 that echoes a corresponding pattern (#1, 3, 2) in the opening vocal phrase of "Dein Bildniss wunderselig." (Cf. Exs. 5-6 and 5-7.) The points of contact between the settings, however, extend beyond this shared motivic detail. Like Schumann's song, Clara's features rich chromatic part writing and pulsing eighths in the accompaniment. In addition, the tonal curve of both pieces is fundamentally the same, proceeding from tonic to dominant and submediant regions (enriched by the mediant in Clara's song) and returning to the tonic by way of melodic emphasis on the flat-sixth and fifth scale degrees. Despite the differences in key (A major in Schumann's song versus E♭ major in Clara's), meter ($\frac{2}{4}$ versus $\frac{3}{4}$), and rhythmic profile (the eighths in Schumann's accompaniment are consistently displaced by one sixteenth note), the motivic, textural, and tonal parallels between the settings suggest that, at some level, Schumann's music has been embedded or enfolded into Clara's.

Of all the products of Schumann's year of song, none had as deeply personal a meaning for him and Clara as the Eichendorff *Liederkreis*. The cycle, he wrote to her on 22 May 1840, "is perhaps the most romantic thing I've written and it contains much of you."[45] Clara responded in kind, not only with "Ihr Bildnis" but also with another song that contained every bit as much of Schumann as her Heine setting of December 1840. Titled "Liebeszauber" and based on a text by Emanuel Geibel, it was offered to Schumann for his thirty-second birthday on 8 June 1842.[46] Here Clara evokes the luminous sound world of Schumann's "Frühlingsnacht," the final song of the Eichendorff *Liederkreis*, not so much in the vocal line as in the propulsive triplets and surging lines of her piano accompaniment. Surely these correspondences were motivated by textual factors, for just as Eichendorff's lyric is set in a magical garden in which a chorus of nightingales proclaims, "Sie ist Deine, sie ist Dein!" ("She is yours, she is yours!"), so Geibel calls up a verdant landscape filled with the "wondrously sweet cry" of the nightingale.[47]

Schumann had the last word in this interchange of love songs. Between June and November 1847 he composed two piano trios, in D minor (Op. 63) and F major (Op. 80), the second of which arguably marks the high point of his creative exchange with Clara. As the boisterous closing gestures of the first movement's exposition dissolve into dreamy figuration, we reach a crucial interstice in the form, a point at which time literally seems to stand still. Like the unfolding fan of Eros, the music draws a deep breath in preparation for its disclosure of "the features of the beloved object within." The moment of revelation then comes as the violin introduces the melody of "Dein Bildniss wunderselig" in C major atop rolling arpeggios in the piano and a pulsing pedal in the cello. (See Ex. 5-8.) Clearly reminiscent of the effect produced

Example 5-6: Clara Schumann, "Ihr Bildnis," mm. 1–2

Example 5-7: Schumann, "Dein Bildniss wunderselig" (Op. 39, no. 2), mm. 1–3

by the "Stimme aus der Ferne" from the eighth *Novellette,* this allusion to a key melodic strand from the Eichendorff *Liederkreis* is the first in a series of similar allusions that span the whole of the movement's development section. Indeed, Schumann conceives the entire section as a succession of interpolations-within-an-interpolation, the *Liederkreis* melody alternating with fugal developments of motives from the exposition. By turns emerging, disappearing, and surfacing again, the melody assumes the character of a dis-embodied image—an image that Schumann strives mightily to make real in the coda, where imitative parries on the melody's head motive, played at a gradually accelerating tempo (*nach und nach schneller*), bring the movement to its jubilant close. The coda thus completes a process whose origins lie in an inner layer of the movement's opening theme. The chromatic motion from C♯ to D (#5–6) in mm. 1–2 (and mm. 4–5) at once lends urgency to the theme and, at a broader level, foreshadows the neighbor-note figure in the first phrase of the *Liederkreis* melody (C♯–E–D = #1–3–2). Embedded deep within the texture at the beginning of the movement, then permitted to reveal its lyrical potential during the development, this figure rises defini-tively to the musical surface only in the coda.

Example 5-8: Schumann, Piano Trio in F (Op. 80), first movement, mm. 105–13

Like so many of the examples we have already considered, the interpolations in the first movement of the F-major Piano Trio are sites of remembrance, musical representations of memory. While the chief token of remembrance crystallizes in an allusion to a song that possessed deep personal
connotations for both Schumann and Clara—"Dein Bildniss wunderselig"—
other aspects of the movement serve to enhance its recollective character.
Chief among these are the fugal episodes that alternate with the allusions to
the song melody in the development section. Contrapuntal writing in general, and fugue in particular, had played an increasingly larger role in Schumann's creative exchange with Clara since early in 1845. Between February
and March of that year he completed four fugues for keyboard (*Vier Fugen*,
Op. 72), the first of several collections in which contrapuntal artifice assumes
a central position, and during the same time Clara composed half a dozen

fugues as well: three on themes from the second book of Bach's *Das wohltem-perirte Clavier* (nos. 7, 9, and 16) and a further set of three on themes provided by Schumann.[48] These forays into the art of counterpoint exercised a notice-able impact on the next major essays in free composition of both husband and wife: Schumann's Symphony No. 2 in C, sketched and elaborated be-tween December 1845 and October 1846, and Clara's Piano Trio in G minor (Op. 17), finished by September 1846. If the effects of Schumann's contra-puntal study of 1845 can be detected in his sophisticated handling of motivic combinations in the C-major Symphony, Clara's honing of her contrapuntal skills bore fruit in the imitative textures and skillfully crafted fugatos of the outer movements of her piano trio.

Although impossible to prove beyond a shadow of a doubt, it is at least a likely hypothesis that Schumann's piano trios of 1847 were conceived in re-sponse to Clara's contributions to the same genre. One series of events in particular may have spurred his creativity. On 15 January 1847, during a con-cert tour in Vienna, Robert and Clara gave a farewell matinee that included performances of Clara's G-minor Piano Trio and several of Schumann's Eichendorff settings. (The poet, who was present on the occasion together with other members of Vienna's cultural elite, reportedly told Clara that her husband "had given genuine life to his poems.")[49] Two weeks later in Prague, Clara accompanied a Herr Emminger in renditions of six of the songs from the Eichendorff *Liederkreis,* among them "Dein Bildniss wunderselig."[50] Is it too much to suggest, therefore, that Schumann's F-major Piano Trio repre-sents a figurative re-creation of these events in memory? If not, then the lyri-cal and fugal episodes that peer out of the folds of the first movement's tex-ture are not only images of Clara but also images of a creative exchange that traversed the whole of the Schumanns' married life up to that point and that embraced the genres of song, fugue, and instrumental chamber music.[51]

IV

Although it could not be said of Brahms, as Barthes said of Schumann, that the "intermezzo" was "consubstantial" with his entire output, the younger composer was quite adept at the art of making interpolations when it suited his expressive purposes. His earlier works in particular are rich in interpola-tions of both the episodic and layered variety, moments that impart to the music the texture of an unfolding fan. While Brahms's tendency in this direc-tion may have intensified after his entry in the Schumann circle in September 1853, it is already evident in some of the music composed before that crucial turning point in his life. Consider, for example, the C-minor Andante of the First Piano Sonata (Op. 1), written as an independent piece sometime in 1852, and cast as a set of variations on a plangent melody in bar form (AAB) under which Brahms underlaid the text of the pseudo folk poem "Verstohlen geht der Mond auf." During the course of the second variation, the theme more than doubles in length, in part through simple phrase extensions but also through the altered repetition of its B section. In varying the *Abgesang*, Brahms pauses twice to muse on a pair of especially striking harmonies—the Neapolitan and the major mediant—interpolating at both points three measures in $\frac{3}{16}$ meter in which the piano meditates quietly on a series of chords in its uppermost register. As George Bozarth has pointed out, these "celestial" chords can be interpreted as a response to the verses in the third strophe of "Verstohlen geht der Mond auf" where the poet asks the moon to peer into his sweetheart's window, thereby enticing her with its glow.[52] In short, the visionary episodes in the Andante of the First Piano Sonata constitute a kind of music of seduction; just as in Schumann's keyboard music, Eros and the art of interpolation go hand in hand.

By the early summer of 1854, Eros saw to it that Brahms's feelings for Clara Schumann had intensified to the point of full-blown passion. Like the smitten lover in Benjamin's miniessay on the fan, Brahms found his beloved's portrait in "nearly every book" that came into his hands. Of course, many of the books that he was perusing at the time were musical scores, and it was here that Clara appeared to him most vividly. To cite a passage from a letter of 27 August 1854 quoted earlier in this chapter: "I too gaze ever more deeply into a pair of wondrously beautiful eyes, which gaze at me now from out of the *Davidsbündlertänze* and the *Kreisleriana*."[53] Several weeks later, he had a similar experience while arranging Schumann's Piano Quintet for piano, four hands, a project undertaken at Clara's request: "I immersed myself ever deeper into [the Quintet] as if into a pair of dark blue eyes."[54] A passage from a letter to Clara of 8 December 1854 (also quoted earlier) describes the phenomenon even more explicitly: "After all, I do see you often, as good as in person; for instance, at the trill in the final passages of the Andante of the C-major Symphony [the third movement of Schumann's Symphony No. 2, Op. 61], and at the pedal points of great fugues, when you suddenly appear to me as St. Cecaelia!"[55] Adding to the psychological complexity of these visions is the fact that Schumann played a decisive role in them as well: in nearly every instance, Brahms perceived an image of Clara in one of her husband's works. His erotic longing for Clara was thus inextricably bound up with (and complicated by) a longing of an entirely different sort: a desire for union, on a spiritual plane, with *both* Schumanns. Brahms addressed this side of the equation in a letter to Clara of 24 October 1854: "I dream and think only about the glorious time when I can live with both of you, I am living out this whole period as though I were travelling a road to the most splendid land."[56]

Brahms gave artistic expression to both kinds of yearning—the sensual and the spiritual—in his Variations on a Theme by Robert Schumann (Op. 9). The original title, affixed to the manuscript copy that Brahms dated 15 June

1854 and sent to Clara at about the same time, reads as follows: *Kleine Varia-
tionen über ein Tema von Ihm. Ihr zugeeignet* (Little variations on a theme by
him. Dedicated to her). While the diminutive, "Kleine," gives a sense for the
intimate atmosphere out of which the piece arose, the fact that Brahms could
not bring himself to utter the names of either Schumann or Clara is a sign of
the reverence he had for both. The theme of Brahms's variations is the first of
two *Albumblätter* from Schumann's *Bunte Blätter* (Op. 99), a short piece in F♯
minor on which Clara herself had written a set of variations (Op. 20) almost
exactly a year before. The family tree of Brahms's work thus consists of two
principal branches, one pointing to Schumann, the other to Clara. Ultimately,
however, these branches were deftly intertwined, and nowhere is this process
more clearly in evidence than in the first of two variations (Nos. 10 and 11) that
Brahms added to the original set later in the summer of 1854, just in time for
presentation to Clara on her name day (12 August) and that he headed with
the suggestive inscription: "The roses and heliotropes exhaled that fragrance."

Like several of the other variations in the set, Brahms's variation 10 is a
contrapuntal tour de force, opening with the combination of the bass line of
the theme, displaced into the treble register, with its inversion, and proceeding with a free canon on the bass melody. During the final four bars of the
variation Brahms couples that melody, still poised in the treble, with an inner
layer in which the melody of Clara's *Romance variée* emerges from the folds of
the texture like a voice from afar. (See Ex. 5-9.) Brahms was especially proud
of this passage, exclaiming to Joachim in a letter of 12 September 1854: "I've
added another set of two to my Variations—through one of them *Clara
speaks!*"[57] Yet Schumann also puts in a word—by proxy, as it were—Clara's
theme having served as the basis for his Impromptus (Op. 5). And obviously,
as the author of this deft combination of thematic strands, Brahms, too, adds
his voice to the duo.[58] Hence, the layered interpolation in the tenth variation
makes for a triple image in which the young Brahms fulfilled his desire to
enter into spiritual communion with the older couple.

The voice from afar in variation 10 occupies only a few moments in a
larger interpolation of the episodic type that embraces variations 10 and 11 in

Example 5-9: Brahms, Variations on a Theme by Robert Schumann, Op. 9,
variation 10, mm. 29–33

their entirety. Grounded in part on genetic factors—the later addition of the two variations—this observation is also borne out by the aural experience of the whole variation set. The larger design of Brahms's Op. 9 is articulated by three structural pillars: the theme, the canonic variation 8 (where the treble melody appears in a form that closely approximates that of its first presentation), and the concluding variation 16 (where Brahms ensures a sense of finality by turning decisively to the major mode and restoring the bass melody to its "proper" register). Brahms then fills out this scheme by arranging the intervening movements so that they form pairs with their neighbors, thus establishing connections between adjacent movements through a variety of means, including elision, shared meters or tempos, related motivic or figurational patterns, and complementary moods.[59]

Although variations 10 and 11 are also paired—the latter is seamlessly linked with the former—they both depart from and amplify the overall scheme in a number of ways. The inner voice of variation 10, a distant relative of the treble theme, is coupled with another descending line so as to produce horn fifths; imbued with a quality of removal in space and time— owing in part to the affective connotations of the horn motive—this inner voice then provides the principal motivic materials of variation 11. Tonal factors also contribute to the sense of distance. In the set as originally conceived, nearly all the variations remain in either F♯ minor or major, the only exception being no. 9, in B minor, which Brahms modeled on the second *Albumblatt* from Schumann's *Bunte Blätter*.[60] Continuing the process of tonal digression already set in motion in variation 9, variation 10 is in D major, while variation 11 transforms that harmony into the dominant seventh of G. Then, invoking one of the Romantics' favored modulatory strategies, Brahms reinterprets the dominant-seventh-sonority as the German augmented-sixth chord in F♯, thereby preparing for the return to the tonic in variation 12.

With variation 11 (the first half is given as Ex. 5-10), Brahms arrives at the furthest point of removal from the theme: melodically (all that remains of the theme is a dim memory of the treble melody, while the original bass line is completely absent), tonally (a highly attenuated G major), and formally (a freely repeated AB pattern as opposed to the ABA design of the theme). The result is an evocative musical rendering of total absorption into a dreamworld—or, better yet, of total immersion "into a pair of wondrously beautiful eyes." Like no other variation in the set, the eleventh projects an almost magical aura whose primary musical agency is a curious blend of steady motion and stasis: for nine bars, the melodic line circles dreamily over a dominant pedal in the bass, which in turn gives way to a five-bar prolongation of subdominant harmonies that supports a suspension chain in the right hand. Brahms aims to hold fast, to freeze in time, in short, to emulate the effect of a photo portrait from the early days of photography, when the subject was often required to hold his or her pose before the camera for minutes at a

Example 5-10: Brahms, Variations on a Theme by Robert Schumann, Op. 9, variation II, mm. 1–13

time. This procedure, in Benjamin's words, "caused the subject to focus his [or her] life in the moment rather than hurrying on past it; during the considerable period of the exposure, the subject . . . grew into the picture, in the sharpest contrast with appearances in a snapshot."[61] Benjamin's description seems tailor-made for a photograph of Clara taken in 1853, just around the time of her meeting with Brahms. Deeply sunk in thought, her head tilted to the side and resting on her hand, her large eyes projecting a just barely suppressed sadness, Clara appears to have completely "grown into the picture."[62] (See Fig. 5-1.) The same turn of phrase offers a potent metaphor for the eleventh variation of Brahms's Op. 9, a tiny slice of musical time to which Brahms imparts the depth of an auratic photo portrait.

It may be more than pure happenstance that Brahms's—and Schumann's—practice of the art of interpolation coincides almost precisely with the rise of portrait photography in the 1840s and 1850s. Both phenomena, after all, are manifestations of one and the same impulse: a desire to arrest the temporal flow and thus to preserve a cherished image for eternity. Although Schumann and his circle were literally surrounded by pictorial representations of one

Figure 5-1: Clara Schuman (calotype, ca. 1853.). Reprinted by permission of Robert-Schumann-Haus, Zwickau.

another—formal oil paintings, miniature oil portraits mounted on ivory, lithographs, pencil sketches, silhouettes, engravings, watercolor and silverpoint drawings—chances are that they, like the rest of the European bourgeoisie, were most captivated by the magical blend of realism and aura that characterized the earliest photo portraits. "Never before has a picture seemed so alive to me," Brahms wrote to Clara on 24 January 1855 about a photo of her that he had recently found and immediately appropriated. "When I gaze at it for a while, you positively step out of it, I believe I could give you my hand."[63]

It is against this background that we might consider Brahms's claim that the Adagio of his First Piano Concerto, composed between December 1856 and January 1857, originated as a "gentle portrait" of Clara. Like the Variations, Op. 9, the Adagio is also a double—or even a triple—portrait, evoking as it does not only the image of Clara but those of Schumann and Brahms as well. It is a well-known fact that in his autograph of the movement Brahms underlaid the text "Benedictus qui venit in nomine Domini" to the opening melody in the violins and violas, a gesture that has given rise to a fair amount of speculation as to the programmatic content of the Adagio. Some have interpreted the "Benedictus" text (and the music associated with it) as a reference to Clara, while others, noting that Brahms sometimes addressed Schumann as "Mynheer Domine" in his correspondence, view it as a reference to Brahms himself.[64] Both interpretations are problematic. Clara may have been "Bendedicta" but surely not "Benedictus." Furthermore, it seems improbable that the self-effacing Brahms would have pronounced himself "Benedictus," that is, "the blessed one who comes in the name of the Lord" (especially in print: as late as the 1870s, he considered leaving the text in the published score). Why not simply take the text for what it is—a phrase from the Sanctus of the Mass or Requiem Mass—and attend to the hymnlike, devotional character and the darkly hued timbre (featuring muted violins, pedal tones, and bassoons in descending thirds) of the opening passage for orchestra? It was no doubt these qualities that led Tovey to state outright: "The slow movement [of the D-minor Piano Concerto] is a Requiem for Schumann."[65] Tovey, however, was only partially correct, for while it makes good sense to conclude, on the basis of both the textual and musical evidence, that the Adagio was a kind of Requiem for Schumann, who had died just months before the movement was written in July 1856, it was also conceived, in Brahms's words, as a "gentle portrait" of Clara. These "programs" do not contradict each other; on the contrary, Brahms arguably intended to synthesize them.

Here it may be helpful to reflect on the design of the movement as a whole. Brahms shaped the Adagio as a greatly expanded ABA form, the main elements of which consist of the opening and closing elegies for orchestra, in D major, and a central elegy for both soloist and orchestra on a contrasting idea that is alternately presented in F♯ minor and B minor. In fleshing out this basic plan, Brahms introduces reflective commentaries, transitional passages, and, just before the orchestral coda, a cadenza for piano alone. While the underlying structure is articulated by the orchestra or by the combined efforts of orchestra and piano, the interpolations in that structure are allotted, by and large, to the solo piano. (Two of the transitions are in fact conceived as interlocking "interpolations-within-an-interpolation." Both passages—mm. 27–36 and mm. 85–94—consist of alternating two-bar phrases in which the piano responds to fragments of the orchestral hymn with dreamy interludes that one might theoretically omit without damaging the musical syntax.) At the risk of interpreting the movement's overall design in an overly schematic manner, I will suggest that the elegiac passages for orchestra, or for orchestra and piano together, comprise Brahms's Requiem music for Schumann, while the "gentle portrait" emerges in the soloist's interpolated commentaries on the orchestra's music.

Example 5-11a: Brahms, Piano Concerto No. 1 in D minor, Adagio, mm. 1–5

In the first of these commentaries (mm. 14–18), the piano ruminates on the initial phrase of the opening orchestral passage (mm. 1–5). (See Exs. 5-11a and 5-11b.) To my ears, the soloist's rendering of the phrase sounds like an expansion of the orchestral model, though in actuality both phrases are precisely the same length: five measures. How does Brahms create this effect? On the one hand, the piano solo *does* enlarge the beginning and end of the orchestra's phrase, by means of both canonic imitation and the melodic exten-

Example 5-11b: Brahms, Piano Concerto No. 1 in D minor, Adagio, mm. 14–18

sion of the initial bassoon duo in descending thirds. On the other hand, and by way of compensation, the middle portion of the orchestra's first phrase (from just after the downbeat of m. 2 through m. 3) is without an equivalent in the pianist's commentary. In other words, the commentary embodies the interplay of "intensity" and "extensiveness"—or "compressed fullness"— that Benjamin attributed to the image worlds that emanate from the interstices of the unfolding fan. At the same time, the piano solo is also distinguished by its revelatory power. A musical counterpart of the "optical unconscious" revealed in the photographic image, it makes manifest that which was latent in the initial orchestral elegy. And it is in this sense that the soloist's music provides the first of several "gentle portraits" of a cherished being.

By the time that Brahms drafted the Adagio of his First Piano Concerto, that being was no longer the object of his erotic longing. For reasons that we may never know, his passion for Clara cooled considerably not long after Schumann's death in the summer of 1856.[66] George Bozarth has suggested that Brahms perhaps learned a lesson from the ill-fated portrait painter Leonard Ettlinger in E. T. A. Hoffmann's *Kater Murr*, a novel that exercised a profound influence on the young composer's developing sensibilities. Not satisfied merely to paint his unattainable beloved (the princess at the court where he was employed) but intent on possessing her as well, Ettlinger was transformed from a "mild, good man" into a raving psychopath.[67] Brahms escaped this fate. By placing Clara in a group portrait with Schumann in the Adagio of the D-minor Piano Concerto, he accomplished two goals, at once sublimating his physical desire through artistic means and crafting an image of his beloved that would endure. Thus in at least one important respect, the

Adagio surpasses the photographic portrait as a repository for the preservation of cherished memories. As Barthes reminds us, the photo is perishable; subject to the forces of material decay, it gradually fades before vanishing entirely.[68] Brahms circumvented this dilemma by choosing a medium of expression in which images unfold and endure in time. Like Robert Schumann, he proved to be a craftsman of durable images.

Part III.

A NOBLE MODEL

CHAPTER 6.

TRANSCENDENTAL CHESS GAMES

*W*HAT BRAHMS OWED to Schumann cannot be overestimated and has not, up to now, been properly appreciated." The "now" of this quotation, from Edward Lippman's article on Schumann in the venerable encyclopedia *Die Musik in Geschichte und Gegenwart*, (henceforth *MGG*) fell during the early 1960s.[1] Lippman's assertion comes under the category of wishful thinking, for at the time he made it, received opinion maintained that as the "third B," Brahms traced his musical heritage in a more-or-less straight line though Beethoven all the way back to Bach. This critical commonplace was long in the making. Firmly entrenched a full century before the publication of the *MGG*, it informed Hanslick's review of the 1867 Vienna performance of the first three movements of Brahms's *Ein deutsches Requiem* (Op. 45), which the critic viewed as an outgrowth of "the style of Beethoven's late works" and of the "harmonic and contrapuntal art" of J. S. Bach.[2] If Hanslick's claim was motivated by a desire to promote his own musical-political crusade on behalf of the supremacy of "absolute" music, the still-prevalent force of the "three Bs" as a viable music-historical construction stems from a common-enough tactic: the tendency of historians, even in our hypercritical age, to practice high-powered games of "connect-the-dots," the connective lines linking one cultural icon to the next. Schumann, however, has yet to achieve iconic status.

I

Granted, shortly before Hanslick set about installing Brahms in the pantheon next to Bach and Beethoven, another writer was in the process of giving a somewhat different spin to Brahms's artistic patrimony. In a lengthy five-part essay published in 1862 in the *Neue Zeitschrift für Musik,* the polyglot jurist and avid music lover Adolf Schubring singled out Brahms as the most gifted representative of the "Schumann school," a loosely knit group comprised of both genuine pupils and those who perpetuated the legacy of the older composer, including Joachim, Theodor Kirchner, and Woldemar Bargiel.[3] A self-avowed *Schumannianer,* Schubring located the essence of the "school" in its attempt to steer a middle course in a highly politicized musical scene that pitted "conservatives" on one side against "progressives" on the other. As he explained in an earlier article in his *Schumanniana* series, the former group "consists of those who cultivate the (old) forms," whereas the latter "emphasize (new) content." Poised between these two factions, the Schumann school strives instead "to fill the old forms with new content," without thereby precluding that "the content expands, breaks through, or transcends these forms."[4] (Later in this chapter, we will see that the act of "breaking through" is a key aspect of the forms, and not just the content, associated with the Schumann school.)

While Schubring's thesis represents a milestone in the critical literature on the Schumann–Brahms relationship, its juxtaposition and synthesis of form and content will probably strike modern critics as too schematic, too pat. Furthermore, although Schubring's analyses include many insightful observations on the role of motivic elaboration (*thematische Arbeit*) in Brahms's earlier works (Opp. 1–18), they are rather low on commentary regarding the relationships between Brahms's musical language and that of his mentor. The same could be said of much criticism from the later nineteenth century, which routinely cast Schumann in the role of intermediary between Beethoven and Brahms.[5] Over the years, this sketch has been amplified with a number of supporting details. During the past two decades in particular, scholars such as Constantin Floros and Siegfried Kross have furthered our understanding of the affinities between Schumann's and Brahms's keyboard music, while both Reinhold Brinkmann and David Brodbeck have recently authored suggestive commentaries on Brahms's reception of Schumann's orchestral music in his own symphonic output. Moreover, thanks to Floros's work, we are now in a position to appreciate more fully the degree to which both composers shared the same aesthetic posture.[6] At the same time, some areas of inquiry, which include many of the hermeneutic readings based on Schumann's and Brahms's putative cryptographic methods, have proven to be cul-de-sacs. Other topics, such as the meaning of Schumann's controversial late music for Brahms, have hardly been broached. Likewise, apart from scattered references in the secondary literature, rather little of substance has been devoted to questions of compositional technique. Clearly, much work remains to be done.

What did Brahms have to offer on the subject? Predictably enough, given his reputation as one of the most tight-lipped figures in an age whose artists delighted in wearing their hearts on their sleeves, the yield is slight. Exhibit A comes from a letter of January 1873 to an acquaintance named Friedrich Heimsoeth: "The memory of Schumann is sacred to me. That noble, pure artist serves me constantly as a model."[7] These lines are not entirely characteristic of an individual who was aptly compared by one of his associates to a hedgehog—ever "poised for attack"[8]—and who more often than not hid his innermost feelings, even from his intimate friends, under layers of irony and sarcasm. The utter absence of these defensive mechanisms in his remarks to Heimsoeth indicates to me that the hedgehog was baring his soft underbelly. In other words, Brahms must have meant what he wrote about Schumann in January 1873—without qualification. The hedgehog assumes his more typical guise in Exhibit B, a remark transmitted by Kalbeck. When asked late in his life what he learned from Schumann, Brahms is supposed to have responded: "Nothing, apart from how to play chess" [*nichts als Schachspielen*].[9] Though relayed at second hand by a not always reliable source, the riposte rings true. With this prickly rejoinder, Brahms (or at least the Brahms we have come to know through legend and anecdote) was obviously attempting to muzzle his curious inquisitor. He was not, however, denying Schumann's importance in shaping his attitude to the art of composition. Quite the contrary. For even if Brahms learned only the rules of chess from Schumann, he learned quite a bit. Chess, after all, demands a considerable amount of foresight, advance planning, and cool calculation on the part of the player. It is, in short, a metaphor for the strategic thinking that musical composition requires in equal measure.

Thus Exhibits A and B do not so much contradict as complement each other. While the letter of 1873 touches on matters of aesthetic stance and, by implication, of musical expression, the quip reported by Kalbeck points toward the nitty-gritty of compositional technique. Together they suggest that what Brahms learned from Schumann arose from the interplay of strategy and affect, of technique and expression. Bearing this in mind, we will begin in a "formalist" vein, focusing on more purely musical processes, and only then continue with some thoughts on the affective connotations of those processes.

II

"Very deep is the well of the past. Should we not call it bottomless?" These opening lines of Thomas Mann's massive tetralogy on the biblical story of Joseph and his brothers[10] have often been compared to the sounding of the low E♭ that sets Wagner's *Ring* cycle in motion. The image of the bottomless well is also an appropriate metaphor for the potentially endless pursuit of sources for Brahms's musical language. Take, for instance, his fondness for constructing melodies out of chains of descending thirds. Among the most frequently cited examples of this technique is the first theme of the opening movement of the Fourth Symphony, where the chain alternates descending thirds with rising sixths in regular succession. It was probably this feature that one sharp-tongued critic (who also happened to be a great composer in his own right) had in mind when he claimed that Brahms, in his Fourth Symphony, raised the "art of composing without ideas" to new heights.[11] One might just as well extend Hugo Wolf's observation to the first theme of Mozart's Symphony No. 40 (K. 550) or to several passages in Beethoven's "Hammerklavier" Sonata (Op. 106), and any number of critics have done just that, though without assuming the negative tone of Wolf's critique.[12] Less frequently noted is Schumann's talent for this brand of "composing without ideas" as manifested in the first-movement development section of the Piano Trio in F and the concluding phases of the last movements of the *Ouverture, Scherzo und Finale* (Op. 52), the Piano Quartet in E flat, the Second Symphony, and the Piano Trio in D minor. In the last of these, Schumann heightens the mood of triumph at the close of the work by coupling two complete cycles of thirds in headlong descent in the upper line with a sequentially rising pattern in the bass. (See Ex. 6-1.) We have already had occasion to examine another of these examples: the fugato in the coda of the Piano Quartet, where Schumann pairs a sharply accented subject built largely from falling thirds and rising sixths with a countersubject whose figurational sixteenths also elaborate a descending chain of thirds.[13]

At the risk of taking a nosedive into a bottomless well, let me suggest a few ways in which Brahms's handling of third chains resonates with Schumann's. As is evident from the instances cited earlier, Schumann tended to reserve this strategy for the ends of movements. Unlike Mozart and Beethoven (or Bach, Handel, Haydn, and Mendelssohn, for that matter), who made use of the technique as a means of presentation or development, Schumann employed it to rally his forces, one last time, at grand moments of peroration. Brahms did likewise, and in precisely the same genres as Schumann: symphonic music (e.g., the coda of the finale of the First Symphony) and chamber music (the coda of the first movement of the Piano Trio in C minor). There is, in addition, a rough-hewn quality about many of Schumann's third-based melodic constructions, stemming from his unwillingness to smooth over their rough edges by filling in the thirds with passing tones. A comparably severe attitude often characterizes Brahms's approach, resulting in the brittle character of several of the third-derived configurations in the First Symphony (first movement, development section), the Piano Trio in C minor (first movement, coda), and the Fourth Symphony (finale, mm. 233–44).

Example 6-1: Schumann, Piano Trio in D minor, Op. 63, finale (Mit Feuer), coda

(continued)

Example 6-1. *continued*

Complementing Brahms's predilection for melodies spun out of thirds, though at a higher structural level, is his pairing of melodic ideas in third-related tonalities. When this principle regulates an entire paragraph (or series of paragraphs) of a larger form, it hearkens to Schubert's "three-key" plans, and to be sure, as James Webster has shown in a now-classic two-part study, Schubert's unique slant on the tonal disposition of the sonata form was a decisive factor in Brahms's accession to his "first maturity."[14] As we have observed earlier in this study, it was equally as decisive a factor in Schumann's approach to the tonal narrative of his sonata forms.[15] In at least some instances, it seems as though Brahms's evocation of the Schubertian strategy was filtered through his experience of Schumann's adaptation of the same technique. In the second group of the finale of his Piano Concerto No. 2 in B flat, Brahms alternates a wistful, appoggiatura-laden idea in A minor with a pair of ideas—one reflective, the other playful—in F major. While this yields an overall three-key plan moving from tonic to dominant via the latter's mediant, the specific realization of the plan points less directly to Schubert than to Schumann, who had already tried something similar in the finale of one of his orchestral works in B♭, the First Symphony. Schumann's second group opens with an idea in the clarinets and bassoons that looks forward, in both character and rhythmic gesture, to the wistful melody from Brahms's concerto. Moreover, it traces the same harmonic path—from A minor to F major—that Brahms would project over a larger span in his concerto movement.

Few strategies are as quintessentially Brahmsian as the binding together of successive phrases by recycling the tail of the first as the head motive of the second—a procedure that Heinrich Schenker called *Knüpftechnik*, or "linkage technique."[16] As it would be tedious to rattle off the many cases from Brahms's output where one phrase dovetails with the next in this way, one will have to serve as a paradigmatic example. To set the stage for the entrance of the expressive second theme in the first movement of his String Quintet in G

(Op. 111), Brahms foreshadows its opening gesture (a falling second and rising third that an overly zealous allusion hunter might well interpret as a reference to the *Todesverkündigung* motive from Wagner's *Die Walküre*) in the immediately preceding measure, the final bar of a transitional phrase in the first violin. Of the many precedents for this strategy in the classical canon, one of the most deftly conceived occurs in the Minuetto of Mozart's String Quintet in G minor (K. 516), where the languid closing cadence of the minuet proper, transformed into major, provides the opening gesture of the Trio. The device was also favored by Schumann, who was apt to use it, like Brahms after him, as a means of effacing the boundary between transitional and thematic passages. In the first movement of his Piano Trio in D minor, for example, the yearning eighth-note figure E–F at the close of the transition is immediately absorbed into the sweeping motive that initiates the second theme.[17]

Of course, not all of Brahms's efforts to ensure motivic continuity occur at such close quarters as in the example cited from the String Quintet in G. His deisre to forge thematic links over far broader spans is evident, among other areas, in his handling of the relationship between slow introductions and the music that ensues. The lengthy introductions to both the opening and closing movements of the First Symphony in fact serve a dual purpose, acting not merely as neutral (though appropriately grand) preparations for the quicker music to come but also as the primary sources for the subsequent thematic argument.[18] This tendency is particularly marked in the finale, whose "Allegro non troppos, ma con brio" derives its entire thematic substance from what Tovey called the "magnificent cloudy procession" of ideas in the preceding introduction ("Adagio" and "Più Andante").[19] While Brahms may have taken his cue from any number of works in the Classical and early Romantic repertory—including Haydn's Symphony No. 103, Schubert's "Great" C-major Symphony, and Mendelssohn's "Scottish" Symphony (Op. 56)—or even from the technique of thematic transformation employed to such brilliant effect by Liszt, he would have found models closer to home in the works of Schumann. All of Schumann's symphonies but one (the "Rhenish") open with slow introductions, as does the *Ouverture, Scherzo und Finale,* and in every case the ostensibly prefatory music functions as a motivic repository for what follows.[20] Two of these works occupy especially important positions in the lineage of Brahms's First Symphony: the D-minor Symphony (No. 4), which, with its slow introductions to both the opening and closing movement, may well have been the model for the double frame of Brahms's work; and the Second Symphony, from whose introductory "Sostenuto assai" Schumann extrapolated all of the major ideas of the ensuing "Allegro ma non troppo."

It will not have escaped notice that each one of the strategies considered thus far represents an attempt to establish some sort of connection—either between successive points in a phrase, or between adjacent phrases, or between widely separated moments in time. These strategies, in short, are products of a musical consciousness that desires to join ideas with ideas. And indeed, nowhere did Schoenberg proclaim his apostleship to Brahms more categorically than when he used just those words: "I wish to join ideas with ideas."[21] No doubt the art of joining (apparently unrelated) ideas—or the practice of "musical logic," to cite Schoenberg's rather more highfalutin locution for the same thing—was a fundamental property of a long tradition of which Brahms was but a single representative. Yet in Brahms's hands the forging of connections between disparate entities became something of an obsession, amounting to an absolute distaste for the introduction of a thought that was without future consequences or that could not be traced back in some way to a thought that preceded it.

What I would like to suggest at this point is that Brahms inherited the obsessive streak in his desire to join ideas with ideas primarily from Schumann. On the one hand, Schumann reinforced a broad range of techniques that Brahms would have found amply represented in the Classical canon. But on the other hand, and more significantly, several of the connective strategies that we think of as Brahms's own speak to his absorption of tactics that, as we shall see, are plainly stamped with Schumann's imprimatur. In the following section, I shall focus on two of these tactics, the first pertaining to form; the second, a function of both texture and structure.

III

In several recently published articles, the theorist Peter Smith offers both a detailed description and a compelling rationale for one of Brahms's more notable deviations from the conventional rhetoric of sonata form: his tendency to blur the line between development and recapitulation, thereby subverting what in the Classical incarnation of the form had generally been a moment of high drama.[22] A manifestation of the same impulse that led him to bind transitional and thematic passages through motivic linkage, this strategy creates a genuine overlap between formal divisions insofar as Brahms prolongs the harmonic instability characteristic of the development section well past the point of thematic return that signals the onset of the recapitulation. Moreover, the return is undercut further by various processes of motivic fragmentation—or "liquidation," to use Schoenberg's term—the most significant of which invokes the opening gesture of the main theme in augmented note values.

As with so many of Brahms's formal ploys, a clinical definition only imperfectly conveys the subtlety of the musical method. To address this inadequacy, Examples 6-2a and 6-2b present the opening theme of the first movement of the C-minor String Quartet (Op. 51, no. 1) and the statement of that

Example 6-2a: Brahms, String Quartet in C minor, Op. 51 no. 1, first movement, mm. 1–6

theme at the point where development and recapitulation merge. In comparing the two, we can easily identify all the features of Brahms's overlapping technique: the displacement of C-minor, tonic harmony with a prolonged $A\flat^6$ (VI^6) chord, the liquidation of the head motive (mm. 133ff.), the appearance of the motive in augmentation (mm. 134–35), and, finally, the resumption of the theme at its initial, brisk pace (mm. 137ff.). The effect during the moments of overlap is quite extraordinary, at once marking a low point in the subject's energy and a gradual gathering of steam for the plunge into a reprise whose commencement we only perceive in retrospect.[23]

In explicating this and other instances where rhythmic augmentation figures in Brahms's dovetailing of development and recapitulation (the first movements of the Cello Sonata in F, Op. 99, and the Fourth Symphony), Smith isolates two underlying rationales for Brahms's employment of the strategy. First, it afforded him the opportunity to explore aspects of the main subject that had only been touched on earlier (e.g., the $A\flat$ harmony in the quartet theme).[24] Second, and perhaps more crucial, by withholding the mo-

Example 6-2b: Brahms, String Quartet in C minor, Op. 51 no. 1, first movement, mm. 133–39

ment of definitive return from its customary spot (the beginning of the recapitulation) and reserving it for a later point in the form (often the coda), Brahms achieved what Smith calls a "continuous linear evolution" from one end of a movement to the other.[25] In this instance then, Brahms's desire to join ideas with ideas resulted in the transformation of a sectional design into one nearly uninterrupted discourse.

While there is some precedent for this strategy in Beethoven's sonata forms—Smith cites the first movement of the Piano Sonata in E minor (Op. 90)[26]—Brahms would have found a wealth of models in the works of Schumann. In at least a half-dozen cases, Schumann undercuts the articulative force of the thematic return at the moment of reprise by coupling it with dominant or tonic-six-four harmony, thus prefiguring the means whereby Brahms would ensure continuity on the large scale in the finale of his Violin

Sonata in D minor.[27] The recapitulatory overlaps in the first movement of Schumann's Piano Trio in F and Cello Concerto (Op. 129) are characterized by more pungent harmonies, the diminished-seventh and German augmented-sixth chord, respectively. Schumann's merger of development and reprise in three other instances—the opening movements of the Violin Sonata in A minor (Op. 105), the String Quartet in A (Op. 41, no. 3), and the finale of the F-major Piano Trio—is especially noteworthy for the line of argument we are pursuing. Indeed, it may not be fanciful to assume that the first of these examples provided a kind of template for Brahms's handling of the interface between development and recapitulation in the opening movement of his C-minor String Quartet. All of the markers that we observed in that work are firmly in place in Schumann's sonata movement (see Ex. 6-3): "liquidation" (effected by the dreamy repetition, in mm. 108–9, of a motivic fragment from the first theme group), tonal instability at the point of return (the appearance of the brooding main theme, in m. 110, over the tonic chord in first inversion), and rhythmic augmentation (at both of the head motive's attempts to reassert itself, mm. 110–13 and 113–15, the second attempt emphasized by the indication *etwas zurückhaltend*)—all of which conspire to ensure that we realize the formal sleight of hand only after the fact, with the resumption of the original tempo, at the *second* measure of the main theme, in m. 116. In light of our earlier discussion of Brahms's C-minor Quartet, the rationale for Schumann's blending of developmental and recapitulatory qualities will also strike a familiar note: while the presentation of the head motive in augmented note values allows Schumann to luxuriate in harmonies only lightly touched upon when the main theme was first heard (one of these harmonies, the F-major sixth chord of m. 111, has an exact parallel in the A♭-major sixth chord of Brahms's movement; both function as VI⁶), his purpose in withholding definitive tonal-thematic articulation at this juncture in the design is to reserve it for the last four bars of the movement, where the head motive is absorbed into an emphatic cadence in the tonic, A minor, the only such cadence in the piece. In sum, Schumann aims for precisely the sort of "continuous linear evolution" that has been identified as a hallmark of Brahms's sonata forms, a claim further borne out by the recapitulatory overlaps, cited earlier, in Schumann's String Quartet in A (first movement) and Piano Trio in F (finale).[28]

If the opening movement of Schumann's A-minor Violin Sonata points forward to Brahms, it also points back to another of Schumann's late works in A minor, the first movement of the Cello Concerto. Embedded in the languid and finely spun main theme is the same affective pitch configuration—C–F–E–E–D♯—that Schumann would later use to initiate the sonata. Furthermore, as we have seen, the concerto movement is one of the family of pieces where Schumann attenuates the passage from development to recapitulation, in this instance by substituting an augmented-sixth chord (actually two of them in succession) for the obligatory tonic. (See Ex. 6-4.) Another aspect

Example 6-3: Schumann Violin Sonata in A minor, first movement, mm. 108–17

Example 6-4: Schumann, Cello Concerto, first movement, mm. 176–78

of this overlap is worthy of attention. Sounding simultaneously with the soloist's restatement of the main theme is a reference to the four-bar "curtain" of woodwind chords that had *preceded* the presentation of the theme at the beginning of the movement. While this telescoping effect hardly represents a major display of contrapuntal skill (the "curtain" and the head motive of the theme are essentially one and the same), it nudges us in the direction of a textural strategy shared by Schumann and Brahms in which contrapuntal thinking—the art of joining ideas with ideas in vertical combination—assumes a position of central importance.

After Bach, Brahms was one of the few composers for whom counterpoint was a native tongue and not a second language. Even when his music takes a lighthearted turn—as in the String Quartet in B flat (Op. 67)—Brahms could not resist the temptation to enrich its texture as only a born contrapuntist would. Embedded in the serpentine figuration with which the first violin accompanies the second violin's statement of a transitional theme in the first movement of the Quartet in B flat (mm. 37–38) is the melodic pattern of that theme in rhythmic diminution. Similarly, in the development section of the finale of the Piano Quartet in C minor (Op. 60)—an altogether more serious affair than the string quartet—Brahms combines both the main theme and its figurational accompaniment with doubly diminished and augmented variants of their original forms. As David Brodbeck points out in a recent study, Brahms's chief model for this sort of decorative counterpoint was another nineteenth-century composer who tended to think in contrapuntal terms: Felix Mendelssohn, whose string quartets were very much on Brahms's mind while he was drafting his String Quartet in B flat, and whose Piano Trio in C minor (Op. 66) Brahms seems to have plundered for motivic ideas in the finale of his Piano Quartet in C minor.[29]

The manifestation of Brahms's contrapuntal thinking that interests me most, however, is not merely decorative but structural, and here, as I will argue, Schumann was almost certainly his chief model.[30] The generative ideas for many of Brahms's sonata-style works are not "themes" in the conventional sense but rather thematic combinations, aggregate constructions that resulted from the vertical merger of distinct melodic strands. The F-minor third movement, Allegretto, of the String Quartet in C minor opens with just such a construction: the confluence of a sighing melody in the first violin (marked **a** in Ex. 6-5a) and an insistent counterline in the viola (**b**). Upon arriving at the minor dominant in this tightly compressed sonata-form movement,[31] Brahms introduces an apparently new combination (see Ex. 6-5b), coupling a sinuous motive in the first violin (**c**) with a descending chromatic line in the viola (**d**). Four bars later, this "new" combination is turned on its head, motive **d**, now in the first violin, sounding above motive **c** in the second. At the midpoint of the development section (mm. 38ff.; see Ex. 6-5c) motive **b** from the original combination undergoes a remarkable metamor-

Example 6-5a: Brahms, String Quartet in C minor, Op. 51, no. 1, Allegretto, mm. 1–2

Example 6-5b: Brahms, String Quartet in C minor, Op. 51, no. 1, Allegretto, mm. 15–17

Example 6-5c: Brahms, String Quartet in C minor, Op. 51, no. 1, Allegretto, mm. 37–40

Example 6-5d: Brahms, String Quartet in C minor, Op. 51, no. 1, Allegretto, mm. 55–57

phosis. Having subjected the initial four-note model (F–D–E♭–F) to retrograde inversion and animated its earlier rhythmic pattern with triplets, Brahms allows the resultant melodic line to unfold in leisurely canons supported by pizzicati from the bystanders in the ensemble. This transformation in turn exercises a direct impact on the varied restatement of the opening melodic complex (a/b) at the point of reprise (mm. 55ff.; see Ex. 6-5d), for motive b now adopts the triplet rhythm it had acquired during the development. Finally, after recapitulating the second complex (c/d) in the tonic (mm. 66ff.), Brahms twice alludes to the first complex in the coda (mm. 76ff.), both in its initial registral disposition (a/b) and with the relative placement of the motivic strands reversed (b/a).

What can be gleaned from this clinical description? Viewed through the lens of Schoenberg's theoretical principles, Brahms's movement enacts a synthesis of two diametrically opposed methods of elaborating the fundamental "idea" of a musical work: the procedures associated with contrapuntal composition, on the one hand, and music of the "homophonic-melodic" style, on the other. Schoenberg used the term *Abwicklung* (variously translated as "unravelling," "unfolding," or "envelopment") to designate the first of these methods, claiming that in contrapuntal genres such as canon or fugue "a basic configuration or combination taken asunder and reassembled in a different order contains everything which will later produce a different sound than that of the original formulation." In contrast, music of the "homophonic-melodic" type was governed by the principle of *Entwicklung* (development) or *entwickelnde Variation* (developing variation), whereby "variation of the features of a basic [melodic] unit produces all the thematic formulations which provide for fluency, contrasts, variety, logic and unity . . . and character, mood, expression, and every needed differentiation."[32]

Both principles obviously come into play in the Allegretto of Brahms's C-minor String Quartet. The notion of *Abwicklung* addresses the initial combinative idea (a/b) and the various guises it assumes through the application of contrapuntal techniques that include canon (in the development section) and *Stimmtausch*, or voice exchange (in the coda). At the same time, the principle of *Entwicklung*, or developing variation, is at work in Brahms's evolution of the movement's subsidiary motivic combination (c/d) from elements of the basic form (the drooping chromatic line of motive d is a clear derivative of the sighs of motive a). Nor are these principles merely juxtaposed. On the contrary, it was Brahms's aim to fuse them as thoroughly as he could, an ideal that emerges not only at the local level, with the development of individual lines in the contrapuntal texture, but also in terms of the design as a whole: a "homophonic-melodic" form, the sonata-allegro, whose principal sections are articulated by contrapuntal combinations and whose narrative trajectory turns on the presentation, development, and restoration of a basic motivic complex.

Like all of Brahms's compositional strategies, this one has numerous precedents. Mozart had already negotiated a rapprochement between contrapuntal and homophonic procedures in the finales of his String Quartet in G (K. 387) and "Jupiter" Symphony (K. 551), both of which are sonata-form movements characterized by the alternation of passages in the "learned" style and the up-to-the-minute "galant" idiom.[33] This dochotomy in turn had consequences both for Beethoven (Andante scherzoso quasi Allegretto of the String Quartet in C minor, Op. 18, no. 4; finale of the String Quartet in C, Op. 59, no. 3; second movement of the First Symphony, Op. 21) and for Brahms as well (finale of the String Quintet in F, Op. 88). What distinguishes Brahms's achievement in the Allegretto of the C-minor String Quartet, however, is its more complete synthesis of the two styles—homophonic-melodic and contrapuntal—and in this endeavor his chief teacher was Schumann.

During the mid-1840s, Schumann experienced something of a stylistic epiphany, or, at the very least, his approach to the act of putting notes to paper underwent a decisive transformation. He described this shift in a passage entered into his diary later in the same decade: "Only from the year 1845 on, when I began to invent and work out everything in my head, did a completely new manner of composing [eine ganz andere Art zu componiren] begin to develop."[34] Schumann's more cerebral attitude toward the compositional process also entailed a fundamental rethinking of the nature of the musical idea, the first signs of which can be detected in his turn to the venerable contrapuntal genres of fugue (Vier Fugen, Op. 72; Sechs Fugen über den namen BACH, Op. 60) and canon (Studien für den Pedal-Flügel, Op. 56). Before long, these impulses went underground, so to speak. Far from abandoning the techniques he had honed by way of this detour into the art of contrapuntal composition, Schumann assimilated them to the parameters of the homophonic-melodic forms he would cultivate in the later 1840s. Having equated "modern fugues" with "artistic ruins" in a sketchbook entry that dates from this period, Schumann set about transforming "artistic ruins" into more imposing musical edifices.[35]

One of the first—and most illuminating—products of this process of sublimation is the first movement (Mit Energie und Leidenschaft) of the Piano Trio in D minor. The germinal idea of the movement (see Ex. 6-6a) is a motivic complex that occupies just over a single bar, the first, in which a cadential gesture in the violin (a) is combined with an unsettled turning figure in the bass register (b). In generating the second bar through the technique of voice exchange, Schumann creates a duality that will become more prominent as the movement proceeds: the ability of the basic combination to serve as both a vertical (a/b) and a horizontal (a+b) unit. The next major station in the form, the unfolding of the second group in F major, features another combination, this one involving a canonic presentation of a new, upwardly striving chromatic gesture (c). Then, in an effort to reveal the latent connec-

Example 6-6a: Schumann, Piano Trio in D minor, first movement (Mit Energie und Leidenschaft), mm. 1–2

tions between these contrasting ideas, Schumann combines the basic unit in its horizontal incarnation, **a+b,** with a variant of motive **c** (see Ex. 6-6b). The parting shot occurs within the first ending (which performers are therefore obliged to take), where Schumann's treatment of **a+b** in a canon at the distance of one measure naturally results in the reconstitution of the initial vertical combination. The sheer number of points of contact between the strategies employed here and those we have noted in Brahms's Allegretto—the grounding of both movements in a terse motivic complex, their exploration of both dimensions of musical space, their adaptation of contrapuntal textures to the unfolding narrative of a "homophonic-melodic" form—makes it difficult for me to believe that Schumann's movement did not serve, at some level, as a model for the synthesis enacted in the later work.

The joining of ideas with ideas in vertical combination is ideally suited to a medium in which every line in the polyphonic web is delivered by a single

Example 6-6b: Schumann, Piano Trio in D minor, first movement (Mit Energie und Leidenschaft), mm. 42–43

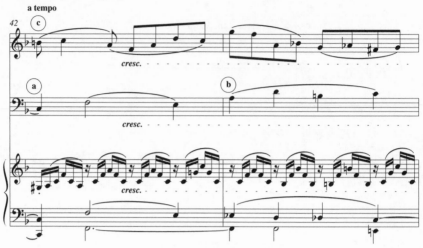

player, hence its prominence in Schumann's and Brahms's chamber music.[36] More surprising, at least at first blush, is the use of the same strategy in the symphonic works of Brahms in particular. The Allegro section of the opening movement of his First Symphony, to cite the most obvious example, is a tour de force of contrapuntal craft, each of the major points of articulation in its design set in relief by a basic two-voice combination (consisting of a sweeping gesture in the first violins coupled with a rising chromatic line and a flourish in the bass-register instruments) or one of its derivatives (generated by voice-exchange, melodic inversion, and/or the addition of new voices).[37] This movement, more than any other in his orchestral output, amply justifies Paul Bekker's often-quoted characterization of Brahms's symphonies as "monumental chamber music."[38]

Though less rigorously maintained than in the opening movement of the First Symphony, contrapuntal textures are much in evidence in the finale of the same work. Its slow introduction begins straightaway with a motivic combination that projects an aura of Baroque severity. (See Ex. 6-7a.) Comprised of a languid gesture in the violins' upper register (**a**) and a descending tetrachord in the bass instruments (**b**), this combinative unit is the first element in that "magnificent cloudy procession" whose chief ideas also include the celebrated Alphorn melody and a solemn chorale intoned by the trombone choir. (See Exs. 6-7b and 6-7d.) Among the tasks of the ensuing "Allegro no troppo, ma con brio," is the disclosure of the latent connections between and among these diverse elements and their variants, the most significant of which is the transformation of motive **a** into the C-major melody that, according to nearly every critic, alludes to the *Freudenthema* of Beethoven's

Example 6-7a: Brahms, Symphony No. 1, finale, mm. 1–3

Example 6-7b: Brahms, Symphony No. 1, finale, Alphorn melody, mm. 30–38

Example 6-7c: Brahms, Symphony No. 1, finale, mm. 47–51

Ninth Symphony in its ninth through eleventh measures. (See Ex. 6-7c.) One such demonstration of motivic kinship occurs at the climax of the developmental expansion within the reprise (mm. 277–89), as a dynamic elaboration of the head motive of **a** evolves, with inexorable logic, into a varied return of the Alphorn melody.[39]

An even more stunning revelation takes place within the first three bars of the coda (see Ex. 6-7e.) As the strings hammer out a neighbor-note figure culled from motive **a,** the winds respond with a gesture that performs no fewer than three functions. While its melodic pattern (A–G) complements the C–B–C figure in the strings to yield nearly the whole of motive **a**'s head motive ([G]–C–B–C–A–G), its harmonization (vii°⁷–I) points back to the climactic restatement of the Alphorn melody (in mm. 285ff.).[40] In addition, melody and harmony together prefigure the massive Amen cadences that cap off the subsequent return of the trombone chorale and bring the symphony to its triumphant conclusion. The contrapuntal and motivic processes unfolded in the coda are fraught with referential meaning. As Reinhold Brink-

Example 6-7d: Brahms, Symphony No. 1, finale, mm. 62–66

Example 6-7e: Brahms, Symphony No. 1, finale, mm. 391–93

mann has observed, the major-mode derivative of motive **a** is a musical embodiment of freedom and brotherhood, whereas the Alphorn melody and the chorale serve as emblems of nature and religion, respectively.[41] Hence the combinative gesture that initiates the coda—a jubilant counterpart of the movement's austere opening combination—reveals the essential unity of these three domains, while the final Amen cadence elevates religion to the position of *primus inter pares.*[42]

The chief precedent for Brahms's symbolic statement—and for the technical means through which he articulated it—lies without question in another orchestral work in C that culminates in a grandiose Amen cadence: Schumann's Second Symphony. Nor are these the only features that the two works hold in common. Schumann's symphony as a whole turns on a strategy that Brahms would later localize in his finale: the gradual displacement of a somewhat unsettled combination of ideas by a more stable configuration. At the very opening of his C-major Symphony, Schumann combines a dignified tune in the brass with a restless countermelody that moves in even quarter notes in the strings. (See Ex. 6-8.) Poised between military fanfare and chorale, the brass melody puts in a striking appearance in the finale as well. Roughly midway through that movement (at m. 280), the winds, led by the oboe, introduce a new chorale tune in E♭—or, more precisely, they offer the first intimations of what will soon evolve into a full-blown tune. More intimate, a touch homelier than its counterpart at the opening of the symphony, the new chorale subsequently unfolds in C major (mm. 394ff.), its phrase endings serving as the pedestals on which Schumann mounts the solemn strains of the first movement's chorale. The underlying symbolism of this gesture could hardly be clearer: in revealing the combinative potential of these two rather different conceits, Schumann enacts a fusion of the martial-heroic with the lyrical-hymnic, the secular and the sacred.

Thus in both Brahms's First Symphony and Schumann's Second the art of joining ideas with ideas in contrapuntal combination is charged with symbolic import, and in both works the chorale is a crucial factor in the equation. In some ways, however, the strategy whereby the chorale enters the musical discourse is the very antithesis of the integrative art of joining disparate ideas. That strategy, in turn, is worth a closer look.

Example 6-8: Schumann, Symphony No. 2, first movement, mm. 1–4

IV

The most memorable moment in Brahms's First Symphony—the moment at which even an inattentive listener will sit up and take notice—occurs during the coda of the finale, at the spot where the sober trombone chorale from the slow introduction is given out, *fortissimo,* by the full orchestra. The chorale enters with a jolt, in terms of both sonority (the brass erect a nearly impenetrable wall of sound) and harmonic effect (the chorale's opening A-major chord responds deceptively to the preceding dominants of C and F). Despite Brahms's preparation for this climactic stroke with the chromatically distorted Amen cadences described earlier, its appearance is unforeseen, unexpected. In short, it displays several of the features of what Paul Bekker and, later, Theodor W. Adorno would call the symphonic "breakthrough" (*Durchbruch*). Associated primarily with the symphonies of Mahler, the breakthrough is a messianic gesture, offering a momentary glimpse of the utopian realm that, in Adorno's words, seeks to overcome the "vain commotion" of "the world's course."[43]

Genuine breakthroughs are few and far between in Brahms's symphonic output. To my ear, there are only two: the sonorous reprise of the chorale at the conclusion of the First Symphony and the comparable gesture at the analogous spot in the Third Symphony, the second of these passages a reminder that the breakthrough need not be a noisy affair.[44] More decisive than sheer volume are the visionary quality and the element of reversal, either from low to high comedy, the mundane to the otherworldly, or from the heroic to the reflective. While Brahms represents a byway in the history of the symphonic breakthrough, his contributions were significant nonetheless, and his models for both incarnations of this strategy—the brassy and the serene—come straight out of the works of Schumann.

All four of Schumann's symphonies—and the *Ouverture, Scherzo und Finale*—feature at least one breakthrough, one point at which the narrative trajectory of a movement takes an unexpected turn toward transcendence. While in the last movement of the *Ouverture, Scherzo und Finale,* this point arrives in the coda, with the transformation of the opening fugue subject into a full orchestral chorale, Schumann generally situates his breakthroughs earlier in the design. In the first movement of the First Symphony, for example, the closing phase of the development precipitates the breakthrough of the introductory brass motto at the juncture normally articulated by the recapitulation of the opening theme—a juncture Schumann once described as "the touchstone of a composer's consummate mastery of form."[45] Here, in other words, breakthrough entails structural reorientation, and its effect is most radical when the structure-in-progress is displaced by a contrasting frame of reference. This is precisely what happens in the development section of the first quick movement (*Lebhaft*) of the Fourth Symphony, as a fanfare theme in the winds gives way to a "new" lyrical idea in the strings, the latter in turn usurping the role of the movement's opening theme at the point of reprise. (The fanfare will recur as the first theme of the finale.) Heralded by the winds' presentation of a lyrical hymn tune in E♭, the central breakthrough in the finale of the Second Symphony marks the chief turning point in the design, the moment at which the preceding rondo form on a martial theme evolves into the freely conceived series of contrapuntal variations, featuring canonic and ostinato techniques, that bring the movement to a close.[46]

The breakthrough theme in the last movement of Schumann's "Rhenish" Symphony—an upwardly surging brass tune presented during the development (see Ex. 6-9)—generates a more-or-less complete design of its own comprised of: (1) introduction (breakthrough theme in B major; mm. 130ff.); (2) exposition (breakthrough theme in E♭; mm. 150ff.); (3) apotheosis-reprise (brass fanfare and chorale, both derived from the breakthrough theme, followed by the recall of themes from the first and fourth movements; mm. 255ff.); and (4) coda (breakthrough theme treated in stretto, leading to the final E♭ cadences; mm. 199ff.).[47] In an 1836 review of Moscheles's Piano Concertos No. 4 and No. 5, Schumann maintained that

> a genuine, artfully wrought musical movement will always have a certain focal point toward which everything gravitates and in which all the spiritual threads converge. Many composers put it in the middle (the Mozartean manner), others toward the end (like Beethoven). The total effect, however, is dependent on its force. If previously one was listening expectantly and breathlessly, then here arrives the moment where, for the first time, one can breathe freely: the summit has been reached and one casts a glance forward and backward, at once luminous and contented.[48]

In the finale of the "Rhenish" Symphony Schumann had it both ways, placing "focal points" in the "middle" of the movement (the first two appearances of the breakthrough theme) and "toward the end" (in the apotheosis-reprise) as well. This tactic had not only structural but also affective consequences. Since it incorporates transformed recurrences of leading ideas from earlier movements in the cycle, the entire design from the initial emergence of the breakthrough theme serves as a fitting capstone for the symphony as a whole. In terms of affect, the breakthrough design projects a shift from the popular, folkish tone prevalent throughout much of the work to a more heroic vein,

Example 6-9: Schumann, Symphony No. 3 ("Rhenish"), finale, mm. 130–33

and ultimately, with the unfolding of the chorale during the apotheosis-reprise, it infuses that heroism with more than a touch of religiosity.[49]

While Brahms did not embrace the full range of Schumann's break-through techniques, he clearly drew on some of them.[50] Schumann's Second and Third Symphonies and the last movement of his *Ouverture, Scherzo und Finale* (Op. 52) were of particular importance in this regard. Both the terminal placement of the breakthrough in the *Finale* of Op. 52 and the fusion of martial and religious topics in that movement and the finale of the "Rhenish" Symphony prefigure the climactic breakthrough of the chorale in the last movement of Brahms's First Symphony. At the same time, the more reflective preview of the breakthrough chorale in the finale of Schumann's Second Symphony may well have been a model for the closing paragraphs of the last movement of Brahms's Third Symphony. Likewise, the conclusions of both works are notable for their deft employment of contrapuntal textures and of thematic recall on the large scale. In the finale of his Second Symphony, Schumann combines the breakthrough chorale with the brass chorale heard at the very beginning of the work. Brahms in turn combines a variant of his finale's main theme with the ascending motto of the symphony's first movement (see Ex. 6-10) just before and after the wind band solemnly intones the breakthrough chorale in a modally tinged F major. The chorale itself has a long history within the symphony, harking back to what Walter Frisch calls the elusive or gnomic second theme of the slow movement (mm. 41–50), a theme that subsequently recurs as a parenthetical aside in the first group of the finale, builds to a climax during a later developmental passage, and ultimately achieves a state of transcendent repose in the breakthrough chorale of the coda.[51]

Hence the breakthrough in the finale of Brahms's Third Symphony is closely implicated with the process whereby the leading thematic threads of the entire symphony are woven into a single diaphonous tapestry. Put another way, with a typical gesture of resolution Brahms demonstrates that the apparently antithetical strategies of "joining ideas with ideas" and breakthrough

Example 6-10: Brahms, Symphony No. 3, finale, mm. 271–74

are in fact complementary. And while Schumann's Second Symphony would have pointed him in that direction, Brahms may well have found an even more powerful inspiration in the apotheosis-reprise of the finale of the "Rhenish." In this context, Brahms's allusion to a melodic detail from the earlier work assumes additional layers of meaning. As many listeners have observed, the main theme of Brahms's first movement is an almost direct steal from a passage in the recapitulation of Schumann's first movement where the head motive of the energetic opening theme gives way to a more lyrical idea. (See Exs. 6-11a–c.) Brahms imbues *his* theme with a similarly lyrical-reflective quality when it recurs to round off both the first movement and finale of the Third Symphony, a further sign that the "Rhenish" was intended as a primary point of reference.[52]

Of course, the endings of both works could hardly be more different in character; whereas Schumann's "Rhenish" strikes a note of unbridled jubila-

Example 6-11a: Schumann, Symphony No. 3 ("Rhenish"), first movement, mm. 1–6

Example 6-11b: Schumann, Symphony No. 3 ("Rhenish"), first movement, mm. 449–56

Example 6-11c: Brahms, Symphony No. 3, first movement, mm. 3–4

Example 6-12a: Schumann, *Nachtlied*, Op. 108, closing section

tion, Brahms's Third dissolves into dreamy reflection. Was Brahms aiming to "take back" Schumann's boisterous peroration, much as Adrian Leverkühn, the protagonist of Thomas Mann's *Doktor Faustus*, attempted a "taking back" (*Zurücknahme*) of Beethoven's setting of the "Ode to Joy" in the final adagio of his symphonic cantata, *Dr. Fausti Weheklag*?[53] Perhaps—though an alter-

Example 6-12b: Schumann, *Nachtlied*, Op. 108, orchestral postlude

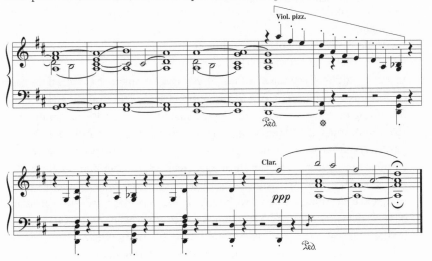

nate and rather more positive interpretation is also possible. At the conclusion of his Third Symphony, Brahms does not so much negate the heroic closing gestures of Schumann's "Rhenish" as raise them to a higher, more transcendent plane. If the emphatic breakthrough of the "Rhenish" points decisively toward a utopian future, Brahms's serene breakthrough and its aftermath project a vision of the future colored by pastness.

V

The final bars of Brahms's Third Symphony call to mind another, far less well known item from Schumann's catalog of works: the *Nachtlied* (Op. 108), composed in 1849, a brief setting for chorus and orchestra of a poem by Friedrich Hebbel. After invoking the "welling, swelling night" in the first strophe and "waxing, waning life" in the second, the poet apostrophizes the approach of sleep (a metaphor for death) in the third and final stanza. Whereas Schumann sets the first strophe to hushed, mysterious music and works toward a grim climax, replete with ominous trumpet fanfares, in the second, he portrays the transition from consciousness to sleep in the third strophe with a descending triadic motive, gently passed from voice to voice in the choral texture. (The motive in its initial form is given as Ex. 6-12a.) In the orchestral postlude, the same gesture is softly echoed by the violins, playing pizzicato, as the music dissolves into nothingness. (See Ex. 6-12b.) Given the similarities in motivic profile, coloristic detail, and mood between this ending and that of Brahms's Third Symphony, is it too much to suggest that the younger composer was attempting to re-create the atmosphere of transcendent calm so delicately portrayed in Schumann's choral-orchestral hymn to the night?

While we are probably not dealing with a bona fide allusion, an interpretation of the kind offered earlier would not have been uncommon within Brahms's circle of intimate friends. Drawing a comparison between another of Brahms's symphonies and Schumann's choral-orchestral magnum opus, his setting of seven scenes from Goethe's *Faust,* Theodor Billroth noted in a letter to Brahms of 5 March 1890: "The last movement of your C-minor Symphony recently put me once again into a state of tremendous excitement (similar in this respect to the third part [scene 7] of Schumann's *Faust*). . . . At last the horn returns with its rapturous cry of desire, as in the introduction, and everything trembles with longing, transcendental sensuousness and bliss!"[54] Billroth's comments highlight a fact that has been somewhat obscured by the twists and turns of reception history: the tremendous importance of Schumann's choral-orchestral music for the development of Brahms's artistic sensibility. Though only spottily represented on today's concert programs,[55] this repertory was very much alive for Brahms, first seizing his imagination not long after he entered the Schumann circle in the early 1850s. "If only I could have heard the *Manfred* music with you!" he wrote to Clara on 21 March 1855. "That, along with the *Faust* scenes, is the most magnificent thing your husband has created."[56] Over forty years later, Brahms's opinion had not altered much. Responding in March 1896 to Richard Heuberger's claim that some of the passages in Schumann's *Faust* scenes were not particularly well orchestrated, Brahms retorted: "Yes, . . . there's much room for improvement in that area. . . . But what splendid music; and that, after all, is the chief point. Even when it comes to orchestral sonority, there are many highly original, individual strokes."[57] Although Brahms was never involved with a performance of the *Faust* scenes, he concluded his first concert as *Chormeister* of the Vienna Singakademie on 15 November 1863 with another of Schumann's Goethe settings for vocal soloists, chorus, and orchestra, the *Requiem für Mignon,* Op. 98b (composed in 1849 on a text from *Wilhelm Meisters Lehrjahre*), and during his tenure as artistic director of the Gesellschaft der Musikfreunde (1872–75) he led performances of *Des Sängers Fluch,* Op. 139 (a ballade for vocal forces and orchestra based on a text by Ludwig Uhland) and the music for Byron's *Manfred*.[58] These and other choral-orchestral works by Schumann, which included the fairy-tale oratorio *Das Paradies und die Peri,* came up frequently in Brahms's correspondence from the 1870s and beyond, especially with Billroth.[59]

In one of the maxims from his *Musikalische Haus- und Lebensregeln,* Schumann encouraged young instrumentalists to "keep in mind that there are also singers, and that the highest in musical expression is achieved through the chorus and orchestra."[60] Brahms would have agreed wholeheartedly. Convinced, like Schumann, that the choral-orchestral medium provided an

ideal venue for the musical realization of the monuments of German literature, he set texts from the works of Goethe (*Rinaldo*, Op. 50; *Alto Rhapsody*,
Op. 53; *Gesang der Parzen*, Op. 89), Hölderlin (*Schicksalslied*, Op. 54), and Schiller
(*Nänie*, Op. 82). The Lutheran Bible—which was just as much a poetic as a
sacred volume for Brahms—in turn provided the textual basis for *Ein
deutsches Requiem* (Op. 45) and the *Triumphlied* (Op. 55).

When asked about his attraction to the Bible by the Viennese reporter
Arthur Abell, Brahms is supposed to have responded: "It was Schumann who
first aroused my interest in the Holy Writ. Schumann always was quoting the
Bible."[61] If Schumann opened Brahms's eyes to the beauties of biblical verse,
his approach to the setting of more purely literary texts for voices and orchestra undoubtedly served as a touchstone for the younger composer's efforts in that direction. Schumann's blending of religious and martial gestures
in works such as the *Adventlied* (Op. 71, composed in 1848) and *Neujahrslied*
(Op. 144, 1849–50) echoes with Brahms's fusion of the same topics in his *Triumphlied*. Moreover, Schumann's musical projection of the theme of redemption from earthly suffering—a topic that looms large in the *Peri*, *Manfred*, and
Faust—has a counterpart in Brahms's interest in the related themes of hope
and consolation.

Hence the relationship between Schumann's and Brahms's works for chorus and orchestra turns largely on matters of tone, character, and mood—
qualities that, by their very nature, do not lend themselves to precise definition in musical terms. [62] Nonetheless, there are a number of connections
between affect and musical technique that Schumann and Brahms—like so
many of their predecessors—exploited to the full. Just as many of Beethoven's pieces in C minor emit an aura of high tragedy, so Schumann seems to
have made his most tragic utterances when writing in D minor.[63] Dark and
brooding, Schumann's "D-minor mood" is most commonly associated with
orchestral works that include the Fourth Symphony and the Violin Concerto,
though it also erupts with full force in the *Faust* scenes: witness the Overture,
a compact and affectively charged preview of coming attractions, the cathedral scene (no. 3), where Gretchen cowers to the ominous strains of the *Dies
irae*, and the sixth scene, where Mephistopheles and his grotesque helpers
prepare for Faust's burial. The grim tone of the burial scene was perhaps
ringing in Brahms's ears when he set to work on the *Gesang der Parzen* in 1882.
Also in D minor, this work opens with an orchestral introduction whose
somber hues and tortuous chromaticism evoke the dusky affect of Schumann's scene. Likewise, the solemn march tune subsequently presented by
the chorus (supported by bassoons, timpani, and lower strings) resonates
with the almost identically scored grave-digging songs from the initial
tableau of Schumann's sixth *Faust* scene.

Brahms's "Tragic" Overture (Op. 81) also projects a somber atmosphere
that owes something to Schumann's D-minor mood in general and to the

Faust music in particular. At the climax of the work, Brahms unleashes a cascading series of interlocked fourths (see Ex. 6-13), thus invoking a figure that appears often in Schumann's *Faust* as a musical emblem for Mephistophelean trickery (no. 1), Gretchen's guilt (no. 3), Faust's anxiety (no. 5), and yearning for the divine (no. 7, Pater ecstaticus's monologue, "Ewiger Wonnebrand").[64]

At the other end of the affective spectrum from the D-minor mood lies the consolatory tone that pervades much of Schumann's and Brahms's choral-orchestral writing and that served to embody what, for lack of a better term, I will designate as the Requiem idea. Few composers were as frequently drawn to that idea as Schumann. Apart from his liturgical (or quasi-liturgical) setting of the actual words of the Mass for the Dead—the Requiem (Op. 148) of 1852—he made dramatic use of portions of the Latin text in the final scene (no. 15) of *Manfred* and the cathedral scene (no. 3) of *Faust*. Goethe's poetic rendering of the funeral ceremonies for Mignon (the mysterious young girl with long black hair in *Wilhelm Meisters Lehrjahre*) elicited music of a correspondingly ritualistic character in the *Requiem für Mignon*, Op. 98a (composed in 1849). Likewise, Schumann conceived the concluding apostrophe to the "Ewig-Weibliche" (eternally feminine) in the *Faust* scenes as a kind of otherworldly Requiem service for the eponymous hero of Goethe's drama. Finally, Schumann's luminous setting for voice and piano of "Ruh' von schmerzensreichen Mühen"—titled "Requiem (altkatholisches Gedicht)" and published as Op. 90, no. 7 (1850)—also deserves mention as an embodiment of the Requiem idea.

Schumann's attraction to the Requiem and to Requiem-related texts is all too easily interpreted as a sign of a morbid obsession with death. This is a mistake, for nearly all of his Requiem settings are affirmative in tone, underscoring as they do the poetic themes of redemption (*Manfred, Faust*), hope in the future (*Requiem für Mignon*), and comfort ("Ruh' von schmerzensreichen Mühen" and Requiem, Op. 148). Schumann's realization of the Requiem idea in the *Requiem für Mignon* perhaps best exemplifies his largely positive stance. This work is not a morose lament for the dead but rather an exhortation to the living to cease mourning and cultivate their own innate abilities instead, a point that Schumann emphasizes with his dignified, choralelike setting for male voices of the key line: "In euch lebe das bildende Kraft" ("May the formative power reside in you"). The overriding message can be summarized in four little words: get on with it.

Much the same attitude informs Brahms's Requiem-related works, of which the key representative is of course *Ein deutsches Requiem* itself. A fulfillment of Schumann's prophecy, in "Neue Bahnen," that Brahms would someday "lower his magic wand where the massed forces of chorus and orchestra lend him their strength,"[65] it is also a continuation—and completion—of Schumann's long line of Requiems. Even though Brahms claimed to be unaware of Schumann's plan to write a "Deutsches Requiem" to words by

Example 6-13: Brahms, "Tragic" Overture, mm. 379–83

the poet Friedrich Rückert,[66] his own *Deutsches Requiem* turned out to be the work of this type that Schumann never composed. As one of the critics noted in response to the premiere of Brahms's Requiem on April 10 (Good Friday) 1868 at Bremen Cathedral: "In order to be able sufficiently to estimate its worth, one must intimately understand the spirit of Schumann's compositions. Our opinion is that Brahms seeks to develop this spirit, the special inclination of the master."[67] "Spirit," no less than mood or tone, is an elusive concept. Still, it is possible to identify more precisely a few of the places where the spirit of Schumann's choral-orchestral works is most pronounced in Brahms's Requiem.

In at least two respects—its overall seven-movement structure and its allusion to a specific chorale melody ("Wer nur den lieben Gott läßt walten")—the Requiem betrays the influence of Schumann's cantatalike *Neujahrslied*.[68] The Handelian jubilation of Brahms's setting of the lines "Aber des Herrn Wort bleibet" (from the second movement) calls to mind Schumann's treatment of the words "Und Freuden ohne Zahl läßt blüh'n" in his motet for double male choir, *Verzweifle nicht im Schmerzensthal* (Op. 93, composed in 1849). Like the fifth movement of Schumann's Requiem ("Qui Miriam absolvisti"), the corresponding movement of Brahms's ("Ihr habt nur Traurigkeit") features a contemplative soprano solo in G major. Brahms's terror-stricken rendering of "Denn es wird die Posaune schallen" (sixth movement) is remarkably similar in character to the music for the Evil Spirit's "Die

Posaune tönt" from the cathedral scene in Schumann's *Faust*. Finally, the serene F-major close of Brahms's Requiem resonates with Schumann's tapering off into silence, in the same key, at the conclusions of both the *Requiem für Mignon* and the *Faust* scenes. No doubt other listeners might argue for further parallels—and indeed, several already have done so.[69] And while none of these parallels counts as a bona fide allusion, together they suggest some of the ways in which Brahms developed the "special inclination" of his mentor.

When Brahms chided Joachim for his failure to ensure a performance of the *Deutsches Requiem* at the Schumann Festival held in Bonn in 1873, reminding his friend that he "ought to know how deeply and intimately a work like the *Requiem* belongs to Schumann,"[70] he all but conceded that the work was first and foremost a memorial to the older composer. (No doubt the death of Brahms's mother on 2 February 1865 also played into the genesis of the composition, though, as Michael Musgrave puts it, this personal loss was more of a "stimulus to the completion of existing ideas . . . than the source of them."[71]) In all probability first conceived in response to Schumann's death in July 1856, Brahms's Requiem was the first in a series of elegies to his departed mentor. As we have already observed in chapter 5, the Adagio of the First Piano Concerto (drafted between December 1856 and January 1857) also belongs in this group.[72] Viewed in light of Brahms's pursuit of the Requiem idea—and of the resonance of that idea with Schumann's Requiem-related works—his initial underlaying of the Benedictus text to the movement's opening melody takes on additional significance. In both tone and shape, Brahms's Adagio is comparable to the final movement (no. 9) of Schumann's Requiem (Op. 148), a setting of the *Benedictus* and *Agnus Dei* texts. Largely devotional in character, Schumann's choral-orchestral movement opens quietly in D♭ major, grows more agitated as it turns to C♯ minor for the *Agnus*, reaches a climax (again in D♭ major) with a powerfully rising perfect fourth on the words "Et lux perpetua," and tapers off with a reflective coda at "quia pius est." In nearly every respect—the overriding hymnic tone, the tripartite design, the climax on an ascending fourth, the contemplative close—Schumann's music might well have been a template for Brahms's. The climactic gesture of Brahms's Adagio, where the winds rise confidently from A to D over extravagant arpeggios in the piano (mm. 79ff.), resonates with another of Schumann's Requiem settings as well: the jubilant choral delivery of "Et lux perpetua," just after the death of the title character, in the final scene of *Manfred*.

Brahms embodied the Requiem idea in another purely instrumental work that has an even more palpable connection with the older composer, the Variations on a Theme by Robert Schumann for Piano, Four Hands (Op. 23). Composed in 1861, the work is based on Schumann's so-called last musical idea, the E♭-major theme upon which he wrote a set of variations in the days that immediately preceded his suicide attempt in February 1854. Although

Schubring probably went too far in suggesting that Brahms's variation cycle as a whole was a musical representation of Schumann's struggle with the forces of physical and mental decline that ultimately consumed him, the critic's programmatic reading of the coda of the tenth and last variation as a *Trauermarsch* rings true.[73] Here Brahms supports the head motive of the theme with solemn dotted rhythms in the bass, thus lending to these final moments the mood of a cortege. Moreover, the appearance of the motive in B♭ and its sequential treatment both recall an earlier manifestation of the same idea in the slow movement of Schumann's Violin Concerto. (See Exs. 6-14a–c.) The message is clear: Brahms's coda is at once an elegy for Schumann and a rechannelling of Schumann's late work toward new expressive ends.[74]

Example 6-14a: Schumann, Theme of 1854 Variations for Piano, mm. 1–4

Example 6-14b: Brahms, Variations on a Theme by Schumann, Op. 23, variation 10, coda (*piano primo* part only)

Example 6-14c: Schumann, Violin Concerto, second movement (Langsam), mm. 4–7

"When Brahms is in a good mood," the violinist Joseph Hellmesberger once quipped, "he sings: 'The grave is my joy'"[75] Underlying the not so subtle irony in this remark is a grain of truth. Yet at the same time, Brahms's "joy" in the "grave" was hardly representative of a grim fixation on death. For Brahms, the essence of the Requiem idea lay not in maudlin lamentation but in the situation of death in a cycle of dissolution and renewal. Nowhere is this outlook more apparent than in his musical eulogies for Schumann, both texted and untexted, of which the most profound perhaps occurs at the conclusion of his Third Symphony. Beautifully described by Peter Smith as an "ethereal reverie" on the opening theme of the "Rhenish" Symphony and the "ultimate resting place for Schumann,"[76] these bars also conjure up (as noted at the beginning of this section) the transcendent calm of Schumann's *Nachtlied*, his choral-orchestral hymn to night, sleep—and death. Brahms's recreation of this visionary world, within the parameters of his own music style, is a fitting monument to the composer who, among other things, taught him how to play chess.

CHAPTER 7.

BRAHMS, THE SCHUMANN CIRCLE,

AND THE STYLE HONGROIS:

CONTEXTS FOR THE "DOUBLE"

CONCERTO, OP. 102

. . . where they wander springs transform the rock,
these vagabonds in front of whom unfurl
familiar empires of oncoming night.
—*Charles Baudelaire,*
  "Gypsies on the Road" ("Bohemiens en voyage"),
  from Les Fleurs du mal

HAVING TRIED THE READER'S PATIENCE by hopping nervously from piece to piece in the previous chapter, I would now like to focus on a single work: Brahms's Concerto in A minor for Violin, Cello, and Orchestra, Op. 102. The last of his orchestral works, it was completed, according to a notation in the autograph score, in the summer of 1887 in Thun and received its public premiere on 18 October in Cologne, with Joseph Joachim and Robert Hausmann (the young cellist in Joachim's quartet) as soloists and the composer conducting. The "Double" Concerto, as it is commonly known, has generally fared better with performers and listeners, who tend to respond intuitively to its sinewy beauties, than with critics and scholars. Granted, with forty-four currently available LPs and CDs listed in the *R. E. D. Classical 2000 Catalogue*, it is the least recorded of Brahms's concertos. (The Violin Concerto leads with 102 entries, followed by the two piano concertos, with 66 and 75, respectively.)[1] Still, forty-four is a more than respectable number of recorded renditions of a piece whose most obvious logistical difficulty involves coordinating the schedules of two star string players. While for the latter and their audiences the "Double" Concerto has long been part of the canon, most critics, whether writing for the popular or the academic press, hedge their praise. Among recent commentators, Malcolm MacDonald is one of the few who does not. The entire concerto, he writes in his 1990 biography of Brahms, is "virtually continuous love music," while the first movement possibly represents "Brahms's most perfect fusion of symphonic dynamism and lyrical ardour."[2] For most critics, however, the "Double" Concerto is somehow not exemplary, at least not in the sense that Brahms's other concertos and the symphonies are. And yet perhaps it is precisely this fact that makes the "Double" Concerto such a compelling object for criticism.

My intent in this chapter is not to act as an advocate for Brahms; at this point he hardly needs one. Proceeding from the premise that we come to understand compositions better by understanding the musical contexts from which they arose, I would rather like to sketch a musical family tree for the "Double" Concerto—a network of models in which Robert Schumann and the members of his extended creative family play a crucial role. My sketch will focus on two levels of the concerto's genealogy. On the one hand, it will address the extent to which the work was bound up with Schumann's aesthetic of the concerto in general and with his late works for soloists and orchestra in particular. On the other hand, it will attempt to reveal Brahms's debt to an idiom—transmitted to him principally through Joachim—about which most critics of the concerto have said little of substance: the *style hongrois,* that is, the musical language employed by Western composers to evoke the performing manner of the Hungarian gypsies. The late Schumann and the gypsy style would seem to make for uncompatible relatives, but on reflection we will have to admit that they share at least one trait in common. Both of them are situated on a fringe area: the late Schumann, on the fringe of the musical canon; the gypsy and his creative legacy, on the fringe of Western culture. And as we will see, Brahms's embrace of the quintessentially "outsider" style of the Hungarian gypsy has not only musical but more broadly cultural and ideological resonances as well. To set the stage, I will begin with some observations on the reception history of the "Double" Concerto.

I

Although the literature on the "Double" Concerto pales in comparison with that devoted to most of Brahms's other orchestral compositions, it is still possible to isolate a number of recurrent motifs in discussions of the work. For better or worse, these motifs, like so many others in Brahms criticism, can be traced to the writings of Eduard Hanslick and Max Kalbeck.

Hanslick, one of Brahms's closest friends and the most influential critical voice among his supporters, was left almost completely cold by the "Double" Concerto. He did not mince words in his review of the December 1888 performance of the work in Vienna under Hans Richter: "I cannot put [the concerto] in the front rank of Brahms's creations." In the first place, the genre of the new work, "a symphony embellished by the passagework of the violin and cello," was itself "somewhat dubious," comparable to a drama with two heroes who are continually "getting in each other's way." Picking up on a theme that runs through many of his discussions of Brahms's larger works, Hanslick was also critical of the concerto's display of prodigious compositional technique at the expense of expressive immediacy: "This work strikes me more as the fruit of a great combinative intellect than of an irresistible outpouring of creative imagination and feeling." But Hanslick reserved his sharpest censure for the first movement, which, though "the most artful of all, never breaks free from its half-defiant, half-depressed mood, nor from its A-minor tonality. Daylight only seldom shines through its many suspensions, syncopations and rhythmic jolts, its augmented and diminished intervals. We are almost reminded of Schumann's late manner."[3] With the last sentence Hanslick delivered the kiss of death: for him as well as for most of his contemporaries, the music of Schumann's last years was a signifier for exhaustion and decay.

Hanslick's remarks were in line with the negative reactions of some of the other members of Brahms's circle. Theodor Billroth, who had got to know the "Double" Concerto through the piano four-hand arrangement, dismissed it as "cheerless, boring, a product of old age." "I know of no less significant work of our dear friend," he wrote to Hanslick in December 1887, "and yet he has grown especially fond of just this piece."[4] Uncharacteristically for her, Clara Schumann vacillated between diametrically opposed views. Present at a preliminary reading on 20 September 1887 with the composer at the piano, she found the concerto "impossible to grasp"—and for good reason: Brahms played sloppily and Joachim simply failed to appear. Upon hearing it with both solo parts on the following day, however, she "warmed to it totally," judging the concerto "an original work through and through." Although the trial performance with the Baden-Baden Kurorchester on 23 September elicited a similar response, Frau Schumann eventually came round to the opinion that Hanslick would take about a year later. Stating her "definite judgment" after the November 1887 performances in Wiesbaden and Frankfurt, she concluded that the concerto was "interesting" and perhaps even "inspired" but "in no way as refreshing and warm as many of Brahms's other works."[5]

At the same time, not all of Brahms's intimates were put off by his new concerto. Though it has often been said that Joachim's reaction was cool, this is not quite the case. When he wrote to Brahms on 27 July 1887, just after receiving the draft solo parts, that the piece struck him as "lively and ingratiating," he was not merely being diplomatic. Three months later he praised the "especially beautiful and powerful" first movement in a letter to Heinrich von Herzogenberg. True, in the same letter Joachim noted that "the subsidiary themes in the finale are not as substantial as they could be" and also expressed his displeasure over "a few harsh spots," but then he immediately qualified his criticisms: "With Brahms I will gladly withhold a final judgment until I have a better sense for the whole. I've been mistaken many times before!" Moreover, the reservations voiced in this letter do not resurface in Joachim's subsequent correspondence on the concerto with the von Herzogenbergs, Eduard Bendemann, Philipp Spitta, or Clara Schumann. In fact, shortly after the turn of the century, Joachim is supposed to have told Andreas Moser that he would "almost give the Double Concerto priority over the Violin Concerto."[6]

Elisabeth von Herzogenberg, who could be just as exacting a judge as Clara Schumann, was particularly impressed by the slow movement, while the Fellingers, a wealthy (and musical) family with whom Brahms was on close terms during his later years in Vienna, described the Viennese premiere of the "Double" Concerto as a success that "in no way corresponded to the work's intrinsic value."[7] Commenting on the same performance, the critic and composer Richard Heuberger reported that even though "a few rogues hissed," Brahms was summoned for seven or eight curtain calls. Furthermore, Heuberger found this to be a fitting reception for a work that, in marked contrast to Hanslick's appraisal, was "easy to comprehend, altogether inventive, rich in spirit, wonderfully orchestrated, and skilfully written for the soloists."[8]

Likewise Max Kalbeck, in his monumental though not always reliable biography of Brahms, put a decidedly positive spin on some of the issues raised in Hanslick's critique of the "Double" Concerto. The generic pedigree of the work, for instance, was not in the least "dubious" in Kalbeck's estimation. A modern-day counterpart of Bach's *concerti grossi* and the classical *sinfonia concertante*, Brahms's concerto was in essence a "symphony with concerting voices" that actually surpassed its models by achieving a "perfect equilibrium" between the orchestral and solo forces. And far from "getting in each other's way," as Hanslick had maintained, the soloists in Brahms's concerto often seemed to behave like "a single, gigantic, eight-stringed fiddle." Kalbeck's efforts to explain the work's relationship to the traditions of the concerto and the symphony bore directly on what was, for him, the underlying meaning of the composition. In Kalbeck's words, the "Double" Concerto was a token of "peaceful reconciliation," an attempt to heal the rift between Brahms and Joachim caused by the former's support of Amalie Joachim in the divorce proceedings between the singer and her violinist husband. And how better for Brahms to "reclaim the lost friend of his youth" than by deriving the thematic fabric of his concerto from a work that both Brahms and Joachim held dear: G. B. Viotti's Violin Concerto No. 22 in A minor? According to Kalbeck, the opening theme of Viotti's concerto served as the motivic source for both the main and subsidiary ideas of the first movement of the "Double" Concerto, though, as shown in Examples 7-1a–c, Brahms apparently took up the motivic elements of Viotti's theme in reverse order. But Kalbeck went even further, claiming that not only the first movement but in fact the entire "Double" Concerto grew from this "unpretentious source," a source that embodied Brahms's and Joachim's regard for the tradition of the Classical concerto.[9]

Example 7-1a: G. B. Viotti, Violin Concerto No. 22 in A minor, first movement, mm. 1–9
b: Brahms, "Double" Concerto, first movement, principal theme (head motif)
c: Brahms, "Double" Concerto, first movement, subsidiary theme (head motif)

Almost all of the motifs of reception raised by Hanslick and Kalbeck have been echoed in more recent commentaries on the "Double" Concerto. Indeed, it would be fair to say that the critical discourse that surrounds the work has essentially remained within the bounds prescribed by these influential writers. For many modern critics, as for Hanslick, the "Double" Concerto represents an unresolved conflict, either between the genres of the concerto and the symphony[10] or between Brahms's art and the spirit of his times.[11] For those who, like Kalbeck, have attempted to justify the generic struggle enacted in the work by situating it within the orbit of hybrid genres that involve soloists and orchestra, the principal models remain the *concerti grossi* of Bach and the classical *concertante* as represented by Mozart's Sinfonie concertante for Violin, Viola, and Orchestra, K. 364, and Beethoven's "Triple" Concerto for Piano, Violin, and Cello, Op. 56.[12] Finally, it has become nearly obligatory in discussions of the "Double" Concerto to cite Brahms's (supposed) allusions to Viotti's A-minor Concerto as signs of the work's reconciliatory nature.[13]

Like all critical traditions, the one engendered by the writings of Hanslick and Kalbeck is characterized by insight and blindness in equal measure. Although Hanslick recognized the tension between expression and technique in the Double Concerto—a tension it shares with many of Brahms's larger works—he hadn't the slightest inkling of what to make of it.[14] Similarly, in limiting the connection between Brahms's style and that of the late Schumann to the affective character they supposedly held in common ("half-defiant" and "half-depressed"), he failed to realize that Brahms may have turned to Schumann to help himself out of a compositional dilemma.

Kalbeck in turn laid the foundation for a fruitful line of inquiry by noting the interdependence of genre, texture, allusiveness, and meaning in the "Double" Concerto. That the work was intended in part as a peace offering for Joachim is all but certain. In his typically offhand way, Brahms implied as much in his correspondence, and Clara Schumann, who was in a position to know such things, said so outright: "The concerto is, to an extent, a work of reconciliation [*ein Versöhnungswerk*]—Joachim and Brahms have spoken to one another for the first time in years."[15] Furthermore, Brahms's conception of the work for *two* soloists and orchestra, after the manner of the classical *concertante,* gave him the opportunity to create textural scenarios that were, in themselves, emblematic of reconciliation. Both on the small and the large scale, Brahms tends to first present the soloists as individuals and then gradually bring them together in either rhythmic unison or octaves. (He does precisely this in the first movement's opening pair of cadenzas: the solo cello leads; the violin responds after a brief orchestral interlude; then both instruments, acting as one, usher in the first major orchestral tutti.) In short, the textural trajectory often proceeds from segregation to unanimity. Over the course of the concerto, Brahms mediates these extremes in any number of ways, sometimes by treating the solo violin and cello as if they were "a single, gigantic, eight-stringed fiddle." Indeed, Kalbeck's phrase aptly describes a passage from the solo exposition of the first movement (mm. 180–87), where one soloist picks up at precisely the point where the other leaves off, while together the violin and cello span the upper and lower limits of their respective registers. In a passage toward the beginning of the recapitulation, Brahms beautifully interlaces the solo parts by having them trade off melodic and accompanimental roles at the time interval of a mere two beats. (See Ex. 7-2.) In both examples, the aim is much the same: the generation of unity out of duality.[16]

Likewise it is entirely possible, as Kalbeck argued, that Brahms might have underscored the reconciliatory nature of the "Double" Concerto by invoking Viotti's A-minor Concerto, a work that Joachim placed "in the foremost rank of violin concertos" due to its "wealth of beautiful melodies and original form" and which Brahms praised for its "remarkable freedom of invention."[17] Indeed, in the first movement of the "Double" Concerto, the emphatic orchestral statement of the main idea at m. 57 reproduces not only the melodic outline of the head-motif from the second phrase of Viotti's theme, but its contrapuntal framework as well. (See Exs. 7-3a–b.)

Yet while it can be illuminating to place genre and the other factors that surround it at the service of meaning, Kalbeck and those who followed in his critical footsteps did not always consider these matters from an altogether convincing perspective. To view the "Double" Concerto as a species of symphony—an orientation shared by Kalbeck and Hanslick alike—is inappropriate for a work that is symphonic in only the loosest sense of the term and that in most ways behaves just as a concerto should.[18] Similarly, although the "Double" Concerto may well incorporate references to Viotti's A-minor Concerto, criticism has placed undue emphasis on the narrowly thematic parallels between the works, while largely ignoring their more broadly compositional affinities—that is, the most interesting ones. After all, when Brahms wrote approvingly of the Viotti concerto to Clara Schumann in May 1878 it was to a compositional issue—the mediation of freedom and structure—

Example 7-2: "Double" Concerto, first movement, mm. 300–303

that he called her attention: "[It sounds] as if [Viotti] were improvising, yet everything is so masterfully thought out and constructed."[19]

The tendency of critics to interpret thematic cells as bearers of meaning is also reflected in the widely held assumption that Brahms's use of motives based on the pitches F, A, and E in the first and last movements of the "Double" Concerto represents a translation of Joachim's motto "frei aber einsam."[20] As we observed in testing the "rules" of Brahms's "game" with musical ciphers

Example 7-3a: "Double" Concerto, first movement, m. 57
b: Viotti, Concerto No. 22, first movement, mm. 6 (with upbeat)–7

in Chapter 4,[21] the problem with this assumption is twofold. First, the "basic form" of the musical cipher (the pitch configuration F–A–E) plays a negligible role in the "Double" Concerto. As shown in Examples 7-4a–d, which present the thematic ideas most frequently linked with Joachim's motto, the pitches in the basic form are either reordered (Ex. 7-4b and 7-4c), reordered and transposed (Ex. 7-4a), or reordered and interspersed with arbitrary repetitions (Ex. 7-4d). Second, and more important, the extraction of these cells from their context does no little violence to the aural reality of the music. Surely it is more significant to hear the supposed Joachim motives in the first movement as varied responses to the immediately preceeding musical material (responses that, incidentally, are shaped much like the tonal answer of a fugue subject) than as derivatives of a pattern that is not even stated explicitly.

As David Epstein has noted, the "Double" Concerto "displays a historical view of concerto form, seen through the filter of Brahms's imagination."[22] To date, however, Brahms criticism has offered only a spotty account of the history embedded in the work and of the ways in which the composer molded that history to his purposes. For most critics, the "Double" Concerto is a late Romantic counterpart of the leading lights of the classical *concertante:* Mozart's Sinfonie concertante, K. 364, and even more emphatically, Beethoven's "Triple" Concerto, which Brahms first got to know intimately in the late 1850s during his tenure as court musician in Detmold. In the selection and treatment of the solo instruments, Brahms's practice represents something of a cross between Mozart's and Beethoven's. While the pairing of high and lower solo strings in the "Double" Concerto obviously recalls Mozart's Sinfonie concertante, the presence of the cello, highlighted through Brahms's exploitation of the instrument's entire range, calls to mind the "Triple" Concerto. Yet in terms of texture and form, Brahms's concerto is certainly closer to the Mozartean than the Beethovenian model. Beethoven's use of the piano trio as *concertino* group raises issues of balance and relative weight that simply do not figure in works, like Mozart's and Brahms's, that turn on the repartee between a pair of string instruments and between that body and the orchestra. (Comparisons between the texture of the "Double" Concerto and that of Brahms's own piano trios are equally problematic. Given its dependence on the equation of piano and orchestra, the view that Brahms's trios in some sense provided models for the concerto does not square well with the fact that only rarely does his chamber music with piano accord the keyboard the accompanimental role often assumed by the orchestra in the "Double" Concerto.)[23] Likewise, when it came to concerto form, particularly first-movement form, Brahms seems to have had a closer affinity with Mozart than with Beethoven. (Comparing the design of Beethoven's Piano Concerto No. 3, Op. 37, with that of Mozart's C-minor Piano Concerto, K. 491, in conversation with Richard Heuberger, Brahms described the later work as "much smaller, weaker," than the earlier one; Beethoven's concerto was perhaps

Example 7-4a: "Double" Concerto, first movement, mm. 1–2
b: "Double" Concerto, first movement, mm. 57–58

Example 7-4c: "Double" Concerto, first movement, mm. 112–17

Example 7-4d: "Double" Concerto, third movement, mm. 1–5

"more modern" but ultimately "not as significant" as Mozart's.)[24] Brahms betrays his debt to the Mozartean paradigm most clearly in the opening movement of the "Double" Concerto, where he conceives the recapitulation as a field of resolution for the textural tensions between soloists and orchestra in the "double exposition." His strategies toward this end—modeling the earlier stages of the recapitulation after the *orchestral* exposition; reordering ideas from the exposition to lend further emphasis to the close of the movement—were Mozart's strategies as well.[25]

If the relationship of the "Double" Concerto to the classical *concertante* is beyond dispute, its affinities with the Romantic cousins of the genre are less clear. Although it is unlikely that Brahms was familiar with the *Grande Sinfonie militaire concertante* for violin, cello, and orchestra, a collaborative effort by Anton and Max Bohrer, there is a possibility, given his early training as a cellist, that he knew Bernhard Heinrich Romberg's Concertino for the same forces. Having taken cello lessons at his father's insistence, Brahms acquired enough skill on the instrument to play some of Romberg's cello concertos, or so he told Julius Klengel several decades after the fact.[26] The "double" concertos of Bohrer and Romberg, like several others composed during the nineteenth century, were quite literally family affairs (Anton and Max Bohrer were brothers, the former a violinist, the latter a cellist; Romberg's Concertino was conceived as a vehicle for the composer and his cousin Andreas Jakob Romberg, a violinist),[27] and so, too, in a sense, was Brahms's concerto. According to Kalbeck, Robert Hausmann, the talented young cellist in Joachim's quartet, had urged Brahms in 1884 "to endow the often-neglected cello with a gift, and to compose—if not a concerto—then at least a companion piece to the splendid E minor Sonata [Op. 38]."[28] While the immediate result of this suggestion was the Cello Sonata in F major (Op. 99), Brahms was hardly oblivious to the fact that Hausmann was nudging him in the direction of a cello concerto. Writing to the cellist in August 1887, soon after sending along the draft solo parts of the "Double" Concerto, Brahms felt sure that "they must have made a bleak impression at first, or that you found it highly ungracious, even offensive, that I added a solo violin to a cello concerto!"[29] Hence with the "Double" Concerto Brahms managed to address two personal matters at a single stroke: mending fences with his old friend Joachim and satisfying (at least partially) the desire of a young artist whom he had recently drawn into his circle for a virtuoso work that involved cello and orchestra.

This brings us to a final and as yet little-explored branch of the family tree of Brahms's work: the virtuoso concerto. As Boris Schwarz has rightly observed, the virtuoso violin concerto in particular counts among the most disparaged of nineteenth-century genres, and something similar could probably be said of the even less well known pieces for cello and orchestra.[30] Viewed condescendingly by most music historians, these genres had a more decisive position in Brahms's creative universe than may have been suspected.

II

As a composer of concertos, Brahms had to deal with a phenomenon that his classical predecessors did not have to face: the rise of an ultra-virtuoso idiom whose heyday extended from the years around 1830, when Paganini took continental Europe by storm, to 1847, when Liszt retired from the concert stage. While the origins of instrumental virtuosity reach back well into the eighteenth and even the seventeenth century, the virtuoso style attained a fever pitch between 1830 and 1850 that it had never known before. Furthermore, the style was primarily driven by advances in the realm of writing for the violin: many of the devices with which Liszt enriched the pianist's stock of virtuoso effects were conceived in direct imitation of Paganini's pyrotechnical feats. Brahms was not immune to these developments. He, too, attempted to transfer Paganini's virtuosity to the keyboard, most obviously in his *Studien,* Op. 35, twenty-eight variations on the famous theme of Paganini's Caprice No. 24. Completed in 1863 and every bit as demanding as Liszt's Paganini-inspired efforts, Brahms's variation set also owes something to Schumann, who had issued keyboard arrangements of a dozen Paganini caprices as *Etudes pour le pianoforte* (Op. 3, 1832) and *VI Etudes de Concert* (Op. 10, 1835). Nor was Brahms unfamiliar with the purely violinistic manifestations of the virtuoso idiom. Included in the repertory for his tour of April–June 1853 with the colorful—though musically and ethically dubious—Hungarian-Jewish violinist Eduard Hoffmann, known to his contemporaries as Reményi, was the flamboyant Violin Concerto No. 1 in E of Henri Vieuxtemps, one of the leading violinist-composers of the generation just after Paganini.[31] In addition, Brahms received an insider's view of the virtuoso violin idiom through his contact with Joachim.

For seriously minded composers born in and around 1810, the virtuoso manner of Paganini and his successors was at once a blessing and a curse. As Carl Dahlhaus has argued, Liszt discovered in the scintillating effects of Paganini's playing (and his music) a perfect counterpart for the "experimental," "avant-garde" materials whose eruptive force he was attempting to master in the late 1830s.[32] Schumann was more circumspect. While by no means indifferent to the blandishments of the new style (and a great admirer of Paganini's artistry), he feared that virtuosity could all too easily degenerate into shallow display and cheap trickery. In other words, the rise of the instrumental virtuoso posed a problem that required the seriously minded composer to strike the proper balance between technical brilliance and musical substance. Both the problem, as articulated by Schumann, and its possible solutions, as reflected in his compositions, must have struck a deep chord with Brahms. For this reason, it will be worthwhile to consider Schumann's attitude somewhat more closely.

Schumann offered his fullest account of the problems posed by the "new" virtuosity in a review-essay of 1839 on the piano concerto. Bemoaning the relative dearth of recently published works in that genre, he looked forward to the arrival on the musical scene of a "genius" who would effect "in a new and brilliant way" the union of piano and orchestra such that the soloist "will be capable of displaying the riches of his instrument and his art, while the or-

chestra will act as more than a mere bystander." In advocating for the replace-
ment of the "serious and worthy concerto form" with more freely conceived
designs, Schumann made a highly suggestive comment on the potential for
future developments of one of the concerto's most conventional elements:
"The old cadenza, in which virtuosos of former times indulged their taste for
bravura, now rests on much sounder principles, and might even be put to
good use today." But while "the opportunity for flashy display in novel and
virtuoso passagework should not be excluded from a concerto," for Schumann the final word went to "*Music*, [which] should stand above everything
else."[33] Within a few years, Schumann would confront the issues raised in
this essay head-on in his Phantasie in A minor for Piano and Orchestra, a
single-movement work in which the cadenza relinquishes its former role as a
"poltergeist in the stately home of Classical music" (to quote Kerman) and is
reconstrued as a site of development near the end of the piece.[34] Moreover,
Schumann continued to explore the problematic relationship between soloistic display and musical integrity in a whole series of *concertante* works composed toward the end of his career: the *Concertstück* for four horns and orchestra, Op. 86 (1849), the *Introduction und Allegro appassionata* for piano and
orchestra, Op. 92 (1849), the Cello Concerto, Op. 129 (1850), the Phantasie for
Violin and Orchestra, Op. 131 (1853), the *Concert-Allegro mit Introduction* for
piano and orchestra, Op. 134 (1853), and the Violin Concerto, WoO 23 (1853).

A number of these pieces bear directly on our attempt to reconstruct a
musical family tree for Brahms's "Double" Concerto. Given Brahms's intimate knowledge of Schumann's output, we can be confident that he had a
more than passing familiarity with this repertory. Indeed, Schumann's late
concertante pieces may have been much on his mind just as he set to work on
his last orchestral composition: the volume of the Schumann *Gesamtausgabe*
(a project for which Brahms served as unofficial editor) that contained the
Concertstück for four horns and orchestra, the Phantasie for Violin and Orchestra, and the *Concert-Allegro mit Introduction* for Piano and Orchestra, appeared in 1887, the year in which Brahms composed the "Double" Concerto.[35] In at least one case, Brahms's relationship with the later *concertante*
works of Schumann takes on a decidedly personal flavor. Early in 1855, during
a visit with the ailing composer at the sanatorium at Endenich, Brahms received the dedication of the *Concert-Allegro mit Introduction,* a gesture he cherished deeply. In a letter of 30 January 1855, he thanked his mentor for the dedication of this "magnificent concert-piece" and went on to reveal why he
took special delight in seeing his name appear in this way: like Joachim, the
dedicatee of the Phantasie, Op. 131, Brahms now had a piece by Schumann
that he could call his own.[36]

For obvious reasons, we will want to give special attention to Schumann's
works that involve solo strings, all of which Brahms must have come to know
soon after entering the Schumann circle in the autumn of 1853. When he first

arrived at the Schumanns' Düsseldorf town house on 30 September 1853, Schumann was just days away from completing his Violin Concerto, which, like the Phantasie, was inspired by and intended for Joachim. Moreover, it is likely that Brahms was on hand when Joachim read through the concerto, in Schumann's presence, with the Hannover court orchestra on 30 January 1854.[37] The Cello Concerto—which, incidentally, shared the bill with the Leipzig Gewandhaus premiere of Brahms's Second Symphony in January 1878—came up in a conversation between Schumann and Brahms in February 1855.[38] As for the Phantasie, Brahms may well have been in the audience when Joachim performed it with the Hannover orchestra on 21 January 1854, but even if he was not, his correspondence with Joachim, Clara Schumann, and Schumann himself between December 1854 and January 1855 speaks to his knowledge of the work.[39] Indeed, Brahms seems to have maintained a fondness for the Phantasie well into his career: he and Joachim collaborated on a performance of the piece on 10 January 1875 in Vienna, during Brahms's third and last season as director of the concerts of the Gesellschaft der Musikfreunde.[40]

To suggest that the mature Brahms might have drawn inspiration from Schumann's very last works, a repertory whose aesthetic worth is still a matter of debate, will no doubt occasion the raising of more than a few eyebrows. Yet there is no question that Brahms held at least some of these pieces in genuinely high regard. It is hard to believe that piety alone led him to program the Phantasie, Op. 131, in 1875, or to encourage Joachim to play the same work for the 1880 concert that commemorated the unveiling of the Schumann monument in Bonn,[41] especially in light of the fact that when he was not convinced of the worth of one of Schumann's later pieces—as was almost surely the case with the Violin Concerto—he acted accordingly.[42] But more to the point, why assume that Brahms could not have learned something even from music that he viewed as flawed in some way? The most compelling evidence that Brahms learned quite a bit from the late Schumann—especially as regards the relationship between virtuosity and musical substance—lies in the music itself.

In his *concertante* works for strings, Schumann's efforts to allow the soloist free reign without thereby jeopardizing the aesthetic integrity of the musical conception are particularly evident in his approach to those moments when the spotlight shines most brightly on the soloist: brief rhapsodic or improvisatory outbursts, evocations of the vocal recitative, and, of course, full-fledged cadenzas. In the Cello Concerto, Schumann binds the second movement with the finale by means of a passionate recitative for soloist and orchestra that calls up motives from both the first and second movements. The finale in turn culminates in an accompanied cadenza that merges with the coda (both the rebounding arpeggios in the cello and the welding together of formal units recall Mendelssohn's transition from cadenza to recapitulation in the first movement of his Violin Concerto); and here, as in the connecting recitative between the second and third movements, Schumann includes references to motivic particles from earlier in the piece. The soloist is introduced in the first movement of Schumann's Violin Concerto in an altogether striking manner. After opening with a bravura variant of the main theme in sonorous quadruple and triple stops, the solo violin proceeds with a declamatory passage that leads to a powerful statement of the main theme, now at its original pitch level. It is worth noting that Brahms adopted nearly the same plan in the opening movement of his Violin Concerto: following on the traditional orchestral exposition, the soloist enters with a rhapsodic, minor-mode variation of the head motif of the main theme, engages in a heated, recitativelike exchange with the orchestra, and then, after a lengthy passage of ornamental filigree, presents the main theme in something more closely akin to its original form.

The bravura cadenza and its relatives figure in both parts of Schumann's Phantasie for Violin and Orchestra: an introductory section, moderately paced and in ternary form, and a quick section (Lebhaft) in sonata form. In the introduction, an improvisatory accompanied recitative serves at the middle term in an ABA′ pattern whose flanking A sections feature orchestral presentations of a languid A-minor theme. The main body of the piece (Lebhaft), like the finale of the Cello Concerto, builds toward a cadenza that leads into the coda by way of richocheting arpeggios, a figuration that Schumann had alread introduced in the development section of the Lebhaft.[43] In sum, all three of Schumann's late concertante works for strings and orchestra demonstrate the composer's concern to devise strategies for integrating the chief tokens of virtuosic display with the formal and thematic argument of the musical work.

Brahms demonstrated similar concerns in his "Double" Concerto, and, as in Schumann's concertante pieces, his strategies for addressing them are most evident in his approach to the cadenza. Traditionally an emblem of closure, the cadenza actually serves as an agency of presentation in the "Double" Concerto. In grappling with the problem of how best to introduce two soloists, Brahms hit upon a compelling solution that might be described as a double cycle of call and response. (See Ex. 7-5.) Answering the orchestra's forceful call, the solo cello enters with an affective and rhapsodic passage, which, according to Brahms's indication, is to be rendered in modo d'un recitativo, ma sempre in tempo (in the manner of a recitative, but always in tempo). The orchestra's second call is considerably milder than the first, featuring the mellow sonority of horns, solo clarinet, and the other woodwinds. To this the solo violin responds with a recitativelike gesture of its own, and before long both soloists are engaged in a dialogue of growing intensity. Repartee gives way to unamimity as the soloists together usher in the orchestral exposition that begins at m. 58 with propulsive scales that lead up to clipped multiple stops. The net effect is thus a reversal of the traditional scheme whereby the orchestra makes way for the solo exposition.

Example 7-5: "Double" Concerto, first movement, mm. 1–56

(continued)

Example 7-5. *continued*

(continued)

(continued)

Example 7-5. *continued*

Two qualifications are in order at this point. First, the novel framework for the introduction of the soloists in the "Double" Concerto derives from a pattern that Brahms had already employed in his own Piano Concerto No. 2 in B flat (Op. 83); there, too, an orchestral call and soloistic response preface a cadenza that drives urgently toward the orchestral exposition. Second, precedents for this framework are not difficult to find in the opening movements of concertos by Mozart and Beethoven. Mozart's Piano Concerto in E flat, K. 271, opens with a call-and-response pattern, while in his D-minor Piano Concerto, K. 466 (a favorite of Brahms), the soloist enters, after the orchestral exposition, with an expressive recitativelike passage. Likewise, both the call and response and the reversal of orchestral-soloistic protocols occur in the majestic opening of Beethoven's "Emperor" Concerto (Op. 73), where the soloist's extravagant, improvisatory responses to a cadential progression rendered grandly by the orchestra (I–IV–V) prepare for the orchestral exposition proper. Yet these two works hardly constitute a complete genealogy for Brahms's opening. If its form hearkens to similar designs in Mozart and Beethoven, its content and spirit resonate just as powerfully with Schumann.

With the entrance of the cello in the "Double" Concerto, Brahms establishes an unmistakable link with the opening of Schumann's Cello Concerto. The latter is also conceived as a soloistic response to the orchestra's call, though Schumann's orchestral preface is far more reflective than Brahms's and his cello soloist enters with a full-blown melody, not a recitative. More striking, however, than the formal parallels between the two openings are the affinities they share in both mood and instrumental color. Schumann allows the cello to dip into the sonorous nether regions of the C string, the register from which Brahms takes off with a gesture whose brooding encirclement of the pitch E (mm. 5–6: D–E–F–D♯–E) distantly echoes a similar melodic turn in Schumann's concerto (mm. 7–8: E–[C]–F–E–D♯). The A-minor tonality common to both works helps to firm the parallel.

Thus, among other things, the cello's opening gesture in the "Double" Concerto is a kind of manifesto: a statement of Brahms's further exploration of a path already traversed by Schumann. Moreover, that path leads in the direction of motivically integrating the cadenza with the musical substance of the work. As we have seen, this was precisely Schumann's intention in crafting the connective recitative and terminal cadenza of the Cello Concerto, the initial phase of the soloist's exposition in the first movement of the Violin Concerto, and the violin's entry and final cadenza in the Phantasie, Op. 131. In much the same spirit, Brahms mediated between display and substance in the first movement of the "Double" Concerto by treating the opening pair of cadenzas as sites of motivic presentation and elaboration. The orchestra's initial gesture—a brash preview of the movement's main theme—becomes the object of rhythmic and sequential variation in the latter half of the cello's recitative-cadenza. (See Ex. 7-5, mm. 13–18.) In complementary fashion, the orchestra's ensuing call foreshadows the first phrase of the movement's lyrical second theme, the final measure of which—a gracefully arching sigh figure—becomes the point of departure for the violin's recitative and the subsequent dialogue between violin and cello. Far from allotting his soloists merely neutral passagework, Brahms engages them in the thematic discourse of the piece, thus betraying his debt to Schumann's example.

Brahms's unique synthesis of recitative and cadenza also recalls the Cello Concerto in A minor (Op. 33) of Robert Volkmann, a composer who had important ties with the Schumann circle.[44] Composed between 1853 and 1855, Volkmann's concerto was obviously admired by Brahms, who had every intention of programming it on a February 1875 concert of the Gesellschaft der Musikfreunde, though for reasons that are not entirely clear the performance failed to materialize.[45] In addition to its compact one-movement form, the most striking feature of Volkmann's Cello Concerto—and one not lost on Brahms—is its high concentration of recitatives and recitativelike cadenzas. Both accompanied and unaccompanied, these passages employ practically the entire range of virtuoso string techniques (rapid runs and arpeggios, wide leaps, pizzicato, expressive double stops), making abundantly clear that the cello is just as much a vehicle of display as its higher-pitched cousin. Furthermore, the cadenzas are crucial to the unfolding form of the work, offering elements of contrast within the first theme group, serving a transitional function between first and second groups, framing the development, bridging the gap between development and recapitulation (much as in Mendelssohn's Violin Concerto), and, in the boldest stroke of all, bringing the concerto to a close. Yet, a few exceptions aside, Volkmann's recitative-cadenzas are lacking in genuine thematic substance,[46] so that at least in this sense they stand somewhat apart from the principal discourse of the piece. Or, put another way, what seems to be absent in Volkmann's concerto is the will toward maximal integration of virtuoso effects that characterizes Schumann's approach—and Brahms's.

Despite the congruences between Schumann's and Brahms attitude toward virtuoso writing for strings, there are some important differences as well. These can be clarified by imagining the soloist in a bravura concerto for violin (or, by extension, for string instruments in general) as an embodiment of one of four personae: the ballet dancer (as in many of the concertos by the early nineteenth-century French violinist Charles de Beriot), the opera singer (the classic example being Spohr's Violin Concerto No. 8, Op. 47, subtitled *in modo di scena cantante*), the wizard or sorcerer (as in the concertos of Paganini and his followers), and, finally, the gypsy.[47] Of course, a single work may evoke any number of these personae. Max Bruch's ever-popular Violin Concerto no. 1 (Op. 26) begins in a frankly operatic vein (the first movement, rich in recitativelike passages for the violinist, is even designated *Vorspiel,* a term associated with the orchestral opening of many nineteenth-century operas) but concludes with music that the soloist must toss off with all the panache of a gypsy fiddler. As a rule, however, one of the personae will dominate in a given instance.

Hence, for Schumann, violin virtuosity was essentially a kind of sorcery, a conceit nurtured by one of the unforgettable experiences of his younger years: when, on 11 April 1830 he heard Paganini in Frankfurt, he was overcome by an "incredible enchantment" whose effects proved to be long-lasting. For years to come his dreams were haunted by images of the captivating Italian virtuoso "in a magic circle."[48] Moreover, Paganini exercised a decisive impact on Schumann's creativity at all levels: as an aspiring writer of imaginative prose (Paganini was one of the characters in *Die Wunderkinder,* a novel Schumann began sketching in 1831), as a music critic (where Paganini served as a touchstone of instrumental virtuosity), and, most significantly, as a composer. In addition to the Paganini transcriptions Opp. 3 and 10 and an incomplete set of variations for piano on Paganini's *Campanella* theme, Schumann called up the image of the celebrated virtuoso in the "Paganini" movement from *Carnaval* and in many of the pyrotechnical flights of fancy from his keyboard works of the 1830s, including the Toccata (Op. 7) and the Phantasie (Op. 17). Both the later Phantasie for Violin and the Violin Concerto abound in gestures representative of Schumann's own idiosyncratic evocation of the Paganinian manner: catapulting arpeggios, wide leaps, *ricochet* bowing effects, and breathtaking scale passages. Finally, one of Schumann's very last projects was intimately linked with Paganini: the composition of piano accompaniments for the violinist's 24 Caprices (Op. 1), an activity that occupied him even while he was confined to the asylum for the mentally disturbed at Endenich.

As we have already observed, Brahms, too, fell under Paganini's spell, attempting to emulate the violinist's inimitable wizardry in his *Studien* for piano (Op. 35).[49] All the same, Brahms's notion of bravura writing for strings was even more decisively shaped by another *persona:* the gypsy. It is to this image, and to its importance for the "Double" Concerto, that we now turn.

III

Oddly enough, the early commentators on Brahms's "Double" Concerto were uniformly silent about one of the work's most salient features: its implication with the Hungarian gypsy style, or *style hongrois*. It is difficult to believe that the members of the composer's inner circle failed to recognize it. The Hungarian element is even more pronounced in the "Double" Concerto than it is in the G-major String Quintet (Op. 111) and the Clarinet Quintet (Op. 115), works whose evocation of the gypsy manner did not fail to elicit reactions from Clara Schumann and Joachim.[50] Perhaps the professional writers among Brahms's intimates felt that the role of the *style hongrois* in the "Double" Concerto was simply not worth mentioning, that it was somehow beneath contempt. In his analysis of the "Double" Concerto, even Tovey did not refer to the gypsy style, and something of his attitude toward it can be gleaned from a parenthetical aside in his essay on Joachim's Violin Concerto "in ungarischer Weise," a work of which he was extraordinarily fond: "The ornaments of the Hungarian Concerto (quite apart from the Hungarian formulas which I purposefully refrain from quoting in the musical examples) are like Bach's."[51] In other words, the "Hungarian formulas" are less germane to a critical appraisal of the piece than an understanding of its relationship to the tradition associated with the German masters. We can safely infer that Tovey's thinking on the Hungarian-gypsy style of the "Double" Concerto proceeded along similar lines.

Modern writers have been less reluctant to acknowledge the "Double" Concerto's connection with the *style hongrois*. Several have called attention to the strong gypsy coloring of the rondo finale—its central episode in particular—observing further that this feature underscores the reconciliatory function of the work vis-à-vis Joachim, as ardent a proponent of the *style hongrois* as was Brahms.[52] Still, in reading these accounts one is left with the impression that the gypsy element in the "Double" Concerto is little more than a layer of veneer applied here and there to touch up an essentially finished piece of workmanship. To my ear, however, the *style hongrois* penetrates to the very essence of Brahms's concerto, a work that in spirit, if not in actuality, bears the epithet "in ungarischer Weise." Furthermore, a closer consideration of the gypsy elements in the "Double" Concerto will afford us a richer sense of the work's meaning for Brahms. As we will see, the concerto may be interpreted not only as a token of reconciliation with Joachim, but also, at an even deeper level, as an emblem for the renewal of his youthful ties with the Schumann circle.

It is a well-established fact that Brahms's passionate attraction to the gypsy style—or, as Joachim humorously put it in a letter of October 1860, "friendly predilection for Hungarian vintages" [*das ungarische Gewächs*][53]—had powerful repercussions on his productivity. As is apparent from Table 7-1, where I have listed the works (or portions thereof) where the gypsy influence is most strongly present, Brahms's essays in the *style hongrois* are clustered around the initial and closing phases of his creative life. Moreover, as Brahms proceeded from one phase to the next, there was a notable shift both in the range of genres for which the *style hongrois* was deemed suitable and in the relative emphasis it was accorded within a multimovement cycle. In the earlier part of Brahms's career, the gypsy idiom was regularly associated with *Hausmusik*, that is, music intended primarily for domestic entertainment (the Hungarian Dances offer a classic example)[54] and with its generic cousins: chamber music and "concert music" for solo piano. In the Violin Concerto, one of the few works from his middle years in which the *style hongrois* plays more than a casual role, Brahms first explored the potential of the gypsy manner for a large-scale, "serious" genre that involved the orchestra. Finally, in his later period, he extended the generic range of the style to include vocal chamber music as well (*Zigeunerlieder*). And whereas in the earlier multimovement works listed in Table 7-1 Brahms generally reserved the *style hongrois* for use in finales, the traditional spot for lighter fare in cyclic compositions, in the later works it infiltrates larger spans of the total form. Indeed, in the "Double" Concerto, the piece that initiates the burst of gypsy-style compositions toward the end of Brahms's career, it is all-pervasive.

What were the sources for Brahms's appreciation of the *style hongrois?* As a young man in the early 1850s, he would have encountered it firsthand as accompanist for Reményi, who often included a generous sampling of popular Hungarian "Lieder und Tänze" on his recital programs.[55] Not surprisingly, the gypsy style crept into Reményi's renditions of the classics as well: according to some reports, he was known to cap off a Beethoven sonata theme with "a cadential flourish from a *czardas*" ("Czardas-Schlußfloskel").[56] As a mature composer in Vienna, Brahms was literally surrounded by the seductive strains of the gypsy fiddlers who were fast becoming a staple of the Austrian capital's restaurant and coffeehouse culture.[57] Of course, we should exercise caution in distinguishing actual gypsy fiddling from the evocations of that practice by composers of art music, that is, from the *style hongrois* in the strict sense, and here, too, Brahms would have had many models ready to hand.

The first of the great nineteenth-century composers to cultivate the *style hongrois* with some regularity was Franz Schubert. Of the many compositions in which he evoked the gypsy manner, the one that had the most direct

Table 7-1: Brahms: Works that incorporate the gypsy style

Early phase

21 Hungarian Dances for Piano, Four Hands (1852–69, several arranged for piano solo and for orchestra)

Variations on a Hungarian Song for Piano, Op. 21 [no. 2] (1853)

Piano Concerto No. 1 in D minor, Op. 15 (1854–58): Finale

String Sextet No. 1 in B-flat, Op. 18 (1858–60): second movement (*Andante, ma moderato*)

Piano Quartet in G minor, Op. 25 (1861): Finale (*Rondo alla Zingarese*)

Variations on a Theme by Robert Schumann for Piano, Four Hands, Op. 23 (1861): Variation 8

Variations and Fugue on a Theme by Handel for Piano, Op. 24 (1861): Variations 13 & 14

Piano Quartet in A, Op. 26 (1861–62): Finale

Piano Quintet in Fm, Op. 34 (1861–64): Finale

Middle phase

Violin Concerto, Op. 77 (1878): first movement and finale

Piano Trio in C, Op. 87 (1883): second movement (Andante con moto)

Late phase

"Double" Concerto, Op. 102 (1887)

Zigeunerlieder, Op. 103 (vocal quartet and solo versions, 1887–88)

String Quintet No. 2 in G, Op. 111: movements 2, 3, 4

Clarinet Quintet, Op. 115 (1891): second movement (Adagio)

impact on Brahms's approach to writing for strings—and which therefore occupies a special place in the genealogy of the "Double" Concerto—was his Fantasie in C Major for Violin and Piano (D. 934), a work that Brahms suggested to Joachim for inclusion in their Viennese programs of the autumn of 1867.[58] The A-minor theme of the Fantasie's Allegretto movement and the violin's first statement of the main idea of the "Double" Concerto's finale are close relatives (cf. Exs. 7-6 and 7-4d), not so much because of similarities in melodic contour, which are in fact minimal, but rather due to affinities in character and tone (and also in the way the themes lie in the player's hand). The pointed rhythms of both themes project the self-confident swagger that constitutes one of the many affective poses of the gypsy style, an impression heightened by the brilliant sonority of the violin's E string.

Although he was less of a connoisseur of the *style hongrois* than Schubert (or Brahms, for that matter), Schumann made some notable contributions to it as well. His *Zigeunerleben* for "small chorus" (or vocal quartet), piano, and

Example 7-6: Schubert, Fantasie for Violin and Piano (D. 934), Allegretto, mm. 1–8

ad libitum, triangle, and tambourine (Op. 29, no. 3) may have served as a model for the original vocal-quartet-and-piano version of Brahms's *Zigeunerlieder,* not only as regards scoring but also in matters of harmonic color (a predilection for the ♯4 of the so-called gypsy-minor scale) and imitative effect (evocations of the dulcimerlike *cimbalon* of the gypsy band). The *style hongrois* also left its mark on the soloist's introductory passage in Schumann's Phantasie for Violin and Orchestra, with its sudden rhapsodic outbursts, ornamental flourishes, and ultra-expressive, sigh-laden melodic gestures often spiced with diminished and augmented intervals. The soloist's opening phrase, for instance, owes its unmistakably gypsy character to a combination of these features.

Although, as we have already observed, Brahms was perhaps drawn to the Phantasie by Schumann's attempts to adapt its bravura materials to a musically substantive argument, an even more direct source for his understanding of this process was Joachim's Violin Concerto "in ungarischer Weise." True to the expectations raised by its subtitle, the work is rich in elements of the *style hongrois,* extending from the plaintive opening idea—its melancholy affect highlighted by dark orchestral colors and the characteristic augmented seconds of the gypsy-minor scale (Ex. 7-7)—to the prototypically "Hungarian" rhythms of the slow movement's main theme and reaching a fever pitch as the soloist launches into the gypsy-inspired *moto perpetuo* of the finale. As other commentators have noted, Brahms harbored a special fondness for his friend's composition. Soon after perusing the full score in November 1859, he accorded it nearly unstinting praise—an extraordinary reaction even for the young Brahms: "I like [the concerto] exceedingly much, especially the first two movements. On the whole I understand the last movement less well. . . . The first movement is simply fabulous [*wunderschön*]; the melody in major [presumably the second theme, mm. 64ff.] is absolutely splendid."[59] Nearly twenty years later, he held to much the same opinion. In December 1878 Brahms wrote to Joachim that the pieces on one of the latter's upcoming concerts were "all things I would passionately like to hear"; among those pieces was the "Hungarian" Concerto.[60] In due course we will examine more closely the specific resonance of Joachim's work for Brahms's "Double" Concerto.

According to Jonathan Bellman, our most eloquent spokesperson for the *style hongrois,* composers of European art music viewed the gypsy idiom above all as a symbol of "freedom, nonconformity, and independence from the constricting mores of society,"[61] though as Bellman further notes, the liberating force of the gypsy style manifested itself in a wide variety of ways. For great Romantic exponents of the style such as Schubert and Liszt, it primarily meant "deep grief and proud defiance," serving them as a means either of externalizing somber psychological states (Schubert) or of registering frustration over an increased sense of marginalization in the world of high culture (Liszt)—feelings closely associated with the plight of the Romany people themselves.[62] If, to quote Bellman again, Schubert and Liszt discovered in the *style hongrois*

Example 7-7: Joachim, "Hungarian" Concerto, first movement, opening (strings only)

"a language of the soul's darkest cries," most of Brahms's essays in the Hungarian manner evince "a lighter, more popular Gypsy vein," rising at times to the level of "wild celebration."[63] The finale of his Violin Concerto—"merry and vigorous to the point of wantoness," in Joachim's colorful description[64]— is but one of many examples where this is surely the case.

At the same time, Brahms was not indifferent to the more affectively charged possibilities of the gypsy style. The soloist's entrance music in the first movement of the Violin Concerto, for instance, is a transformation of the placid D-major main theme into an improvisatory flourish in the gypsy-minor mode (note the augmented second between 3 and #4), projecting at a stroke the characteristic blend of abandon, defiance, and pathos that is one of the hallmarks of the *style hongrois*. (Cf. Exs. 7-8a–b.) Nor is this the only time in the movement when the darker side of the gypsy style makes its presence felt. It surfaces again in the brooding interlude that separates the A-major and A-minor portions of the second group, in the brilliant passage-work (again in the gypsy-minor mode) at the conclusion of the soloist's exposition, and in the languid C-minor theme (a derivative of material from the earlier interlude) that the soloist presents in expressive double stops near the beginning of the development section. But if, in the first movement of the Violin Concerto, the *style hongrois* serves a largely articulative function, marking off the soloist's entrance and exit music, and if, in the finale of the same piece, it lends a "merry" or even wanton character to the proceedings, then in the "Double" Concerto it contributes to the reenactment of an archetypal gypsy narrative that embraces the entire work. The formula with which Bell-man summarizes this narrative—"Gypsy music = suffering + defiance + animal-level joys and griefs"[65]—seems tailor-made for the "Double" Concerto, given that the work's overall affective trajectory progresses from deep melancholy and searing passions (first movement), to noble defiance and bittersweet musings (second movement), and finally to utter abandon and exuberant celebration (third movement).

Analysis of the gypsy idiom has been greatly facilitated by Bellman's formulation of a "lexicon" for the *style hongrois,* a body of features grouped under the general headings of "Performance Style," "Rhythm," "Harmony and Tonality," and "Form."[66] One of the most significant yields of this categorization is a clearer sense for the highly imitative nature of the *style hongrois,* for when composers set about evoking the art of the Hungarian gypsy, they took as their point of departure a musical language that itself thrived on mimicry. Whether imitating the distant echo of the horn call (with the "Kuruc" fourth) or adapting the rhythms of his performance to the speech accents of the Hungarian language, the gypsy musician engages in a special sort of ventriloquism, speaking with a voice that is not quite his own. Hence many of the evocations of the gypsy style in a composition such as Brahms's "Double" Concerto are in fact twice removed from their original source.

Table 7-2 offers a representative sampling of the gypsy elements in that work. The categories listed in the left-hand column are drawn largely from Bellman's lexicon, which I have slightly amplified to include the techniques of the gypsy fiddler that were most commonly echoed in the virtuoso string music of the nineteenth century. (Although these are designated as "violinistic" effects, nearly all of them transfer easily to the cello.) Here, too, we note many imitative tendencies: with his melting *glissandi* and affective shifts of color on repeated notes, the gypsy fiddler becomes an impassioned singer;

Example 7-8a: Brahms, Violin Concerto, first movement, mm. 1–3 (cellos)

Example 7-8b: Brahms, Violin Concerto, first movement, mm. 90–94

Table 7-2: Elements of the *style hongrois* in Brahms's "Double" Concerto

Lexicon	Example
Performance style	
hallgató style	i. 5–26, 30–57* (cadenzas)
(Rhapsodic improvisations on song melody)	ii. 71–78, 112–118 ("kleine Kadenz")
imitations of instruments and instrumental techniques:	
soloist/gypsy-band dialogue	i. opening "call-and-response"
	ii. B section/50–63
	iii. central episode/127–36, 137–47, 206–14
"Kuruc"-fourth	ii. opening gesture & *passim*
(horn call)	
dronelike effects	iii. central episode/127–34, 180–84,
(bagpipe)	206–18
cimbalon	i. close of solo exposition 189–92
(Percussive alternation of mallets)	iii. transition/56–65
gypsy-band woodwind color	i. 26–28, 147–52
	iii. 148–64
Rhythm (evocations of speech accents)	
spondee	i. first group/61, 63
(Long + long)	iii. central episode/122, 126
bókazó rhythm or cadence	
(Clicking of spurs)	—
"Lombard" and "choriambus" rhythms	
(Accented short + unaccented long, long + short + accented short + long)	—
alla zoppa or "limping" rhythms	i. first group/77–78
(4/4: short + long + short)	i. development/*passim*
	i. coda/416
	iii. central episode/148–79
"Hungarian" anapest	
(2 shorts + long)	—
dotted rhythm	iii. central episode/118–47, 197–214 (central episode)
ornamental triplets	iii. central episode/127–36
Scalar Formations, Harmony, and Tonality	
modal progressions	i. opening gesture/1, 57 (melodic and/or harmonic) 112, 290, 396 (Aeolian)
	i. coda/410–16 (Phrygian, Aeolian)
gypsy-minor scale	i. cello cadenza/5–26
	iii. central episode/164–72
major-minor scalar formations and attendant harmonic clashes	iii. central episode/118–22, 137–41, 148–201
tonal ambiguity: 5th relationships	i. 1–4 (Em/Am)
	i. coda/410–16 (Dm/Am)

Table 7-2: *(continued)*

Lexicon	Example
static pedal effects	See earlier: dronelike effects
repetition of minor-key melody in relative major	—
Form	
Czardas (*lassu* + *friss*)	i. cadenzas (*lassu*) + exposition (*friss*)
Medley	iii. central episode (ABA)
Variation principle	iii. B section of central episode (theme + 2 variations)
Violinistic effects and techniques	
In *hallgató* style or *lassu* sections:	
expressive *portamento*, ascending	i. second theme / 155–156, 169–70
glissando, descending	i. second theme / 153–54, 167–68
Color shifts on repeated notes	—
Rhapsodic interpolations	i. cadenzas
	ii. cadenzas
	iii. transition / 56–65
Extravagant arpeggiation	i. cadenza / 46–52
	i. second group / 180–89
	i. development / 258–59, 262–63
	iii. central episode / 180–96
	iii. from recap / 237–56
	iii. coda / 298–304
In *cifra* ("flashy") style or *friss* sections:	
moto perpetuo	iii. coda / 313–19
In both *hallgató* & *cifra* styles:	
"Sul G"	i. coda / 415–16
	ii. main theme
Double-stopping (often 3rds and 6ths)	i. cadenza / 39–45
	ii. cadenzas
	iii. transition, second group, central episode, *passim*
Punctuating triple or quadruple stops	iii. 49–51, 54–56
Incessant trills	i. development / 242–58
Pizzicato	i. cello cadenza
	i. coda (orch. strings)
	iii. A section of central episode (orch. strings)
Pizzicato and bowed notes in rapid alternation	—
Harmonics, natural and artificial	i. cello cadenza / 10–11
	iii. retransition / 100–101
Combinations:	
Sul G + arpeggios + harmonics	i. coda

*Lowercase Roman numerals = movements; measure numbers are given in Arabic numerals.

likewise, his penchant for harmonics, flamboyant arpeggios, and rapid pizzicati lends to his violin the quality of a flute, *cimbalon,* and guitar, respectively.

A glance at the right-hand column of Table 7-2 indicates that hardly a major thematic idea or formal division of the "Double" Concerto was left untouched by some aspect of the *style hongrois.* Of course, some portions of the work are denser in markers of the gypsy style than others. The initial phase of the first movement constitutes one such section. (See Ex. 7-5.) Its organization as a double cycle of call and response might well be construed as an evocation of the dialogue between a gypsy band and its leader or, in this case, leaders. The "band" strikes a defiant tone to which the modal, Aeolian quality of the opening gesture lends a touch of primitivism. In contrast, the brooding, melancholy character of the solo cello's answer derives in part from the almost immediate emphasis on the #4 of the gypsy-minor scale (mm. 6, 9–10), while the closing measures of this passage in the *hallgató* (or improvisatory) style feature the characteristic augmented second of the same scale (mm. 23–26).

The second cadenza of the double cycle is even more directly imitative of *hallgató* playing, which, strictly speaking, refers to the gypsy fiddler's art of embellishing a song melody,[67] often with the most extravagant ornaments. Here the "song" melody appears in the interlude between the soloists' cadenzas (mm. 25–30), where the orchestral winds offer a foretaste of the movement's lyrical second theme. Initiated by the clarinet, one of the more popular wind instruments in the nineteenth-century gypsy band, the melody (specifically, its graceful closing gesture) serves as a catalyst for the ensuing improvisations of the soloists. Bálint Sárosi, a noted specialist on Hungarian gypsy music, has compared the *hallgató* style to an "instrumental fantasy" in which the structure of the original song tune is virtually torn asunder "with runs, touching, languid pauses, and sustained or snapped off notes."[68] This is precisely what happens in the second cadenza of Brahms's double cycle: the violin's rhapsodizing is interrupted by "touching, languid pauses" that are in turn filled in by the solo cello; both instruments share in an outburst of extravagant arpeggios and runs; and finally, as the soloists' abrupt, "snapped off" chords bring in the orchestra, all traces of the melody that inspired the earlier flights of fancy seem to have been obliterated. In retrospect, we might even interpret the double cycle as part of a larger pattern that replicates the bipartite structure of the czardas, the Hungarian national dance. Although I would not press the point too far, the cadenzas evince the gravity, fantasy, and rhythmic irregularity of the first section of the czardas (the *lassu*), while the subsequent entrance of the orchestra is analogous in some ways to the czardas's rhythmically driving second section (or *friss*).

A somewhat different configuration of elements from the lexicon characterizes the coda of the first movement. Prepared by a "gypsified" Phrygian cadence on A in mm. 414–15 (note the B♭ *minor* chord) and a suspenseful

Example 7-9: "Double" Concerto, second movement, mm. 1–6

pause, the final *in tempo* section opens with a passionate outpouring of gypsy bravado. The modal flavor is now Aeolian, while the *alla zoppa* or "limping" rhythm adds a further bit of gypsy spice to the coda theme (mm. 416 ff.). This theme also reminds us that some elements of the *style hongrois* may not be inscribed in the music but must be brought to it by the performers. In order to capture the proper spirit of the passage, both soloists should play the head motif of the theme on the G string, swooping upward with a dramatic *portamento*. Similarly, the special character of the figuration in mm. 421–422 resides in the contrast between rugged, driving triplets played *sul G* on the violin and *sul C* on the cello, and the catapulting arpeggios which the violinist will want to top off with an E harmonic, thus rendering the passage with all the élan of a gypsy fiddler.

The sonorous tone of the soloists' lower strings also assumes a significant role in establishing the gypsy character of the central Andante. This movement begins with a horn call, which, spanning a perfect fourth and played *forte*, is echoed *piano*, a fifth higher, by the entire wind section. From these gestures (obvious allusions to the "Kuruc" fourth of the *style hongrois*) the soloists spin out a long-breathed tune the first phrase of which is given in Example 7-9. While verging on the sentimental, this melody acquires the noble quality that is equally decisive for its character by being played *sul G*. After the movement's ruminative B section (mm. 30–70), Brahms prepares for the return of the opening melody with a passage for the soloists that reveals other facets of the *style hongrois*. Designated in the composer's corrrespondence as the "kleine Kadenz im Andante" ("little cadenza in the Andante"),[69] the passage begins with a broad rendering, in octaves, of the mottolike horn call out of which the violin enacts a graceful descent in chromatically inflected tenths, sixths, and thirds—a foil for the cello's dominant pedal, enlivened by trills. Never prone to squander a good idea, Brahms rounds off the movement with a subdued reminiscence of the same music.

It is easy to understand why nearly all the commentaries on the gypsy flavor of the "Double" Concerto cite the central episode of the finale (mm. 118–214). Indeed, it would be possible to extrapolate a sizable body of *style hongrois* effects from this music alone. Occupying nearly one-third of the

Example 7-10: "Double" Concerto, third movement, mm. 118–26

movement's total length, the episode falls into the sort of loosely structured
medleylike design typically found in the *friss* section of a czardas: an ABA'
form whose middle part is cast as a theme plus two variations.[70] Rhythmically, the main idea of the A section features the dotted gestures and emphatic spondees of the gypsy style, while a piquant blend of major and minor
characterizes its tonal-harmonic idiom. (See Ex. 7-10.) Adopting the *alla zoppa*
as its chief rhythmic figure, the main theme of the B section is also colored

by modal mixture, while the first variation (mm. 164ff.) foregrounds the middle segment of the gypsy-minor scale (3–♯4–5–♭6). (See Exs. 7-11a–b.) Imitative effects featured in the episode include evocations of the dialogue between fiddler and band in the A sections and droning pedal tones in both the A and B sections. Finally, the episode is rich in virtuoso fiddle techniques, which range from expressive double-stopping to the dramatic arpeggios of the B section (variation 2, mm. 180–96).

Just as telling, however, as the many elements from the gypsy lexicon that Brahms incorporates into the "Double" Concerto are those that he underplays or eschews. Totally absent are such common emblems of the *style hongrois* as the cadential *bókazó* rhythm (in imitation of clicking spurs: ♩ ♪ ♫ ♩) and the "Lombard rhythm in its basic (♪♩.) and amplified form (♩.♪♪♩.). Only seldom does Brahms highlight what is perhaps the most universally recognized calling card of the style—the augmented second between ♭6 and ♮7 of the gypsy-minor scale—opting instead to foreground the half steps that encircle the fifth scale degree (♯4–5–♭6). Of the elements in the gypsy fiddler's arsenal of special effects, Brahms either avoids or allows few opportunities for the use of harmonics, pizzicato, glissandi, and coloristic shifts on repeated notes. The frantic *moto perpetuo,* a hallmark of the *cifra* or "flashy" style, is likewise confined to a brief appearance as counterpoint to the soaring melodic lines of the finale's coda.

Even those stylistic features of the "Double" Concerto that owe the most to the gypsy idiom are often handled with a certain reserve. The arpeggios that erupt at various spots in the solo parts of the first movement and finale are precisely rhythmicized, neatly parsed into groupings of four or six pitches. Similarly, the cello's imitation of the *hallgató* style at the very opening of the concerto is to be played, according to the composer's directions, *sempre in tempo.* One has the impression that Brahms has somehow tamed the *style hongrois,* making it fit for use in a highbrow genre and appropriate for consumption by the refined bourgeois class that would have constituted his audience. Furthermore, we sense that the style has been submitted to a kind of chemical process of transformation, the result being a far cry from the popularizing treatment of the idiom in Brahms's own Hungarian Dances or Liszt's Hungarian Rhapsodies (not to mention such overt displays of gypsy excess as those in the *Zigeunerweisen* for Violin and Orchestra of the violinist-composer Pablo de Sarasate). In short, the *style hongrois* in the "Double" Concerto transcends style: it has been totally absorbed into Brahms's personal idiom. How did this take place?

In part, the process of assimilation was facilitated by the underlying correspondences between Brahms's temperament and his technical proclivities on the one hand and those associated with the gypsy style on the other. For a composer who purportedly sang, "The grave is my joy," when he was in a good mood, the melancholy side of the *style hongrois* would have had a natu-

Example 7-11a: "Double" Concerto, third movement, mm. 148–56

Example 7-11b: "Double" Concerto, third movement, mm. 165 (with upbeat)–72

ral appeal. Likewise, an art that thrives on extempore elaboration would have obviously been attractive to a composer who channeled his improvisatory gifts into the technique of developing variation. In turning again to the introductory paragraphs of the "Double" Concerto's first movement, we realize that these fifty-six bars constitute a veritable treasure trove for analysts of Brahms's practice of motivic evolution. The orchestral calls and soloistic responses, for instance, are bound together by the linkage technique that was one of Brahms's favored means of establishing continuity between apparently dissimilar musical ideas. The opening gesture (marked **A** in Ex. 7-5) gives way to a series of sequentially rising quarter-note triplets, each spanning the interval of a third (**B**). The latter figure in turn provides the point of departure for the opening of the cello cadenza, which ends with a derivative of the same three-note motive (**B′**), its concluding sigh serving as a catalyst for the initial gesture (**C**) of the orchestra's lyrical interlude. Finally, the second cadenza, like the first, grows directly from the immediately preceding motive in the orchestra. The motivic relations within each of the cadenzas are no less carefully wrought. Just as the solo cello's variations on motive **B** (mm. 8–10) lead to a reinstatement and development of the opening gesture (**A**, mm. 13ff.), so does the elaboration of the violin's first phrase (**D**) eventually regenerate motive **B′** from the end of the cello cadenza (cf. mm. 24–26, 36, and 38–39). Taken as a whole, the second cadenza is thus governed by a process of "liquidation," here involving a systematic compression of the phrase first stated by the violin. Initially occupying a full six bars (mm. 31/with upbeat–36), the phrase is halved by the cello (mm. 36–38), reduced to two bars by the violin (mm. 38–39), halved again (m. 42), and at last disappears entirely with the outburst of arpeggios and scales that brings the cadenza to a close.

"Evolution," "linkage," "regeneration," "compression," "liquidation": all of them are just so many metaphoric terms that can be called into service for a descriptive analysis of Brahms's motivic techniques. None of them, however, touches on the extraordinary freedom with which these techniques are employed in the opening pages of the "Double" Concerto, a passage that seems to bear out Schoenberg's claim that, for Brahms, "organizational order" went hand in hand with "daring courage" and "bizarre fantasy."[71] Even more important for our purposes, the passage suggests that devices such as developing variation and its complement, liquidation, represent a kind of frozen or fixed improvisation, making palpable the kinship between the gypsy fiddler's hallgató-style rhapsodizing and the fundamental elements of Brahms's compositional idiom.

If the opening cadenzas of the "Double" Concerto's first movement point to the coincidence of Brahms's personal style and the *style hongrois,* other passages disclose a combination of Brahmsian and gypsy traits that borders on synthesis. The central episode in the finale, for example, shows the process at work in the domains of harmony, tonality, and rhythm. In considering the first two of these parameters, we might keep in mind the lively description of the tonal-harmonic language of the gypsy that Liszt provided in his book on the gypsies and their music (*Des bohémiens et de leur musique en Hongrie,* 1859),[72] which, he claimed, was especially notable for its "wild harmony, fantastic and full of discords." Characterized as well by "sudden change and quick transformation," and by the performer's "habit of passing suddenly to a remote key," the strange but alluring harmonies of the gypsy style seemed intentionally to defy the "most treasured scientific . . . tenets" of the "civilised musician."[73] The main theme of Brahms's central episode captures more than a little of this volatility. (See Ex. 7-10.) Note, in particular, the "wild and fantastic" inflection of diatonic harmonies toward the flat side (mm. 120–21), the "discords" that result from the clash between the soloists' suave parallel thirds and the underlying harmonies (mm. 120–21), the "sudden change and quick transformation" at the end of the first phrase, where Brahms unceremoniously juxtaposes F- and A-major chords (m. 122), and the highly "unscientific" motion of the second phrase toward a G-major cadence (m. 126).

This passage caught the attention of the music historian and theorist Hugo Riemann (a "civilised musician" if ever there was one), who traced the tonal peculiarities of its first phrase to Brahms's employment of an artificially constructed scale on F from which both major tonic and minor subdominat harmonies could be extracted. According to Riemann, this "minor-major key" [*Molldurtonart*] possessed distinctive poetic qualities, "resonating as if from long-gone centuries and distant realms."[74] This description is of special interest for us because it draws a connection between the tonal foundation of the phrase and its "otherness"—an otherness that, given the "sudden change" from one modal quality to another implicit in the minor-major scale, calls up the realm of the gypsy. Yet Riemann's analysis does not go quite far enough: his "minor-major" tonality on F governs the center of the phrase but not its end points, and in ignoring these we will fail to recognize how deeply the otherness of the music is implicated in Brahms's personal harmonic language.

The beginning and end of the phrase suggest not F minor-major but D minor: the central episode is preceded by a half-cadence on the dominant of that key, and its first phrase closes with the same dominant chord (on A). Hence the phrase is characterized not only by the duality between major and minor but also by the pairing of tonalities a minor third apart (D and F), a by-product of another typically Brahmsian gesture: the descending chain of melodic thirds. Both phrases of the theme from the central episode open with just such a chain in the supporting parts, the first filling in the space between A and G^1 (A–F–D–B$\flat^1$–G^1), the second proceeding from e to F (e–c–A–F). And just as the first chain can be interpreted as either a D-minor or an F-major formation, so the second wavers between A minor and C.[75]

Although neither the minor-major scale nor the tonal pairs that result from melodic chains of thirds have precise equivalents in the lexicon of *style hongrois* harmonic effects, both configurations can be viewed as either close relatives of these effects or means of arriving at similar ends. The minor-major scale evinces a modal quality not far removed from that of a number of gypsy scalar formations, while the pairing of third-related keys embodies the tonal and affective ambiguity that, as Bellman has observed, is part and parcel of gypsy harmony.[76] Ultimately, then, it is difficult to say where the "civilised" composer leaves off and the gypsy begins.

Brahms achieves a similar sort of synthesis in the domain of rhythm as well, and here, too, an excellent example is at hand in the central episode of the "Double" Concerto's finale. As noted earlier, the gypsy character of the episode's middle part, a theme and variations embedded in a larger design, derives in large part from Brahms's use of the *alla zoppa* ("limping") rhythm. Repeated again and again throughout the course of the main theme (see Ex. 7-11a), this rhythmic pattern persists in the first variation, initiated by the soloists alone (m. 165/with upbeat). One might hear these passages as echoes of the several spots from the first movement where the *alla zoppa* rhythm plays a leading role, such as the transitional theme from the exposition (mm. 77–80) and the coda theme (mm. 415ff.).[77] Yet there is a significant difference between Brahms's treatment of the rhythm in the first and last movements of the concerto. Whereas in the former the metric accents fall squarely on the first and third beats of the $\frac{4}{4}$ measure, in the latter the situation is somewhat more complicated. In a classic display of his penchant for metric ambiguity, Brahms conceives the finale's central idea as a compound of three layers of activity.[78] In the first and principal layer (located, naturally enough, in the main melody as presented by the clarinets and supported by the bassoons), the metric accent is displaced from the first to the fourth eighth note of the $\frac{2}{4}$ bar. The second layer, centered in the soloists' triplet figures, at once reinforces and rubs mildly against the first: while the phrasing of the triplets nudges the accent toward the end of the bar, as in the first layer, the introduction of a triple division of the beat, grouped in pairs, increases the level of metric dissonance. The third layer, in cellos and basses, intensifies the dissonance level even further, displacing the metric accent to the second beat of the bar.

This combination of metrical layers then serves as the starting point for a broader strategy. At the outset of the first variation (m. 165/with upbeat), Brahms affirms the primacy of the first layer in the strongest manner possible by simply eliminating the other two, so that the accent appears to have shifted definitively to the last eighth note of the bar (see Ex. 7-11b). With the second variation, however, the first layer disappears and the third comes to the fore, thus effecting an accentual shift to the second beat of the bar. Finally, when the orchestra enters with a varied reprise of the episode's initial idea (m. 197/with upbeat), metric equilibrium is restored as the accent reverts to the beginning of the measure. In sum, the middle part of the episode is governed by a process of metric evolution roughly analogous to Brahms's techniques of motivic development. Starting from a point of maximal metric ambiguity, Brahms gradually displaces the beat further "back" in the bar until, at the moment of reprise, he forcefully reinstates metric stability. Moreover, the entire process is built around a key term from the lexicon of gypsy rhythmic effects, a syncopated figure whose inherent metric ambivalence Brahms exploits to the fullest.

There is a degree of detachment in Brahms's handling of the *alla zoppa* rhythm, a sense in which the pattern is approached as an "object" that the composer configures and reconfigures as he pleases. This objective stance is particularly in evidence when an element from the gypsy lexicon is granted long-range significance. Consider, as one example among many, the role of the gypsy-minor scale in the "Double" Concerto. As we know, rather than emphasizing its most characteristic feature (the augmented second between ♭6 and ♯7 in its upper tetrachord), Brahms chose to highlight the intervallic cell from its lower hexachord in which the fifth scale degree is surrounded by its chromatically inflected lower and upper neighbors (♯4–5–♭6). Brahms wastes no time in exploring the melodic and harmonic potential of these materials. Indeed, D♯ (♯4) is the root of the first genuine chord that we hear, the vii°⁴/³ on the downbeat of the third bar of the orchestral introduction. A reordered version of the three-note cell (6–♯4–5) is in turn embedded in the cello's opening gesture, and here, too, Brahms accords the pitch D♯ special emphasis, in terms of both metric placement (on the downbeat of m. 6) and duration. At the same time, the first two bars of the cello cadenza invite an alternate interpretation. Growing directly from the preceding three-note gesture in the orchestra (D–E–F yields D–E–F–D♯–E), they can be heard as an expanded variant of the pitch cell D–D♯–E. And as it turns out, this chromatic cell—either with or without its first member but with its central term (D♯) almost invariably absorbed within a vii° chord—appears at major junctures throughout the first movement: the high point of the violin-cello cadenza (mm. 45–46); the orchestra's preparation for the soloists' next entry (mm. 110–11); the close of the soloists' exposition, where D♯ is replaced by its enharmonic equivalent, E♭ (mm. 188–90); the close of the lyrical phase of the second group in the recapitulation (mm. 340–41); and the climax of the orchestral passage that leads into the soloists' final statements (m. 388).

Both melodic cells in which the irksome D♯ is embedded play a stunning part in the coda. As a rugged counterpoint to the orchestra's clipped, minor-mode presentation of the second theme, the soloists offer a propulsive ostinato on the D♯–E–F cell (mm. 420–21). Soloists and orchestra then converge on the closely related D–D♯–E cell (m. 421), a move intensified at first by repetition and next by rhythmic augmentation until, finally, the urgency generated by these operations is expended in the closing A-minor cadence. Thus a single bit of melodic color—the ♯4 of the gypsy-minor scale—is intimately bound up with the tonal and motivic narrative of the movement as a whole.

Yet Brahms still has unfinished business to attend to. The coda of the last movement echoes that of the first, the melodic-tonal preoccupations of the earlier movement appearing in a new and brighter light, shifted as they are from a minor-mode to a major-mode context. The finale's coda (mm. 324–40) opens with a major-mode variant of the movement's opening theme, but tellingly enough, the music seems to stall on the theme's third pitch: the D♯ that figured so powerfully in the first movement. Once again Brahms harmonizes the pitch with a vii°7 chord, but he then "purges" it of its chromatic character through melodic motion to a D, which is then subsumed within a brash A-major cadence. Furthermore, the cadence dovetails with a variant of the ♯4–5–6 cell in the soloists' parts (mm. 328ff.), now firmly ensconced in major: $E_{(5)}–D♯_{(♯4)}–E_{(5)}–F♯_{(6)}–E_{(5)}$.[79] In the end, the irksome D♯ is literally swallowed up in the flourish with which the solo violin leads into the final A-major hammer strokes. By resolving the residual tensions of the first movement in this way, the coda of the finale serves as a fitting capstone for the entire piece. There is perhaps no better example in the "Double" Concerto of Brahms's recourse to the gypsy lexicon for "objects," which he then employed toward his own ends, in this case a desire for tonal and motivic continuity on the largest scale.

Brahms's relationship to the *style hongrois,* as exemplified in the "Double" Concerto, is thus a multilayered one, comprised in equal parts of self-identification or coincidence, assimilation or synthesis, and objectification. Bearing this in mind, we may pick up a thread from earlier in our discussion: the position of Joachim as man and artist in the genealogy of the work.

Example 7-12: Joachim, cadenza to the first movement of Brahms's Violin Concerto, mm. 9–13

While it is a well-established fact that the concerto was conceived in a spirit of reconciliation, our analysis of its relationship to the *style hongrois* will allow us to understand more clearly how Brahms hoped to effect this rapprochement: through an act of renewal not only of a collaborative enterprise with a friend who happened to be one of the great violinists of his age but also of a *compositional* exchange initiated many years before. Even though Joachim left his mark on history mainly as a performing artist, we should recall that Brahms thought of him just as much as a fellow composer, particularly in the earlier years of their friendship. Upon receiving Joachim's Variations on an Original Theme (Op. 10) in February 1855, Brahms claimed that his friend's work affected him "in the same way as Beethoven's."[80] Thirty-two years later, in the same letter to Clara Schumann in which he informed her of his "jolly idea of writing a concerto for violin *and cello*," he expressed regret over the fact that "Joachim, unfortunately, has stopped composing."[81]

That Brahms meant to address Joachim as both performer and composer in the "Double" Concerto is apparent from the violin's entrance with a gesture that resonates both within and beyond its immediate context. A wistful response to the preceding phrase in the orchestral winds, it also echoes a passage near the beginning of Joachim's cadenza to Brahms's Violin Concerto.[82] (Cf. Ex. 7-5, mm. 30–34, and Ex. 7-12) In both passages, a pedal on the violin's open A string is surrounded by a pair of conjunct melodic lines (while they descend in Brahms's cadenza and proceed in contrary motion in Joachim's, a chromatic descent from g' is common to both spots). Moreover, each passage fits into the player's hand in much the same way. Hence the violin entry in the "Double" Concerto would have jogged Joachim's memory on two levels: the physical and the more purely musical, each reinforcing the other.

The "Double" Concerto would have called up memories of a far more ambitious product of Joachim's compositional efforts as well: his D-minor Concerto "in ungarischer Weise." As we have observed, Brahms held this piece in very high regard, and his enthusiasm for it seems not to have abated over the years. From our perspective, Brahms's opinion is a bit difficult to fathom. History has determined, and not without justification, that Joachim's "Hungarian" Concerto is not the masterpiece that Brahms thought it was, and although a few enterprising violinists have taken the trouble to meet its technical challenges, it is unlikely that too many others will follow suit.[83] Still, there can be no doubt that Brahms's affection for his friend's concerto was genuinely felt. Tovey, another ardent fan of the work, put it well when he maintained that the "Hungarian" Concerto was "a composition from which Brahms was proud to learn."[84] Indeed, Brahms was still putting its lessons to good use nearly three decades after he first perused the score.

What attracted Brahms to the "Hungarian" Concerto, and what did he derive from it? Obviously, he was struck by its all-pervasive gypsy atmosphere, its embodiment of that "love for the spirit of Hungarian music" he shared with Joachim.[85] In addition, Brahms would have learned much from Joachim's deft handling of the violin in general and from his knack for crafting richly ornamental lines for the soloist in particular.[86] This supposition is born out by numerous features of the string writing in Brahms's Violin Concerto and "Double" Concerto, including the series of persistent trills that appear in the development section of the first movements of both works (recalling the retransition to the recapitulation of the "Hungarian" Concerto's first movement) and the whirling triplets over an open-string drone that figure in the central episode of the "Double" Concerto's finale (an echo of the closing stages of the soloist's exposition in the first movement of the "Hungarian" Concerto).[87]

Yet Brahms's debt to the "Hungarian" Concerto involved more than passing references to its glittering surface. Ultimately it was his friend's grasp of the technique of composition that would have meant the most to him. Joachim's use of the same rhythmic framework for both the main and subsidiary themes of the "Hungarian" Concerto's first movement, for instance, demonstrates just the sort of economy that Brahms prized so highly. (See Exs. 7-13a–b.) Another feature that must have caught Brahms's attention was Joachim's introduction of the soloist with a *hallgató*-style accompanied cadenza, a passage that he integrated with the thematic argument by supporting the violin's rhapsodic musings with motives from the close of the orchestral exposition. (See Ex. 7-14.) Given his proclivity for contrapuntal textures, Brahms was probably also impressed by Joachim's artful combination, in the development section of the concerto's first movement, of its lyrical second theme with a suave countermelody in the orchestral violins. And when, in a letter of 7 December 1858, Brahms praised the slow movement of the "Hungarian" Concerto for its "charm and affability," noting that "one idea grows so beautifully from its predecessor,"[88] he must have been thinking of passages such as the one given in Example 7-15, where the closing figure of the movement's A section generates the opening gesture of its middle section, thus forging the sort of motivic link in which Brahms's own music abounds.

Not surprisingly, all of these examples draw liberally on the lexicon of gypsy figures and effects, which Joachim strove to fold into the ongoing musical argument, at times with genuine panache. His attitude toward the *style hongrois* was characterized by both proximity and distance: recall, for in-

Example 7-13a: Joachim, "Hungarian" Concerto, first movement, mm. 10–17, main theme (strings only)

stance, how in the slow movement a stock cadential figure from the lexicon is treated as the object of a rather sophisticated motivic strategy. In short, Joachim's relationship to the gypsy idiom involved the elements of self-identification, stylistic synthesis, and objectification that defined Brahms's approach as well.

In adducing these compositional points of contact as evidence for an "exchange" that culminated in the "Double" Concerto, I am of course using the term in a figurative sense. Yet the dialogue that Brahms's final concerto was intended to renew can also be construed as an exchange in the literal sense. Joachim set to work on the "Hungarian" Concerto no later than the autumn of 1857 and had completed a draft by November 1859, when he sent a copy of

Example 7-13b: Joachim, "Hungarian" Concerto, first movement, subsidiary theme
(winds only)

the score to Brahms; after submitting the draft to extensive revision in the ensuing months, Joachim gave the premiere performance of the work, with the
Hanover Court Orchestra, on 24 March 1860. Therefore, the concerto was
conceived just on the heels of the period when Joachim and Brahms were engaged in trading exercises in counterpoint (and longer contrapuntal pieces)
for each other's inspection. Formally proposed by Brahms in February 1856,
this contrapuntal exchange elicited a series of canons, fugal fragments, and
fugues from Joachim and a group of even more ambitious works from his
younger colleague, including a number of movements from the so-called

Example 7-14: Joachim, "Hungarian" Concerto, first movement, violin entrance

(continued)

"Missa canonica," preludes and fugues, and the "Geistliches Lied" (Op. 30) for chorus and organ.[89]

The genesis of the "Hungarian" Concerto also overlapped with Brahms's efforts to complete his Piano Concerto in D minor, a work with a long and not entirely certain history. Begun in 1855, it drew to an extent on materials from the D-minor symphony that Brahms had provisionally drafted in the second half of 1854 and which itself was based on a three-movement sonata for two pianos composed earlier in the same year. Although our knowledge of the precise relationships among the piano concerto, the symphony, and the two-piano sonata is riddled with gaps (drafts of the symphony and sonata

Example 7-14. *continued*

do not survive), it is still clear that Brahms's D-minor Piano Concerto, in its final form, and Joachim's "Hungarian" Concerto, also in D minor, constitute something of a pair. This, in any event, was Brahms's view: already in December 1858, well before Joachim's concerto was anywhere near completion, Brahms had decided that "it would be wonderful if we could arrange for a performance of *both our concertos* somewhere on the same evening."[90] Together the concertos formed an exchange in "free" composition that complemented the exchange of fragments and full-fledged works in the strict, contrapuntal style. Just as Brahms's concerto benefited from Joachim's advice on matters of pacing and orchestration, so Joachim sought Brahms's opinion on the instrinsic musical worth of *his* concerto.[91] And just as the gypsy style is everywhere evident in Joachim's work, so does it make a strong showing in the finale of Brahms's.[92]

Example 7-15: Joachim, "Hungarian" Concerto, second movement, mm. 26–27 (soloist and strings only)

In a letter of 8 October 1860, Joachim offered the dedication of his concerto to Brahms, noting his friend's predilection for "Hungarian vintages" and humorously admonishing him that the offering "isn't exactly a glass of Tokay."[93] A week later, Brahms responded warmly: "The dedication of your concerto has given me great joy. Were I ever so satisfied with one of my own works, your name would appear on it."[94] In fact, Joachim's name had already appeared on one of Brahms's works some seven years before: as dedicatee of his first published composition, the Piano Sonata in C, Op. 1. But it would take Brahms many years to reach the level of satisfaction to which he alluded in the letter of October 1860. In October 1879 his Violin Concerto was published with a dedication to Joachim, whose part in shaping the finished product can be traced through the correspondence between the friends and the extant manuscript sources of the work itself. On the basis of his close study of these materials, Boris Schwarz rightly concludes that in the Violin Concerto we find "an intangible interplay between the art of Brahms and that of Joachim: Brahms seems to have projected his concerto through Joachim's image of [what Hanslick called] 'modest, unadorned greatness'."[95] What is perhaps most remarkable about this interplay is Joachim's double role, both as performing artist (whose suggestions on matters of violin technique

Brahms anxiously sought and often adopted, in whole or in part)[96] and as composer. While it was Joachim the violinist who made minor adjustments in the soloist's initial passagework to allow for a more idiomatic use of the open strings, only a violinist with compositional expertise could have re-fashioned the soloist's cadenzalike excursion over the dominant pedal point in the finale (mm. 259–64) in the way he did and have offered suggestions for changes in the original orchestration that Brahms was willing to accept.[97] Taken together with Brahms's efforts, at various points in the concerto, to integrate the gypsy style with the musical argument in ways that recall Joachim's similar aims in the "Hungarian" Concerto, these factors allow us to recognize in the Violin Concerto a rekindling of the spirit of the compositional exchange initiated in the mid-1850s.

In writing the "Double" Concerto Brahms once again must have thought back on the promise he had made after learning that he would be the dedicatee of Joachim's "Hungarian" Concerto, for his final concerto was inscribed: "An den, für den es geschrieben ist" ("To him for whom it was written").[98] Paradoxically enough, this phrase is all the more deeply personal than an overt dedication precisely because Joachim's name was not explicitly mentioned. And with this gesture, Brahms once again addressed his old friend as both a performing *and* a creative artist. Much as he had with the Violin Concerto, Brahms drew Joachim into the compositional process by encouraging him (and Hausmann as well) to examine the solo parts "with an eye toward playability [*Spielbarkeit*]."[99] But even more important, Brahms's approach to the gypsy style in the "Double" Concerto resonates powerfully with Joachim's embodiment of the idiom in the "Hungarian" Concerto—so powerfully, in fact, that it suggests an interpretation of the "Double" Concerto as an even more profound fulfillment than the Violin Concerto of the promise Brahms made to Joachim in 1860. For if the Violin Concerto is a piece in which the *style hongrois* assumes a significant but circumscribed role, the "Double" Concerto, more than any of Brahms's other works, merits the descriptive phrase "in ungarischer Weise."

Thus Brahms's last orchestral work emerges as the final (or nearly final) term in a compositional exchange of long standing.[100] And it is against this backdrop that we should consider a remark from a letter to Joachim of 5 March 1888 in which Brahms let down his usual defenses, thereby affording us a rare glimpse into his inner world. After acknowledging Joachim's reports on the recent performances of the "Double" Concerto in London under Georg Henschel, he added: "For me, f.a.e. has always remained a symbol that, in spite of everything, I still cherish."[101] This remark is not, as some have taken it to be, a license to hunt for musical encodings of Joachim's motto, "frei aber einsam," in the "Double" Concerto,[102] but rather a statement of the profoundly symbolic nature of a work in which Brahms—with that blend of melancholy, wistfulness, and defiance he shared with the archetypal gypsy fiddler—looked back on an irrecoverable past. For Brahms, the "Double" Concerto thus spelled both reconciliation and renewal: of something he knew was forever lost.

IV. PRECISION AND PASSION

In constructing the genealogy of Brahms's "Double" Concerto, I have given special emphasis to two branches of its family tree, one of which embraces the aesthetic of virtuosity embodied in Schumann's later works for soloists and orchestra, while the other involves the evocation of the gypsy idiom in nineteenth-century art music. Joachim emerges as the chief mediator between these apparently unrelated branches. On the one hand, his attempts to strike a balance between virtuoso display and musical substance were just as firmly rooted in Schumann's aesthetic as were Brahms's comparable efforts;[103] on the other hand, his approach to composition was decisively shaped by his desire to emulate a gypsy style. Both tendencies came together in the D-minor Violin Concerto "in ungarischer Weise," which, as we have seen, served as an important model for Brahms's own *concertante* works for solo strings.

As I also intimated earlier in this chapter, Schumann's later music and the *style hongrois* share common ground in a further sense as well: both are emblems of exclusion. The major part of Schumanns's late output lies well beyond the body of works that have come to constitute the Western musical canon, a situation that prevailed in Brahms's time and which still holds today. The gypsies, in turn, have occupied a place on the periphery of Western culture for nearly a millennium. From their point of origin on the Indian subcontinent they wandered steadily westward, often the object of scorn, derision, and harsh decrees that forced them to embark on a seemingly endless series of peregrinations. Even when they managed to establish something of a sedentary existence, they often wound up in what were, quite literally, border areas. (One of these was the Burgenland, a geographical location directly south of Vienna, nestled among the Alps, the Carpathians, and the Balkan Highlands; a meeting point between East and West, the Burgenland was comprised in the late nineteenth century of about 325 townships, over a third of which had gypsy camps just outside their limits.[104]) Little wonder, then, that the Romantic sensibility—with its fascination for alienated characters of all types—was magnetically drawn to the gypsies, that race of vagabonds, as Baudelaire called them, "in front of whom unfurl familiar empires of oncoming night."[105] And little wonder that Brahms's creative sensibility drew sustenance from the Romantic image of the gypsy. Writing to Billroth on 22 July 1886, he declared: "For a long time, perhaps always, I've been and continue to be an incorrigible 'outsider' [*Abseiter*]!"[106] Brahms, Schumann, and the gypsy: each, in his own way was indeed an outsider.

Issues of genealogy are thus inextricably linked with meaning: biographical, musical, and more broadly cultural. Yet the deeply personal message of the "Double" Concerto appears to have fallen on some deaf ears. And it is a noteworthy fact that those members of Brahms's circle who reacted most negatively to the work—Hanslick and Billroth—at the same time enthusiastically embraced a group of pieces written just after the "Double" Concerto, and, like it, strongly indebted to the gypsy style: the *Zigeunerlieder*. For Hanslick, few of Brahms's compositions made "such an immediately enchanting effect" as these songs.[107] Likewise Billroth, who had dismissed the "Double" Concerto as "cheerless, boring, a product of old age," praised the *Zigeunerlieder* for their "freshness," "warmth," and "buoyant" spirit.[108] The discrepancy between these reactions to two works that bear the same stylistic pedigree may be framed in terms of an opposition that lies at the heart of Romantic aesthetics: that between art (*Kunst*) and nature (*Natur*). Simply put, in the eyes of some of Brahms's intimates, the "Double" Concerto failed to establish an appropriate relationship between these terms. While we may choose to disagree with them, the concerto's critics put their finger on an aspect of the work that proves to have considerable cultural resonance.

It was a commonplace of the Romantic aesthetic that the artwork should conceal its artfulness, that the highest manifestations of art were those in which the beholder mistook art for nature. When Hanslick, in his review of the "Double" Concerto, claimed that the work struck him "more as the fruit of a great combinative intellect than of an irresistible outpouring of creative imagination and feeling," he was essentially saying that the composition displayed its artfulness too blatantly, while stinting on the natural side of the formula.[109] In contrast, Hanslick traced the "enchanting effect" of the *Zigeunerlieder* to Brahms's having "completely dissolved [his] artistic mastery into the freshest feeling." Devoid of the complexity that (supposedly) marred much of Brahms's other music, these songs struck Hanslick "with the immediacy of a charming creation of nature." Taking the nature metaphor a step further, he attributed to the *Zigeunerlieder* "the fragrance and color of fresh roses."[110] To be sure, the "nature" that Hanslick prized in the songs was a highly idealized affair. Far removed from the primitive and eroticized nature of bona fide gypsy music, it aimed to impart the spirit of that music in a form that would not offend the sensibilities of the bourgeois consumers for whom the collection was intended. Thus for Hanslick—and, we can infer, for some of Brahms's other friends as well—the absence of raw "naturalism" (*Naturalismus*) from the *Zigeunerlieder* was a welcome omission. In Brahms's songs Hanslick found neither "the frantic, insect-like scurrying of rapid passagework" nor the "chaotic whining and wailing" of the gypsy bands, features that "drive us crazy after a quarter-hour of listening."[111]

With the "Double" Concerto, however, Brahms must have hit a raw nerve. His offense lay not so much in the calling of forbidden passions to the surface and not only in an overzealous display of intellect but rather, I think, in demonstrating that passion could be treated as a worthy object of the intellect. This is the subtext of Hanslick's complaint that "the thematic material [of the "Double" Concerto] does not seem to be significant enough for so ambitious a work."[112] Embodying a whole lexicon of gypsy effects, the motivic substance of the concerto struck the critic as peculiarly at odds with the highfalutin techniques to which it was subjected. And although Hanslick made no mention of the *style hongrois* in his review of the "Double" Concerto, the implications of his remarks are clear when we read them together with his comments on the *Zigeunerlieder*: while the gypsy was a welcome guest in the charming but "lower" art of *Hausmusik*, an art embodied in the songs,[113] he threatened to taint the rarefied atmosphere of a "high" artform such as the classical concerto. Ultimately then, it may have been Brahms's effort to stage a full-scale synthesis of these two worlds that caused the critic's discomfort (and that also, by the way, poses the greatest challenge to performers who attempt to strike a satisfactory balance between gypsy abandon and "classical" restraint in their renditions of the "Double" Concerto).

Hanslick's tendency to view art and nature (or intellect and raw passion) as oppositional terms in turn reflects one of the major ideological and political rifts in late nineteenth-century Viennese culture: the conflict between the adherents of liberalism on the one hand and the various antiliberal groups on the other. Espousing equality before the law, religious freedom, and German cultural hegemony, the liberals were guided by the belief that "the spread of rational culture would one day provide the prerequisite for a broadly democratic order."[114] During the 1880s, however, the rationalist point of view came under increasing fire from all directions. Attacked by Pan-Germans and Christian Socialists from the right and by Social-Democrat Marxists from the left, the liberal cause was further undermined by the rise of Czech nationalism and Zionism. Yet as different as these mass movements may have been in character and intent, they shared at least two features in common: a deep-seated mistrust of the liberals' ultrarational outlook and an urge to embrace the "life of feeling" that was conspicuously absent from the liberal agenda.

Though by no stretch of the imagination a political activist, Brahms nonetheless participated, albeit indirectly, in this conflict between the rational order and the cult of feeling. In a nuanced and insightful essay, Margaret Notley has revealed the extent to which Brahms, like many of his colleagues and friends from the upper bourgeois classes, shared in the liberal system of belief. As Notley has convincingly argued, even his music conveys some of the values of that system: while his concern for the "logical" development of motivic ideas goes hand in hand with the rationalist thrust of the liberal program, his strong association with the various genres of instrumental chamber music resonates with the liberals' emphasis on individualism.[115] At the same time, Brahms was hardly the cold and calculating composer of "brain-music" (*Gehirnmusik*) that some of his critics made him out to be.[116] No doubt he could be a cerebral artist, but he was also something of a sentimentalist as well.[117] The melodic sweep and harmonic lushness of even his most intellectually demanding works are emblems of an approach that strove to mediate between the claims of reason and sentiment, of cerebralism and sensuality. To put it bluntly: there is good reason to believe that Brahms recognized the opposition of these terms as a false one.

In this, his outlook foreshadowed that of the Austrian writer Robert Musil, a figure who waged a lifelong battle against the retrogressive tendency of Austrian culture to erect a barrier between intellect and feeling: "To set the [creative] spirit in opposition to reason," he wrote in 1921, "is a pernicious misunderstanding; the humanly essential questions are only confused by all the scribbling about rationalism and antirationalism."[118] For Musil, the way out of this false dichotomy led in two complementary directions: toward the eroticization of the intellect and the rationalization of Eros. Speaking through Ulrich, the passive protagonist of his unfinished magnum opus, *The Man without Qualities*, Musil described his search for the "missing expression" that would resolve the moral crisis of contemporary culture: "Such an expression is always risky, not yet justified by the prevailing state of affairs, a combination of precision and passion."[119] Brahms, too, endeavored to synthesize precision and passion at many points in his creative life, but perhaps never as dramatically as in the "Double" Concerto, where the hot-blooded gypsy and the man of reason prove to be closer relatives than we might have imagined.

EPILOGUE:

CROSSING PATHS AND MODES

OF EXPERIENCE

*R*EVIEWING A NUMBER of Schubert's late keyboard works in 1838, Schumann maintained that their composer would always be a favorite among the young because he possessed a youthful spirit. Moreover, Schubert "tells to youth what it loves the best: romantic stories, full of knights, maidens, and adventures."[1] The ability to spin a yarn in tones was obviously a gift that Schumann held in high regard. A year after publishing this review, he referred to himself, in a letter to Clara, as "deinem alten Märchenerzähler"[2]—a phrase that translates literally as "your old teller of fairy tales" and that he would echo in the titles of a number of his own late compositions: the musical *Märchen, Der Rose Pilgerfahrt* (Op. 112), the *Märchenbilder* for viola and piano (Op. 113), and the *Märchenerzählungen* for clarinet, viola, and piano (Op. 132). Schumann's narrative talents were recognized by one nineteenth-century critic in particular. Writing in 1861, Adolf Schubring claimed that "as important as Schumann is in his lyric works . . . he is at his greatest in his epic works," citing as examples several of his poetic cycles for piano (*Carnaval, Kreisleriana*) and a number of his larger works for vocal and orchestral forces (*Das Paradies und die Peri, Der Rose Pilgerfahrt, Manfred, Faust, Der Königssohn,* and *Vom Pagen und der Königstochter*).[3] If the storyteller—or crafter of epic works, to use Schubring's more formal terminology—draws from the past, making it a vivid presence for the listener, then one of his close relatives, the fortune-teller, peers into the future. And that relative, of course, is nothing other than a gypsy, a persona that played a vital part in the creative output of Brahms.

In short, all three of the central characters of this book—Schubert, Schumann, and Brahms—contributed in varying degrees to the art of storytelling. In doing so, they made their mark on a practice that, according to Walter Benjamin, entered a period of decline in the nineteenth century and was clearly in danger of coming to an end in the twentieth. The storyteller, Benjamin wrote in a 1936 essay on the tales of the Russian writer Nikolai Leskov, "is by no means a present force. He has already become something remote from us and something that is getting even more distant."[4] Why was this phenomenon a source of concern? For Benjamin, the demise of the storyteller and his art was closely bound up with a gradual disintegration of human values. On the one hand, it was an index of our increasing inability "to exchange experiences," while on the other, it suggested that experience itself had "fallen in value."[5] In a slightly earlier essay, Benjamin sounded an even more dire alarm, observing ruefully that "our poverty of experience is not merely poverty on the personal level, but poverty of human experience in general. Hence, a new kind of barbarism."[6]

The key term in Benjamin's diagnosis is "experience." A rather ambiguous word in English, it may refer either to a striking event located at a specific point in time ("Today I had an incredible experience") or to the accumulated wisdom that results from sustained engagement in a particular type of activity ("Job Requirement: Only those with experience need apply"). In German, these two meanings are conveyed with the terms *Erlebnis* and *Erfahrung,* respectively. As a critic of culture, Benjamin was interested in both, arguing that modern life was rich in *Erlebnisse* but dismally lacking in *Erfahrung,* thus his diagnosis of the contemporary condition as one of *Erfahrungsarmut* (poverty of experience). Doubtful that it was possible to acquire *Erfahrung* through natural means in the modern world, Benjamin located it in a medium where it was produced synthetically: the literary work of art. He interpreted the lyric poems of Baudelaire's *Les Fleurs du mal,* for instance, as an attempt to endow the disorienting *Erlebnisse* of big-city life with the weight and depth of *Erfahrung.* Similarly, in Proust's *À la recherche du temps perdu,* Benjamin noted that the chance event triggers the *mémoire involontaire* as if with an electric shock (an *Erlebnis* on the smallest scale), thus opening the floodgates of memory and revealing the continuity between present and past that is a necessary condition of genuine experience (*Erfahrung*). To be sure, the primary medium for this sort of continuity is the story—or network of stories—where the isolated occurrence is embedded in the consciousness of a narrator who then "pass[es] it on as *Erfahrung* to those listening."[7] Operating under the sign of Mnemosyne (mother of the Muses), "The Rememberer," a master teller of tales like Leskov added new links to that "chain of tradition which passes a happening from generation to generation."[8]

These reflections can be brought to bear on a number of issues touched upon in this book. To return to a topic first broached in the introductory chapter, it might be instructive to consider the role of allusiveness in nineteenth-century music in terms of a distinction between various approaches to the experience of listening. From this perspective, the tendency to hear the musical text as a web of allusions speaks to a perception geared toward the gestural immediacy of the individual moment. Yet in granting primacy to the part at the expense of the larger whole in which it is embedded, the practice of allusion hunting promotes a mode of listening insufficiently attuned to the possibility that the stimulating detail—the musical *Erlebnis*—may be nothing more than a signifier for the stylistic continuity between the work at hand and the tradition—the musical *Erfahrung*—of which it partakes.

At this stage, I do not propose to reopen the debate on the value of identifying musical allusions—a debate that is still far from settled. Rather, I would like to consider one final intersection of the crossing paths of our protagonists, the art of musical storytelling, as a sign of their efforts to preserve the integrity of experience. Granted, the preservation of experience was not as pressing a concern in the early, middle, or even the later years of the nineteenth century as it was in the wake of the cataclysmic events of the first part of the twentieth century, the period that called forth Benjamin's diagnosis of *Erfahrungsarmut*. Nonetheless, it may not be pure coincidence that the self-conscious adoption of the storyteller's persona on the part of composers followed almost immediately on the social and political upheavals caused by the late eighteenth-century French Revolution and its aftermath. Nearly every nineteenth-century composer was gripped by the urge to tell stories—often in response to a social crisis—and of this group, Schubert, Schumann, and Brahms would display a special affinity in their approach to the task.

We have already had occasion to observe all three composers in their storytelling mode. The practice of making interpolations into an ongoing discourse that we identified, for instance, in the opening movements of Schumann's Fantasie (Op. 17) and F-major Piano Trio and in the Adagio of Brahms's First Piano Concerto, is a characteristic aspect of the storyteller's art. It would be a mistake for us to hold the storyteller to the strictures of the Aristotelian plot paradigm, insisting that the beginning, middle, and end of his narrative follow from one another with inexorable logic. On the contrary, the natural storyteller loves to digress, to linger reflectively on a pertinent (and sometimes impertinent) detail, to reminisce, to dart backward and forward in time, in short, to engage in precisely the sort of temporal play that Brahms and especially Schumann invoked in their musical works and that finds a precedent in Schubert's fondness for "musing on the past" in his later piano music.[9] In every case, the aim is much the same, namely, to lend the substance of *Erfahrung* to the ephemeral *Erlebnis*, whether in the form of an erotic daydream (the "Im Legendenton" of Schumann's Fantasie), a dimly remembered song melody (Schumann's evocation of "Dein Bildniss wunderselig" in the F-major Piano Trio), or the image of a beloved object (Brahms's "gentle portrait" of Clara in the Adagio of his First Piano Concerto). Likewise, each of these moments embodies a profound revelatory power, disclosing with striking clarity half-forgotten events and images, all of them preserved in unconscious memory and awaiting the storyteller's magic touch to bring them to light again. In sum, the digressions and interpolations in the music of Schubert, Schumann, and Brahms are no less agencies of *Erfahrung* than the efforts to simulate genuine experience in the poetry and prose of Baudelaire and Proust.

It practically goes without saying that storytellers must possess a prodigious memory, that they must have at their command a whole arsenal of tales, ready for the telling at a moment's notice. But while storytellers thrive on the past, the best of them are hardly sentimentalists. Moreover, the effects of their narratives must extend well into the future. Acording to Benjamin, the genuine storyteller will adopt a neutral, dispassionate stance, relating the most "extraordinary things . . . with the greatest accuracy," but without forcing "the psychological connection of the events . . . on the listener." Furthermore, the objectivity with which the tale is delivered contributes to its longevity, ensuring that it will continue to "release its strength"—in the form of wise counsel to future listeners—long after the teller of the tale is dead and gone.[10]

Both the objective attitude of the storyteller and the future-oriented quality of his work are in evidence in a group of works by Schubert, Schumann, and Brahms that drew on a common source: a body of poetry that first appeared in print in the late eighteenth century but was said to trace its origins to the epic poetry of Ossian, the legendary Gaelic bard of the third century who celebrated the exploits of his father, Fingal, and son, Oscar, in recitation and song. Within a few years of James Macpherson's publication of *The Works of Ossian* in 1765, Europe was overtaken by a veritable Ossianic fever, the results of which included translations of Macpherson's redactions into all the major European languages (from German, French, and Italian to Hungarian, Russian, and Greek), hundreds of poetic imitations, and, not least of all, an impressive array of musical works inspired by Ossianic texts and themes. Schubert, Schumann, and Brahms were only three of a large cast of composers—including, most notably, Mendelssohn and Niels Gade—who were affected in one way or another by the Ossianic craze. While translations of actual Ossianic poetry were set to music by both Schubert (*Ossians Gesänge*, ten songs in five volumes, published in 1830 and composed between 1815 and 1817 or so) and Brahms (*Gesang aus Fingal* for women's chorus, two horns, and harp, Op. 17, no. 4; *Darthulas Grabgesang* for six-part chorus, Op. 42, no. 3), Ossian-inspired verses provided the point of departure for the cycle of four ballades for chorus, vocal soloists, and orchestra that Schumann composed between 1851 and 1853: *Der Königssohn* (Op. 116), *Des Sängers Fluch* (Op. 139), and *Das Glück von Edenhall* (Op. 143), all based on poems by Ludwig Uhland; and *Vom Pagen und der Königstochter* (Op. 140), on a ballad cycle by Emanuel Geibel.[11]

According to a number of nineteenth-century critics, Schumann among them, music that took its cue from Ossianic themes was imbued with a distinct "Nordic character" or "tone." Evident not only in texted compositions but also in purely instrumental works (such as Mendelssohn's "Hebrides" Overture, Op. 26, and Gade's Overture, *Nachklänge von Ossian,* Op. 1), the harmonic, melodic, and textural factors that together constitute "Nordic character" were intended primarily to conjure up images of the past, the temporal counterpart of the forlorn, mist-enshrouded landscapes in which the happenings related by the ancient Gaelic bard played themselves out. In the Ossianic music of Schubert, Schumann, and Brahms, this temporal (and topographical) orientation is often projected by melodies conceived in direct imitation of folk song; melancholy in tone, they frequently include deliberately archaic, modal touches that help to create an aura of pastness.

The voice of the past in most of these works generally emanates from the Ossianic bard himself or from one of his poetic descendents, who, in Schumann's ballades, appear in the guise of a blind minstrel (*Der Königssohn*), an aged harper (*Des Sängers Fluch*), a "merman" (*Vom Pagen und der Königstochter*), and a venerable cupbearer of a noble house (*Das Glück von Edenhall*). Moreover, that voice assumes a self-consciously objective pose in nearly every case—dignified and austere in Schubert's *Ossians Gesänge,* solemn and detached in Brahms's *Darthulas Grabgesang,* boldly declamatory in Schumann's ballades, all the better to fulfill the bardic imperative: the imprinting of past deeds on the memories of the community of listeners, the elevation of a singular event (*Erlebnis*) to the level of universal experience (*Erfahrung*).

Although set in the past, the Ossianic compositions of Schubert, Schumann, and Brahms do not wallow in it. On the contrary, the essence of this music lies in its deft interweaving of past and present, recollection and prophecy, archaic and modern. Indeed, the urge to evoke what lay in the recesses of the past inspired all three composers to bold experimentation in the areas of form (the intricate through-composed designs of many of Schubert's *Ossians Gesänge*), harmony (the searing chromaticism of several passages in Schumann's *Des Sängers Fluch*), and texture (the otherworldly sonority produced by the combination of women's voices, horns, and harp in Brahms's *Gesang aus Fingal*). "It sounded so old, yet was so new": what Hans Sachs said of Walther's "Trial Song" in Wagner's *Die Meistersinger* holds true for the Ossianic repertory as well. In offering an intimation of the future—no less than in making the past meaningful for the present—it fulfills another requirement of genuine experience: the realization that the three temporal modes are not so much markers of discrete, precisely measurable time spans as they are signifiers for interdependent states of mind.[12]

Nikolai Leskov, the central figure of Benjamin's essay on the storyteller, once claimed that he approached writing as a craft and not a "liberal art." Benjamin underscored the craftsmanly nature of the writer's work with an aptly chosen metaphor: "The traces of the storyteller cling to the story the way the handprints of the potter cling to the clay vessel."[13] The conviction that artistic production was a heightened form of craft would have hit home with our triumvirate of composers, Brahms in particular. In her Brahms biography, Florence May relates an anecdote that speaks volumes on this point. In response to reports of the academic progress of three gifted young ladies, the daughters of his friend Hugo Conrat, Brahms is supposed to have shown them a worn tablecloth. "My old mother did this," he told the girls. "When you can do such work you may be prouder of it than of all your other studies."[14]

If storytelling offers a discursive medium for genuine experience, then the guild—an alliance of craftsmen—provides that experience with an institutional framework. And while the notion of an artist guild may at first strike us as an oxymoron (artists, after all, pride themselves on their individuality, whereas the members of a guild must submit to a canon of time-honored procedures), it proved to be remarkably attractive to the Romantic sensibility. Already at the turn of the nineteenth century, Friedrich Schlegel suggested that "the artists of the present, like the merchants of the Middle Ages, should band together in a Hansa in order to defend themselves."[15] Schumann's Davidsbund—both in its original form, established in the 1830s as a vehicle for his music criticism, and in its later incarnation, hinted at in his proclamation of Brahms as the new musical messiah in 1853[16]—was conceived in the spirit of just such a Hanseatic league. At the same time, there is a crucial difference between the medieval guilds and their latter-day counterparts. While the older organizations were founded on the principle of preservation (both of communal values and of the individual's right to practice his craft), their romantic analogues situated this principle in a dialectic with the imperative for originality. This is what Schumann was getting at when, in an 1836 review of Chopin's piano concertos, he noted the progress of artists toward a "spiritual aristocracy" whose aim was the promotion of musical *Bildung*, namely, "that capacity for eager reception and re-creation from which arises the marriage . . . of productivity and reproductivity to artisthood."[17] Once again, genuine artistic experience—creative *Erfahrung*, as it were—arises at the point where past, present, and future intersect.

It is in this light that one of Brahms's favorite expressions should be interpreted. In conversation with his pupil Gustav Jenner, Brahms made it clear that, for him, the only variety of musical composition worthy of the name was that which fell under the category of "dauerhafte Musik"—"enduring music." Defined as "music rooted in the deep interior of the musical spirit, in contrast to music that clings unsteadily to superficial and subordinate elements,"[18] Brahms's concept of "dauerhafte Musik" suggests a conservative, even reactionary stance. While open to interpretation as a thinly veiled apology for the primacy of "absolute" over "program" music, it is also an endorsement of an aesthetic that recognizes *Erfahrung*, as opposed to *Erlebnis*, as its foundational premise. This premise was shared by all of the members of Schumann's extended musical family. It underlies the young Joachim's belief that the artistic yield of those "who have a sense for what endures eternally . . . will be esteemed and valued by people of all lands for years to come, even if it only survives as a ruin."[19] A similar point of view appears earlier in Mendelssohn's correspondence with Schubring. "But even now," he wrote in February 1841, "I cannot muster much interest in music that I consider to be bound merely to the here-and-now"—that is, the musical *Erlebnis*—"and from which I cannot expect anything of enduring value."[20] Finally, the same conceit lies at the center of Schumann's artistic credo, the essence of which found succinct expression in the plaintext of his diminutive "Rebus" for piano: "Lass das Fade, fass das Ächte" ("Don't concern yourself with trifles, seize only what's genuine"). The implication is clear: only what is genuine endures.

These pronouncements are more than the idealistic musings of a band of archconservatives. The main characters in this book neither renounced the present nor turned their backs on the future. Rather, they used their musical storytelling skills to transform the momentary into the visionary, the ephemeral into the enduring, the *Erlebnis* into *Erfahrung*. Nor did they merely replicate the tradition that nurtured their development; like the great poets in T. S. Eliot's model of literary history, they created it. As advocates of musical *Erfahrung*, they could not accomplish this task unaided, realizing all too well that the absolutely independent path—the one that never crosses with another—leads directly into a dead end.

NOTES

INTRODUCTION

1. Richard Heuberger, *Erinnerungen an Johannes Brahms: Tagebuchnotizen aus den Jahren 1875 bis 1897*, ed. Kurt Hofmann (Tutzing: Schneider, 1971), p. 94.

2. *JBr*, p. 82.

3. *NZfM* 39 (28 October 1853), p. 185.

4. See Brahms's letter of January 1873 to Friedrich Heimsoeth, in *BBw* 3, p. 121; and Gustav Jenner, "Johannes Brahms as Man, Teacher, and Artist," trans. Susan Gillespie, in Walter Frisch, ed., *Brahms and His World* (Princeton: Princeton University Press, 1990), p. 197.

5. See Michael Musgrave, *Brahms: A German Requiem* (Cambridge: Cambridge University Press, 1996), p. 62.

6. Marie Luise Maintz, *Franz Schubert in der Rezeption Robert Schumanns* (Kassel: Bärenreiter, 1995).

7. James Webster, "Schubert's Sonata Form and Brahms's 'First Maturity'," *19th Century Music* 2 (1978), pp. 18–37, 3 (1979), pp. 52–71.

8. See Christopher Wintle, "The 'Sceptred Pall': Brahms's Progressive Harmony," in Michael Musgrave, ed., *Brahms 2: Biographical, Documentary and Analytical Studies* (Cambridge: Cambridge University Press, 1987), pp. 197–222; and Peter H. Smith, "Brahms and the Neapolitan Complex: ♭II, ♭VI, and Their Multiple Functions in the First Movement of the F-minor Clarinet Sonata," in David Brodbeck, ed., *Brahms Studies*, vol. 2 (Lincoln: University of Nebraska Press, 1998), pp. 169–208.

9. Donald Francis Tovey, "Franz Schubert (1797–1828)," in *The Main Stream of Music and Other Essays* (Cleveland: Meridian, 1959), orig. publ. in *The Heritage of Music*, vol. 1 [Oxford University Press, 1927]), p. 123.

10. See Constantin Floros, *Brahms und Bruckner: Studien zur musikalischen Exegetik* (Wiesbaden: Breitkopf und Härtel, 1980), pp. 115–30; and the same author's *Johannes*

Brahms: "Frei aber einsam"—ein Leben für eine poetische Musik (Zurich: Arche, 1997), pp. 145–82.

11. See Siegfried Kross, "Brahms und Schumann," *Brahms Studien* 4 (1981), pp. 27–29.

12. See Reinhold Brinkmann, *Late Idyll: The Second Symphony of Johannes Brahms,* trans. Peter Palmer (Cambridge, Massachusetts: Harvard University Press, 1995, orig. publ. *Johannes Brahms—die Zweite Symphonie—späte Idyll* [Munich: edition text + kritik GmbH, 1990]), pp. 206–11, 215–17; and David Brodbeck, *Brahms: Symphony No. 1* (Cambridge: Cambridge University Press, 1997), pp. 40–50, 72–73. Walter Siegmund-Schultze also touches on Schumann and Brahms's shared attitudes as composers of symphonic music in "Zu den Beziehungen Robert Schumanns und Johannes Brahms," *Robert-Schumann-Tage 1985,* p. 20.

13. See Walter Frisch, *Brahms and the Principle of Developing Variation* (Berkeley: University of California Press, 1984), pp. 91–92; and Harald Krebs, *Fantasy Pieces: Florestan, Eusebius and Metrical Dissonance* (New York: Oxford University Press, 1999), pp. 219–24.

14. E. M. Forster, "The *Raison d'etre* of Criticism in the Arts" (1947), in *Two Cheers for Democracy* (San Diego: Harcourt Brace, 1979), p. 116.

15. Harold Bloom, *The Anxiety of Influence—a Theory of Poetry* (London: Oxford University Press, 1973), p. 5.

16. See Kevin Korsyn, "Towards a New Poetics of Musical Influence," *Music Analysis* 10/1–2 (1991), pp. 3–72; Mark Evan Bonds, *After Beethoven: Imperatives of Originality in the Symphony* (Cambridge, Massachusetts: Harvard University Press, 1996); and Joseph Straus, *Remaking the Past: Musical Modernism and the Influence of the Tonal Tradition* (Cambridge, Massachusetts: Harvard University Press, 1990).

17. Richard Taruskin, "Revising Revision" (review of Korsyn, "Towards a New Poetics of Musical Influence," and Straus, *Remaking the Past*), *JAMS* 46 (1993), p. 114. For an astute critique of Bloom's concept of "misreading," see Martin Scherzinger, "The 'New Poetics' of Musical Influence: A Response to Kevin Korsyn," *Music Analysis* 13/2–3 (1994), p. 305. Scherzinger pinpoints a logical flaw in Bloom's theory by reasoning as follows: If a strong poet "misreads" his predecessors, then a weak one fails to misread them. Yet how is it possible to arrive at a *failed* misreading?

18. *Webster's Third New International Dictionary of the English Language, Unabridged,* ed. Philip Babcock Grove (Springfield, Massachusetts: Merriam-Webster, 1993), p. 59.

19. The more important contributions in this area include: David Brodbeck, "Brahms's Mendelssohn," in Brodbeck, *Brahms Studies,* vol. 2, pp. 209–31; Kenneth Hull, "Allusive Irony in Brahms's Fourth Symphony," in Brodbeck, *Brahms Studies,* vol. 2, pp. 135–68, and "Brahms the Allusive: Extracompositional Reference in the Instrumental Music of Johannes Brahms," Ph.D. dissertation, Princeton University, 1989; Raymond Knapp, "Brahms and the Anxiety of Allusion," *Journal of Musicological Research* 18/1 (1998), pp. 1–30, *Brahms and the Challenge of the Symphonic Tradition* (Stuyvesant, New York: Pendragon, 1997), pp. 81–141; and Raymond Knapp, "Utopian Agendas: Variation, Allusion, and Referential Meaning in Brahms's Symphonies," in *Brahms Studies, Volume 3,* ed. David Brodbeck (Lincoln and London: University of Nebraska Press, 2001), pp. 129–89.

20. Translation quoted from Brodbeck, "Brahms's Mendelssohn," p. 227.

21. The same pattern of usage appears from time to time in Schumann's writings as well. Painting a none too rosy picture of the post-Beethovenian symphony, he observed in 1839: "We find reminiscences [*Anklänge*] to be sure—reminiscences in too

great a number . . . especially of Beethoven's earlier symphonies." *NZfM* 11 (2 July 1839), p. 1.

In one of the first major essays on the music of Brahms, the music lover and critic Adolf Schubring identified several "reminiscences of the old masters" (Haydn, Beethoven, Schubert, and Mendelssohn) in the Serenades for Orchestra (Opp. 11 and 16) and the First Piano Concerto (Op. 15). See Schubring's "Schumanniana Nr. 8. Die Schumann'sche Schule. IV. Johannes Brahms," *NZfM* 56 (1862), p. 111.

22. Max Kalbeck relates the anecdote in *Johannes Brahms*, 2nd ed., vol. 3 (Berlin: Deutsche Brahms-Gesellschaft, 1912–21), p. 109.

23. Brahms's remark was occasioned by Dessoff's offer to recompose a passage from his String Quartet in F major, whose resemblance to the theme from Brahms's Second Symphony he realized after the fact. Brahms responded by telling Dessoff that he "would have said nothing and then simply taken the free goods" for himself. See Brodbeck, "Brahms's Mendelssohn," p. 227.

24. Brahms's setting of Goethe's text offers a delightful example of the "ludic" quality that genuine allusions often display. While the poem humorously compares wine and women, Brahms playfully exploits the contrapuntal possibilities of Scarlatti's gavottelike theme. Just as the narrator-poet cannot resist either drink or feminine charms, so Brahms is unable to pass up an opportunity to display his contrapuntal prowess.

25. From this perspective, Charles Rosen may well be right in claiming that "Brahms's intentional or unintentional borrowing of melodies is no greater than that of most composers from Bach to Stravinsky." See Charles Rosen, "Brahms: Classicism and the Inspiration of Awkwardness," in *Critical Entertainments: Music Old and New* (Cambridge, Massachusetts: Harvard University Press, 2000), p. 195.

26. T. S. Eliot, "Tradition and the Individual Talent," in Frank Kermode, ed., *Selected Prose of T. S. Eliot* (New York: Harcourt Brace Jovanovich, 1975), p. 40.

27. Ibid., p. 38.

28. Of Bloom's six "revisionary ratios"—the "modes" in which later poets "misread" their precursors—the third and fourth are linked with the psychic defense mechanism of repression: "kenosis" (the poet's "movement towards discontinuity" with his predecessors) and "daemonization" (the "movement towards a personalized Counter-Sublime, in relation to the precursor's "Sublime"). Whereas the ratios called clinamen ("poetic misreading or misprision proper") and tessera ("completion and antithesis") address the aspiring poet's desire to "complete or correct the dead," kenosis and daemonization involve an attempt to "repress the memory of the dead" (*The Anxiety of Influence*, p. 122). The connection between repression and "daemonization" is particularly strong. Indeed, Bloom opens his chapter on that ratio by asserting that poetry "is not a struggle against repression but is itself a kind of repression" (p. 99). Operating under the aegis of daemonization, the younger poet strives to repress the past in order to make himself appear more godlike and his predecessors more human. In this way, the latecomer imagines that he has revealed his *"precursor's relative weakness"* (p. 100, Bloom's emphasis). For a synopsis of the six revisionary ratios, see *The Anxiety of Influence*, pp. 14–16.

29. Friedrich Schlegel, *Athenäum Fragments*, no. 53, translation slightly modified, in *Friedrich Schlegel's Lucinde and the Fragments*, trans. Peter Firchow (Minneapolis: University of Minnesota Press, 1971), p. 167.

30. Walter Benjamin, "The Storyteller: Reflections on the Works of Nikolai Les-

kov" (1936), in *Illuminations: Essays and Reflections,* ed. Hannah Arendt, trans. Harry Zohn (New York: Schocken, 1969), pp. 83–109.

31. Walter Benjamin, "Literary History and the Study of Literature" (1931), in *Walter Benjamin: Selected Writings, vol. 2: 1927–1934,* trans. Rodney Livingstone and others, ed. Michael W. Jennings, Howard Eiland, and Gary Smith (Cambridge, Massachusetts: The Belknap Press of Harvard University Press, 1999), p. 464.

CHAPTER 1

1. See David Brodbeck, "Brahms's Schubert," *American Brahms Society Newsletter* 15/1 (1997), p. 1; and Brian Newbould, "Schubert," in D. Kern Holoman, ed., *The Nineteenth-Century Symphony* (New York: Schirmer, 1997), p. 15.

2. Alex Ross, "Great Soul," *New Yorker* (3 February 1997), p. 78.

3. Georg Eismann, *Schumann: Ein Quellenwerk über sein Leben und Schaffen,* vol. 1 (Leipzig: Breitkopf und Härtel, 1956), p. 44.

4. See Martin Schoppe, ed., *Robert Schumann—selbstbiographische Notizen—Faksimile* (Zwickau: Robert-Schumann-Gesellschaft, n.d.). One of four similar manuscripts now at the Robert-Schumann-Haus in Zwickau, this autobiographical sketch probably dates from 1840, when Schumann was assembling application materials for a doctorate from the University of Jena.

5. *TB* 1, p. 111.

6. Clara Schumann, ed., *Jugendbriefe von Robert Schumann,* 2nd ed. (Leipzig: Breitkopf und Härtel, 1886), p. 82.

7. Ibid., p. 83. A diary entry for 31 October 1831 includes another suggestive passage. Commenting on the diverse ways in which genius manifests itself among composers, Schumann associates Bach's artistry with "gravity," Mozart's with "lightness," Beethoven's with "warmth," and Schubert's with "darkness," though he adds "even darkness isn't the right word." *TB* 1, p. 375.

8. *AmZ* 48 (July 1846), col. 472.

9. Marie Luise Maintz, *Franz Schubert in der Rezeption Robert Schumanns* (Kassel: Bärenreiter, 1995).

10. Eismann, *Schumann,* vol. 1, p. 44.

11. *TB* 1, pp. 96, 119.

12. *TB* 1, pp. 116, 165, 166. Schumann's poetic description comes from a diary entry of 19 August 1828 (*TB* 1, p. 119). In late May 1831, he similarly described Schubert's Polonaises as "the pinnacle of Romantic rapture" (*TB* 1, p. 333).

13. *TB* 1, p. 113.

14. *TB* 1, p. 113.

15. Letter of 6 November 1829, in Schumann, *Jugendbriefe,* p. 85.

16. *TB* 1, p. 178.

17. *TB* 1, p. 420.

18. *NZfM* 13 (1840), p. 3.

19. To judge from his diary, the eighteen-year-old Schumann was probably enamored of Agnes Carus (see, e.g., the entries for 20 August 1828: "Dreams about Agnes" [*TB* 1, p. 119] and for 11 December 1828: "my melancholy bliss and [Agnes's] eyes" [*TB* 1, p. 153]). Eight years his senior and a gifted singer, she was the chief interpreter of the half-dozen or so settings of texts by Justinus Kerner that Schumann composed during the summer of 1828.

Schumann either heard or was involved in the performance of the following Schubert songs at the Carus home: "Gretchen am Spinnrade," D. 118; "Über allen Gipfeln ist Ruh'," D. 768; "Erlkönig," D. 328; "Das Heimweh," D. 851; "Die Allmacht," D. 852; and "Im Freien," D. 880 (see the entries of 11 and 14 December 1828, in *TB* 1, pp. 153 and 156). In a diary entry from this time, Schumann even berated Heinrich Marschner, then serving as music director of the Leipzig Theater, because he "seemed not to value Schubert's songs highly enough" (12 December 1828, *TB* 1, p. 155).

20. *NZfM* 19 (1843), pp. 34–35.

21. *NZfM* 8 (1838), p. 177; and *NZfM* 11 (1839), p. 71. On the potentially adverse effects of a poor poem on the resultant musical setting, see *NZfM* 13 (1840), p. 119. Schumann's view of Schubert's lieder cannot be attributed to limited familiarity. In an amusing diary entry from late May 1831, he wrote: "Bellowed through about twenty volumes of Schubert's songs with Christian Glock" (*TB* 1, p. 335). Though Schumann mentioned few specific Schubert songs in his critical writings—see the references to "Erlkönig" in *NZfM* 12 (1840), p. 103, and "Der Wanderer," D. 489, in *NZfM* 13 (1840), p. 156—his comments on the wide range of Schubert's poets, who run the gamut from Aeschylus and Klopstock to the "easygoing" Wilhelm Müller, show an awareness of the extent of the repertory. See "Aus Franz Schubert's Nachlass," *NZfM* 8 (1838), p. 177.

22. Letter of 6 January 1839 to Breitkopf und Härtel, in *BNF*, pp. 424–25.

23. See Newbould, "Schubert," p. 11.

24. Letter of 11 December 1839, in *BNF*, p. 175.

25. Letter of 11 December 1839, in *BrKG*, vol. 2, p. 826. Not everyone found the length of Schubert's symphony to be as heavenly as Schumann did. According to Anton Schindler, for instance, the finale was "stretched out to the point of fatigue." Early attempts to perform the whole symphony or individual movements in Vienna (in 1828, 1836, and 1839) failed to materialize due to the complaints of orchestral players about the work's inordinate length. Even Mendelssohn felt compelled to make cuts for the Leipzig premiere of the symphony in March 1839. See Thomas Denny, "Too Long? Too Loose? and Too Light? Critical Thoughts about Schubert's Mature Finales," *Studies in Music* 23 (1989), pp. 25, 48.

26. "Und diese himmlische Länge der Symphonie, wie ein dicker Roman in vier Bänden etwa von Jean Paul, der auch niemals endigen kann und aus den besten Gründen zwar, um auch den Leser hinterher nachschaffen zu lassen." *NZfM* 12 (1840), p. 82. Schumann also alludes to the symphony's "heavenly length . . . like a novel in four volumes, longer than [Beethoven's] Ninth Symphony" in a letter to Clara of 11 December 1839. See *BrKG*, vol. 2, p. 826.

27. *NZfM* 12 (1840), p. 83.

28. Ibid.

29. See Mark Evan Bonds, *After Beethoven: Imperatives of Originality in the Symphony* (Cambridge, Massachusetts: Harvard University Press, 1996), p. 116; and Newbould, "Schubert," p. 11.

30. *NZfM* 12 (1840), p. 83.

31. On the affinities between Schumann's Symphony No. 1 and Schubert's C-major Symphony, see Bonds, *After Beethoven*, p. 117; and my *Robert Schumann: Herald of a "New Poetic Age"* (New York: Oxford University Press, 1997), p. 319.

32. See the entries in Schumann's household account books for 6–28 December 1845 (*TB* 3, pp. 408–10). The "Second" Symphony was in fact the third in order of

composition. In October 1840, about seven months after the premiere of his First Symphony, Schumann finished a D-minor Symphony that he revised and reorchestrated in December 1851. This composition was published as his Fourth Symphony, Op. 120, in 1853.

33. *NZfM* 8 (1838), p. 178.

34. *NZfM* 13 (1840), p. 198.

35. *NZfM* 5 (1836), p. 208. The dating of the Piano Trio in B flat is still a matter of conjecture. According to notations in the autograph of the Piano Trio in E flat, Schubert had completed three movements of that work by November 1827; the entire trio was completed no later than 21 February 1828, when Schubert offered it for publication to Schott in Mainz. In mid-April it was accepted by the Leipzig publisher Heinrich Probst, who issued it as Op. 100 in October 1828; as such, it was the only one of Schubert's works to appear in print outside of Austria during his lifetime. For the Piano Trio in B flat no autograph materials survive, and it was not published until June 1836, when it appeared under the imprint of the Viennese firm of Diabelli as Op. 99. While we know that the first performance of the E♭ trio took place no later than 26 March 1828 (in a concert devoted to Schubert's works), it is impossible to say with certainty which of the trios was performed on two additional occasions: a concert of the Schuppanzigh quartet in late December 1827 and a Schubertiade held at the home of Josef von Spaun on 28 January 1828. Since Schubert himself designated the Piano Trio in B flat as his "First," it was perhaps the first of the two to be performed in public, at the December 1827 concert of Schuppanzigh's group. For a summary of the evidence, see Stephen E. Hefling and David S. Tartakoff, "Schubert's Chamber Music," in Stephen E. Hefling, ed., *Nineteenth-Century Chamber Music* (New York: Schirmer, 1998), p. 109; see also *NA*, series 6, vol. 7: *Werke für Klavier und mehrere Instrumente*, ed. Arnold Feil (Kassel: Bärenreiter, 1975), p. xii.

36. "Innerlich unterscheiden sie sich aber wesentlich von einander. Der erste Satz, der dort tiefer Zorn und wiederum überschwengliche Sehnsucht, ist in unserm anmuthig, vertrauend, jungfräulich; das Adagio, das dort ein Seufzer, der sich bis zur schreienden Herzensangst steigert, ist hier ein seliges Träumen, ein Auf- und Niederwallen schön menschlicher Empfindung. Die Scherzo's ähneln sich; doch gebe ich dem im früher erschienenen zweiten Trio den Vorzug. Ueber die letzten Sätze entscheid' ich nicht. Mit einem Worte, das zweite Trio ist mehr handelnd, männlich, dramatisch, unseres dagegen leidend, weiblich, lyrisch." *NZfM* 5 (27 December 1836), p. 208.

37. See Brian Newbould, *Schubert: The Music and the Man* (London: Victor Gollancz, 1997), pp. 369–70.

38. *TB* 1, pp. 150–52.

39. "Wunderbar rührend spielt öfter die klagende Romanze des zweiten Satzes in das wilde Treiben des Schmerzes und der Lust, und hin und wieder lassen sich mancherley Stimmen der Erinnerung vernehmen, deren Anklang schnell wieder übertäubt wird von der Unruhe der Gegenwart, die ihre Nebel verhüllend über den sonst freundlichen Morgen der Zukunft breitet." *AmZ* 30 (10 December 1828), cols. 841–42.

40. *TB* 1, pp. 152, 168, 171, 180. Schubert's E flat–major Piano Trio continued to play a part in Schumann's convivial music making after his move from Leipzig to Heidelberg later in 1829. In the last week of January 1830, he and two other law students—Hermann Wolff, an amateur violinist, and J. August Lemke, a cellist—

rehearsed the trio and performed it at the home of J. Mitchell, a wealthy Englishman who resided in Heidelberg. See *TB* 1, p. 223.

41. *TB* 1, p. 180. A "gallopade" is a quick dance in duple meter.

42. *TB* 1, p. 182.

43. *TB* 1, p. 184. The draft of the quartet was notated on four staves disposed as follows: piano (right hand only), violin, viola, and cello. Schumann's score contains numerous instrumental designations (flute, oboe, clarinet, bassoon, horn, strings) for the projected orchestral version. See Robert Schumann, *Quartett c-Moll für Pianoforte, Violino, Viola und Violoncello (1829)*, ed. Wolfgang Boetticher (Wilhelmshaven: Heinrichshofen's Verlag, 1979), *passim*.

44. "Sehr gut erinnere ich mich einer Stelle in einer meiner Compositionen (1828), von der ich mir sagte, sie sei *romantisch*, wo mir ein vom der alten Musikcharakter abweichender Geist sich mir eröffnete, ein neues poëtisches Leben sich mir zu erschliessen schien (es war das Trio eines Scherzo eines Clavierquartettes)." *TB* 2, p. 402.

45. These similarities may not be entirely fortuitous. On 25 January 1829, when work on his Piano Quartet was well under way, Schumann and his friends read through all three of Beethoven's piano trios, Op. 1. See *TB* 1, p. 170.

46. *TB* 1, p. 151.

47. *TB* 1, pp. 171, 180.

48. Newbould, *Schubert*, p. 371.

49. See Richard Cohn, "As Wonderful as Star Clusters: Instruments for Gazing at Tonality in Schubert," *19th Century Music* 22/3 (1999), pp. 213–32. Cf. Donald Francis Tovey, "Tonality in Schubert" (1928), in *The Main Stream of Music and Other Essays* (Cleveland: Meridian, 1959), p. 159.

50. Cohn, "As Wonderful as Star Clusters," p. 215.

51. Overt cyclic connections of this sort are relatively rare in Schubert's instrumental music. Two instances come to mind that are as different from each other as they are from Schubert's approach to intermovement recall in the Piano Trio in E flat. In the A-major Piano Sonata, D. 959, the last six bars of the finale allude to the rhythmic profile (and, even more obliquely, to the harmonic progression) of the opening idea of the first movement, thus rounding out the work in a rather obvious sort of way, though not significantly altering its course. The situation in the "Wanderer" Fantasy is quite exceptional. Nearly the whole of the work's thematic substance radiates outward from the song-derived theme of the second movement, an Adagio in C♯ minor. A somewhat looser network of recurrent ideas also informs the Fantasie in C for Violin and Piano (D. 934). One of those ideas is the theme of the slow movement (based on the song "Sei mir gegrüßest," D. 741), which makes a final appearance just before the virtuosic Presto that brings the Fantasie to a close. The similarity between this pattern of recurrence and the cyclic scheme of the Piano Trio in E flat may not be fortuitous: the Fantasie was completed in December 1827, immediately on the heels of the trio. For a thorough—and fair—assessment of this much-criticized piece, see Patrick McCreless, "A Candidate for the Canon? A New Look at Schubert's Fantasie in C major for Violin and Piano," *19th Century Music* 20/3 (1997), pp. 205–30.

52. See Newbould, *Schubert*, p. 370.

53. On Schubert's reconfiguration of the original Swedish melody, see Newbould, *Schubert*, pp. 370–71; and Hefling and Tartakoff, "Schubert's Chamber Music," pp. 116–18. Schubert alludes to the descending fifth of the folk melody at several points in the first movement as well (see, e.g., mm. 72–74, 81–83). As Newbould has

observed, the autograph manuscript reveals that the measures in which these references occur were probably added after the body of the movement was essentially complete. Regardless of whether they were inserted after Schubert had drafted the second movement and finale, they serve to heighten the unity of the cycle as a whole. See Newbould, *Schubert*, p. 372.

54. Pointing to a number of melodic, gestural, and tonal parallels between Schubert's theme and the main idea of the Marcia funebre from the "Eroica" Symphony, Christopher Gibbs has recently interpreted the slow movement of Schubert's piano trio as a "*Tombeau de Beethoven.*" See *The Life of Schubert* (Cambridge: Cambridge University Press, 2000), pp. 157–58, 196 (note 8).

55. See note 39.

56. Translation quoted from Hefling and Tartakoff, "Schubert's Chamber Music," p. 116.

57. *NZfM* 5 (27 December 1836), p. 208.

58. The following comments offer only the bare essentials of a complex and wideranging topic. For a fuller account of Schubert's formal expansiveness, see Denny, "Too Long? Too Loose? and Too Light?" pp. 27–34.

59. See Carl Dahlhaus, "Sonata Form in Schubert: The First Movement of the G-Major String Quartet, Op. 161 (D. 887)," trans. Thilo Reinhard, in Walter Frisch, ed., *Schubert: Critical and Analytical Studies* (Lincoln: University of Nebraska Press, 1986), pp. 1–12. As Dahlhaus convincingly shows, each of the principal sections (exposition, development, recapitulation) of the G-major Quartet's opening movement contains embedded within it one or more theme-and-variation forms.

60. See Donald Francis Tovey, "Franz Schubert (1797–1828)," in *The Main Stream of Music and Other Essays*, orig. publ. in *The Heritage of Music*, vol. 1 [Oxford University Press, 1927], p. 125. In Tovey's view, the problem does not reside in the "scheme" but in the "impossible scale on which it is worked out."

61. In the aptly chosen words of Hefling and Tartakoff, Schubert's development "proceeds with the formulaic regularity of a parabolic curve into infinity." See "Schubert's Chamber Music," p. 115.

62. For Tovey, the "enormous sprawling forms of the typical Schubert finales are the outcome of a sheer irresponsibility that has involved him in little or no strain" ("Franz Schubert," p. 127). In fact, the orginal version of the finale of the Piano Trio in E flat displayed an even greater "irresponsibility" than Tovey might have imagined. Before sending the manuscript to Probst in May 1828, Schubert deleted two long passages from the development section (making for a total of ninety-nine bars), adding in the note he enclosed with his score: "These deletions are to be observed to the letter." See Otto Erich Deutsch, *Schubert: Die Dokumente seines Lebens*, in *NA*, series 8, vol. 5 [Kassel: Bärenreiter, 1964]), p. 516. Performers may be tempted to render Schubert's movement in its original form—a possibility encouraged by the layout of the trio in the *Neue Ausgabe* of Schubert's works—in part because one of the excised passages includes the single instance where Schubert combines the slow movement's main theme with the evocation of the *cimbalon* from the finale's exposition. The earlier version of the finale has been recorded by the Mozartean Players (Harmonia Mundi/France HMU 907095). Of all of Schubert's mature finales, perhaps none has been criticized so harshly for its excessive length as that of the Piano Trio in E flat. For a summary of the critical responses to this aspect of the movement, see Denny, "Too Long? Too Loose? and Too Light?" p. 25.

63. To cite only the most obvious examples: Schumann makes extensive use of the "isorhythmic" technique in the opening movement and finale of his First Symphony, the development sections of the first movements of all four symphonies draw to varying degrees on the strophic variation principle, Schubertian three-key expositions appear in the first movements of the Second and Third Symphonies, and large-scale structural parallelism informs the finale of the First Symphony. Parallel designs also play a major role in Schumann's larger keyboard works of the 1830s. See Linda Roesner, "Schumann's 'Parallel' Forms," *19th Century Music* 14 (1991), pp. 265–78. We will revisit this issue in the next chapter.

64. So, too, might the waltzlike third movement, In mäßiger Bewegung, of Schumann's F-major Piano Trio (Op. 80, composed in 1847). The outer sections of the movement abound in canons between all possible pairings of instruments.

65. See note 8.

66. Examples of Beethoven's use of intermovement thematic recall can be found in the Fifth and Ninth Symphonies, the C-major Cello Sonata (Op. 102, no. 1), and the A-major Piano Sonata (Op. 101). The only instance that I can think of where Beethoven couples the explicit recall of material from an earlier movement with an apotheotic close occurs in the last movement of the Piano Sonata in A flat, Op. 110, but even here the material invoked is not a theme but an abstract intervallic pattern: the falling third and rising fourth of the sonata's opening idea.

67. In his First Symphony, composed a little over a year before, Schumann linked the inner movements of the cycle in a similar manner. The forceful opening theme of the symphony's Scherzo is a transformed variant of the otherworldly trombone chorale that serves as the coda of the preceding slow movement.

68. See *TB* 2, p. 220. Fugal finales occur in Mozart's K. 387 and Haydn's Op. 20, nos. 2, 4, 5, and Op. 50, no. 4. Beethoven integrates fugal rhetoric into the sonata form in the Andante scherzoso quasi Allegretto of Op. 18, no. 4, and the finale of Op. 59, no. 3.

At the same time that Schumann was studying string quartets, he was also "hard at work on counterpoint and fugue." (See *TB* 2, p. 215.) His hard work is much in evidence in the finales of the Piano Quintet and Piano Quartet.

CHAPTER 2

Chapter 2 draws on my article, "'One More Beautiful Memory of Schubert': Schumann's Critique of the Impromptus, D. 935," *Musical Quarterly* 84(4), Winter 2000, pp. 604–18.

1. See chapter 1, p. 20.

2. See chapter 1, pp. 15–18.

3. *JBr*, pp. 82–83.

4. Emil Staiger, *Basic Concepts of Poetics*, trans. J. C. Hudson and L. T. Frank, ed. M. Burkhard and L. T. Frank (University Park: Pennsylvania State University Press, 1991, trans. of *Grundbegriffe der Poetik*, [1946]), p. 186.

5. Ibid., p. 186.

6. Ibid., p. 188.

7. Ibid., p. 187.

8. See chapter 1, pp. 30–31.

9. This is an admittedly schematic characterization of the temporal quality of Beethoven's music. As Karol Berger has recently demonstrated, Beethoven frequently

established a dichotomy between two "ontological levels" in his earlier and later piano sonatas, as well as in his late string quartets: a "real" world of action and dynamism and an "imaginary" world in which the normal laws of musical space and time appear to be suspended. As a realm of reverie, contemplation, and inwardness, the imaginary world is stamped by what I am calling a temporality of pastness. See Karol Berger, "Beethoven and the Aesthetic State," in Mark Evan Bonds, ed., *Beethoven Forum* 7 (Lincoln: University of Nebraska Press, 1999), pp. 17–44. To judge from his critical writings, Schumann located the essence of Beethoven's music in its purposeful motion toward a goal, that is, in temporalities of presence and futurity.

10. *TB* 1, p. 113.

11. Robert Schumann, "Der Psychometer," *NZfM* 1 (26 May 1834), p. 63.

12. Schumann appended a brief paragraph on Liszt's transcriptions of several Schubert lieder to the main body of the review; that section is not translated here. See *NZfM* 9 (1838), pp. 192–93. The original text of the portion of the review devoted to the Impromptus (D. 935) reads as follows:

> Er hätte es noch erleben können, wie man ihn jetzt feiert; es hätte ihm zum Höchsten begeistern müssen. Nun er schon lange ruht, wollen wir sorgsam sammeln und aufzeichnen, was er uns hinterlassen; es ist nichts darunter, was nicht von seinem Geiste zeugte, nur wenigen Werken ist das Siegel ihres Verfassers so klar aufgedrückt, als den seinigen. So flüstert es denn in den zwei ersten Impromptus auf allen Seiten "Franz Schubert" wie wir ihn kennen in seiner unerschöpflichen Laune, wie er uns reizt, und täuscht und wieder fesselt, finden wir ihn wieder. Doch glaub' ich kaum, dass Schubert diese Sätze wirklich "Impromptus" überschrieben; der erste ist so offenbar der erste Satz einer Sonate, so vollkommen ausgeführt und abgeschlossen, dass gar kein Zweifel aufkommen kann. Das zweite Impromptu halte ich für den zweiten Satz derselben Sonate; in Tonart und Charakter schliesst es sich dem ersten knapp an. Wo die Schlusssätze hinkommen, ob Schubert die Sonate vollendet, oder nicht, müssten seine Freunde wissen; man könnte vielleicht das vierte Impromptu als das Finale betrachten, doch spricht, wenn auch die Tonart dafür, die Flüchtigkeit in der ganzen Anlage beinahe dagegen. Es sind also Vermuthungen, die nur eine Einsicht in die Originalmanuscripte aufklären könnte. Für gering halte ich sie nicht; es kömmt zwar wenig auf Titel und Ueberschriften an; anderseits ist aber eine Sonatenarbeit eine so schöne Zier im Werkkranz eines Componisten, dass ich Sch'n. gern zu seinen vielen noch eine andichten möchte, ja zwanzig. Was das dritte Impromptu anlangt, so hätte ich es kaum für eine Schubert'sche Arbeit, höchstens für eine aus seiner Knabenzeit gehalten; es sind wenig oder gar nicht ausgezeichnete Variationen über ein ähnliches Thema. Erfindung und Phantasie fehlen ihnen gänzlich, worin sich Schubert gerade auch im Variationsgenre an andern Orten so schöpferisch gezeigt. So spiele man denn die zwei ersten Impromptus hinter einander, schliesse ihnen, um lebhaft zu enden, das vierte an, und man hat, wenn auch keine vollständige Sonate, so eine schöne Erinnerung an ihn mehr. Kennt man seine Weise schon, so bedarf es fast nur einmaligen Durchspielens, sie vollkommen inne zu haben. Im ersten Satz ist es der leichte phantastische Zierrath zwischen den melodischen Ruhestellen, was uns in Schlummer wiegen möchte; das Ganze ist in einer leidenden Stunde geschaffen, wie im Nachdenken an Vergangenes. Der zweite Satz hat einen mehr beschaulichen Charakter, in der Art,

wie es viel von Schubert gibt; anders der dritte (das vierte Impromptu), schwollend, aber leise und gut: man kann es kaum vergreifen; Beethoven's "Wuth über den verlornen Groschen," ein sehr lächerliches, wenig bekanntes Stück fiel mir manchmal dabei ein.

13. Charles Fisk has recently taken up this invitation in a subtle and nuanced discussion of Schubert's evocation of memory in the Op. 142/D. 935 set as a whole. See his *Returning Cycles: Contexts for the Interpretation of Schubert's Impromptus and Last Sonatas* (Berkeley: University of California Press, 2001), pp. 141–79, *passim*.

14. See Otto Erich Deutsch, *Schubert: Die Dokumente seines Lebens*, in NA, series 8, vol. 5 (Kassel: Bärenreiter, 1964), p. 545. Schubert first broached the possibility of placing the Impromptus with Schott in a letter of 21 February 1828. Among the other pieces that he offered for publication at the same time was the recently completed Piano Trio in E flat.

15. Tomášek's first set of eclogues was composed in 1807 and appeared in print four or five years later as Op. 35. The collection obviously struck a chord with the public, for during the following decade Tomášek issued five more volumes that bore the same title (Opp. 39, 47, 51, 63, and 66); a final volume of eclogues, Op. 83, appeared in 1840. Between about 1810 and 1840 Tomášek also published three volumes of rhapsodies (Opp. 40, 41, and 110) and a collection of three dithyrambs (Op. 65).

16. Although there is no hard evidence that Schubert knew Tomášek's music and while the evidence for his personal contact with Voříšek in Vienna is purely circumstantial, the stylistic points of contact between collections such as Schubert's *Momens musicals*, D. 780 (published in 1828), and Voříšek 's Impromptus are probably not coincidental. On the possible lines of influence that run from Tomášek and Voříšek to Schubert, see Willi Kahl, "Das lyrische Klavierstück Schuberts und seiner Vorgänger seit 1810," *Archiv für Musikwissenschaft* 3 (1921), pp. 111–22.

17. See especially Jeffrey Kallberg, "The Rhetoric of Genre: Chopin's Nocturne in G Minor," *19th Century Music* 10 (1988), pp. 239–46.

18. Likewise, Schumann originally took Schubert's Grand Duo for Piano, Four Hands (D. 812) to be a symphony arranged for piano. Even after seeing the manuscript, Schumann held to this opinion: "Whoever writes as much as Schubert doesn't bother much over titles, so perhaps in haste he called the work a sonata, even though it stood complete in his head as a symphony" *NZfM* 8 (5 June 1838), p. 178.

19. See chapter 1, p. 33.

20. What Fisk has written of the entire set of Impromptus applies equally well to the first one: although D. 935 is not a sonata, "it does represent the integrative, consolidating response of a composer grounded in sonata forms to one of his most extraordinary compositional innovations." See *Returning Cycles*, p. 179.

21. See Schumann's definition of the term "Capriccio" for Herloßsohn's *Damenkonversationslexikon*, in GS 2, p. 207; and his review of Berlioz's *Symphonie fantastique*, in *NZfM* 3 (1835), p. 37. For a discussion of large-scale formal symmetries in Schumann's earlier piano works, see Linda Roesner, "Schumann's 'Parallel' Forms," *19th Century Music* 14 (1991), pp. 265–78. On the finales of the Piano Quintet and Piano Quartet, see chapter 1, pp. 33–46.

22. The "undistinguished theme" of the third Impromptu, in B♭ major, has often been compared to the well-known "Entre'act" (no. 5) from Schubert's incidental music for *Rosamunde* (D. 797) and also to the theme of the slow movement from his A-minor String Quartet (D. 804). See, for instance, William Kinderman, "Schubert's

Piano Music: Probing the Human Condition," in Christopher Gibbs, ed., *The Cambridge Companion to Schubert* (Cambridge: Cambridge University Press, 1997), p. 168. To maintain, as Schumann did, that the variations are "totally lacking in invention and fantasy" is overly harsh. Granted, most of them are of the straightforward, melodic type and two (the second and fifth) are conceived in the virtuoso idiom toward which Schumann had grown increasingly negative over the years. But the third variation, in the minor mode, plumbs genuine emotional depths, and the fourth, in G♭, dissolves the theme into luxurious arabesques.

23. Schubert numbered the Impromptus (D. 935) "5" through "8," suggesting that they merely represented a continuation of the earlier set of Impromptus (D. 899), which he numbered "1" through "4." See Walther Dürr's *Vorwort* to *NA*, series 7 (*Klaviermusik*), section 2 ("Werke für Klavier zu zwei Händen", vol. 5: *Klaviersücke II*), ed. Christa Landon and Walther Dürr (Kassel: Bärenreiter, 1984), p. xiii. Yet as Fisk points out, Schubert wrote out both sets in separate manuscripts; taken together with the musical connections among the pieces in the second set in particular, this indicates that at some level Schubert conceived each group as a quasi-independent set. See *Returning Cycles*, p. 142.

24. "Ein Denkmal ist eine vorwärts gedrehte Ruine (wie diese ein rückwärts gedrehte Monument.)" See Schumann's "Monument für Beethoven—vier Stimmen darüber," *NZfM* 4 (1836), p. 212. Fragments may also point toward the future. For Friedrich Schlegel, a "project" (or "fragment of the future") is "a subjective embryo of a developing object" (*Athenäum Fragments*, no. 22). Pointing forward to its realization as a self-sufficient whole, the fragment in this case makes no attempt to mask its incompletion.

25. Schumann, "Der Psychometer," p. 63.

26. On this point, see also Fisk, *Returning Cycles*, p. 165.

27. Henri Bergson, *Matter and Memory*, trans. N. M. Paul and W. S. Palmer (New York: Zone Books, 1991, trans. of *Matiere et mémoire*, 5th ed., [1908]), p. 13. The passage also resonates with one of Staiger's observations on the tendency of reflective verse to blur the distinctions among temporal modes: "The present, the past, [and] even the future can be interiorized and remembered in lyric poetry." See *Basic Concepts of Poetics*, p. 82.

28. As Peter Gülke has noted, the "actuality" of the piece resides in the A♭-major theme of section D; the sense of arrival is short-lived, however, for the theme soon dissolves into "a backward glance of reminiscence." See Gülke's *Franz Schubert und seine Zeit* (Laaber: Laaber-Verlag, 1991), p. 302.

29. For Fisk, the idea that the music of section B strives to remember is the opening theme (mm. 1–13), which he describes as "a potential emblem for the all-pervasive power of lost or unarticulated memory." This theme, in Fisk's reading, is "impenetrable, signifying a closed past and fateful setting for the music that follows." See *Returning Cycles*, pp. 151, 159.

30. Quoted from Proust's analysis of the *mémoire involuntaire* in *Remembrance of Things Past*, part 8: *The Past Recaptured*, trans. Stephen Hudson and Andreas Meyer (New York: Vintage, 1982), pp. 903–8. For a summary of the structure, content, and function of the *moments bienheureux*, see Roger Shattuck, *Proust's Binoculars* (Princeton: Princeton University Press, 1962), pp. 69–78.

31. As Fisk observes, the duet texture in these sections may represent "different,

only partly articulated voices within a single lone protagonist." See *Returning Cycles*, p. 157.

32. Schubert may well have known Leopold Czapek's *Impromptu brillant* (Op. 6), a set of bravura variations published in 1826 by Mechetti, the same firm that issued Vořišek's Impromptus (Op. 7) in 1822.

33. Friedrich Schlegel, *Fragmente zur Litteratur und Poesie*, no. 587, in *Kritische Friedrich Schlegel Ausgabe* [*KFSA*], vol. 16, ed. Hans Eichner (Munich: Thomas, 1981), p. 134.

34. Among the many fragments from Schlegel's notebooks that pursue this line of thought, I quote only a small sample: "An epical, lyrical, [and] dramatic *form* exists apart from the spirit of the old genres bearing these names" (*Fragmente zur Litteratur und Poesie*, no. 322, in *KFSA*, vol. 16, p. 111). "Even among novels there is a lyrical-epical-dramatic genre" (no. 1073, p. 174). "In Shakespeare's tragedies the form is dramatic, while the spirit and aim are novelistic" (*Philosophische Fragmente. Erste Epoche II*, no. 55, in *KFSA*, vol. 18, ed. Ernst Behler [Zurich: Thomas, 1963], p. 23). See also Peter Szondi's classic study, "Friedrich Schlegel's Theory of Poetical Genres: A Reconstruction from the Posthumous Fragments," in *On Textual Understanding and Other Essays*, trans. Harvey Mendelsohn (Minneapolis: University of Minnesota Press, 1986), pp. 90ff.

35. Robert Schumann, "Sonaten für das Klavier," *NZfM* 10 (1839), p. 134.

36. *NZfM* 3 (1835), p. 208.

37. For a discussion of the earlier incarnations of this title—"Romanza," "Legende," and "Erzählend im Legenden Ton" ("narrated in the tone of a legend")—see Nicholas Marston, *Schumann: Fantasie, Op. 17* (Cambridge: Cambridge University Press, 1992), pp. 17, 20–21.

38. In addition to these reminiscences of previous events we also find premonitions of later ones. The phrase that begins with the upbeat to m. 157, for instance, offers a foretaste of the movement's lyrical coda (Adagio), a passage that has frequently been heard as an allusion to the last song of Beethoven's *An die ferne Geliebte*. Yet even a melodic foreshadowing like this one is imbued with the temporality of pastness: on first hearing, it strikes us as a fragment of a half-remembered tune. Only at the end of the movement are we able to interpret it, retrospectively, as the kind of presentiment that sometimes comes to us in dreams.

39. Composed during the same year, the *Concertstück* for four horns and orchestra (Op. 88) embodies a similar opposition between contrasting sound worlds. Midway through the second movement (Romanze), a sumptuous melody in $B^\flat$ is presented first by the orchestra, then by the solo horns over pizzicato triplets in the cellos. The same melody recurs as a moment of sublime removal in the midst of the boisterous motivic and rhythmic interplay of the finale. Transposed to E major, the music from the slow movement is now punctuated with references to the fanfares that appeared earlier in the finale—reminders of the temporal presence to which the interlude offers a momentary alternative.

40. Berthold Hoeckner, "Schumann and Romantic Distance," *Journal of the American Musicological Society* 50/1 (1997), p. 109.

41. Ibid., pp. 102–4.

42. For a discussion of this passage as an instance of the kind of "voice exchange" that allowed Schumann to overcome the distance that separated him and Clara, see Hoeckner, "Schumann and Romantic Distance," pp. 126–31.

43. Theodor Adorno, *Mahler: A Musical Physiognomy,* trans. Edmond Jephcott (Chicago: University of Chicago Press, 1992, trans. of *Mahler: Eine musikalische Physiognomik,* [1971]), p. 21.

CHAPTER 3

1. *BrKG* 1, p. 33; *CC* 1, pp. 31–32.

2. Berthold Litzmann, ed., *Clara Schumann–Johannes Brahms: Briefe aus den Jahren 1853–1896,* vol. 1 (Leipzig: Breitkopf und Härtel, 1927), p. 198.

3. See, for example, Nicholas Temperley, in "Schumann and the Cipher—Letters and Comments," *Musical Times* 106 (1965), pp. 767–68; George Bozarth, "Brahms's First Piano Concerto, Op. 15: Genesis and Meaning," in Reinmar Emans and Matthias Wendt, eds., *Beiträge zur Geschichte des Konzerts: Festschrift Siegfried Kross zum 60. Geburtstag* (Bonn: Gundrum Schröder, 1990), p. 218, note 39; and Charles Rosen, "Secret Codes—Caspar David Friedrich, Robert Schumann," in *Romantic Poets, Critics, and Other Madmen* (Cambridge, Massachusetts: Harvard University Press, 1998), pp. 93–95. Rosen expresses similar views in "Aimez-Vous Brahms?" *New York Review of Books* 45/16 (22 October 1998), p. 66. See also my *Robert Schumann: Herald of a "New Poetic Age"* (New York: Oxford University Press, 1997), p. 159.

4. See David Brodbeck, "The Brahms-Joachim Counterpoint Exchange; or Robert, Clara, and 'the Best Harmony between Jos. and Joh.,'" in David Brodbeck, ed., *Brahms Studies,* vol. 1, (Lincoln: University of Nebraska Press, 1994), pp. 69–70, and *Brahms: Symphony No. 1* (Cambridge: Cambridge University Press, 1997), pp. 39–41; A. Peter Brown, "Brahms' Third Symphony and the New German School," *Journal of Musicology* 2 (1983), p. 436; Raymond Knapp, *Brahms and the Challenge of the Symphonic Tradition* (Stuyvesant, New York: Pendragon, 1997), p. 82; Malcolm MacDonald, *Brahms* (New York: Schirmer, 1990), p. 226; Michael Musgrave, "Brahms's First Symphony: Thematic Coherence and Its Secret Origin," *Music Analysis* 2/2 (1983), p. 128, and *The Music of Brahms* (London: Routledge and Kegan Paul, 1985), pp. 28, 138–41; Dillon Parmer, "Brahms, Song Quotation, and Secret Programs," *19th Century Music* 19/2 (1995), pp. 185, 189; Christopher Reynolds, "A Choral Symphony by Brahms?" *19th Century Music* 9/1 (1985), pp. 1–2, 7–8, 14–16, 20–22; Elaine R. Sisman, "Brahms and the Variation Canon," *19th Century Music* 14 (1990), p. 149; and Jan Swafford, *Johannes Brahms: A Biography* (New York: Knopf, 1997), pp. 123–24. Kenneth Hull adopts a "stance of cautious acceptance of the 'Clara' cipher in "Allusive Irony in Brahms's Fourth Symphony," in David Brodbeck, ed., *Brahms Studies,* vol. 2 (Lincoln: University of Nebraska Press, 1998), p. 156.

For a recent contribution to the Schumann literature that makes use of the Clara cipher as a hermeneutic point of reference, see Melinda Boyd, "Gendered Voices: The *Liebesfrühling* Lieder of Robert and Clara Schumann," *19th Century Music* 23/2 (1999), pp. 145–62.

5. For a useful glossary of cryptographic terms, see Shawn Rosenheim, *The Cryptographic Imagination: Secret Writing from Edgar Poe to the Internet* (Baltimore: Johns Hopkins University Press, 1997), pp. 253–56.

6. Eric Sams, "Did Schumann Use Ciphers?" *Musical Times* 106 (1965), pp. 584–91; "The Schumann Ciphers," *Musical Times* 107 (1966), pp. 392–400; "The Schumann Ciphers—a Coda," *Musical Times* 107 (1966), pp. 1050–51; "Why Florestan and Euse-

bius?" *Musical Times* 108 (1967), pp. 131–34; "Politics, Literature, People in Schumann's Op. 136," *Musical Times* 109 (1968), pp. 25–27; *The Songs of Robert Schumann,* 1st ed. (New York: Norton, 1969), pp. 23–24 (this material is reproduced, essentially without change, in the second and third editions of 1975 and 1993); "The Tonal Analogue in Schumann's Music," *Proceedings of the Royal Musical Association* 96 (1969–70), pp. 112–14; "A Schumann Primer?" *Musical Times* 111 (1970), pp. 1096–97; "Schumann and the Tonal Analogue," in Alan Walker, ed., *Robert Schumann: The Man and His Music* (London: Barrie and Jenkins, 1972), pp. 398–401; and "Cryptography, Musical," in Stanley Sadie, ed., *The New Grove Dictionary of Music and Musicians,* vol. 5 (London: Macmillan, 1980), p. 80.

7. Eric Sams, "Brahms and His Musical Love Letters," *Musical Times* 112 (1971), pp. 329–30; and "Brahms and His Clara Themes," *Musical Times* 112 (1971), pp. 432–34.

8. Sams, "Brahms and His Musical Love Letters," p. 329.

9. This, at least, is what Schumann told his friend Anton Töpken. See my *Robert Schumann,* pp. 66, 513 (note 52).

10. Sams, "Did Schumann Use Ciphers?" p. 584.

11. Ibid.

12. Robert Haven Schauffler, *Florestan: The Life and Work of Robert Schumann* (New York: Holt, 1945), pp. 310–15; and Roger Fiske, "A Schumann Mystery," *Musical Times* 105 (1964), pp. 574–78.

13. Sams, "Did Schumann Use Ciphers?" p. 584.

14. Sams did, however, treat the pitch sequence C–B–A–G♯–A as the basic form of the cipher in some of his later writings. See note 35.

15. In a letter of 22 September 1837 to Ignaz Moscheles, Schumann observed that Asch, in addition to being the name of a "little Bohemian town" where he had a "musical girlfriend," also contained the "only musical letters" in his last name. See *BNF,* pp. 101–2.

16. Sams, "Why Florestan and Eusebius?" p. 133.

17. "Eusebius an Chiara," in *GS* 1, p. 119. Schumann made sporadic note of the name days in his household account books and diaries until 1853.

18. Sams, "Did Schumann Use Ciphers?" p. 586.

19. Fiske, "A Schumann Mystery," pp. 575–77.

20. Sams, "Did Schumann Use Ciphers?" pp. 584–85.

21. Sams, "The Schumann Ciphers," pp. 395–96.

22. Ibid., p. 496. See *TB* 2, p. 154. Schumann revised the symphony substantially in December 1851; it was published in this form, as Op. 120, in 1853.

23. Sams, "Did Schumann Use Ciphers?" p. 589.

24. Sams, "Politics, Literature, People in Schumann's Op. 136," pp. 25–27.

25. Sams, "Did Schumann Use Ciphers?" p. 590.

26. Ibid., p. 399.

27. Ibid., pp. 399–400.

28. Sams, "The Schumann Ciphers," pp. 399–400, and "A Schumann Primer?" pp. 1,096–97.

29. Sams, "The Schumann Ciphers," p. 399.

30. Temperley, in "Schumann and the Cipher," pp. 767–68.

31. Malcolm Boyd, in "Schumann and the Cipher," p. 770.

32. See, for instance: Nancy Reich, *Clara Schumann: The Woman and the Artist* (Ithaca: Cornell University Press, 1985), p. 200; and R. Larry Todd, "On Quotation in

Schumann's Music," in R. Larry Todd, ed., *Schumann and His World*, (Princeton: Princeton University Press, 1994), p. 109.

33. See Anna Burton, "Robert Schumann and Clara Wieck: A Creative Partnership," *Music and Letters* 69 (1988), pp. 213–14; Nicholas Marston, *Schumann: Fantasie, Op. 17* (Cambridge: Cambridge University Press, 1992), p. 90; and Akio Mayeda, *Robert Schumanns Weg zur Symphonie* (Zurich: Atlantis, 1992), p. 450.

34. Cf. note 4.

35. Sams, *The Songs of Robert Schumann*, p. 24, and "The Tonal Analogue in Schumann's Music," p. 113.

36. During middle age, Gade posed for a photograph under which was printed a musical staff with four pitches in "retrograde-inversion" notation. That is, whether the pitches are read right-side-up (in treble clef) or upside down and backward (in alto clef), the resultant plaintext is the same: **GADE.** This portrait is reproduced in Bernhard Appel, *Robert Schumann's "Album für die Jugend"* (Zurich: Atlantis, 1998), p. 161.

37. Note that Schumann did not attempt to encipher the opening **L** in the expression that serves as the plaintext for his "Rebus" (**Lass das Fade . . .**).

38. *BrKG* 1, p. 229. Consider also the following, one of several "little verses" that Schumann appended to a letter of 1 December 1838 to Clara: "Egmonts Geliebte Klärchen hieß— / O Namen wundersüßes! / Klärchen Schumann / Ein Engel den Namen ersann." ("Egmont's beloved was called Klärchen— / What a wondrously sweet name! / Klärchen Schumann / A name invented by an angel.") *BrKG* 1, p. 312.

39. *TB* 1, pp. 342–44.

40. "Paganini must have a magical effect on Cilia." Diary entry of 15 June 1831, in *TB* 1, pp. 342–43.

41. In a letter to Clara from early April 1838, Schumann wrote: "I just noticed that *Ehe* is a very musical word: it [contains] the interval of a fifth." Schumann then notates the pitches: e–b–e. *BrKG* 1, p. 145. The **Ehe** motive, if it is indeed that, takes a slightly different form in "Mondnacht": e'–b–e.

42. *BNF,* p. 92.

43. *GS* 1, p. 484.

44. *BNF,* pp. 101–2.

45. "Denn ich würde dem talentvollen Komponisten sofort die verwikeltesten Aufgaben stellen . . . Und damit er in Uebung käme, gäbe ich ihm noch etliche Themata dazu, nähmlich ausser den allbekannten *Bach, Fasch,* auch *Eis* (was freilich nur ein Thema aus eine Note wäre) . . . Caffé u. Fisch, Hase, Schaaf, damit ein ganzes Mittagessen daraus würde." Schumann copied the entire review, which appeared in the journal *Iris im Gebiet der Tonkunst*, into his diary. See *TB* 1, pp. 424–25.

46. Sams, "Did Schumann Use Ciphers?" p. 585.

47. *BrKG* 1, p. 75.

48. Letter of 6 February 1838. See *BrKG* 1, p. 93, and *CC* 1, pp. 94–95.

49. Schumann designated the opening two bars of the first piece in the *Davidsbündlertänze* as a "Motto v. C. W." This idea had served as the principal theme of Clara's Mazurka in G, no. 5 of her *Soirées musicales*. Schumann gave Clara's collection a glowing review in the 15 September 1837 of the *Neue Zeitschrift*. See *NZfM* 7 (1837), p. 87.

50. See Sams, "Did Schumann Use Ciphers?" p. 585, and "The Schumann Ciphers," p. 395; and Fiske, "A Schumann Mystery," pp. 575–77.

51. Sams, "The Schumann Ciphers," pp. 395–96.

52. Sams, "The Tonal Analogue in Schumann's Music," p. 114.

53. Sams, "The Schumann Ciphers," p. 399.

54. Sams, "A Schumann Primer?" p. 1096.

55. "Bericht an Jeanquirit in Augsburg über den letzten kunsthistorischen Ball beim Redacteur" ("Report to Jeanquirit in Augsburg on the editor's most recent art-historical ball"), in *NZfM* 6 (19 May 1837), pp. 159–61.

56. See Sams, "The Schumann Ciphers," p. 400, and Klüber, *Kryptographik*, p. 234. This is the only complete passage from Klüber's book that Sams quotes; it bears no relation to Schumann's "Bericht an Jeanquirit" apart from the chance similarity between the names Beda and Bede.

57. Sams, "The Schumann Ciphers," p. 399, and "A Schumann Primer?" p. 1096.

58. Johann Ludwig Klüber: *Kryptographik: Lehrbuch der Geheimschreibekunst (Chiffrir- und Dechiffrikunst) in Staats- und Privatgeschäften* (Tübingen: Cotta, 1809), pp. 278ff., 386–411, 471–72.

59. Sams, "A Schumann Primer?" p. 1096. The comment in Schumann's diary was prompted by Heinrich Dorn's rendition of "Narzisse," one of three character pieces for piano from his *Tonblumen* or *Bouquet musical*, Op. 10 (see *TB* 1, pp. 399–400). For Schumann's review of Dorn's cycle, see *NZfM* 1 (1834), pp. 97–99. Schumann had studied counterpoint with Dorn for about a year beginning in July 1831.

60. Johann Wolfgang von Goethe, *Westöstlicher Divan*, in *Goethes Werke (Hamburger Ausgabe in 14 Bänden), vol. 2: Gedichte und Epen II*, ed. Erich Trunz (Munich: C. H. Beck), p. 190.

61. Ibid., pp. 190–91.

62. Ibid., pp. 193–94.

63. For the reader who is interested in constructing such a lattice, here is an example drawn from Klüber's book: begin with the sequence of integers 1, 2, 3, 4, each of which is designated "n"; replace each integer (n) with ($n^2 + n$), thus yielding: 2, 6, 12, 20; then replace each integer (n) with $(2n + 1)^2$, the result being: 9, 25, 49, 81. See Klüber, *Kryptographik*, p. 217.

64. See *TB* 1, pp. 240–41, and Sams, "A Schumann Primer?" p. 1096. The purpose of Schumann's calculations is somewhat obscure. At the top of the page on which they appear, he wrote: "Rosen–24 Jahr—," perhaps a reference to the age of his friend Gisbert Rosen. The number 24 does indeed set off Schumann's computations, though at the time they were made Rosen was only twenty-two years old.

65. Sams, "The Schumann Ciphers," p. 396. See also Brodbeck, *Brahms: Symphony No. 1*, pp. 40–41, and Musgrave, "Brahms's First Symphony," p. 128, and *The Music of Brahms*, p. 141.

66. *TB* 2, p. 154.

67. *TB* 3, pp. 179–83. On 4 May 1841 he also began sketching an A-minor Phantasie for Piano and Orchestra, which would eventually become the first movement of the Piano Concerto in A minor (Op. 54).

68. *TB* 2, p. 162.

69. See *TB* 2, p. 164, and *BNF*, p. 434.

70. *TB* 2, p. 160.

71. Sams, "The Schumann Ciphers," p. 400.

72. Sams, "Did Schumann Use Ciphers?" p. 590.

73. See Brahms's letter of 25 April 1856 to Joachim, in *BLL*, p. 125.

74. Edgar Allan Poe, "The Gold-Bug" (1843), in *Collected Works of Edgar Allan Poe: Tales and Sketches 1843–1849*, ed. Thomas Ollive Mabbott (Cambridge Massachusetts: Harvard University Press, 1978), p. 806.

75. Thomas Mann, *Doctor Faustus: The Life of the German Composer Adrian Leverkühn As Told by a Friend*, trans. H. T. Lowe-Porter (New York: Random House, 1971), p. 155. *Hetæra esmerelda* is Leverkühn's private name for the prostitute from whom he contracted syphilis.

76. Cf. the description of Schumann as a composer who was well known for his "predilection for every sort of obscure enigma that runs counter to prosaic, mundane experience, from charades and masquerades based on hieroglyphs to symbolic and code names," in Thomas Phleps, " 'In meinen Tönen spreche ich': Biographische Chiffren in Kompositionen von Brahms," in Hanns-Werner Heister, ed., *Johannes Brahms oder Die Relativierung der "absoluten Musik"* (Hamburg: von Bockel, 1997), p. 209. In the footnote appended to his description of Schumann, Phleps cites the German translation of Sams's "Did Schumann Use Ciphers?": "Hat Schumann in seinen Werken Chiffren benutzt?" *NZfM* 127/6 (1966), pp. 218–24.

77. Swafford, *Johannes Brahms*, p. 124.

78. The same behavior characterizes Schumann's approach in what Sams calls a code letter to Clara ("The Schumann Ciphers," p. 400). Schumann leaves about twenty blank spaces in this letter of 10 July 1834 and then, as a postscript, simply writes out the missing words (*BrKG* 1, pp. 13–16; *CC* 1, pp. 11–14). This procedure bears only a superficial resemblance to one of the techniques for writing code letters described by Klüber (see *Kryptographik*, pp. 106–7). Called Heidel's method after the eighteenth-century philologist Wolfgang Ernst Heidel, it involves interweaving a secret message into a letter and providing a numerical key in a postscript. In Schumann's letter, there is no "secret message"; the postscript consists of isolated words that do not in themselves convey a coherent message. Moreover, the postscript can hardly be described as a numerical key; it is merely a string of words that can be easily plugged into the appropriate blank spots in the letter.

79. Walter Benjamin, "Old Forgotten Children's Books" (1924), in *Walter Benjamin: Selected Writings, vol. 1: 1913–1926*, ed. Marcus Bullock and Michael W. Jennings (Cambridge, Massachusetts: Belknap Press of Harvard University Press, 1996), pp. 410–11. Benjamin was not the only thinker to recognize the psychological ramifications of the picture puzzle. Sigmund Freud's comments on a series of eight cartoons originally published in a comic newspaper and titled "A French Nurse's Dream" reveal with particular clarity the close relationship between pictorial representations and the "dream-work." The dream involves a little boy who, suddenly overtaken by the urge to relieve himself while out on a walk with his French nanny, produces a stream large enough to float an ocean liner. Freud cleverly interprets the artist's rendering of the dream as a struggle between the craving for sleep and a stimulus toward waking. See Sigmund Freud, *The Interpretation of Dreams*, trans. and ed. James Strachey (New York: Basic Books, reprint of *The Standard Edition of the Complete Psychological Works of Sigmund Freud*, vols. 4 and 5 [London: Hogarth, 1953]), pp. 367–68. I would like to thank Stuart Feder for calling my attention to this passage.

80. Benjamin, "Old Forgotten Children's Books," p. 410.

81. Lyser did the colored lithographs for A. L. Grimm's *Fabelbuch* (1827) and his *Linas Mährchenbuch* (n.d.), two of the most widely known children's books of the Biedermeier period. He was responsible for both the text and illustrations of the *Buch der*

Mährchen für Töchter und Söhne gebildeter Stände (Leipzig, 1834). Between 1840 and 1860, Richter provided illustrations for nearly fifty children's books. See Appel, *Robert Schumann's "Album für die Jugend,"* p. 83.

82. For a thorough account of the role of illustrations in the genesis of the *Album für die Jugend* and of Schumann's close contacts during the late 1840s with the visual artists of the Dresden Academy, see Bernhard R. Appel, " 'Actually, Taken Directly from Family Life': Robert Schumann's *Album für die Jugend,"* trans. John Michael Cooper, in R. Larry Todd, ed., *Schumann and His World* (Princeton: Princeton University Press, 1994), pp. 184–88; and Appel, *Robert Schumann's "Album für die Jugend,"* pp. 73–92.

83. Seven of these arrangements survive: *Ein Stückchen von J. S. Bach* (from the Partita, BWV 829); *Ein Thema von G. F. Händel* (the theme of the "Harmonious Blacksmith" Variations); *Ein Stückchen von Mozart* ("Vedrai, carino" from *Don Giovanni*); *Eine berühmte Melodie von L. van Beethoven* (the "Ode to Joy" theme from the Ninth Symphony); an Andante by Beethoven (the theme of the slow movement of his Piano Sonata in E, Op. 109); "Ein Ländler von Franz Schubert" (the German dance, D. 783, no. 14); and "Ein Trinklied von Carl Maria von Weber" (Caspar's "Hier im ird'schen Jammerthal" from *Der Freischütz*). For a discussion and transcription of Schumann's "music history in examples," see Appel, *Robert Schumann's "Album für die Jugend,"* pp. 64–67, 299–308.

84. See Appel, *Robert Schumann's "Album für die Jugend,"* p. 95.

85. For an informative discussion of the amplified birthday album, see the commentary by Bernhard Appel in the facsimile edition of the manuscript *Robert Schumann, Klavierbüchlein für Marie: Ein Schumann-Handschrift im Beethoven-Haus Bonn* (Bonn: Beethoven-Haus, 1998), pp. 20–31. See also Dagmar Weise, "Ein bisher verschollenes Manuskript zu Schumanns 'Album für die Jugend,' " in Dagmar Weise, ed., *Festschrift Joseph Schmidt-Görg zum 60. Geburtstag* (Bonn: Beethoven-Haus, 1957), pp. 383–99.

86. The Mozart arrangement thus appears twice in Marie's *Klavierbüchlein:* first in the eight original *Stückchen* and then in the appendix of music-historical examples.

87. See Appel, " 'Actually, Taken Directly from Family Life,' " pp. 190, 198.

88. Walter Benjamin, "Notes for a Study of the Beauty of Colored Illustrations in Children's Books—Reflections on Lyser" (1918–21), in *Walter Benjamin,* vol. 1, p. 264. As Benjamin noted in one of his radio talks, "No pirate stories or ghost stories will grip the adolescent boy as powerfully as his ABC-book did when he was little." See Benjamin, "Children's Literature" (1929), in *Walter Benjamin: Selected Writings, vol. 2: 1927–1934,* trans. Rodney Livingstone and others, ed. Michael W. Jennings, Howard Eiland, and Gary Smith (Cambridge, Massachusetts: Belknap Press of Harvard University Press, 1999), p. 250.

89. Other classic children's texts from the late eighteenth and early nineteenth centuries include Amos Comenius's *Orbis Sensualium Pictus,* Johann Basedow's *Elementarwerk,* and Friedrich Justin Bertuch's *Bilderbuch für Kinder.* The last of these three publications, which was issued in installments between 1792 and 1847, consisted of twelve lavishly illustrated volumes, each with about a hundred colored engravings.

90. Eugenie Schumann, *Memoirs of Eugenie Schumann,* trans. Marie Busch (London: Eulenburg, 1985, orig. publ. *Erinnerungen* [Stuttgart, 1925]), p. 218.

91. The *Lebensregeln* were also issued as an appendix to the second edition of the *Album für die Jugend* (1851).

92. *GS* 2, p. 165.

93. Appel, " 'Actually, Taken Directly from Family Life,' " p. 176. For a transcription of the canon, see Appel, *Robert Schumann's "Album für die Jugend,"* p. 321.

94. The message would have been equally clear had Schumann decided to include the "music history in examples" in the published *Album für die Jugend,* as originally planned. In a preliminary list of the volume's contents, "Rebus" appears directly after one of the items in the little music history course, an arrangement of Mozart's "Vedrai, carino." See Appel, *Robert Schumann's "Album für die Jugend,"* p. 95.

95. Around 1840, the Viennese publisher Tobias Haslinger issued a volume of twenty-five lithograph picture puzzles titled *Rebus aus dem Gebiete der Musik.* Each of the puzzles combines individual letters, fragments of words, musical symbols, and pictorial representations in unusual and fanciful ways. In the twelfth rebus, for instance, the letters "s," "t," "u," "d," and "i" are arranged "around" (= *um,* in German) the pitch D♭ (= *Des*), yielding the plaintext **Studium des** (= "study of"). The plaintext in its entirety reads: **Das Studium des Generalbasses und des einfachen und doppelten Contrapunktes ist nicht zu vermeiden** (The study of figured bass and of simple and double counterpoint is not be be avoided). Haslinger's rebus not only makes explicit what is implicit in Schumann's; it also offers a further instance of the interdependence between a mode of representation (the picture puzzle) and the message it conveys (the centrality of craft). For a reproduction of and commentary on the lithograph, see Appel, *Robert Schumann's "Album für die Jugend,"* pp. 68–69.

96. Games of this sort were not only popular among children. The *Leipziger Illustrirten Zeitung* (1845)—a publication rich in picture puzzles based on proverbs, aphoristic sayings, and brief statements that concerned historical and current events—was directed primarily at an adult audience. As the Leipzig publisher J. J. Weber observed in the preface to the first issue of his *Rebus-Almanach* (1845), such puzzles "occupy the imagination, sharpen the wit, and when they are properly understood and put to good use, they are well suited to provide the spirit with nourishment." See Appel, *Robert Schumann's "Album für die Jugend,"* p. 69.

97. Walter Benjamin, "A Glimpse into the World of Children's Books" (1926), in *Walter Benjamin,* vol. 1, p. 442.

98. See Jean Paul, *Vorschule der Ästhetik,* chapters 31–35, in *Werke,* vol. 5, ed. Norbert Miller (Munich: Carl Hanser, 1963), pp. 124–44.

99. Jean Paul, *Werke,* vol. 2, ed. Gustav Lohmann (Munich: Carl Hanser, 1959), p. 713.

100. Published in the early 1840s, J. P. Lyser's *Musikalisches Bilder = ABC zum Lesenlernen der Noten, Vorzeichen und Schlüssel* reinforces the child's understanding of the basic principles of musical notation by combining pitches and letters of the alphabet to yield humorous sentences, many of which are coupled with equally humorous illustrations. One group of illustrated plaintexts, for instance, concerns an organ-playing ape ("Affe"). For reproductions of and commentary on this playful series of exercises, see Appel, *Robert Schumann's "Album für die Jugend,"* pp. 69, 71. The musical equivalents of "ape" (A–F–F–E) and "sheep" (S–C–H–A–F–E) play an important role in Max Reger's Sonata in C for Violin and Piano, Op. 72 (1903), a work in which the humorous potential of musical ciphers is taken to a biting, sarcastic extreme. As Reger wrote to Theodor Kroyer, the piece "is teeming with strettos and 'contrapuntal jokes,' " the butt of the jokes being the small-minded critics who had derided the modernist tendencies in Reger's compositions. The sonata receives a detailed analysis

in an unpublished paper by Antonius Bittmann, "Between Brahms and Strauss: Munich Modernism and Max Reger's Op. 72."

101. Benjamin, "A Glimpse into the World of Children's Books," p. 442.

102. Schumann was acutely sensitive to the visual appearance of a musical score. Consider the following passage from his celebrated review of Chopin's Op. 2:

> I leafed through the score somewhat distractedly: there is something magical about enjoying music in this veiled way, that is, without actually hearing any sounds. Moreover, it seems to me that every composer conveys to the viewer his own distinctive manner of creating shapes out of tones: Beethoven looks different on the page than Mozart, just as Jean Paul's prose looks different than Goethe's. But here [in Chopin's Opus 2] it were as if altogether strange eyes, the eyes of flowers, of basilisks, of peacocks, of maidens, were wondrously gazing back at me. ("Ich blätterte gedankenlos im Heft: dies verhüllte Geniessen der Musik ohne Töne hat etwas Zauberisches. Überdies, scheint mir, hat jeder Komponist seine eigentümlichen Notengestaltungen für das Auge: Beethoven sieht anders auf dem Papier als Mozart, etwa wie Jean Paulsche Prosa anders als Goethesche. Hier aber war mir's als blickten mich lauter fremde Augen, Blumenaugen, Basiliskenaugen, Pfauenaugen, Mädchenaugen wundersam an.")

See GS 1, p. 5.

103. In a letter of 20 December 1836, Schumann asked Lyser—an experienced and imaginative illustrator of publications for children—to do the graphic design for the title page of Carnaval, an assignment that Lyser apparently did not accept. See Appel, Robert Schumann's "Album für die Jugend," p. 70.

104. On the importance of this scene for Schumann, see my Robert Schumann, pp. 82–87.

105. At the same time, Schumann made a point of differentiating the later from the earlier cycle. As he put it in a letter of 6 October 1848 to Carl Reinecke, the pieces from the Album für die Jugend "are completely different from the Kinderscenen. The latter are reflections of an adult for adults, while the Weihnachtsalbum [Christmas Album, at the time Schumann's projected title for the Album für die Jugend] is made up of foreshadowings and premonitions of future situations for children." BNF, p. 290.

106. Debussy's contribution was titled "Hommage a Haydn"; Ravel called his a "Menuet sur le nom d'Haydn." For the key to the cipher system that allowed Ravel to render **Haydn** as the pitch cell B–A–D–D–G, see Arbie Orenstein, Ravel: Man and Musician (New York: Columbia University Press, 1975), p. 174.

107. See Schumann's article on Gade in NZfM 20 (1 January 1844), pp. 1–2.

CHAPTER 4

1. See Johannes Brahms, Des jungen Kreislers Schatzkästlein: Aussprüche von Dichtern, Philosophen und Künstlern, zusammengetragen durch Johannes Brahms, ed. Karl Krebs (Berlin: Verlag der Deutschen Brahmsgesellschaft m. b. h., 1909), pp. 57–59. The four volumes bear the following titles: Schatzkästlein des jungen Kreislers, Des jungen Kreislers Schatzkästlein, Schöne Gedanken über Musik, and Schöne Gedanken über Musik, book 2. Toward the end of his life, Brahms returned to these notebooks, adding further excerpts from the works of Goethe, Jean Paul, Bismarck, and others. As Krebs notes in

the preface to his edition (pp. viii–ix), the two volumes of *Schöne Gedanken* were perhaps related to Schumann's *Dichtergarten*. A project undertaken in his later years, it was comprised of quotations about music culled from the monuments of world literature, including ancient Greek and Roman writings, Shakespeare's plays, and Jean Paul's novels.

2. *BBw* 6, p. 291. At the time, Agathe was the widow of a member of the Göttingen Board of Health named Schütte.

3. The pitches of the F–A–E cell are also embedded in the opening measures of Dietrich's movement: E–F in the violin, A in the piano.

4. *BBw* 6, p. 187.

5. According to Kalbeck, Brahms knew of Schubring's self-styled musical cipher, D–A–S, a derivative of the plaintext **Dr. A. S**chubring. See Max Kalbeck, *Johannes Brahms* vol. 1, p. 114.

6. The manuscripts of some of Brahms's early works also include signatures related to the composer's Kreisler persona, such as: "Joh. Kreisler jun." (Piano Sonata, Op. 1), and "Kr" (several of the Variations, Op. 9).

7. In honor of Brahms's twenty-first birthday in 1854, his friend Julius Otto Grimm sent him a little piece based on the musical letters in the composer's name (**B** = B♭; **A** = A; **H** = B; **S** = E♭). See David Brodbeck "Brahms-Joachim Counterpoint Exchange; or Robert, Clara, and 'the Best Harmony between Jos. and Joh.,'" in David Brodbeck, ed., *Brahms Studies*, vol. 1 (Lincoln: University of Nebraska Press, 1994), p. 72.

8. See, for instance, Brahms's letter to Schumann of 29 November 1853, in *BLL*, p. 27.

9. *BLL*, pp. 78, 116.

10. On 27 August 1854, Brahms wrote to Clara that he was deeply engrossed in the *Davidsbündlertänze* and *Kreisleriana*: "Almost the whole day I sit in Bilkerstaßese 1032 on the second floor, and I have also assailed your [music] cabinet; I must search through everything!" *BLL*, p. 60. Consider also the following remark from a letter to Clara of 24 October 1854: "I play your husband's things for my teacher a lot; he said that I had never played anything as beautifully as the *Symphonic Etudes!*" *BLL*, p. 67.

11. Brodbeck, "Brahms-Joachim Counterpoint Exchange," pp. 30–80, *passim*.

12. Ibid., pp. 35–47.

13. Joachim spelled out this connection in a letter to Schumann of 29 November 1853: "The last notes [in the second of the *Drei Stücke* for violin and piano], F–A–E, are highlighted with blue ink, and alternate during the piece with three other notes [G♯–E–A]; the first pattern possesses not only an artistic but also a more human, personal significance for me, meaning 'frei aber einsam.' I am not engaged." Johannes Joachim and Andreas Moser, eds., *Briefe von und an Joseph Joachim*, vol. 1 (Berlin, 1911–13), p. 109.

14. Cf. chapter 3, pp. 77–81.

15. Kalbeck, *Brahms*, vol. 1, p. 98.

16. Michael Musgrave, *"Frei aber froh:* A Reconsideration," *19th Century Music* 3 (1979), pp. 251–58.

17. On Brahms's use of the F–A–E cell in these works, see: Constantin Floros, *Johannes Brahms: "Frei aber einsam"—ein Leben für eine poetische Musik* (Zurich: Arche, 1997), pp. 62–63, 65–66; Günter Hartmann, "Vorbereitende Untersuchungen zur Analyse von Brahms' Doppelkonzert a-moll op. 102," in Reinmar Emans and Matthias

Wendt, eds., *Beiträge zur Geschichte des Konzerts: Festschrift Siegfried Kross zum 60. Geburtstag* (Bonn: Gudrun Schröder, 1990), pp. 276–77, 286–92; Peter Jost, "'Gewissermassen ein Versöhnungswerk': Doppelkonzert A-moll, Op. 102," in Renata Ulm, ed., *Johannes Brahms: Das Symphonische Werk—Entstehung, Deutung, Wirkung* (Kassel: Bärenreiter, 1996), p. 173; and Jan Swafford, *Johannes Brahms: A Biography* (New York: Knopf, 1997), pp. 540–41.

18. Benjamin Locke has recently identified a cipher based on the first name of Brahms's mother (**Christiane**) and discussed its use in the first, fifth, sixth, and seventh movements of *Ein deutsches Requiem*. The argument is not convincing. First, it is odd that Brahms would have enciphered the letters **C, H, A,** and **E** (to form the pattern C–B–A–E), but not the letter **S** into tone (cf. rule 2). Moreover, in all instances but one the cipher lacks clear-cut thematic definition and/or is tucked away in a longer idea (cf. rules 3, 6–8). It assumes thematic self-sufficiency only in the fugue subject of the sixth movement, though here the pitches of the basic form are interspersed with other, "noncipher" tones: *C–B–G–A–F–D–E–G–A*. See Benjamin Locke, "Christiane: Cryptography in Brahms's *Ein deutsches Requiem*," *Choral Journal* 39/2 (September 1998), pp. 9–14. On the premises that underlie Sams's hypothesis, cf. chapter 3, pp. 68–69.

19. See chapter 3, note 4. Allen Forte has proposed yet another Clara cipher in an article titled "Motivic Design and Structural Levels in the First Movement of Brahms' String Quartet in C Minor," *Musical Quarterly* 69 (1983), pp. 477, 499–500. In Forte's view, the pitch configuration A–C–E♭ represents an encipherment of three of the musical letters in Clara's name: **Cl**a**ra S**chumann. While this cell functions at various structural levels in the opening movement of Brahms's C-minor String Quartet, there is no reason to assume that the cell was derived from Clara's name.

20. See A. Peter Brown, "Brahms' Third Symphony and the New German School," *Journal of Musicology* 2 (1983), p. 436; David Brodbeck, *Brahms: Symphony No. 1* (Cambridge: Cambridge University Press, 1997), pp. 40–41; Malcolm MacDonald, *Brahms* (New York: Schirmer, 1990), p. 226; Michael Musgrave, *Music of Brahms* (London: Routledge and Kegan Paul, 1985), p. 140; Dillon Parmer, "Brahms, Song Quotation and Secret Programs," *19th Century Music* 19-2 (1995), pp. 185–86; and Eric Sams, "Brahms and His Clara Themes," *Musical Times* 112 (1971), p. 432.

21. As Brahms wrote to Schumann on 30 January 1855, "There is indeed considerable progress from [my] Op. 8 to Op. 9. Both are dedicated to your wife" (*BLL*, p. 84).

22. See James Webster, "The C Sharp Minor Version of Brahms's Op. 60," *Musical Times* 121 (1980), pp. 89–93.

23. Kalbeck, *Brahms*, vol. 1, p. 232.

24. Ibid. and 2nd ed., vol. 3 (Berlin: Deutsche Brahms-Gesellschaft, 1912–21), p. 12.

25. Similar deviations from Brahms's rules occur in the many vocal works in which Sams has discerned various forms of the Agathe motive: *Lieder und Romanzen,* Op. 14, nos. 1, 4–8; *Fünf Gedichte,* Op. 19, nos. 1–3; *Drei Duette,* nos. 1, 3; and *Zwölf Lieder und Romanzen* for women's chorus, Op. 44, nos. 7–9. Like Kalbeck, Sams associates the motive with the plaintext **Agathe, ade,** a connection for which there is no evidence. See Kalbeck, *Brahms* vol. 1, p. 331, and Eric Sams, "Brahms and His Musical Love Letters," *Musical Times* 112 (1971), pp. 329–30.

26. George Bozarth, "Brahms's First Piano Concerto, Op. 15: Genesis and Meaning," in Reinmar Emans and Matthias Wendt, eds., *Beiträge zur Geschichte des Konzerts: Festschrift Siegfried Kross zum 60. Geburtstag* (Bonn: Gundrum Schröder, 1990), p. 218.

27. Brahms, *Des jungen Kreislers Schatzkästlein*, p. 61 (excerpt no. 244): "Die Jünger, welche um einen Meister sich scharend, Schule bilden, sind an dem Himmel der Kunstgeschichte wie die Milchstratze; einzeln würden sie nicht bemerkt, zusammen geben sie freundlich hellen Glanz."

28. At this point in his life, Brahms felt it would be presumptuous of him to dedicate a piece outright to Schumann. Hence, as he noted in a letter to Schumann of 30 January 1855: "I would want to alternate the names Joachim and Clara Schumann [as dedicatees] until I had the courage to set down your name; that probably won't happen to me so soon." *BLL*, p. 84.

29. Brodbeck, "Brahms-Joachim Counterpoint Exchange," pp. 73–75, and *Brahms: Symphony No. 1*, pp. 40–50.

30. On the relationship between Schumann's *Manfred* and his contrapuntal works of 1845, see my *Robert Schumann: Herald of a "New Poetic Age"* (New York: Oxford University Press, 1997), p. 357.

31. Brahms, *Des jungen Kreislers Schatzkästlein*, pp. 58–59 (excerpt no. 230): "**Handwerker und Künstler.** Ihr, die ihr nur das zufällig Alltägliche aufgreift und als modisch brauchbar Gerät wiedergebt, euch wird schon das nächste Geschlecht euer Werk aus der Zeit in die Vergangenheit nachschmeissen, es gegen neue modische Zier vertauschen; aber ihr, die ihr fühlt, was durch alle Zeiten dauernd zieht, Baumeister, die ihr mit urewigen Steinen Tempel der Künste schafft, euer Werk werden auch späte Völker, und wär's als Ruine, halten lieb und wert."

32. Ibid., p. 57 (excerpt no. 226).

33. On Bachian elements in Brahms's A flat–minor Fugue, see Siegfried Kross, *Johannes Brahms: Versuch einer kritischen Dokumentar-Biographie* (Bonn: Bouvier, 1997), p. 241. On Schumann's "B-A-C-H" Fugues as an important chapter in the history of Bach reception, see Bodo Bischoff, "Das Bach-Bild Robert Schumanns," in Michael Heinemann and Hans-Joachim Hinrichsen, eds., *Bach und die Nachwelt*. Vol. 1: *1750–1850* (Laaber: Laaber-Verlag, 1997), pp. 469–72.

34. Translation slightly modified, from Brodbeck, "Brahms-Joachim Counterpoint Exchange," p. 30.

35. Joachim and Moser, *Briefe von und an Joseph Joachim*, vol. 1, p. 356.

36. Quoted in Berthold Litzmann, *Clara Schumann: Ein Künstlerleben*, vol. 2 (Leipzig: Breitkopf und Härtel, 1925), p. 412.

37. See Brahms's letter of 25 April 1856 to Joachim, in *BLL*, pp. 125–26.

38. Eugenie Schumann's *Memoirs* speak to the easygoing familiarity between Brahms and the Schumann children: "We children all liked Brahms, but we treated him as one who had always been there, and this perhaps made us a little perfunctory in manner towards him." *Memoirs of Eugenie Schumann*, trans. Marie Busch (London: Eulenburg, 1985, orig. publ. *Erinnerungen* [Stuttgart, 1925]), p. 147.

39. See Walter Benjamin, "A Glimpse into the World of Children's Books," in *Walter Benjamin: Selected Writings*, vol. 1: *1913–1926*, ed. Marcus Bullock and Michael W. Jennings (Cambridge, Massachusetts: Belknap Press of Harvard University Press, 1996), p. 442.

40. See George Bozarth, ed. and trans., "Johannes Brahms's Collection of *Deutsche Sprichworte* (Proverbs)," in Brodbeck, *Brahms Studies*, vol. 1, pp. 1–29. Brahms also included dozens of maxims—among them, several from Ecclesiastes—in the *Schatzkästlein*. Even the title of the latter collection situates it within the context of the morally edifying children's literature of the Biedermeier period. One of the main-

stays of that genre was a compendium of poetry and prose by Johann Peter Hebel titled *Schatzkästlein des rheinischen Hausfreunds*. See Walter Benjamin, "Children's Literature," in *Walter Benjamin: Selected Writings*, vol. 2: *1927–1934*, trans. Rodney Livingstone and others, ed. Michael W. Jennings, Howard Eiland, and Gary Smith (Cambridge, Massachusetts: Belknap Press of Harvard University Press, 1991), pp. 254, 256.

41. *Des jungen Kreislers Schatzkästlein*, p. 59 (excerpt no. 231): "Wir müssen uns hüten, dass der Geist eines geliebten Genius für uns zur Flamme werde, von der wir armen Schmetterlinge im Umflattern untergehen."

42. For selections from this sketch, see Hans Küntzel, *Brahms in Göttingen* (Göttingen: Edition Herodot, 1985), pp. 89–105.

43. Ibid., pp. 99–100.

44. Max Kalbeck, *Johannes Brahms*, vol. 2, p. 157. According to Kalbeck, Brahms shared this remark with Joseph Gansbächer.

45. Siegfried Kross describes this process very well: "After presenting the [Agathe] motive so emphatically three times, [Brahms] varies and alters it, as though he had been caught making too obvious an allusion and now wanted to render his far too personal statement unrecognizable by quickly covering it up." See Kross, *Johannes Brahms*, p. 446.

46. *BLL*, p. 48.

47. Letter of 15 December 1854, in ibid., p. 79.

48. Styra Avins offers an insightful and clearheaded assessment of the evidence in "Johannes Brahms and Clara Schumann" (*BLL*, Appendix A, pp. 757–64). See also Nancy B. Reich, "Clara Schumann and Johannes Brahms," in Walter Frisch, ed., *Brahms and His World* (Princeton: Princeton University Press, 1990), pp. 37–47.

49. See in particular Brahms's letter to Clara of 22 October 1856, in *BLL*, p. 145.

50. Brahms's letter to Clara of 31 May 1856, the first in which he addresses her throughout with the familiar "du" form, begins like a typical love letter, but in reading further we realize that the love expressed here is a highly idealized one: "My beloved Clara, I wish I could write to you as tenderly as I love you, and give you as much kindness and goodness as I wish for you. You are so infinitely dear to me that I can't begin to tell you. I constantly want to call you darling and all kinds of other things, without becoming tired of adoring you. If this goes on, I will eventually have to keep you under glass, or save money to have you gilded." See *BLL*, p. 134.

51. "Es läßt sich eben nicht Jedes in Buchstaben bringen." *NZfM* 7 (7 September 1837), p. 87.

CHAPTER 5

1. *JBr*, p. 268.

2. *CC*, vol. 1, p. 302 (translation slightly modified).

3. Letter of 19 May 1839, in *CC* 2, p. 201. At the time, the piece was titled "Idylle." It was published in 1840 as the third of Clara's *Trois romances* for piano, Op. 11.

4. Letter to Clara of 27 August 1854, in *BLL*, p. 60 (translation slightly modified).

5. *BLL*, p. 76 (translation slightly modified).

6. See Hector Berlioz, *Berlioz: Fantastic Symphony, Norton Critical Score*, ed. Edward T. Cone (New York: Norton, 1971), p. 23 (translation slightly modified).

7. See Douglas Jarman, "Alban Berg, Wilhelm Fliess and the Secret Programme of the Violin Concerto," *Musical Times* 124 (1983), pp. 218–23.

8. *CC*, vol. 1, p. 225, and vol. 2, p. 285 (translations slightly modified).

9. Berthold Litzmann, ed., *Clara Schumann–Johannes Brahms: Briefe aus den Jahren 1853–1896*, vol 1 (Leipzig: Breitkopf und Härtel, 1927), p. 198.

10. "FÄCHER. Man wird folgende Erfahrung gemacht haben: liebt man jemanden, ist man sogar nur intensive mit ihm beschäftigt, so findet man beinah in jedem Buche sein Porträt. Ja er erscheint als Spieler und als Gegenspieler. In den Erzählungen, Romanen und Novellen begegnet er in immer neuen Verwandlungen. Und hieraus folgt: das Vermögen der Phantasie ist die Gabe, im unendlich Kleinen zu interpolieren, jeder Intensität als Extensivem ihre neue gedrängte Fülle zu erfinden, kurz, jedes Bild zu nehmen, als sei es des zusammengelegten Fächers, das erst in der Entfaltung Atem holt und mit der neuen Breite die Züge des geliebten Menschen in seinem Innern aufführt." Walter Benjamin, *Einbahnstraße*, in *Gesammelte Schriften*, vol. 4-i, ed. Tilman Rexroth (Frankfurt am Main: Suhrkamp, 1972), p. 117.

11. Walter Benjamin, *A Berlin Chronicle* (1932), in *Walter Benjamin: Selected Writings*, vol. 2: *1927–1934*, trans. Rodney Livingstone and others, ed. Michael W. Jennings, Howard Eiland, and Gary Smith (Cambridge, Massachusetts: Belknap Press of Harvard University Press, 1999), p. 597.

12. Walter Benjamin, *One-Way Street* (1928), in *Walter Benjamin*, vol. 2, p. 603; cf. note 10.

13. The phrase comes from an unnamed nineteenth-century source quoted by Benjamin in the materials for his project on the Parisian arcades: "Humanity has also invented, in its evening peregrinations . . . the symbol of memory; it has invented a mirror that remembers. It has invented photography." See *The Arcades Project*, trans. Howard Eiland and Kevin McLaughlin (Cambridge, Massachusetts: Belknap Press of Harvard University Press, 1999), p. 688.

14. Walter Benjamin, "Little History of Photography" (1931), in *Walter Benjamin*, vol. 2, pp. 510, 512. Cf. Roland Barthes, *Camera Lucida: Reflections on Photography*, trans. Richard Howard (New York: Hill and Wang, 1981), p. 32: "The photographic 'shock' . . . consists less in traumatizing than in revealing what was so well hidden that the actor himself [i.e., the subject of the photograph] was unaware or unconscious of it." The revelatory potential of photography was recognized already around 1840 by the French scientist Joseph Guy-Lussac, who insisted that no detail, "even if imperceptible," can escape "the eye and the brush of this new painter." Quoted in Siegfried Kracauer, *Theory of Film: The Redemption of Physical Reality* (1960) (Princeton: Princeton University Press, 1997), p. 5.

15. *BrKG*, vol. 2, p. 562.

16. Roland Barthes, "Rasch," in *The Responsibility of Forms: Critical Essays on Music, Art, and Representation*, trans. Richard Howard (New York: Hill and Wang, 1985), pp. 300, 301–2.

17. "An Anna II," on a text by Justinus Kerner, composed in 1828.

18. *CC*, vol. 1, p. 36.

19. *CC*, vol. 2, p. 320; *BrKG*, vol. 2, p. 640. To quote Anna Burton, the couple "enjoyed a complete dialogue," made possible by Clara's "full initiation into Schumann's poetic fantasies, consensual ideas and new musical vocabulary." See her "Robert Schumann and Clara Wieck: A Creative Partnership," *Music and Letters* 69 (1988), p. 224.

20. See Janina Klassen, *Clara Wieck-Schumann—Die Virtuosin als Komponisten—Studien zu ihrem Werk, Kieler Studien zur Musikwissenschaft*, vol. 37 (Kassel: Bärenreiter,

1990), p. 99. The passage in question from Schumann's *Humoreske* also hearkens back to a moment near the very opening of the piece (mm. 8ff.).

21. Ibid., pp. 103, 110.

22. Cf. chapter 2, p. 59.

23. See Nicholas Marston, *Schumann: Fantasie, Op. 17* (New York: Cambridge University Press, 1992), pp. 7–8.

24. *CC*, vol. 1, p. 129; *BrKG*, vol. 1, p. 126.

25. On this point, see Nicholas Marston, "'Im Legendenton': Schumann's 'Unsung Voice,'" *19th Century Music* 16/3 (1993), p. 238.

26. Berthold Hoeckner, "Schumann and Romantic Distance," *Journal of the American Musicological Society* 50-1 (1997), p. 121. See also Marston, *Schumann: Fantasie, Op. 17*, p. 17, and "'Im Legendenton': Schumann's 'Unsung Voice,'" pp. 230–32. Clara's *Romance variée* was completed in 1833 and published in the summer of that year with a dedication to Schumann, whose variations on the same romance melody—his Impromptus (Op. 5)—also appeared in print in 1833. Although Schumann identified the melody as Clara's, he may have had a hand in its making: the head motive of Clara's theme is nearly identical to a four-bar sketch that Schumann entered into his diary in September 1830. See *TB* 1, p. 321.

27. On the various titles of the "Im Legendenton" section, see Marston, *Schumann: Fantasie, Op. 17*, pp. 20–21, and "'Im Legendenton': Schumann's 'Unsung Voice,'" pp. 234–35. The network of reminiscences in the "Im Legendenton" section has been described in some detail in the secondary literature on Schumann's Fantasie. For a summary of the principal relationships, see my "Schumann's *Im Legendenton* and Friedrich Schlegel's *Arabeske*," *19th Century Music* 11/2 (1987), pp. 157, 159–60.

28. Stephen Downes, "Kierkegaard, a Kiss, and Schumann's *Fantasie*," *19th Century Music* 22/3 (1999), p. 277. In this nuanced discussion of the dialectic between immediacy and reflection in Schumann's musical representations of eroticism, Downes offers a particularly subtle analysis of the phrase that Schumann cited in a letter to Clara of 9 June 1839 and identified as his "favorite melody" in the opening movement of the Fantasie. (See *BrKG*, vol. 2, p. 562, and pp. 277–80 of Downes's article.) First heard in F major during the exposition (mm. 61ff.), the melody assumes the form of an evocative reminiscence in D♭ during the "Im Legendenton" section (mm. 181ff.).

29. *TB* 1, p. 422.

30. *CC*, vol. 1, pp. 76, 95; *BrKG*, vol. 1, pp. 75, 93.

31. *CC*, vol. 1, p. 95.

32. These "ascriptions of authorship" were omitted from the second edition of the *Davidsbündlertänze*, issued in 1850–51.

33. In eliminating the held B from the second edition, Schumann fundamentally altered a key aspect of the cycle's design. This will become more apparent when we consider the "melodic thread" that runs through the original version of the *Davidsbündlertänze*.

34. On Schumann's allusion to Clara's *Valses romantiques* in both the *Davidsbündlertänze* and *Carnaval*, see Hoeckner, "Schumann and Romantic Distance," pp. 101–4.

35. *NZfM* 7 (15 September 1837), p. 87.

36. For detailed discussions of the melodic-harmonic progression that links no. 17 with no. 18, a pattern that capitalizes on the enharmonic equivalence of the German augmented-sixth chord in B minor and the dominant seventh of C major, see Peter Kaminsky, "Principles of Formal Structure in Schumann's Early Piano Cycles," *Music*

Theory Spectrum 11/2 (1989), pp. 217, 222–24; and Hoeckner, "Schumann and Romantic Distance," pp. 105, 109. Hoeckner draws a suggestive connection between this progression and comparable gestures in Clara's *Valses romantiques.*

37. Schumann had a special fondness for this work. "Do you know what my favorite of your pieces is?" he asked in a letter of 11 February 1838. "The Notturno in F major and 6/8 time. What were you thinking when you wrote it? Something quite melancholy I suppose." *BrKG*, vol. 1, p. 100; *CC*, vol. 1, p. 102.

38. See chapter 2, p. 61.

39. Hoeckner, "Schumann and Romantic Distance," p. 128.

40. Benjamin, *A Berlin Chronicle*, p. 597.

41. Letter of 6 February 1838, in *CC*, vol. 1, p. 94.

42. Benjamin, *A Berlin Chronicle*, p. 615.

43. The other songs that comprised Clara's December 1840 Christmas offering included an additional Heine setting—the *Volkslied*, "Es fiel ein Reif," a text set by Schumann in 1841 and published in 1847 as part of the *Romanzen und Balladen* (Op. 64)—and a setting of a poem by Robert Burns in German translation, "Am Strande," that Schumann had probably recommended to her for musical treatment. See *TB* 2, p. 107. When "Ihr Bildnis" was published in 1843, the original title was replaced by the opening line of the poem: "Ich stand in dunklen Träumen."

44. Schumann drafted his Eichendorff *Liederkreis* in May 1840. It is worth pointing out, especially in light of the creative exchange between Schumann and Clara, that she was responsible for the selection of the texts that provided the basis for the Eichendorff cycle.

45. Robert and Clara Schumann, *Briefe einer Liebe*, ed. Hanns-Josef Ortheil (Königstein: Athenäum, 1982), p. 278.

46. The song was published later in that year as the third song in Clara's *Sechs Lieder* (Op. 13), the same collection that included "Ich stand in dunklen Träumen," the revised version of "Ihr Bildnis."

47. Another of Clara's Geibel settings, "Die stille Lotosblume" (composed in July 1843 and published as Op. 13, no. 6), makes oblique reference to two of the songs from Schumann's *Myrthen* (presented to Clara as a wedding gift in September 1840): "Die Lotosblume" and "Du bist wie eine Blume," both on texts by Heine. Given that "Die stille Lotosblume" and "Die Lotosblume" share the same poetic image (lotus blossoms glimmering in the moonlight) and that all three poems play on the tension between innocence and sensuality, it is not surprising that the musical settings should share so many features, which include quietly pulsing accompaniments, chromatic inner voices, and tonal designs that feature excursions to the flat mediant region.

48. Soon thereafter Clara added preludes to the latter group, which was published by Breitkopf und Härtel in October 1845 as *Drei Praeludien und Fugen*, Op. 16. The other collections of Schumann's "contrapuntal year" were the *Vier Skizzen* for pedal piano (Op. 58), the canonic *Sechs Studien* for pedal piano (Op. 56), and the *Sechs Fugen über den Namen BACH* for organ (Op. 60).

49. Litzmann, *Clara Schumann*, vol. 2, p. 151.

50. *TB* 2, pp. 413 and 550 (note 727).

51. Similar claims could be made about the first movement of the slightly earlier Piano Trio in D minor. Just as in the corresponding movement of the F-major work, a voice from afar emerges from the ongoing discourse—and at precisely the same interstice in the form. The development opens with an incredible passage in which the

piano, poised in the upper segment of its range, offers a dreamy rendition of a melody in softly repeated triplet chords. The violin extracts an inner voice from the predominantly four-voice texture, adding to the otherworldly effect by playing *sul ponticello*. Projecting the quality of a disembodied reminiscence, this music alternates with developmental interludes on material from the exposition and also reappears briefly in the coda, offering a ray of D-major sunlight before being extinguished by the brooding cadential flourishes that bring the movement to a close in D minor. Although the distant voice does not allude to a specific song melody, as in the first movement of the F-major Piano Trio, it clearly evokes a family of melodies whose members include the opening motto of the First Symphony, the choralelike Trio theme of the Scherzo from the *Ouverture, Scherzo und Finale* (Op. 52), and, most significant of all, the principal melody of the final song from *Myrthen* ("Zum Schluss"). In other words, the first movement of the D-minor Piano Trio is just as much a repository of buried memories as its F-major counterpart, and Schumann establishes its recollective character in much the same way.

52. George S. Bozarth, "Brahms's *Lieder ohne Worte:* The 'Poetic' Andantes of the Piano Sonatas," in George S. Bozarth, ed., *Brahms Studies: Analytical and Historical Perspectives* (Oxford: Clarendon, 1990), pp. 349–52.

53. *BLL*, p. 60 (translation slightly modified).

54. Letter to Joachim of 12 September 1854, in *BLL*, p. 62.

55. *BLL*, p. 76 (translation slightly modified).

56. Ibid., p. 68.

57. Ibid., p. 62.

58. Clara also interwove a reference to the Romance melody into the final variation of her Op. 20. In all likelihood, however, this gesture was added *after* Brahms presented her with the supplementary variations 10 and 11 in August 1854. (See Klassen, *Clara Wieck-Schumann*, p. 67.)

These two sets of variations were the first products of a creative exchange between Brahms and Clara that invites comparison with the earlier interchange of compositional ideas between Schumann and Clara. Invoking a gesture redolent of her exchange with Schumann in the late 1830s, Clara inscribed one of the autographs of her "Romanze" in A minor (Op. 21, no. 1): "To my dear friend Johannes . . . 2 April 1855." Interestingly enough, another autograph of the same work, preserved in the Robert-Schumann-Haus in Zwickau, bears the inscription: "To my dear husband, 8 June 1855." Contrary to appearances, these unofficial dedications are not in conflict. The first two bars of Clara's wistful "Romanze" evoke the striking progression from tonic harmony to subdominant seventh (enriched with an appoggiatura) that distinguishes the opening of the first *Albumblatt* from Schumann's *Bunte Blätter*—a piece that Brahms had made his own in the Variations, Op. 9.

Clara's "Romanze" in B minor, dated Christmas 1856 and possibly presented to Brahms at that time, takes one of the younger composer's works as its point of reference. The descending triadic melody that Clara evolves out of the murmuring figuration of the "Romanze"'s initial bars is comparable to the main idea of the fourth movement (Intermezzo) of Brahms's Piano Sonata in F minor, Op. 5, which he played at the Schumanns' home in November 1853. For a discussion of Clara's late *Romanzen* for piano and their relationship to Brahms, see Klassen, *Clara Wieck-Schumann*, pp. 103–4, 106; and Nancy Reich, *Clara Schumann: The Artist and the Woman*, Revised Edition (Ithaca: Cornell University Press, 2001), pp. 233–35.

During the same year that Clara wrote her B-minor "Romanze," she and Brahms collaborated on a cadenza for the first movement of Mozart's D-minor Piano Concerto (K. 466). Many years later, when Clara was preparing to issue a cadenza for the movement that drew some of its material from her earlier joint effort with Brahms, she offered to add the following acknowledgment to the published score: "[composed] with partial use of a cadenza by Johannes Brahms." Brahms's response, in a letter of 2 October 1891, speaks volumes to the nature of his creative exchange with Clara: "Even the smallest J. B. would only look peculiar; it really isn't worth the trouble, and I could show you many a more recent work in which there is more than an entire cadenza! What's more, by rights I would then have to add to my loveliest melodies: actually by Clara Schumann!" BLL, p. 687. There is an uncanny resemblance between Brahms's remarks and the sentiments expressed by Schumann upon receiving a copy of Clara's G-minor "Romance" (Op. 11, no. 2) in July 1839: "Each of your ideas comes from my soul, just as I owe all of my music to you." CC 2, p. 307.

59. Brahms highlighted the affective complementarity of the variations in his autograph, signing several of them either "Kr," after E. T. A. Hoffmann's volatile Kapellmeister Johannes Kreisler (nos. 5, 6, 9, 12, 13), or "B," for "Brahms" (nos. 4, 7, 8, 14, 16). The variations of the latter group tend to be more reflective in character and often make conspicuous use of contrapuntal techniques. Brahms's signatures clearly recall Schumann's ascription of the movements of his Davidsbündlertänze to Florestan, Eusebius, or both. The impetus for Brahms's frequent recourse to contrapuntal textures in general and canon in particular (e.g., in variations 8, 10, 14, and 15) no doubt lay in Clara's canonic treatment of Schumann's theme in the sixth variation of her Op. 20. At the same time, the prominent role of counterpoint in Brahms's Op. 9 situates the variation set in a tradition that also includes Schumann's Impromptus (Op. 5) and Variations on an Original Theme (commonly known as the Geistervariationen), written just days before his suicide attempt in February 1854.

60. See Brahms's letter of 11 October 1857 to Clara, in which he takes issue with a critic who claimed that the ninth variation was not written in imitation of Schumann's second Albumblatt (BLL, pp. 158–59). The Op. 9 Variations have provided fertile territory for investigations of Brahms's allusions to Schumann's keyboard music. See Hermann Danuser, "Aspekte einer Hommage-Komposition: Zu Brahms' Schumann-Variationen op. 9," in Friedhelm Krummacher and Wolfram Steinbeck, eds., Brahms-Analysen: Referate der Kieler Tagung 1983, (Kassel: Bärenreiter, 1984), pp. 93, 104; Constantin Floros, Brahms und Bruckner: Studien zur musikalischen Exegetik (Wiesbaden: Breitkopf und Härtel, 1980), pp. 119–31; Oliver Neighbour, "Brahms and Schumann: Two Opus Nines and Beyond," 19th Century Music 7/3 (1984), pp. 266–69; and Elaine Sisman, "Brahms and the Variation Canon," 19th Century Music 14/2 (1990), pp. 145–49.

61. Benjamin, "Little History of Photography," p. 514.

62. Schumann kept a copy of this photo, a reproducible calotype, in his room at the asylum in Endenich. See Ingrid Bodsch and Gerd Nauhaus, eds., Clara Schumann 1819–1896: Katalog zur Ausstellung (Bonn: Stadtmuseum Bonn, 1996), p. 226. Reporting on his visit to Endenich in late February 1855, Brahms wrote to Clara: "Then I fetched your picture for him [Schumann]. Oh, if you could have seen how deeply moved he was, how he almost had tears in his eyes and how he held it ever closer and finally said, 'Oh, how long I have waited for this.'" BLL, p. 92.

63. BLL, p. 82.

64. For a summary of these and related readings, see George S. Bozarth, "Brahms's First Piano Concerto, Op. 15: Genesis and Meaning," in Reinmar Emans and Matthias Wendt, eds. *Beiträge zur Geschichte des Konzerts: Festschrift Siegfried Kross zum 60. Geburtstag* (Bonn: Gundrun Schröder, 1990), pp. 215–16.

65. Donald Francis Tovey, *Essays in Musical Analysis*, vol. 3: *Concertos* (London: Oxford University Press, 1936), pp. 117–18.

66. See chapter 4, p. 123.

67. For a summary of these views, see Bozarth, "Brahms's First Piano Concerto," pp. 230–38.

68. Barthes, *Camera Lucida*, p. 93.

CHAPTER 6

1. Edward A. Lippman, "Robert Schumann," in *MGG*, ed. Friedrich Blume, vol. 12 (Kassel: Bärenreiter, 1965), cols. 315–16.

2. Hanslick's review is quoted in Daniel Beller-McKenna, "How *deutsch* a Requiem? Absolute Music, Universality, and the Reception of Brahms's *Ein deutsches Requiem*, Op. 45," *19th Century Music* 22/1 (1998), p. 15.

3. Schubring's essay on Brahms, which includes analyses of Opp. 1–18, was the eighth in a twelve-part series called *Schumanniana* that appeared between 1860 and 1869 in the *Neue Zeitschrift für Musik* and the *Allgemeine musikalische Zeitung*. For an excellent critical overview of the series in general and of the Brahms essay in particular ("Schumanniana Nr. 8. Die Schumann'sche Schule. IV. Johannes Brahms," *NZfM* 56 (1862), pp. 93–96, 101–4, 109–12, 117–19, 125–28), see Walter Frisch, "Brahms and Schubring: Musical Criticism and Politics at Mid-Century," *19th Century Music* 7/3 (1984), pp. 271–81. Frisch has also translated the introductory portion of Schubring's Brahms essay and the analyses of Opp. 1, 2, 5, 8 (first version), and 15; see Walter Frisch, ed., *Brahms and His World* (Princeton: Princeton University Press, 1990), pp. 103–22.

4. Adolf Schubring, "Schumanniana Nr. 5: Carl Ritter," *NZfM* 55 (1861), p. 53.

5. See, for instance, Carl Kipke's review of the Leipzig premiere (18 January 1877) of Brahms's First Symphony: "In the realm of instrumental music Schumann was Beethoven's most fully entitled heir, and since then Brahms alone has had the power to appropriate so correctly the legacy of both departed ones." Quoted in David Brodbeck, *Brahms: Symphony No. 1* (Cambridge: Cambridge University Press, 1997), p. 83.

6. On the literature pertinent to Brahms's reception of Schumann, see also the introduction to this study, pp. 4–5.

7. *Bw*, vol. 3, p. 121. Brahms went on to say: "It is hardly likely that I will ever love a better human being; nor, hopefully, will I ever observe so closely—and feel with such total compassion—as such a dreadful fate runs its course."

8. The analogy was drawn by Otto Gottlieb-Billroth. See Constantin Floros, *Johannes Brahms: "Frei aber einsam"—ein Leben für eine poetische musik* (Zurich: Arche, 1997), p. 53.

9. Max Kalbeck, *Johannes Brahms*, vol. 1, p. 125. As Schumann noted in his "Erinnerungen an F. Mendelssohn vom Jahre 1835 bis zu s[einem] Tode. (Materialien)" ("Reminiscences of F. Mendelssohn from the year 1835 until his death. [Notes]") (ca. 1847–48), he also enjoyed playing chess—and billiards—with Mendelssohn. See Robert Schumann, "Aufzeichnungen über Mendelssohn," annotated by Heinz-Klaus

Metzger and Rainer Riehn, in *Musik-Konzepte 14/15: Felix Mendelssohn Bartholdy* (Munich: Edition Text + Kritik, 1980), p. 110.

10. Thomas Mann, *Joseph and His Brothers*, trans. H. T. Lowe-Porter (New York: Knopf, 1986), p. 3.

11. Hugo Wolf, *The Music Criticism of Hugo Wolf*, trans. and ed. Henry Pleasants (New York: Holmes and Meier, 1978), p. 186.

12. See, e.g., Raymond Knapp, *Brahms and the Challenge of the Symphonic Tradition* (Stuyvesant, New York: Pendragon, 1997), pp. 97–97. Knapp finds further precedents for Brahms's technique in Handel's *Messiah*, the First Book of Bach's *Well-Tempered Clavier* (Prelude 6), Haydn's Symphony No. 103, and Mendelssohn's Symphony No. 2, "Lobgesang" (Op. 52).

13. See chapter 1, pp. 44–46.

14. James Webster, "Schubert's Sonata Form and Brahms's First Maturity," *19th Century Music* 2 (1978), pp. 18–37, and 3 (1979), pp. 52–71.

15. See chapter 1, p. 38.

16. Heinrich Schenker, *Harmony* (1906), ed. Oswald Jonas, trans. Elisabeth Mann Borgese (Cambridge, Massachusetts: MIT Press, 1973), pp. 11–12. For a discussion of *Knüpftechnik* in selected examples from Brahms's symphonies, chamber music, and songs, see Walter Frisch, *Brahms and the Principle of Developing Variation* (Berkeley: University of California Press, 1984), pp. 16, 79–80, 101, 140.

17. The first movement of the ever-popular Piano Quintet in E flat includes a stunning realization of the same principle. Schumann prolongs the transition's arrival on the V/V with the threefold repetition of a new thematic idea in the piano, which then becomes the point of departure for the second theme, an amorous duo between cello and viola.

18. Although Brahms almost surely wrote the initiatory "Un poco sostenuto" of the symphony's first movement *after* the main "Allegro" section of the movement was complete in some form, one cannot help but perceive the former as a preview of the material unfolded in the latter.

19. Donald Francis Tovey, *Essays in Musical Analysis*, vol. 1, *Symphonies* (London: Oxford University Press, 1935) p. 92.

20. A standard feature of Schumann's sonata forms, this strategy occurs often in his overtures (*Genoveva*, Op. 81; *Manfred*, Op. 115; *Die Braut von Messina*, Op. 100; *Fest-Overtüre über das Rheinweinlied*, Op. 123), single-movement concertante works (*Introduction und Allegro appassionato* for piano and orchestra, Op. 92; *Concert-Allegro mit Introduction* for piano and orchestra, Op. 134; *Phantasie for Violin and Orchestra*, Op. 131), and chamber music (first movements of the String Quartet in A, Op. 41, no. 3; Piano Quartet in E flat; and Violin Sonata in D minor, Op. 120).

21. Arnold Schoenberg, "Brahms the Progressive" (1947) in *Style and Idea*, ed. Leonard Stein, trans. Leo Black (Berkeley: University of California Press, 1984), p. 407.

22. See Peter Smith, "Liquidation, Augmentation, and Brahms's Recapitulatory Overlaps," *19th Century Music* 17/3 (1994), pp. 237–61, and "Brahms and Schenker: A Mutual Response to Sonata Form," *Music Theory Spectrum* 16/1 (1994), pp. 77–103.

23. Cf. also Walter Frisch's comments on the recapitulatory overlap in the Andante of Brahms's Third Symphony: "The whole process by which the recapitulation emerges is so subtle, so carefully drawn out, that one cannot point to a single moment where the return begins." *Brahms and the Principle of Developing Variation* , p. 139.

24. Smith, "Liquidation, Augmentation," pp. 237, 241–47.

25. Smith, "Brahms and Schenker," p. 103.

26. See Smith, "Liquidation, Augmentation," pp. 238, 241. Beethoven brings his development to a close by liquidating the head motive of the movement's main theme and augmenting its note values, but he does not blur the boundary between development and recapitulation. The latter begins unequivocally (in m. 144) with a statement of the opening theme in the tonic.

27. See, e.g., the last movement of the *Ouverture, Scherzo und Finale*, the third movement of the Second Symphony, the *Genoveva* Overture, the first movement of the Third Symphony ("Rhenish"), the first movement of the Violin Sonata in D minor (Op. 120), and the first movement of the Piano Trio in G minor (Op. 110). Joel Lester cites several of these movements as examples of Schumann's conflation of re-transitional and recapitulatory functions in "Robert Schumann and Sonata Forms," *19th Century Music* 18/3 (1995), p. 205. The recurrence of the main theme, *fortissimo*, over a dominant pedal in the first movement of Max Bruch's First Symphony in E flat (Op. 28)—a work that made the rounds of the major Central European orchestras in the later nineteenth century but has since disappeared from the repertory—echoes the similar gesture in the opening movement of Schumann's "Rhenish" Symphony. For a discussion of the Brahmsian resonances in this little-known work, see Walter Frisch, " 'Echt symphonisch': On the Historical Context of Brahms's Symphonies," in David Brodbeck, ed., *Brahms Studies*, vol. 2, (Lincoln: University of Nebraska Press, 1998), pp. 124–30. On Brahms's approach to the reprise in the finale of Brahms's D-minor Violin Sonata, see Smith, "Brahms and Schenker," pp. 101–2.

28. Schumann employs the strategy with a considerably lighter—even humorous—touch in both of these movements. Moreover, as opposed to literal augmentation, he makes use of tempo adjustments—four bars of *un poco più slentando* and four bars of *Più Adagio* capped off by a fermata in the quartet; two bars of *ritard.*, also leading to a fermata, in the piano trio—to achieve a similar end.

29. See David Brodbeck, "Brahms's Mendelssohn," in *Brahms Studies*, vol. 2, pp. 219–21.

30. Not surprisingly, Schumann's works are rich in examples of decorative or ob-bligato counterpoint as well. To cite two instances from his chamber music: Much of the murmuring piano figuration in the development of the first movement of the Piano Quintet is based on a segment of the movement's first theme treated in diminution. Diminution also occurs in the violin's accompaniment to the return of the lush opening cello theme in the slow movement of the Piano Quartet; interwoven with the violin's steadily moving sixteenths is a variant of a subsidiary melody (from mm. 31ff.) rendered at twice its original speed. Schumann's aim in both of these examples was to imbue the accompanying voices in the texture with motivic substance.

31. For a discussion of the "highly economical motivic process" in the Allegretto, see Frisch, *Brahms and the Principle of Developing Variation*, pp. 111–13.

32. Arnold Schoenberg, "Bach" (1950), in *Style and Idea*, p. 397. Schoenberg drew the same distinction in a number of the other essays collected in *Style and Idea*: "Ornaments and Construction" (1923) (p. 312); "National Music I" (1931) (pp. 170–71); "New Music, Outmoded Music, Style and Idea" (1946) (pp. 115–18); and "On Revient Toujours" (1948) (p. 109). His most fully worked-out attempt to conceptualize the difference between contrapuntal and melodic-developmental modes of elaboration occurs in *Der musikalische Gedanke und die Logik, Technik, und Kunst seiner Darstellung*, the

longest of the manuscripts devoted to the "musical idea," which dates from the mid-1930s. See *The Musical Idea and the Logic, Technique, and Art of Its Presentation,* ed. and trans. Patricia Carpenter and Severine Neff (New York: Columbia University Press, 1995), pp. 110–13, 136–37. See also *Fundamentals of Musical Composition* (1937–48), ed. Gerald Strang and Leonard Stein (London: Faber and Faber, 1967), p. 85. For a critique of Schoenberg's notions of "development," "unfolding," and "juxtaposition" or "stringing together" (the foundational principle of folk and popular styles), see Severine Neff, "Schoenberg as Theorist: Three Forms of Presentation," in Walter Frisch, ed., *Schoenberg and His World* (Princeton: Princeton University Press, 1999), pp. 55–84.

33. For a discussion of the stylistic tug-of-war in these works and its rhetorical basis, see Elaine Sisman, *Mozart: The "Jupiter" Symphony* (Cambridge: Cambridge University Press, 1993), pp. 68–79.

34. *TB* 2, p. 402.

35. See Robert Schumann, *NsA,* series 7, group 3, vol. 4: *Studien und Skizzen,* ed. Reinhold Dusella, Matthias Wendt, Bernhard R. Appel, and Kazuko Ozawa-Müller (Mainz: Schott, 1998), p. 3.

36. Another example from Brahms's works in this genre is the powerful first movement of the Piano Trio in C minor (Op. 101). Within the first three bars, the basic motivic combination is twice subjected to voice exchange, thus evoking (and intensifying) Schumann's practice at the opening of his D-minor Piano Trio. As the movement proceeds, Brahms elaborates the components of his initial unit through the application of contrapuntal techniques (including canon) and developing variation (sequence, augmentation, rhythmic displacement) as well. Schumann's attempt to synthesize these two types of procedures is evident not only in the first movement of his D-minor Piano Trio but also in the second movement of the same work and in several other of his late chamber works (Piano Trio in F, finale; Violin Sonata in A minor, first and last movements).

37. For discussions of the contrapuntal-motivic processes in this movement, see especially: Brodbeck, *Brahms: Symphony No. 1,* pp. 33–34; and Giselher Schubert, "Themes and Double Themes: The Problem of the Symphonic in Brahms," *19th Century Music* 18 (1994), pp. 15–16.

38. Paul Bekker, *Die Sinfonie von Beethoven bis Mahler* (Berlin: Schuster and Loeffler, 1918), p. 22.

39. For a detailed discussion of the process through which this transformation is effected, see Brodbeck, *Brahms: Symphony No. 1,* pp. 73–77.

40. Frisch comments on this crucial harmonic detail in *Brahms: The Four Symphonies,* pp. 64–65.

41. See Reinhold Brinkmann, *Late Idyll: The Second Symphony of Johannes Brahms,* trans. Peter Palmer (Cambridge, Massachusetts: Harvard University Press, 1995, orig. publ. *Johannes Brahms—die Zweite Symphonie—späte Idyll* [Munich: edition text and kritik GmbH, 1990]), pp. 36, 41, 44–45.

42. Giselher Schubert arrives at a similar conclusion, though by a different route, in "Themes and Double Themes," p. 23.

43. Theodor W. Adorno, *Mahler: A Musical Physiognomy,* trans. Edmund Jephcott (Chicago: University of Chicago Press, 1992, trans. of *Mahler: Eine musikalische Physiognomik* [Frankfurt am Main, 1971]), pp. 7, 11. Drawing his examples from Mahler's Symphonies 1, 4, and 5, Adorno devotes nearly the whole of the book's first chapter (pp. 3–17) to the breakthrough, a concept first aired by Paul Bekker in his discussion

of the first movement of Mahler's First Symphony in *Gustav Mahlers Sinfonien* (Tutzing: Schneider, 1969, reprint of 1921 ed.), pp. 44–45, 62. For an insightful commentary on Adorno's views and an equally stimulating analysis of the musical and philosophical implications of the breakthrough in the last movement of Mahler's First Symphony, see James Buhler, " 'Breakthrough' as Critique of Form: The Finale of Mahler's First Symphony," *19th Century Music* 20/2 (1996), pp. 125–43. James Hepokoski explicates Richard Strauss's use of this technique in "Fiery-pulsed Libertine or Domestic Hero? Strauss's *Don Juan* Reinvestigated," in Bryan Gilliam, ed., *Richard Strauss: New Perspectives on the Composer and His Works*, (Durham: Duke University Press, 1992), p. 149.

44. On this point, see Adorno's comments (*Mahler*, p. 10) on the delicate waltz, rendered *pianissimo*, that constitutes the breakthrough in the otherwise macabre second movement of Mahler's Fourth Symphony.

45. Robert Schumann, "Sonaten für das Clavier," *NZfM* 10 (1839), p. 135.

46. For a detailed reading of the evolving form of this movement, see Anthony Newcomb, "Once More between Absolute and Program Music: Schumann's Second Symphony," *19th Century Music* 7/3 (1984), pp. 233–50. Cf. Michael Talbot, *The Finale in Western Instrumental Music* (New York: Oxford University Press, 2001). As Talbot has questioned my description, in another context, of Schumann's finale, I should emphasize that I certainly do not mean to suggest that the concluding phase of the movement strictly adheres to the variation form, as in, for example, Bach's Variations for organ on *Von Himmel hoch* (BWV 769). In using the designation "chorale variations," I am merely attempting to capture the affective and structural underpinnings—and the generic character—of this remarkable passage.

47. The breakthrough in the finale of Mahler's First Symphony generates a rather similar form, the phases of which Buhler designates with the terms "model," "rupture," and "reprise." (See " 'Breakthrough' as Critique of Form," pp. 137–43.) That Mahler derived this plan from Schumann is further suggested by the motivic parallel between his "breakthrough motive" (G–A–C) and the brass fanfare that initiates the apotheosis-reprise in the finale of the "Rhenish" Symphony (B♭–C–E♭). Reinhard Kapp comments on this allusion and other correspondences between the symphonies of Schumann and Mahler in "Schumann–Reminiszenzen bei Mahler," *Musik-Konzepte Sonderband: Gustav Mahler* (July 1989), pp. 338–34.

48. "Ein echter musikalischer Kunstsatz hat immer einen gewissen Schwerpunct, dem Alles zuwächst, wohin sich alle Geistes-Radien concentriren. Viele legen ihn in die Mitte (die Mozartsche Weise), Andere nach dem Schluss zu (die Beethovens). Aber von seiner Gewalt hängt die Totalwirkung ab. Wenn man vorher gespannt und gepresst zugehört, so kömmt dann der Augenblick, wo man zum erstenmal aus freier Brust athmen kann: die Höhe ist erstiegen und der Blick fliegt hell und befriedigt vor- und rückwärts." Review of Moscheles, Piano Concertos 4 and 5, in *NZfM* 4 (1836), p. 123.

49. Schumann's aim was to bring an audience to its feet, and in this he succeeded brilliantly. According to one of the critics who reviewed the premiere (6 February 1851), the often-phlegmatic Düsseldorfers broke into "loud exclamations" after every movement and even the orchestra joined in a "three-fold 'hurrah' " "at the conclusion of the performance. Making a point that would surface time and again in discussions of the work, the same critic observed that the "chief character" (*Hauptcharakter*) of the symphony was of the "popular" (*volkstümlich*) sort. Schumann himself implied as much in a letter to Simrock of 19 March 1851, noting that his latest symphony "per-

haps here and there reflects a bit of local color." For an overview of the early reception of the "Rhenish" Symphony, see the "Critical Notes" to Linda Correll Roesner's edition of the work in NSA, series 1, group 1, vol. 3 (Mainz: Schott, 1995), pp. 193–98. Recent analytical accounts that stress the high level of motivic integration across the symphony's five movements include: Michael Musgrave, "Symphony and Symphonic Scenes: Issues of Structure and Context in Schumann's "Rhenish" Symphony," in Craig Ayrey and Mark Everist, eds., *Analytical Strategies and Musical Interpretation: Essays on Nineteenth- and Twentieth-Century Music* (Cambridge: Cambridge University Press, 1996), pp. 120–48; and Linda Correll Roesner, "Schumann," in D. Kern Holoman, ed., *The Nineteenth-Century Symphony* (New York: Schirmer, 1997), pp. 59–67.

50. For a discussion of the impact on Brahms of Schumann's use of "new themes" (an obvious corollary to the breakthrough technique), see Brinkmann, *Late Idyll,* pp. 215–16.

51. Walter Frisch, *Brahms: The Four Symphonies* (New York: Schirmer Books, 1996), pp. 102, 109; see also Frisch, *Brahms and the Principle of Developing Variation,* pp. 129–30, 138, 140–41.

52. Brahms's theme has also been linked with a transitional passage (mm. 70–74) from the Larghetto of Schumann's First Symphony (see, e.g., Knapp, *Brahms and the Challenge of the Symphonic Tradition,* pp. 93, 95). That the "Rhenish" was probably the main allusive source is strengthened by a biographical detail: Brahms drafted the Third Symphony in the late spring and early summer of 1883 while staying in Wiesbaden—on the Rhine. See D. Brodbeck, "Brahms," in Holoman, ed., *The Nineteenth-Century Symphony,* p. 248.

53. Thomas Mann, *Doctor Faustus: The Life of the German Composer Adrian Leverkühn As Told by a Friend,* trans. H. T. Lowe Porter (New York: Vintage, 1971), pp. 489–90.

54. "Der letzte Satz deiner C-Moll-Symphonie hat mich neulich wieder fürchterlich aufgeregt (ähnlich wie der dritte Teil von Schumanns Faust). . . . Zuletzt kommt doch wieder das Horn mit seinem schwärmerischen Sehnsuchtsschrei wie in der Einleitung, und alles zittert in Schnsucht, Wonne und übersinnlicher Sinnlichkeit und Seligkeit!" Otto Gottlieb-Billroth, ed., *Billroth und Brahms im Briefwechsel* (Berlin: Urban, 1935), p. 451. The reference, of course, is to the recurrence of the Alphorn theme in mm. 389ff. of the finale of Brahms's First Symphony.

55. This was not always the case. According to Schubring's 1861 essay on Schumann's place in music history ("Schumanniana Nr. 4: Die gegenwärtige Musikepoche und Robert Schumann's Stellung in der Musikgeschichte"), the composer's works for chorus and orchestra—and his symphonies—were at that time better known than "the more difficult piano works of his first period, up through Op. 23," owing to their "more easily comprehensible thematic content." Schubring went even further, claiming that as important as Schumann was in his "lyrical works" (i.e., lieder), he was at his greatest in "romantic-epic" works such as the *Peri, Manfred, Faust,* and the late ballades for vocal forces and orchestra. See *NZfM* 54 (1861), pp. 213–14.

56. *CS–JB,* vol. 1, p. 100.

57. "Ja, . . . manches dürfte nie gut zu machen sein. . . . Aber was für eine herrliche Musik; und das ist doch die Hauptsache. Und auch im Klang so viel Hochoriginelles, Eigenartiges!" Richard Heuberger, *Erinnerungen an Johannes Brahms: Tagebuchnotizen aus den Jahren 1875 bis 1897,* ed. Kurt Hofmann (Tutzing: Schneider, 1971), p. 99.

58. See Richard von Perger and Robert Hirschfeld, eds., *Geschichte der K. K. Gesellschaft der Musikfreunde in Wien* (Vienna: Holzhausen, 1912), pp. 304–5.

59. In addition to the letter of March 1890 quoted earlier, see Billroth's letters of 16 October 1874 (on Schumann's *Faust*), 20 June 1880 (on *Faust* and the *Peri*), and 3 August 1882 (on *Faust*). *Billroth und Brahms im Briefwechsel*, pp. 207, 300, 332.

60. *GS*, vol. 2, p. 166.

61. The interview took place toward the end of Brahms's life and was documented many years later, in 1931, in an article titled "Brahms As I Knew Him." See Daniel Beller-McKenna, "Brahms, the Bible, and Robert Schumann," *American Brahms Society Newsletter* 13/2 (1995), p. 2.

62. Similarly, Giorgio Pestelli describes Schumann's and Brahms's choral-orchestral works as a species of "philosophical music." Often characterized by attenuated melodic ideas and textures, this music, in Pestelli's view, is at once "secretive" and "difficult." See *Canti del destino: Studi su Brahms* (Turin: Einaudi, 2000), p. 17.

63. For a comprehensive account of the special connotations of the C-minor tonality for Beethoven, see Michael C. Tusa, "Beethoven's 'C-Minor Mood'," in Christopher Reynolds, Lewis Lockwood, and James Webster, eds., *Beethoven Forum 2* (Lincoln: University of Nebraska Press, 1993), pp. 1–28. Reinhard Kapp offers an intriguing commentary on the affective implications of D minor in Schumann's late works—and the possible relationship between that tonality and principles of Gothic architecture—in *Studien zum Spätwerk Robert Schumanns* (Tutzing: Hans Schneider, 1984), pp. 134–44.

64. According to Kalbeck, the "Tragic" Overture owes its existence to a request from the theatrical director Franz von Dingelstedt for incidental music to accompany a production of Goethe's *Faust* in its entirety. (See Max Kalbeck, *Johannes Brahms*, 2nd ed., vol. 3 (Berlin: Deutsche Brahms-Gesellschaft, 1912–21), pp. 257–58.) Even though Brahms contemplated this project—which, in any event, fell through—just *after* completing the "Tragic" Overture in the summer of 1880, the parallels between that work and Schumann's *Faust* scenes are suggestive nonetheless.

65. *NZfM* 39 (28 October 1853), p. 186. Cf. Clara's reaction to the 1868 Bremen premiere of Brahms's work: "The *Requiem* has taken hold of me as no sacred music ever did before. . . . As I saw Johannes standing there, baton in hand, I could not help thinking of my dear Robert's prophecy . . . which is fulfilled today." See Berthold Litzmann, ed., *Clara Schumann–Johannes Brahms: Briefe aus den Jahren 1853–1896*, vol. 3 (Leipzig: Breitkopf und Härtel, 1927), pp. 218–19.

66. Schumann made note of this project while working on his *Missa sacra* (Op. 147) in early 1852. See Bernhard R. Appel, "Critical Notes" to *NSA, Geistliche Werke 2: Missa sacra op. 147* (Mainz: Schott, 1991), p. xv. On Brahm's disclaimer, see Kalbeck, *Johannes Brahms*, vol. 2, pp. 249–50.

67. Quoted in Michael Musgrave, *Brahms: A German Requiem* (Cambridge: Cambridge University Press, 1996), p. 62.

68. On the role of the chorale in Brahms's Requiem and its implications for the composer's reception of Bach, see ibid., pp. 26–34. The close of Schumann's *Neujahrslied* elaborates the chorale "Nun danket alle Gott."

69. Christopher Reynolds, for instance, has detected similarities between the middle section of Brahms's second movement ("So seid geduldig") and the finale of part 2 of Schumann's *Das Paradies und die Peri*. See "A Choral Symphony by Brahms?" *19th Century Music* 9/1 (1985), pp. 8–10. On the textual points of contact between Brahms's Requiem and Schumann's *Requiem für Mignon*, see Klaus Blum, *Hundert Jahre Ein deutsches Requiem von Johannes Brahms* (Tutzing: Schneider, 1971), pp. 101–2.

70. *BBw* 6, p. 88. The organizational committee for the event apparently wanted a new composition, specially tailored for the occasion, an assignment Brahms refused to undertake.

71. Musgrave, *Brahms: A German Requiem,* p. 12. See also Blum, *Hundert Jahre Ein deutsches Requiem,* pp. 101–4.

72. See chapter 5, pp. 148–49.

73. Adolf Schubring, "Schumanniana Nr. 11. Die Schumann'sche Schule. Schumann und Brahms. Brahms' vierhändige Schumann-Variationen [Op. 23]," *AmZ* 3. Jahrgang (1868), p. 51. Schubring's "program" for the last variation reads as follows: "'Trauermarsch: 'Ach, sie haben einen guten Mann begraben, (*coda*)—doch mir war er mehr! [Ah, they have buried a good man, (*coda*)—yet he meant so much more to me!] *Requiescat in pace et lux perpetua luceat ei!'* "

74. Likewise, Siegfried Kross describes Brahms's Op. 23 Variations as a "spiritual monument" to Schumann. See "Brahms und Schumann," *Brahms Studien* 4 (1981), p. 39.

David Brodbeck has drawn some suggestive connections among the hymnic E♭-major theme of the slow movement (Adagio) of Brahms's Violin Sonata in G major (Op. 78), Schumann's "last musical idea," and the slow-movement theme of Schumann's Violin Concerto. In the G-major Sonata, the subject of Brahms's elegy was not Schumann but his fatally ill son Felix, the youngest of Robert and Clara's children. In February 1879, Brahms sent Clara a version of the Adagio's main theme that differs somewhat from its final form, inscribing on the overleaf: "If you play what is on the reverse side quite slowly, it will tell you, perhaps more clearly than I otherwise could myself, how sincerely I think of you and Felix—even about his violin, which however surely is at rest." See "Medium and Meaning: New Aspects of the Chamber Music," in Michael Musgrave, ed., *The Cambridge Companion to Brahms* (Cambridge: Cambridge University Press, 1999), pp. 117–18.

75. See Floros, *Johannes Brahms: "Frei aber einsam,"* p. 32.

76. Smith, "Brahms and Schenker," p. 99.

CHAPTER 7

1. *R. E. D. Classical 2000 Catalogue: Master Edition 1* (London, 2000), pp. 193–94. The statistics gleaned from this catalog make for an interesting comparison with those presented by Siegfried Kross for performances of Brahms's orchestral works between 1890 and 1902. Drawing on reports from Wilhelm Fritzsch's *Musikalisches Wochenblatt,* Kross arrives at the following count for performances of Brahms's concertos during the last decade of the nineteenth century: Piano Concerto No. 1: 58, Piano Concerto No. 2: 67, Violin Concerto: 128, and "Double" Concerto: 40. See Siegfried Kross, "The Establishment of a Brahms Repertoire 1890–1902," in Michael Musgrave, ed., *Brahms 2: Biographical, Documentary and Analytical Studies* (Cambridge: Cambridge University Press, 1987), p. 37.

2. Malcolm MacDonald, *Brahms* (New York: Schirmer, 1990), pp. 322–23. See also the same author's " 'Veiled Symphonies'? The Concertos," in Michael Musgrave, ed., *The Cambridge Companion to Brahms* (Cambridge: Cambridge University Press, 1999), pp. 167–70.

3. "Dieses Kunstwerk dünkt mir mehr die Frucht eines grossen combinatorischen Verstandes zu sein, als eine unwiderstehliche Eingebung schöpferische Phantasie und

Empfindung. . . . Der erste Satz, der kunstreichste von allen, kommt aus der halb trotzigen, halb gedrückten A-moll-Tonart nicht hinaus. Durch seine vielen Vorhälte, Synkopen und rhythmischen Rückungen, seine übermässigen und verminderten Intervalle bricht nur selten das helle Tageslicht. Fast werden wir an Schumanns spätere Manier erinnert." Eduard Hanslick, *Aus dem Tagebuche eines Musikers. (Der "Modernen Oper" VI. Theil).* (Berlin: Allgemeine Verein für Deutsche Litteratur, 1892), pp. 265–66.

Hanslick's view that the "Double" Concerto was high on intellect but low in spontaneous invention was shared by a number of the work's early critics. For a summary of these reactions, see Michael Struck's *Einleitung* to his edition of the "Double" Concerto in Johannes Brahms, *Neue Ausgabe sämtlicher Werke,* series 1, vol. 10 (Munich: Henle, 2000), p. xx.

4. Otto Gottlieb-Billroth, ed. *Billroth und Brahms im Briefwechsel* (Berlin: Urban, 1935), p. 421.

5. Berthold Litzmann, *Clara Schumann: Ein Künstlerleben nach Tagebüchern und Briefen,* 8th ed., vol. 3 (Leipzig: Breitkopf und Härtel, 1923–25), pp. 495–96, 499–500.

6. See BBw 6, p. 232; Johannes Joachim and Andreas Moser, eds., *Briefe von und an Joseph Joachim,* vol. 3 (Berlin: Julius Bard, 1911–13), p. 311; and Gottlieb-Billroth, *Billroth und Brahms im Briefwechsel,* p. 421.

7. For Elisabet von Herzogenberg's reaction, see BBw 2, p. 170, and Joachim and Moser, *Briefe von und an Joseph Joachim,* vol. 3, p. 315. On the Fellingers, see Imogen Fellinger, ed., *Klänge um Brahms: Erinnerungen von Richard Fellinger* (Mürzzuschlag: Österreichische Johannes Brahms-Gesellschaft, 1997), p. 58.

8. Richard Heuberger, *Erinnerungen an Johannes Brahms: Tagebuchnotizen aus den Jahren 1857 bist 1897,* ed. Kurr Hoffmann (Tutzing: Schneider, 1971), p. 41.

9. Max Kalbeck, *Johannes Brahms,* vol. 4, pp. 62–63, 65, 68.

10. See Karl Geiringer, *Brahms: His Life and Work,* 3rd ed., in collaboration with Irene Geiringer (New York: Da Capo, 1982), pp. 263, 265; and Hans Gál, *Johannes Brahms: His Work and His Personality,* trans. Joseph Stein (New York: Knopf, 1963), p. 129.

11. See Jan Swafford, *Johannes Brahms: A Biography* (New York: Knopf, 1997), p. 542.

12. See, e.g., Geiringer, *Brahms,* p. 263; MacDonald, *Brahms,* p. 322; and Michael Musgrave, *The Music of Brahms* (London: Routledge and Kegan Paul, 1985), p. 235.

13. See Hans Engel, *Das Instrumentalkonzert: Eine musikgeschichtliche Darstellung,* vol. 2 (Leipzig: Breitkopf und Härtel, 1971, 1974), pp. 419–21; Constantin Floros, *Johannes Brahms: "Frei aber einsam"—ein Leben für eine poetische Musik* (Zurich: Arche, 1997), p. 65; Geiringer, *Brahms,* p. 263; Günter Hartmann, "Vorbereitende Untersuchungen zur Analyse von Brahms' Doppelkonzert a-moll op. 102," in Reinmar Emans and Matthias Wendt, eds., *Beiträge zur Geschichte des Konzerts: Festschrift Siegfried Kross zum 60. Geburtstag* (Bonn: Gudrun Schröder, 1990), pp. 278–81; John Horton, *Brahms Orchestral Music* (London: BBC, 1968), p. 62; Peter Jost, " 'Gewissermassen ein Versöhnungswerk': Doppelkonzert A-moll, op. 102," in Renata Ulm, ed., *Johannes Brahms: Das Symphonische Werk—Entstehung, Deutung, Wirkung* (Kassel: Bärenreiter, 1996), p. 173; MacDonald, *Brahms,* p. 321; Simon McVeigh, "Brahms's Favourite Concerto," *Strad* 105 (April 1994), p. 347; Musgrave, *The Music of Brahms,* p. 235; and Swafford, *Johannes Brahms,* pp. 540–41. Oddly enough, most of these writers focus on the hardly compelling resemblances between the first phrase of Viotti's theme and the second main theme of Brahms's first movement.

14. As Donald Francis Tovey put it, "It is pathetic to see the struggles of such a

critic as Hanslick with this excursion beyond the lines laid down by his apostleship." *Essays in Musical Analysis*, vol. 3: *Concertos* (London: Oxford University Press, 1936), p. 140.

15. Diary entry of 21 September 1887, in Litzmann, *Clara Schumann*, vol. 3, p. 496. See also Brahms's letter to Simrock of 23 August 1887, in *BBw* 11, p. 158.

16. Both passages also exemplify what Joseph Kerman, in his recently published Charles Eliot Norton Lectures, calls coplay, the sharing of material by the "agents" in a concerto. See *Concerto Conversations* (Cambridge, Massachusetts: Harvard University Press, 1999), p. 43.

17. Together with the violin concertos of Bach, Mozart, Beethoven, Mendelssohn, and Brahms, Viotti's concerto appeared among the ten "Meisterwerke der Violinliteratur" ("masterworks of the violin repertory") that comprise the third and final volume (*Vortragsstudien*) of the *Violinschule* of Joachim and Andreas Moser (Berlin: Simrock, 1905). I have quoted from Joachim's introductory essay to his edition of the work (*Violinschule*, vol. 3, part 1, p. 39). Brahms was even more enthusiastic about the Viotti concerto than Joachim. See his letter of May 1878 to Clara Schumann, quoted in Litzmann, *Clara Schumann*, vol. 3, p. 274; and the discussion of Brahms's and Joachim's reception of Viotti's work in McVeigh, "Brahms's favourite concerto," pp. 343–47.

18. To quote Tovey, the "Double" Concerto "does not make any confusion between the lines of a concerto and those of a symphony." See his *Essays in Musical Analysis*, vol. 3, p. 141.

19. Günther Hartmann provides an exhaustive (and exhausting) analysis of the motivic similarities between the "Double" Concerto and Viotti's Concerto No. 22; see "Vorbereitende Untersuchungen," pp. 278–81, 286–92.

For Brahms's June 1878 letter to Clara Schumann, see Litzmann, *Clara Schumann*, vol. 3, p. 274.

It is instructive to observe how Joachim dealt with the issue of allusions in Brahms's works. In the prefatory essay to Joachim's edition of the Violin Concerto, he noted a thematic parallel with—or, in his words, an "unconscious echo" of—Viotti's concerto in the first movement of Brahms's. What struck him as most important about the parallelism between the passages in question (mm. 120–123 of Viotti's first movement and mm. 236–45 of Brahms's) was not their similarity in melodic contour but their comparable functional roles: both phrases act as transitions, either between first and second theme groups (Viotti) or between two distinct paragraphs of the second group (Brahms). See Joachim and Moser, *Violinschule*, vol. 3, part 3, p. 27.

20. Again, Hartmann offers the most thorough exposition of this view in "Vorbereitende Untersuchungen," pp. 276–77, 286–92. Cf. also Floros, *Johannes Brahms*, p. 65–66; Jost, " 'Gewissermassen ein Versöhnungswerk,'" p. 173; Musgrave, *The Music of Brahms*, p. 225; and Swafford, *Johannes Brahms*, pp. 540–41.

21. See chapter 4, pp. 108–14.

22. David Epstein, "Concerto in A Minor for Violin and Violoncello ["Double" Concerto], Opus 102," in Leon Botstein, ed., *The Compleat Brahms* (New York: Norton, 1999), p. 56.

23. See Christian Martin Schmidt, *Johannes Brahms und seine Zeit* (Laaber: Laaber-Verlag, 1983), p. 77; and MacDonald, *Brahms*, p. 322.

24. Heuberger, *Erinnerungen*, p. 93.

25. I consider this point at greater length in my "From 'Concertante Rondo' to

'Lyric Sonata': A Commentary on Brahms's Reception of Mozart," in David Brodbeck, ed., *Brahms Studies*, vol. 1 (Lincoln: University of Nebraska Press, 1994), pp. 127–29.

26. For comprehensive and engaging accounts of Brahms's knowledge of the cello and its repertory, see Styra Avins, "Brahms the Cellist," *Newsletter of the Violoncello Society* (Summer 1992), pp. 1–5, and "An Undeniable Gift," *Strad* 107 (October 1996), pp. 1,048–53. In a conversation with Heuberger of 8 December 1894, Brahms reported: "At one time I played the violin a bit [*gegeigt*], but my instrument was the cello. I even played some cello concertos." Heuberger, *Erinnerungen*, p. 73.

27. Romberg reworked his Doppelconcertino for Two Celli, Op. 72, as the Concertino for Violin and Cello precisely so he could play it with his cousin. See Engel, *Das Instrumentalkonzert*, vol. 2, p. 415.

28. Kalbeck, *Brahms*, vol. 4, p. 33.

29. "Die Stimmen Ihnen vorläufig einen trostlosen Eindruck gemacht hätten, oder aber Sie hätten es höchst ungnädig u. übel vermerkt dass ich zu einem V'Cell-Concert gar noch eine Solo-Violine nehme!" Quoted from Friedrich Bernhard Hausmann, "Brahms und Hausmann," *Brahms Studien* 7 (1987), p. 29.

30. Boris Schwarz, "Joseph Joachim and the Genesis of Brahms's Violin Concerto," *Musical Quarterly* 69 (1983), p. 508.

31. In a review of 28 April 1834, Schumann made a direct comparison between the then fourteen-year-old Vieuxtemps and Paganini, describing both as "artist-magicians" who possessed the uncanny ability to draw their audience into a "magic circle." See *NZfM* 1 (1834), p. 31.

32. See Carl Dahlhaus, *Nineteenth-Century Music*, trans. J. Bradford Robinson (Berkeley: University of California Press, 1989), pp. 135–37.

33. Robert Schumann, "Das Clavier-Concert," *NZfM* 10 (4 January 1839), pp. 5–6. Schumann's essay includes critiques of piano concertos by Moscheles (Op. 93) and Mendelssohn (Op. 40).

34. Kerman, *Concerto Conversations*, p. 72.
In 1845 Schumann added a slow movement and finale to a somewhat revised version of the Phantasie, the result being his A-minor Piano Concerto (Op. 54).

35. Linda Correll Roesner, "Brahms's Editions of Schumann," in George Bozarth, ed., *Brahms Studies: Analytical and Historical Perspectives* (Oxford: Clarendon, 1990), p. 251; and Michael Struck, *Robert Schumann: Violinkonzert d-Moll (WoO 23)* (Munich: Wilhelm Fink, 1988), p. 19.

36. Brahms also reported that he and Joachim had "often discussed both [pieces] and which might be our favorite—we could not settle it"; see *BLL*, p. 84. See also Brahms's letter to Clara Schumann of 23–24 February 1855, where he wrote out the dedication as Schumann had notated it for him: "Concertpiece for Pianoforte & Orchestra, / Op. 134 / dedicated to Johannes Brahms / by Robert." In November of the previous year, Clara had performed the work in The Hague. See *BLL*, p. 94.

37. The Schumanns visited Hannover, where Joachim was concertmaster of the court orchestra, between 19 and 30 January 1854. As Schumann noted in his diary, he and Clara had daily contact with Joachim and Brahms and were also joined by the young composer Julius Otto Grimm. During the many evenings of informal music making at the Schumanns' lodgings, Joachim and Clara played through all of Schumann's major chamber works for violin and piano: the Sonata in A minor, Op. 105; the Sonata in D minor, Op. 121; and the posthumously published "Third" Sonata in A minor. Brahms was certainly present for most, if not all, of these sessions; Schu-

mann's diary entry for 29 January makes reference to the reading of several movements from sonatas by Brahms (probably including some no longer extant works for violin). As Schumann also related, Joachim, Grimm, and Brahms departed from Hannover immediately after the run-through of his Violin Concerto on the morning of 30 January. See *TB* 2, pp. 447–49.

38. Letter of 23–24 February 1855 to Clara Schumann, in *BLL*, p. 94.

39. See *BLL*, p. 84, and Michael Struck, *Die umstrittenen späten Instrumentalwerke Schumanns* (Hamburg: Wagner, 1984), pp. 251–252.

40. Richard von Perger and Robert Hirschfeld, eds., *Geschichte der K. K. Gesellschaft der Musikfreunde in Wien*, vol. 2: *1870–1912* p. 305.

41. Letter to Joachim of 5 April 1880, in *BLL*, p. 560. It is worth noting that critical opinions of the Phantasie, and of many of Schumann's other late works as well, varied widely in the years just before and after his death. The critic for the *Neue Zeitschrift für Musik* who reviewed Joachim's January 1854 performance of the work in Leipzig described the Phantasie as a "splendid piece," which offers "the performer an opportunity to show himself as a multifaceted artist" and allows "the listener to take pleasure in its genuine beauty." See *NZfM* 40 (1854), p. 42. In marked contrast, an October 1856 review by Richard Pohl in the same journal judged the work to be "poorly conceived for the violin" and "insignificant in terms of its inner musical value." See *NZfM* 45 (1856), p. 199. Writing in 1861, Hanslick viewed the Phantasie in a similar light: "It is a dark abyss across which two great artists clasp hands. Martyr-like, gloomy, and obstinate, this Fantasy struggles along, depending upon continuous figuration to make up for its melodic poverty." See Eduard Hanslick, "Joseph Joachim" (1861), in Henry Pleasants, trans. and ed., *Hanslick's Music Criticisms* (New York: Dover, 1988), p. 80. Michael Struck, noting the remarkable fact that the critical about-face from positive to negative perceptions occurred soon after Schumann died, arrives at the plausible conclusion that this shift was prejudiced by the belief that Schumann's final illness must have had an adverse effect on his creativity. (See Struck, *Robert Schumann*, pp. 17, 72.) Musical party politics probably also played a role. Elsewhere in the review in which he commented on the Phantasie, Richard Pohl, soon to be an ardent advocate for the "New Germans," denigrated Schumann's alignment with the "Mendelssohn School," a group whose creative efforts "border on weakness." See *NZfM* 45 (1856), p. 199.

42. Although there is no extant written documentation of Brahms's view of the Violin Concerto, it is likely that he, Clara, and Joachim jointly decided to exclude it from Schumann's *Gesamtausgabe*. See Struck, *Robert Schumann*, p. 19; and *Die umstrittenen späten Instrumentalwerke*, pp. 252, 305.

43. The *Concert-Allegro mit Introduction* for piano and orchestra, completed just before the Phantasie in August 1853, exhibits a similar overall design (slow introduction in tripartite form + *Lebhaft* in sonata form) and introduces passages of soloistic display at analogous points. Moreover, both pieces fall into more or less the same overall form as the *Introduction und Allegro appassionata* for piano and orchestra of 1849.

44. In 1836 the twenty-one-year-old Volkmann began taking composition lessons with the organist C. F. Becker in Leipzig; during the course of his three years of study there he had personal contact with Mendelssohn and Schumann, both of whom exerted a lasting impact on his compositional style. Except for a brief period in Vienna (1854–58), he was active mainly in Budapest, where he settled in 1841 and died in 1883.

See Thomas Brawley, "The Instrumental Works of Robert Volkmann (1815–1883),"
Ph.D. diss., Northwestern University, 1975, pp. 13–14.

45. In a letter to Volkmann of November 1874 that concerned the projected performance of his Cello Concerto with Reinhold Hummer, the cellist of the Rosé
Quartet, Brahms sought the composer's opinion on the cuts prescribed in David Pop-
per's edition of the work. Not surprisingly, Volkmann expressed his preference for an
unabridged rendition. See BLL, pp. 470–71. As early as 1856, Brahms wrote approvingly to Volkmann of the latter's A-minor String Quartet (Op. 9) and B flat–minor
Piano Trio (Op. 5), though the two did not meet until 1866 in Vienna. Apparently they
enjoyed more than a passing acquaintance: over the course of the next decade or so
they remained in fairly close touch, either through correspondence (of which only a
little over a dozen letters, mostly from Volkmann to Brahms, survive) or through actual social contact in Vienna and Budapest. No doubt their friendship was fueled by a
mutual veneration for the "classics" and disapproval of the tenets of the "New Germans." See Brawley, "Instrumental Works," pp. 18–21, 218.

46. The exceptions include the brief recitative-cadenza before the coda, which alludes to thematic material from its counterpart at the beginning of the development
section.

47. For an engaging discussion of the many roles a concerto "agent" may assume—including "master and servant," "mentor and acolyte," "pleurant," "minx,"
"diva," and "cad"—see Kerman, Concerto Conversations, pp. 52–58.

48. See TB 1, pp. 282–83, 404. I explore the resonance of this metaphor for Schumann in "Il circolo magico: Schumann e la musica di Paganini," forthcoming in Atti
del Convegno Internazionale della Accademia Nazionale dei Lincei: Schumann, Brahms e
l'Italia (Rome, 2001), pp. 41–58.

49. Paganini's Caprices were among the few items from the virtuoso violin repertory in Brahms's library. See Kurt Hofmann, Die Bibliothek von Johannes Brahms:
Bücher- und Musikalienverzeichnis (Hamburg: Wagner, 1974), p. 160.

50. For Clara, the conclusion of the String Quintet (Op. 111) called to mind "just
the sort of magnificent confusion that one hears in a dream after a Zigeuner evening
in Pest." See Berthold Litzmann, ed., Letters of Clara Schumann and Johannes Brahms
1853–1896, vol. 2 (New York: Longmans, 1927), p. 188. Writing (in English) to Sir Charles
Villiers Stanford about possible performances of the Clarinet Quintet in Britain,
Joachim insisted on the participation of Richard Mühlfeld, whose playing had inspired the work in the first place: "There is so much of the Gypsy-stile in it [the quin-
tet]: I don't think they [English clarinettists] would find the right expression." See
Joachim and Moser, Briefe von und an Joseph Joachim, vol. 3, pp. 406–7.

51. Tovey, Essays in Musical Analysis, vol. 3: Concertos, p. 110.

52. See Joan Chissell, "The Symphonic Concerto: Schumann, Brahms and Dvořák,"
in Robert Layton, ed., A Companion to the Concerto (New York: Schirmer, 1988), p. 168;
Horton, Brahms Orchestral Music, p. 64; Jost, "'Gewissermassen ein Versöhnungswerk,'" p. 178; MacDonald, Brahms, p. 322; and Swafford, Johannes Brahms, pp. 540–41.
Michael Musgrave goes somewhat further than these writers in noting the "sharp inclination to the gypsy manner" in both of the outer movements and even detects similarities in key and shape between the main theme of the slow movement and variation 4 (though he must mean variation 10) of Brahms's Variations on a Hungarian
Song for Piano (Op. 21 [no. 2]). See Music of Brahms, pp. 235, 237.

53. *BBw* 5, p. 290.

54. Brahms issued his Hungarian Dances in a number of versions: all twenty-one appeared in arrangements for piano, four hands, in four volumes published in 1868 (vols. 1 and 2: Dances 1–10) and 1880 (vols. 3 and 4: Dances 11–21); arrangements of the first ten dances for piano solo were published in 1872; Brahms also transcribed nos. 1, 3, and 10 for orchestra (published 1874). Dozens of other transcriptions, by figures who included Joachim (who arranged all twenty-one for violin and piano) and Dvořák (arranger of nos. 17–21 for orchestra), appeared before the end of the century. Obviously this flood of publications answered to a market-driven need: the passion of the music-loving public for alien, exotic cultures. In Brahms's Hungarian Dances, gypsy culture was made fit for domestic consumption; needless to say, the bourgeois consumers of piano, four-hand, and other arrangements never would have dreamed of allowing a real gypsy into their drawing rooms.

55. See Renate and Kurt Hofmann, *Johannes Brahms Zeittafel zu Leben und Werk* (Tutzing: Schneider, 1983), pp. 12, 14. Brahms may have been present for Reményi's concerts of 10 and 19 November 1849 in Hamburg; on both occasions the violinist played his own arrangements of "Ungarische Nationalmelodien." See Max Kalbeck, *Johannes Brahms*, vol. 1, p. 59.

56. Siegfried Kross, *Johannes Brahms: Versuch einer kritischen Dokumentar-Biographie* (Bonn: Bouvier, 1997), pp. 64–65.

57. Many of these musicians had probably come to Vienna by way of the Burgenland, an area directly south of the city that had been under Hungarian control since 1867. See Andrew F. Burghardt, *Borderland: A Historical and Geographical Study of Burgenland, Austria* (Madison: University of Wisconsin Press, 1962), pp. 3–5, 266–67. One of the Burgenland's main regions, Alföld, turns up in the following line from the song "Röslein dreie" from Brahms's *Zigeunerlieder:* "Schönstes Städtchen in Alföld ist Ketschkemet" ("Kecskemét is the loveliest little town in Alföld").

On Brahms's enthusiasm for the music of gypsy bands and his ties to Budapest, see Wolfgang Ebert, "Brahms in Ungarn: Nach der Studie 'Brahms Magyarorsagón' von Lajos Koch," in *Studien zur Musikwissenschaft: Beihefte der Denkmäler der Tonkunst in Österreich*, vol. 37 (Tutzing: Schneider, 1986), pp. 103–64.

58. See Brahms's letter to Joachim of 26 September 1867, in *BBw* 6, p. 47. Joachim kept the piece in his repertory even though he admittedly had reservations about its aesthetic worth. As he explained to Hans von Brosart in April 1879, "The Fantasie is not among Schubert's most profound creations, yet in addition to much pale material, it contains many stimulating and charming things." See Joachim and Moser, *Briefe von und an Joseph Joachim*, vol. 3, pp. 207–8.

59. Letter of 24 November 1859, in *BBw* 5, p. 252.

60. Letter of 21 December 1878, in *BBw* 6, p. 152.

61. Jonathan Bellman, "Toward a Lexicon for the *Style Hongrois*," *Journal of Musicology* 9/2 (1991), p. 214.

62. See Jonathan Bellman, "The Hungarian Gypsies and the Poetics of Exclusion," in Jonathan Bellman, ed., *The Exotic in Western Europe* (Boston: Northeastern University Press, 1998), pp. 96–98, 103. The Hungarian gypsies called themselves *rom*, meaning "man," "husband," or "gypsy man"; hence *romany*, the adjectival form, means "of or pertaining to the gypsies."

63. See Jonathan Bellman, *The Style Hongrois in the Music of Western Europe*

(Boston: Northeastern University Press, 1993), p. 202, and "The Hungarian Gypsies," p. 103.

64. Quoted from Joachim's introductory essay on Brahms's Violin Concerto in Joachim and Moser, *Violinschule*, vol. 3, part 3, p. 28.

65. Bellman, "The Hungarian Gypsies," p. 100.

66. See especially Bellman, *The Style Hongrois*, pp. 93–130, and "Toward a Lexicon for the *Style Hongrois*," pp. 214–37.

67. See Bellman, *The Style Hongrois*, pp. 102–4.

68. Quoted in Bellman, "Toward a Lexicon," p. 221.

69. Letter of early October 1887, in *BBw* 6, p. 241.

70. Other paradigmatic examples from the *style hongrois* repertory include the closing Allegro molto vivace of Pablo de Sarasate's *Zigeunerweisen*, Op. 20, for Violin and Orchestra (the framing sections of its ABA' form make prominent use of variation techniques) and the "Moderato" and "Meno vivo" sections of Ravel's *Tzigane* for Violin and Orchestra (each section is cast as a theme-and-variations form).

71. Arnold Schoenberg, "Brahms the Progressive" (1947) in *Style and Idea*, ed. Leonard Stein, trans. Leo Black (Berkeley: University of California Press, 1984), p. 401.

72. Although Liszt's monograph is often inflammatory in tone and not always reliable in content, it contains may useful insights. A later, expanded version appeared in English translation as *The Gypsy in Music* (London, 1881). Princess Caroline Sayn-Wittgenstein had a major hand in both versions. See Bellman, "Toward a Lexicon," p. 215.

73. Quoted in Bellman, *The Style Hongrois*, p. 124.

74. See Hugo Riemann, "Einige seltsame Noten bei Brahms und anderen," in *Präludien und Studien: Gesammelte Aufsätze zur Aesthetik, Theorie und Geschichte der Musik*, vol. 3 (Leipzig: H. Seemann Nachfolger, 1901), pp. 109–111. Riemann borrowed the notion of a "minor-major key" from Moritz Hauptmann and also considered its role in the slow movement of Brahms's Fourth Symphony.

75. Other examples of this pattern in Brahms's output occur in the first and last movements of the Fourth Symphony, the third song of the *Vier ernste Gesänge* ("O Tod, wie bitter bist du"), and the B-minor Intermezzo for piano, Op. 119, no. 1. Descending third chains figure in many other passages in the "Double" Concerto as well, including the cello's opening cadenza in the first movement (mm. 16–20: $e–c–A–F–D–B^1–G^1–E^1$) and the first tutti of the finale (mm. 45–47: $g^1–e^1–c^1–a^1–f^1–d^1$).

76. Bellman, *The Style Hongrois*, pp. 122–26.

77. Other examples include the close of the soloists' exposition and recapitulation (mm. 193–95, 363–65) and the last phase of the development (mm. 270–78).

78. My description of the rhythmic character of the passage borrows several terms from Harald Krebs, *Fantasy Pieces: Metrical Dissonance in the Music of Robert Schumann* (New York: Oxford University Press, 1999).

79. As is evident from the autograph manuscript, this passage underwent a number of revisions before it achieved its final form. Three layers can be discerned: (1) Brahms's original conception (where the violin and cello proceed throughout with the triplet pattern established in mm. 328–29); (2) a very different version, in Joachim's hand, which features ornamental sextuplets and trilled Es in both parts; and (3) a variant, in Brahms's hand, of the violin line from Joachim's version. In the final, published version, Brahms essentially returned to his first conception, reinforcing the violin part at

the lower octave from m. 330 on. Both the first and final versions highlight the motivic connection with the first movement more clearly than do versions (2) and (3). For transcriptions of and commentaries on the relevant passages, see the Critical Report to Michael Struck's edition of the "Double" Concerto, in Brahms, *Neue Ausgabe,* series 1, vol. 10, pp. 258–59.

80. *BBw* 5, p. 85.

81. Letter of August 1887, in *BLL,* p. 649.

82. Joachim began working on the cadenza about two weeks before the concerto's premiere on New Year's Day, 1879. According to Brahms, Joachim's cadenza was "so beautiful that people applauded right into my coda." See Schwarz, "Joseph Joachim and the Genesis," p. 508.

83. The violinists Charles Treger and Aaron Rosand issued recordings of the "Hungarian" Concerto in the 1970s, though both made cuts, some of them rather extensive, in the first and third movements. The only complete rendition (and a very convincing one) I know of is Elmar Oliveira's 1991 CD recording with Leon Botstein and the London Philharmonic Orchestra (IMP Classics 30367 02092).

84. Donald Francis Tovey, "Joachim: Hungarian Concerto for Violin with Orchestra," in *Essays in Musical Analysis,* vol. 3, p. 109.

85. Letter of 9 May 1860 from Joachim to Otto Goldschmidt, in Joachim and Moser, *Briefe von und an Joseph Joachim,* vol. 2, p. 93.

86. According to Tovey, violinists would discover, in playing the concerto's passagework slowly, that the ornaments produced "living melodies with real harmonic meanings." *Essays in Musical Analysis,* vol. 3, p. 110.

87. The patterned sextuplet figuration in the slow movement of Brahms's Violin Concerto and the double-stopping in the coda of the finale may have been modeled after similar features in corresponding spots from Joachim's "Hungarian" Concerto.

88. *BBw* 5, pp. 224–25.

89. For a detailed account, see David Brodbeck, "The Brahms-Joachim Counterpoint Exchange; or Robert, Clara, and 'the Best Harmony between Jos. And Joh.,'" in David Brodbeck, ed., *Brahms Studies,* vol. 1 (Lincoln: University of Nebraska Press, 1994), pp. 30–80; see also the discussion in chapter 4, pp. 109–10. The exchange proceeded most intensely between April and July 1856, resumed briefly in the summer of 1857 (with five fugues by Joachim), and was then suspended until September 1861, when Brahms sent Joachim a copy of the Credo from the "Missa canonica."

90. Letter of 7 December 1858, in *BBw* 5, p. 225.

91. See, for instance, Joachim's letter to Brahms of 4 December 1858. After reporting on his progress on the first and last movements, Joachim promised to send along a copy of the recently completed slow movement, adding, somewhat timidly: "Let me know if you agree that there isn't much to it apart from the Hungarian flavor." *BBw* 5, p. 224.

92. According to MacDonald, both works emerged "out of a shared concern to restore Beethovenian dignity and architectonic logic to the concerto form" (see "'Veiled Symphonies'?" pp. 160–61).

Although Tovey was correct in underscoring the importance of the "Hungarian" Concerto for Brahms, his argument for the direct influence of Joachim's finale on Brahms's does not hold up well. (See *Essays in Musical Analysis,* vol. 3, pp. 108–9.) So far as can be inferred from the surviving correspondence, Brahms did not examine the finale of the "Hungarian" Concerto until late in 1859. (See *BBw* 5, p. 252.) By this time the premiere of his D-minor Piano Concerto (on 22 January 1859 in Hanover) was well behind him.

93. *BBw* 5, p. 290. Joachim acknowledged Brahms's mastery of the gypsy style in a letter of 15 October 1861. Commenting on the finale (*Rondo alla Zingarese*) of Brahms's Piano Quartet in G minor (Op. 25), he noted wryly: "You have given me a sound thrashing on my own territory." (*BBw* 5, p. 312).

94. *BBw* 5, p. 292.

95. Schwarz, "Joseph Joachim and the Genesis," p. 506.

96. See ibid., pp. 515–16, 518–20, 522–23; and Günter Weiss-Aigner, "Komponist und Geiger: Joseph Joachims Mitarbeit am Violinkonzert von Johannes Brahms," *NZfM* 135 (1974), pp. 232–36.

97. See Schwarz, "Joseph Joachim and the Genesis," pp. 513–14, 522–23.

98. See Joachim's letter of thanks, dated 3 July 1888, in *BBw* 6, p. 248.

99. Letter of 24 July 1887, in *BBw* 6, pp. 230–31. In late July, Joachim reported that on the whole, he and Hausmann found "everything quite manageable"; he returned the parts with only "a few trifling suggestions for note changes" (Letter of 31 July 1887, in *BBw* 6, p. 233). Brahms subsequently asked for further suggestions on bowings, dynamics, and articulation, to which Joachim responded, in his letter of 14 August 1887 (*BBw* 6, pp. 235–36), with a bowing for the main theme of the finale "in the style of Ferdinand David": ♩♫ ♩♫ ♪). (Brahms retained his original articulation: ♫♩ ♫♩). Although the draft solo parts are no longer extant, Brahms's autograph manuscript contains a number of corrections to the parts that may stem from Joachim and Hausmann and which, on the whole, were intended to enhance the idiomatic character or heighten the brilliance of certain passages. These spots include the coda of the first movement (mm. 407, 409), the "kleine Kadenz" in the slow movement (mm. 73ff.), and the D-major portion of the central episode in the finale (mm. 180–95). For details, see Michael Struck's commentary in Brahms, *Neue Ausgabe*, series 1, vol. 10, pp. 228, 236–37.

100. The spirit of this exchange is evident in a letter of 27 November 1890 from Brahms to Joachim: "As you can see, I keep my word about G major better than you do—here is mine!—?—" The G-major pieces to which Brahms alluded were his own String Quintet, Op. 111, enclosed with the letter, and Joachim's G-major Violin Concerto, completed in 1864 but not published until 1890. Joachim sent Brahms a copy of the published score of his concerto in December of that year. The gypsy style figures in both works.

101. "Für mich ist f.a.e. ein Symbol geblieben, und darf ich, trotz allem, wohl segnen." *BBw* 6, p. 245.

102. See, for example, Hartmann, "Vorbereitende Untersuchungen," pp. 282–83, 288–92.

103. This tendency is much in evidence in the orchestrally accompanied cadenza of the first movement of the "Hungarian" Concerto. Supported by quietly echoing "Kuruc" fourths in the strings and snippets of earlier themes in the winds, the violin part presents an imaginative synthesis of a polyphonic idiom derived from the solo sonatas of Bach with the virtuoso figuration of the *style hongrois*. Like Schumann and Brahms, Joachim also took pains to imbue the "old bravura cadenza" with genuine musical character.

104. See Burghardt, *Borderland: A Historical and Geographical Study of Burgenland, Austria*, pp. 266–67.

105. From Charles Baudelaire, "Gypsies on the Road" ("Bohemiens en Voyage"), in *Les Fleurs du Mal,* trans. Richard Howard (Boston: Godine, 1983), p. 22.

The alienation of the Romany people from anything that remotely resembled bourgeois European culture is a major theme of Liszt's book on the gypsies. To quote Susan Bernstein: "In Liszt's view, the Gypsies are attached to no property or geographical territory; they report no history or origin. . . . The Gypsies thus represent the persistence of the ahistoric within the civilized world; they are defined against the culture whose standards and structures they reject." See Bernstein's *Virtuosity of the Nineteenth Century: Performing Music and Language in Heine, Liszt, and Baudelaire* (Stanford: Stanford University Press, 1998), p. 102.

106. Gottlieb-Billroth, *Billroth und Brahms im Briefwechsel,* p. 390.

107. Eduard Hanslick, "Neue Gesänge von Brahms" (1888), in *Musikalisches und Litterarisches (Der "Modernen Oper" V. Theil) Kritiken und Schilderungen,* 2nd ed. (Berlin: Allgemeiner Verein für Deutsche Litteratur, 1889), p. 146.

108. Letter to Brahms of 22 August 1888, in Gottlieb-Billroth, *Billroth und Brahms im Briefwechsel,* p. 427. Writing to Brahms from Nice on 28 October 1888, Elisabet von Herzogenberg offered a similar appraisal of the songs: "They sway and throb and stamp and flow, tripping along with the delicacy of a caress." *BBw* 2, p. 208.

109. Hanslick, *Aus dem Tagebuche,* p. 266.

110. Hanslick, "Neue Gesänge," pp. 146–47, 149.

111. Ibid., p. 147. Elisabet von Herzogenberg touched on precisely the same points—the elevation of nature to art, the suppression of overt artfulness, and the avoidance of crude naturalism—in her response to Brahms's second set of Hungarian Dances: "You have ennobled what was originally mere noise as a beautiful *fortissimo* without thereby making it an annoyingly cultivated [*fatal gebildete*] *fortissimo.*" Letter to Brahms of 23 July 1880, in *BBw* 1, p. 126.

The power of gypsy music to both attract and repel is aptly summed up in the composer Samuel Barber's description of an encounter with an actual gypsy band in the 1920s: "It swept me off my feet; for it was not music; it was an expression of a directness too naïve, too naked and living to be music. It is something I shall never forget, and I left Budapest early for I did not wish to hear it again." Quoted in Bellman, "The Hungarian Gypsies," p. 74.

112. Hanslick, *Aus dem Tagebuche,* p. 266. As noted earlier, Billroth leveled the same charge in even more damning terms: "I know of no less significant work of our dear friend." Letter to Hanslick of December 1887, in Gottlieb-Billroth, *Billroth und Brahms im Briefwechsel,* p. 421.

Interestingly enough, Hanslick's criticism of the "Double" Concerto echoes his opinion of Joachim's "Hungarian" Concerto, which, in a review of 1861, he described as "too expansive and complicated" for a work that was relatively low in "melodic invention." See Hanslick, "Joseph Joachim," in *Hanslick's Music Criticisms,* trans. and ed. Henry Pleasants (New York: Dover, 1988).p. 79.

113. Brahms made the point, with more than a touch of self-deprecation, in calling these songs "a bit of jolly, high-spirited nonsense." Letter of March 1888 to Elisabet von Herzogenberg, in *BBw* 2, p. 173.

114. Carl Schorske, *Fin-de-siècle Vienna: Politics and Culture* (New York: Vintage, 1981), p. 117.

115. Margaret Notley, "Brahms as Liberal: Genre, Style, and Politics in Late Nineteenth-Century Vienna," *19th Century Music* 19 (1993), pp. 109–115.

116. Hugo Wolf dismissed Brahms's creative efforts with this term in conversation with the writer Hermann Bahr, who himself recalled that during the 1880s and 1890s he and his friends had dubbed Brahms the cold one (*der Kalte*). See M. Notley, " 'Brain-Music' by Brahms: Toward an Understanding of Sound and Expression in the Allegro of the Clarinet Trio," *ABS Newsletter* 16/ii (1998), p. 1. It is interesting to observe that several of the criticisms directed at Brahms's music by the antiliberal press (e.g., its lack of emotional immediacy and melodic invention) were echoed by critics who ostensibly shared Brahms's liberal ideals, Hanslick among them. For a compelling discussion of the antiliberal assault on Brahms, see Notley, "Brahms as Liberal," pp. 117–23.

117. See Peter Gay, "Aimez-vous Brahms? Polarities in Modernism," in *Freud, Jews, and Other Germans: Masters and Victims in Modernist Culture* (Oxford: Oxford University Press, 1978), pp. 247–51.

118. Robert Musil, "Mind and Experience," in *Precision and Soul: Essays and Addresses,* ed. and trans. Burton Pike and David S. Luft (Chicago: University of Chicago Press, 1990), p. 142.

119. Robert Musil, *The Man without Qualities,* trans. Sophie Wilkins (New York: Knopf, 1995), p. 272.

EPILOGUE

1. Review of Schubert's Grand Duo for Piano, Four Hands (D. 812), and piano sonatas in C minor (D. 958), A (D. 959), and Bb (D. 960), in *NZfM* 8 (5 June 1838), pp. 177–78.

2. Letter of 9 June 1839, in *BrKG* 2, p. 558.

3. Adolf Schubring, "Schumanniana Nr. 4: Die gegenwärtige Musikepoche und Robert Schumann's Stellung in der Musikgeschichte," *NZfM* 54 (1861), p. 213.

4. Walter Benjamin, "The Storyteller: Reflections on the Works of Nikolai Leskov" (1936), in *Illuminations: Essays and Reflections,* ed. Hannah Arendt, trans. Harry Zohn (New York: Schocken, 1969), p. 83.

5. Ibid., pp. 83–84.

6. Walter Benjamin, "Experience and Poverty" (1933), in *Walter Benjamin: Selected Writings,* vol. 2: *1927–1934,* trans. Rodney Livingstone and others, ed. Michael W. Jennings, Howard Eiland, and Gary Smith (Cambridge, Massachusetts: Belknap Press of Harvard University Press, 1999), p. 732.

7. Walter Benjamin, "On Some Motifs in Baudelaire" (1939), in *Illuminations,* p. 159.

8. Benjamin, "The Storyteller," p. 98.

9. Cf. the discussion of Schumann's review of Schubert's Impromptu in F minor (D. 935, no. 1), in chapter 2, pp. 49–58.

10. Benjamin, "The Storyteller," pp. 86–90.

11. I discuss the Ossianic pedigree of Schumann's choral-orchestral ballades in "Schumann's Ossianic Manner," *19th Century Music* 21/3 (1998), pp. 260–73. For a thoughtful account of the engagement of another important nineteenth-century composer with Ossianic themes, see R. Larry Todd, "Mendelssohn's Ossianic Manner, with a New Source—*On Lena's Gloomy Heath,*" in Jon W. Finson and R. Larry Todd, eds., *Mendelssohn and Schumann: Essays on Their Music and Its Context* (Durham: Duke University Press, 1984), pp. 137–60.

12. Italo Calvino, an eloquent twentieth-century storyteller, was getting at the

same thing when he wrote: "Memory truly counts only if it holds together the imprint of the past and the plan for the future." Quoted in Michael Wood's review of Calvino's *Why Read the Classics?* in *New York Review of Books* 57 / 4 (9 March 2000), p. 44.

13. Benjamin, "The Storyteller," p. 92.

14. Florence May, *The Life of Johannes Brahms*, vol. 2, 2nd rev. ed. (London: Reeves, ca. 1948), p. 638.

15. Friedrich Schlegel, *Ideen*, fragment no. 142, translation, slightly modified, from *Friedrich Schlegel's Lucinde and the Fragments*, trans. Peter Firchow (Minneapolis: University of Minnesota Press, 1971), p. 255.

16. Apart from Brahms, the members of the "new" Davidsbund included Joachim, Gade, Albert Dietrich, and Robert Franz. See "Neue Bahnen," *NZfM* 39 (28 October 1853), p. 253.

17. *NZfM* 4 (22 April 1836), p. 139.

18. Gustav Jenner, *Johannes Brahms als Mensch, Lehrer und Künstler* (Marburg: Elwert, 1930), p. 75.

19. Johannes Brahms, *Des jungen Kreislers Schatzkästlein: Aussprüche von Dichtern, Philosophen und Künstlern, zusammengetragen durch Johannes Brahms*, ed. Karl Krebs (Berlin: Verlag der Deutschen Brahmsgesellschaft m. b. h., 1909), p. 57 (excerpt no. 230).

20. Quoted in Wulf Konold, *Felix Mendelssohn-Bartholdy und seine Zeit* (Laaber: Laaber-Verlag, 1984), p. 140.

INDEX